REWARD MANAGEMENT

REWARD MANAGEMENT

A HANDBOOK OF REMUNERATION STRATEGY & PRACTICE

SECOND EDITION

Michael Armstrong & Helen Murlis

Published in association with the
Institute of Personnel Management

First published in 1988

Second Edition 1991 (fully revised)

Kogan Page Limited
120 Pentonville Road
London N1 9JN

British Library Cataloguing in Publication Data

A CIP record for this book is available from the British Library.

ISBN 0 7494 0220 2

Typeset by J&L Composition Ltd, Filey, North Yorkshire
Printed and bound in Great Britain by Biddles Ltd, Guildford and Kings Lynn

Contents

LIST OF FIGURES

LIST OF TABLES

Acknowledgements

We would like to thank the following people for their professional advice and contributions to this book:

John Beadle, Compensation and Benefits Manager, Glaxo Pharmaceuticals UK Ltd for details of the Glaxo pay curve and job family structure;

Vicky Wright and Cliff Weight, Hay Management Consultants – Incentives;

Derek Pritchard, Hay Management Consultants – Computer Assisted Job Evaluation;

John Baker, Hay Management Consultants – New Trends in computerized salary systems;

Alan Judes, Director, CC&P – Tax considerations and the UK share option pricing model;

Isabel Kerr, New Bridge Street Consultants – Appendix A;

Peter Crutchett, Senior Actuary, KPMG Peat Marwick McLintock Actuarial Services – Pensions;

Lucy McGuire, KPMG Peat Marwick Human Resources Consultancy – International remuneration.

We would also like to thank all the consultancies who have allowed us to refer to or reproduce summaries of their approaches to job evaluation (Hay Wyatt, Link Group Consultants Ltd, PA Consulting, Mercer Fraser, PE International, Towers Perrin Forster and Crosby, Price Waterhouse, KPMG Peat Marwick McLintock and Saville and Holdsworth), also Company Benefits Analysis Ltd, Monks Partnership and Employment Conditions Abroad for allowing us to quote from their work. The support of our families and many other colleagues is also gratefully acknowledged.

Introduction: The Basis of Reward Management

This book is about rewarding people in relation to their actual or potential value to the organization as measured by their contribution. It is also about recognizing that individuals have their own needs and goals, and that the organization must be constantly aware that it has to match its incentives and rewards to those needs.

Reward management is not just about money. It is concerned with intrinsic as well as extrinsic motivation; with non-financial as well as financial rewards. That is why we have not given this book the title of 'remuneration management', which implies that pay and benefits are the only things that matter. Neither have we called it 'salary administration', because this implies a mechanistic approach to reward which seldom, if ever, works. We have also avoided the use of the word 'compensation', although we have to accept that it has crept across the Atlantic from the USA into the vocabulary of a number of people in the reward field and is becoming an established term in the UK. We have, however, to declare a prejudice against this term because, according to the Oxford Dictionary, to compensate means 'to make amends' and we should ask if we are really in the business of making amends to people for the unfortunate fact that they have to go to work? We prefer the more positive connotations of 'reward' because we believe, fundamentally, that reward management is above all a dynamic concept. It is based on the proposition that organizations are in a constant state of change, and any system of management they practise must therefore be capable of adapting and responding quickly to new circumstances.

Definition

Reward management is the process of developing and implementing strategies, policies and systems which help the organization to achieve its objectives by obtaining and keeping the people it needs, and by increasing their motivation and commitment.

It is concerned with both financial and non-financial rewards and, although this book is mainly concerned with remuneration, this does not mean that we underestimate the significance of the non-financial elements in the system. We agree with the following views expressed by Michael Beer:

> 'Organizations must reward employees because, in return, they are looking for certain kinds of behaviour: they need competent individuals who agree to work with a high level of performance and loyalty. Individual employees, in exchange for their commitment, expect certain extrinsic rewards in the forms of promotions, salary, fringe benefits, perquisites, bonuses or stock options. Individuals also seek intrinsic rewards such as feelings of competence, achievement, responsibility, significance, influence, personal growth, and meaningful contribution. Employees will judge the adequacy of their exchange with the organization by assessing both sets of rewards.'

The reward management system – strategy and processes

The reward management system is illustrated in Figure I.1 as a set of relationships between the various reward management processes and corporate strategy. This shows that reward management strategies and policies are driven by corporate and human resource management strategies. These provide guidance on the processes required in four main areas: (a) non-financial rewards; (b) employee benefits; (c) pay structures; and (d) performance management. All of these contribute as follows to the ultimate aim of improved performance:

- non-financial rewards satisfy individual needs for variety, challenge, responsibility, influence in decision-making, recognition and career opportunities
- employee benefits satisfy employees' needs for personal security and provide remuneration in forms other than pay, which meet other needs and which are also frequently tax efficient
- pay structures, by combining the results of market surveys (which also contribute to decisions on benefit levels) and job evaluation, define levels of pay and differentials and pay progression limits
- performance management, on the basis of continuing as well as formal reviews of performance against targets and standards, leads to the design of performance-related pay (PRP) systems and development and training programmes
- employee benefits and basic and performance-related pay combine to form total remuneration.

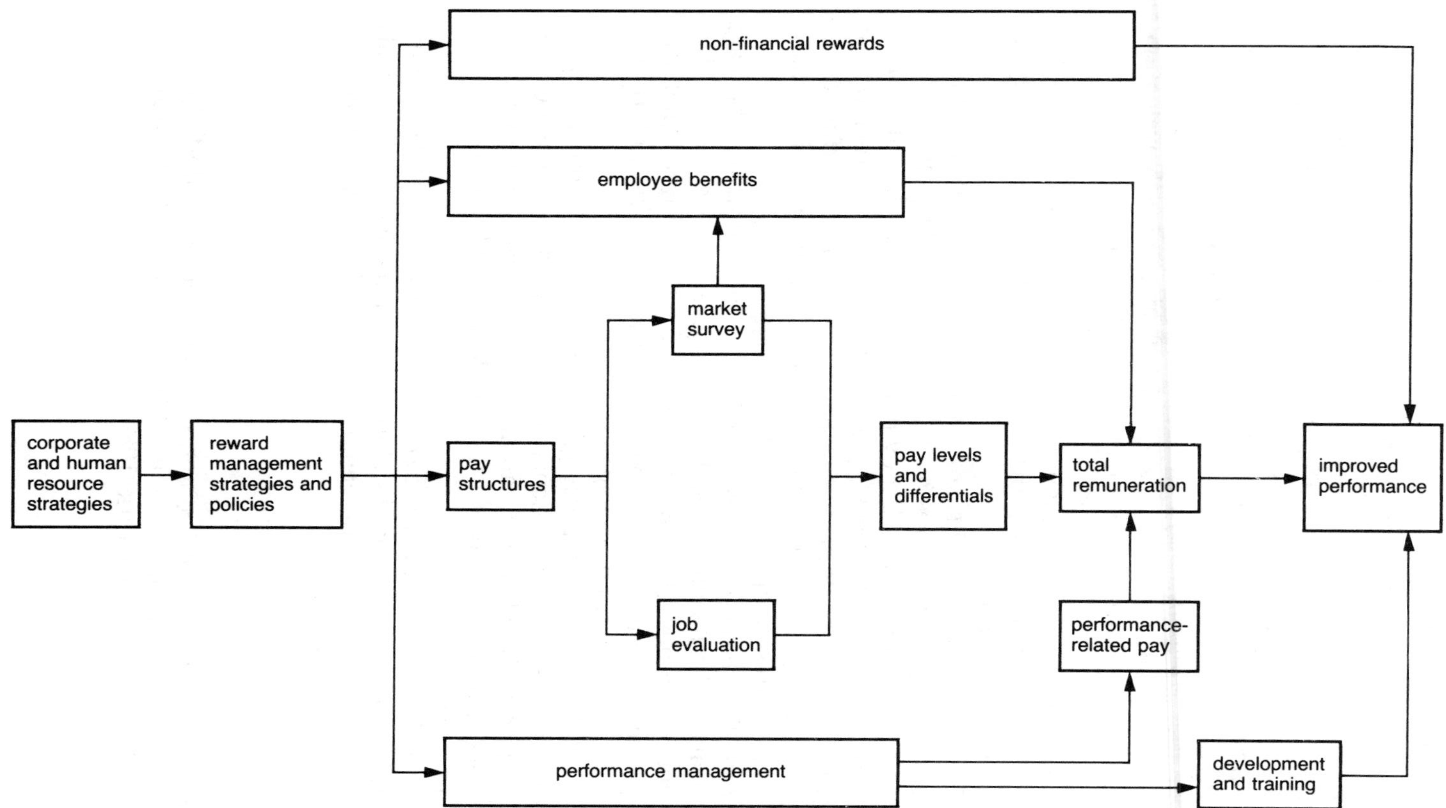

Figure I.1 *Reward management – strategy and processes*

Plan of this book

This book covers reward management in the following parts:

- *Part 1 – reward management strategies and policies*: this includes a discussion in Chapter 2 of the role of money as a motivator and of the significance of non-financial benefits. A summary of the main approaches that can be used to implement strategies and policies is set out in chapter 3
- *Part 2 – determining pay levels and relativities*: this covers the key processes of assessing market rates, and job evaluation. In the latter area (see Chapter 5), the important topic of equal pay for work of equal value is discussed. Part 2 ends with a description of the techniques of job analysis used to prepare the job descriptions which provide the basis for market comparisons and job evaluation
- *Part 3 – designing reward structures*: this part deals with the design of pay structures by reference to the data on pay levels and differentials provided by pay surveys and job evaluation
- *Part 4 – paying for performance*: this major part reviews the whole area of performance management including performance-related pay systems, incentives, other cash payments, share ownership schemes and profit sharing
- *Part 5 – employee benefits and total remuneration*: this part deals with the employee benefits package, pensions, the tax considerations affecting pay in general and employee benefits in particular, and how all aspects of reward combine to form the total remuneration package
- *Part 6 – special aspects of reward management*: this part covers a number of particular areas of reward management such as international remuneration, and the impact of mergers and organization start-ups on the development of pay policies and practices
- *Part 7 – managing the reward system*: this part describes how the system should be developed and maintained. It also deals with administration procedures and the important subject of communications.

References

1. Beer, Michael 'Reward systems' in Michael Beer, Bert Spector, Paul R Laurence, and D Quinn Mills, *Managing Human Assets*, The Free Press, New York, 1984.

Part 1

Reward Management Strategies and Policies

Chapter 1

Reward Management Strategies

Definition

Reward management strategies define the intentions of the organization on the remuneration policies and systems required to ensure that it continues to obtain, motivate and retain the committed and competent people it needs to accomplish its mission.

Purpose and aim

Reward management strategies address critical longer term issues concerning how employees should be rewarded. As declarations of intent they provide the basis for deciding how the reward system can help to achieve the objectives of the organization and how the system should be designed and managed.

For a business, the aim of reward management strategies should be to help it to achieve sustainable competitive advantage. In a non-profit making organization the aim should be to enable it to reach higher levels of service and performance. These aims will be achieved by developing and reinforcing high levels of performance to meet the requirements of the organization.

The basis of reward strategies

Reward management strategies must:

- be congruent with and support corporate values and beliefs
- emanate from business strategy and goals
- be linked to organization performance
- drive and support desired behaviour at all levels
- fit desired management style
- provide the competitive edge needed to attract and retain the high level of skills the organization needs
- be anchored to the realities of the labour market.

The contribution of reward strategies

Reward strategies can make a significant contribution to the achievement of corporate and functional objectives by:

- developing a positive culture – in Rosabeth Moss Kanter's words, 'A culture of pride and a climate of success'
- underpinning the organization's values, especially those concerned with excellence, performance, team-work and quality
- conveying a message to prospective high-calibre employees that the organization will satisfy their reward expectations
- ensuring that the right mix and levels of reward are provided in line with the culture of the organization, the needs of the business, the needs of employees and the economic, competitive and market environment in which the business operates
- linking reward policies, systems and procedures to the key business and human resource strategies for innovation, growth, development and the pursuit of excellence
- developing a strong orientation toward the achievement of sustained high levels of performance throughout the organization by recognizing successful performance and increases in levels of competence, thus contributing to the processes of empowering, enabling, and energizing all employees
- indicating to existing employees what types of behaviour will be rewarded and how this will take place, thus increasing motivation and commitment and improving performance.

Behavioural implications

All the contributions mentioned above are important, but the impact of reward management on behaviour is particularly significant. In general, behaviour modification takes place in five stages:

1. *Pinpoint* – specify the behaviour to be changed in terms of what people are expected to do.
2. *Record* – obtain data on performance.
3. *Identify* – identify influences on behaviour such as the reward system, corporate culture and values, the quality of leadership and training.
4. *Arrange* – arrange for reinforcement of desired behaviour by intrinsic or extrinsic motivation.
5. *Evaluate* – record and measure performance to generate new data.

Reward strategy, as the basis of reward policies and practices, is involved in all these stages. The development of reward systems means exercising choice between a number of different approaches.

Desired behaviour	Reward systems					
	Rules	Common intrinsic rewards	Group rewards	Individual extrinsic rewards	Individual intrinsic rewards	Goals
Join						
Remain						
Perform to standard						
Perform beyond standard						
Spontaneity of action						
Cooperation						

Figure 1.1 *Behaviour/reward grid*

Conceptually, these choices can be related to desired behaviours by using the behaviour/reward grid shown in Figure 1.1. How the grid is completed will depend on the culture, pay philosophy and requirements of the organization and the needs of its employees. Particular importance would be attached to the factors affecting reward policies as discussed in Chapter 2 and the development of performance management strategies as described in Chapter 9.

The rest of this chapter considers how reward management strategies can be developed to make a full contribution to organizational success. It describes the components of strategy and how it is evolved and integrated with business and human resource strategy.

The development of reward strategy

The determinants of reward management strategy are shown in Figure 1.2. These indicate that the strategy should be based on an analysis of:

- the external factors affecting the organization – market practice, the characteristics of the industry or sector, and the national and international social and political environment
- the organizational requirements for performance in the short- and longer term as expressed in its strategies and goals
- the operational environment within the organization – its structure and ownership, culture, employees and future employees (their present and future needs, expectations and attitudes), and the personnel policies so far developed and implemented.

These will all affect the organization's ability to deliver, ie to achieve its goals. And this, plus the results of the analysis, will determine the intrinsic and extrinsic reward strategy. Both these aspects of reward should be covered. The intrinsic reward strategy will deal with how the motivation and commitment of staff can be improved by such means as increasing responsibility and by enabling and empowering them to achieve high levels of performance. The extrinsic rewards include financial rewards and benefits, and non-financial rewards such as status and recognition.

The components of reward management strategy

Reward management strategy covers the following areas:

1. *Reward policies* – the objectives and roles of different elements of the reward system: how the system should fit the culture of the organization and can help to reinforce or re-shape it; the types and levels of rewards to be offered; the design of the

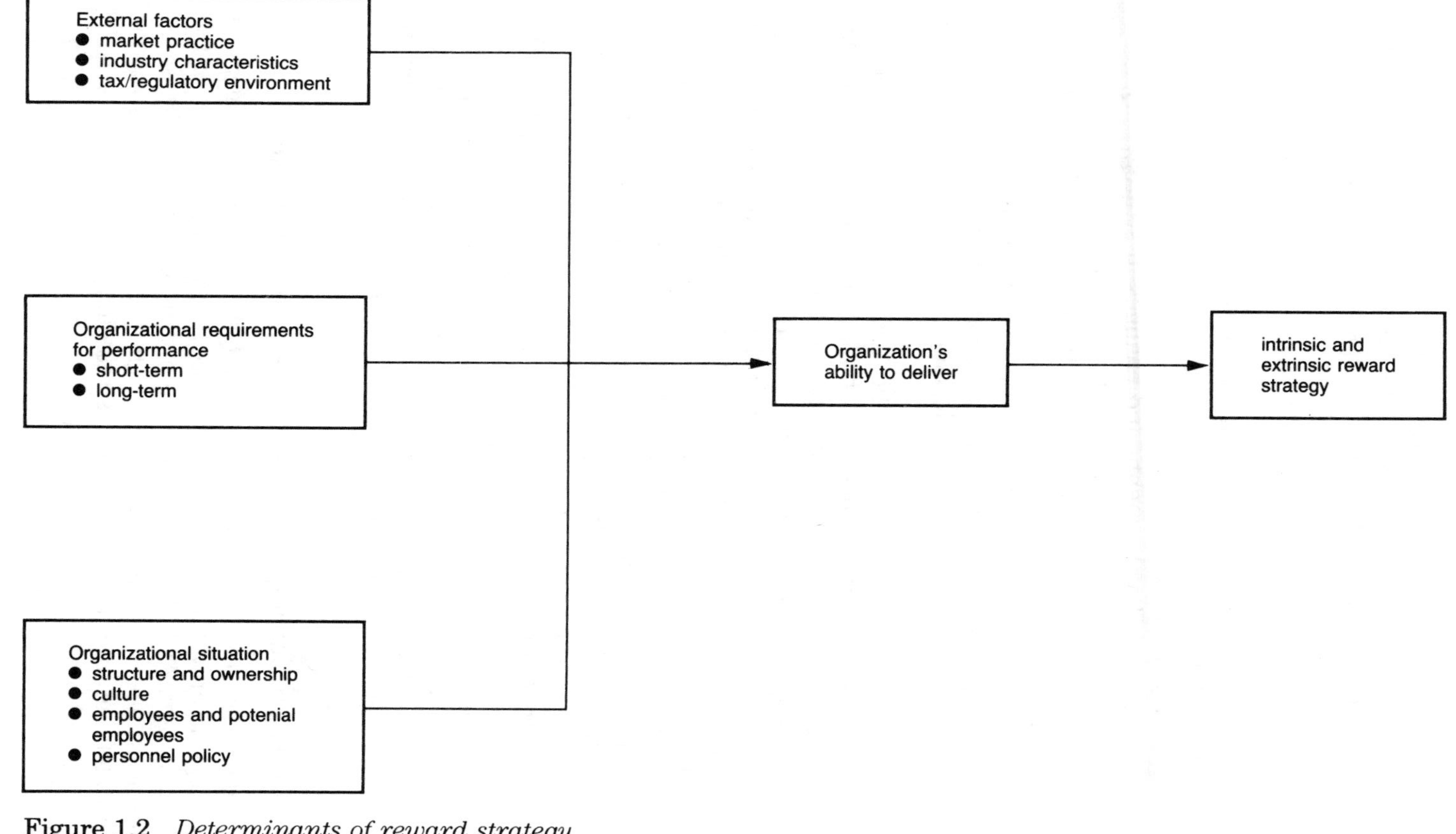

Figure 1.2 *Determinants of reward strategy*

system; how the system relates to the external environment; and how the tension between the aims of a reasonable degree of internal equity and external competitiveness can be managed (see Chapter 2).

2. *Reward practices* – the analysis of current practices in relation to:
   (a) business requirements and priorities
   (b) changes in the political, competitive, social and economic (including tax) environment
   (c) internal developments and changes in strategy, organization, technology and performance criteria
   (d) the need for people with particular levels of competence (see Chapter 3).
3. *Pay levels and relativities* – the analysis of market rates and the use of job evaluation to develop pay structures (see Part 2).
4. *Reward structures* – the development and design of pay structures (see Part 3).
5. *Paying for performance* – the design and management of systems of performance-related pay, relating to individual, group or corporate achievements (see Part 4).
6. *Employee benefits and total remuneration* – the development of the employee benefit package and the use of a total remuneration approach to reward management (see Part 5).
7. *Special reward management programmes* – the design of programmes to deal with special aspects of reward management strategy, for example boardroom pay, international remuneration, and dealing with mergers, acquisitions and business start-up situations (see Part 6).
8. *Programmes for managing the reward system* – maintaining the structure and its operational procedures, delegating more authority to line managers to enable them to make effective pay decisions concerning their staff, developing an employee relations and communications strategy and dealing with reward management issues and challenges (see Part 7).

The integration of reward management strategies

Fundamental to this book is the belief that reward management strategy is an integral part of the human resource strategy of the organization. And this human resource strategy must be driven by business needs as expressed through the process of strategic management and its expression in strategic plans.

Strategic management

A strategic approach to reward management is part of the process of strategic management, in which the organization and its managers determine:

- where they are going in the medium and longer term – the strategic intent
- how they are going to get there – strategic or long-range planning
- what they are going to do to ensure that they will get there – the direction of operations so that they move steadily towards the achievement of the strategic plan.

Managers who think strategically are looking ahead at what they need to achieve in the longer term. Although they know that businesses, like managers, must perform well in the present to succeed in the future, they are aware of the broader issues they are facing and the general direction in which they must go to deal with these issues. They then set long- and medium-term business and personal goals, and initiate and co-ordinate the actions required to achieve them.

Strategic planning

Strategic management is expressed through strategic plans which aim to relate the company's internal resources, strengths, weaknesses and values to the opportunities and threats present in the external environment in the pursuit of competitive advantage.

Strategic plans may be concerned with innovation, development and growth, but they must also be concerned with the capacity of the business to achieve its goals. And this capacity will depend largely on the distinctive competences of the business and the quality, motivation and commitment of its human resources. It is, after all, people who implement the business plan.

Strategic human resource management

Strategic human resource management helps the organization to achieve its objectives by:

- ensuring that all business planning processes recognize from the outset that the ultimate source of value is people – the concept of gaining added value from the effective use of resources is fundamental to strategic planning
- achieving a close match between business objectives and the objectives of the human resource function

- identifying the organization's distinctive competences and the type of people who will be needed to build and maintain them
- providing the quality and quantity of human resources which the business needs
- assessing the performance requirements needed to reach the company's goals, and deciding how these requirements should be satisfied
- developing particular strategies for improving the motivation and commitment of members of the organization.

Integrating reward management strategies

Reward management strategies should flow directly from these human resource strategies which, in turn, are derived from the overall strategies of the organization. The following are ten ways in which reward management strategies can help to implement human resource and business strategies:

1. Stimulate and direct effort toward the achievement of corporate goals for added value and competitive gain.
2. Convey clear messages on corporate values relating to innovation, endeavour, performance, team-work and quality.
3. Underpin these values by linking rewards to accomplishment and contribution.
4. Establish and clarify priorities for people in terms of their principal accountabilities.
5. Attract high-quality people who fit the culture of the organization and grow and contribute to its success.
6. Encourage enterprise and strategic thinking.
7. Ensure that high-quality staff prosper and stay with the organization.
8. Deliver messages to poor performers that they must improve or go.
9. Avoid demotivating the people the company wishes to retain.
10. Motivate the majority of reliable 'core' performers as well as the minority of high-flyers.

Examples of reward management strategies

Cadbury Schweppes

The following is the 'reward strategy for high performance' devised by Cadbury Schweppes.

The strategic approach to the design of pay and benefit systems:

- is geared to individual business strategies and practices but recognizes the increasingly international nature of the business
- is an integral part of an overall human resource strategy geared to those business requirements
- is market-driven within each country, thus enabling us to attract, select and retain world-class employees
- is designed to motivate and reinforce superior performance
- is flexible and increasingly individually orientated, yet soundly constructed, providing a relevant framework and basis for proper control and reasonable equity
- is the subject of regular review as to its continuing relevance and effectiveness in meeting strategic business requirements
- provides, over and above existing national pay and benefit arrangements:
  - for an effective framework for international moves
  - for situations where there is multi-business presence in a particular country
  - for trans-national arrangements to meet business needs.

The key elements in this reward strategy are:

- a basic salary structure which is competitive in the market and in which individual salary is performance-driven via regular reviews geared to the business cycle. Performance is assessed against clear and consistent standards relating to the achievement of individual business objectives and competence development
- variable pay in the form of bonuses geared to the success of the business. This needs to reflect both the performance of the team at each senior level of the business and also the achievement against annual budget
- benefit programmes geared to local market requirements, while recognizing the multi-national nature of the business.

ICL executive reward strategy

The executive remuneration strategy at ICL had to be designed to recognize the considerable individual contribution that senior directors and managers can make to the bottom line.

The ICL approach was to develop a sharply focused high-leverage plan which would help to pull the organization together. ICL, because of the highly integrated nature of its organization, needs to have a group of managers with shared and interlocking objectives. Without them, as Don Beattie, the then Personnel Director, said, 'the organization would fly apart'.

The main features of the ICL strategy were:

- base salary slightly below the market

- on-target incentive earnings to produce total cash payments ahead of the market, with significant over-achievement potential on top
- long-term incentives – typically share options – to focus people's attention on the longer term health of the company
- benefits broadly market-competitive.

National Westminster Bank

The reward strategy of the National Westminster Bank has concentrated on the introduction of performance-related pay. The prime reason for its introduction was to improve the business performance of the bank. The stated aim of the scheme was 'to provide a greater concentration on corporate objectives and the resulting business and personal objectives.' To achieve this aim, the intention is to clarify key objectives at each level, rewarding managers according to how well they achieve them.

Shell

The new remuneration system recently introduced by Shell (the 'Multi point maxima' system) stated its aims as being 'to provide better rewards for better performance and continue to recognize personal accountability and responsibility within a more flexible salary structure. This will help the company to retain a strong competitive position as an employer.'

Chapter 2

Reward Management Policies

Policies on how rewards should be managed need to be formulated as guidelines on the implementation of reward management strategies.

Reward policies will cover such areas as: levels of reward; paying for performance; the reconciliation of the tension between the need to achieve external competitiveness as well as a reasonable degree of internal equity; the extent to which decisions on pay can be delegated to line managers; the type of salary structure which is most appropriate; and the degree to which a flexible approach can realistically be adopted toward total remuneration – allowing some element of choice for employees on the level and mix of employee benefits and cash.

The starting-point must be the philosophy of the organization toward rewards and the strategy adopted. The policies can then be developed within a broad framework which brings an understanding of the factors affecting: (a) reward policies; and (b) actual and potential satisfaction with the reward system.

Reward philosophies

As was stated in the Top Pay Unit's 1990 publication, *Putting pay philosophies into practice*[1]:

> 'Behind every pay system is a pay philosophy – a set of aims and assumptions which underpin the reward structure and determine its form. A pay philosophy can reflect an existing company culture, or it can be used as an agent for change. ... Having a well-considered pay philosophy is the first step towards creating a salary structure which will assist in the recruitment and retention of high quality executives and specialists.'

The pay philosophy should be articulated because it will govern the company's approach to how it rewards its employees, the objectives it wants the pay system to achieve and the way in which it wants to manage the system.

Reward philosophies have been influenced strongly by changes in the environment in which companies operate. The enterprise culture as a product of the 1980s may not seem so relevant in the less aggressive 1990s, although it has created the strong pressures for flexibility, performance-related pay and responsiveness to the market which still prevail. However, pay philosophies increasingly recognize that financial rewards are not the only way to increase motivation and commitment. Many people responsible for human resource management know that attention has to be paid to adopting an integrated approach to reward and performance management which makes use of intrinsic as well as extrinsic motivators.

Contributions from the 'gurus'

A number of gurus, especially American ones, have made contributions recently to the debate on reward philosophies. Rosabeth Moss Kanter, for example, has suggested in *When giants learn to dance*[2] that, in the new 'post-entrepreneurial 1990s', de-layered organizations with less hierarchical structures which have to respond more quickly to change will design pay systems to match remuneration more closely to the company's earnings rather than to reflect position or job title. She rejects merit pay as expensive, unfair, relying too much on subjective judgements, divisive and not a reliable motivator. She believes that the pay mix should include a guaranteed small amount based on level and position and a large proportion of cash from gain-sharing, profit sharing and bonus schemes, the latter being awarded for exemplary team and individual contributions.

Tom Peters, in *Thriving on chaos*,[3] believes in incentives for everyone, comprising:

- pay-for-knowledge incentives to encourage employees to learn several skills (this links up with the movement to develop competency-based pay progression systems which we describe in Chapter 10)
- productivity and quality-based incentives, based on team performance
- profit-distribution incentives, based on profit centre performance
- a simple and understandable bonus formula, with the incentive bonus constituting at least 20 per cent of total pay, to be distributed monthly, separate from base salary
- an employee share ownership scheme, with the employer contributing 8 to 10 per cent of payroll.

These prescriptions may not be universally applicable, but they give plenty of food for thought. Ultimately, however, every company has to work out its own approach, and this will be contingent upon its culture, values, strategies, structure, technology and environment.

Recurring themes in the UK

There may be no such thing as a universal pay philosophy, but the recent research carried out by the Top Pay Unit (1990) did reveal the following recurring themes:

- salary policy is increasingly seen as a tool for bringing about cultural change within organizations
- much greater flexibility in salary systems is now required to enable employers to recruit and retain high-quality executives
- for managers and professionals, some link between pay and performance is increasingly taken for granted
- relating pay to performance increases the responsibilities of line managers, who have to live with the consequences of their recommendations on salaries for their staff
- careful monitoring is necessary to ensure fairness and consistency, both within and between groups if a performance-related system is used
- computerization has made possible the introduction of more sophisticated ways of calculating individual performance-related salary increases for large numbers of employees
- as labour markets become more competitive, personnel departments are having to work harder to provide up-to-date information on market rates
- bonus schemes, especially for senior managers, are being introduced by many companies, but the reason may have more to do with market pressures than a belief that a bonus scheme will increase motivation or secure better results.

The factors that affect the development of reward policies

Within the framework of the organization's pay philosophy, reward policies should be developed on the basis of an understanding of:

1. The factors affecting employee performance and motivation.
2. The factors affecting reward levels.
3. The influence of corporate culture and organization.
4. The factors influencing employee satisfaction with the reward system.

The factors that affect performance and motivation

The ingredients of high performance

High performance requires that employees are:

- energized to perform because they are well motivated and highly committed
- empowered to perform because they have the ability, skills and know-how needed to achieve the levels of competence required
- enabled to perform through the guidance and support provided to them, the quality of leadership and the autonomy they are given to decide, to act and to exercise control over their work.

All these ingredients are important but, as reward management is very much concerned with motivation and commitment, we propose to concentrate on these aspects of the process.

Motivation

The basis of motivation

Motivation is about what makes people act or behave in the way they do. It is anchored in two basic concepts:

1. The *needs* that operate within the individual.
2. The *goals* towards which the individual moves.

In its simplest form, the process of motivation is initiated by the conscious or unconscious recognition of a need. A goal is then established which, it is thought, will satisfy that need and a course of action is determined that will lead to the attainment of that goal. But, as goals are satisfied, new needs emerge and the cycle continues.

Motivation as goal-directed behaviour

Motivation and performance will be higher when individuals are set specific goals, when goals are difficult but accepted and when there is feedback on performance. Participation in goal-setting is important as a means of getting agreement to the setting of higher goals. Stretching goals must be agreed and their achievement reinforced by guidance and advice. Feedback is vital in maintaining motivation, particularly towards the achievement of even higher goals.

Expectancy theory

The assumption of the needs–goals concept is that people will direct their efforts towards the goals they value. But people will only act when they have a reasonable expectation that their actions will lead to desired goals.

Motivation is only likely when a clearly perceived and usable relationship exists between performance and outcome and the outcome is seen as a means of satisfying needs.

The strength of motivation, therefore, depends on:

- the value of the rewards available to individuals for achieving goals in so far as they satisfy their needs
- the expectations which individuals have that their actions will lead to desired goals; in other words, that rewards depend on effort, as perceived by the individual.

Motivation and performance

The link between motivation and performance is more complex than most people believe. This is partly because individual needs, expectations and goals are highly variable, but it also arises because there are a number of factors which impinge on performance. These were summed up in the motivation model developed by Porter and Lawler.[4]

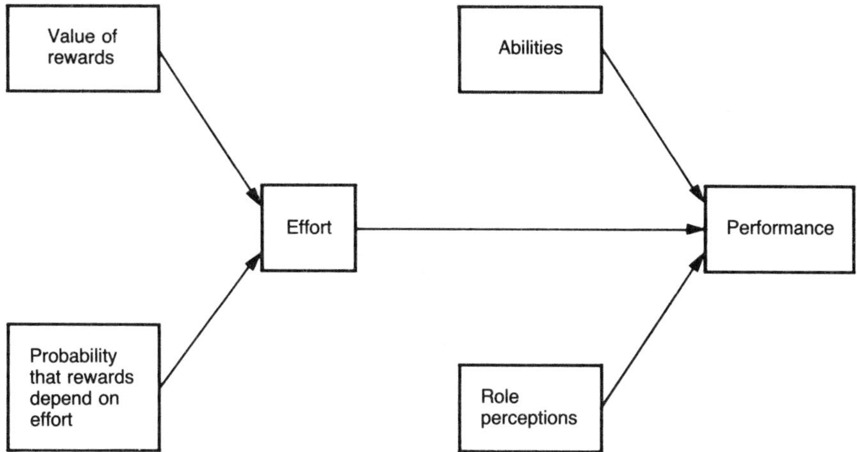

Figure 2.1 *Motivation model*

Source reproduced with permission from L W Porter and E E Lawler, *Managerial Attitudes and Performance*, Irwin – Dorsey, Homewood, Illinois, 1968.

The model in Figure 2.1 suggests that effort will be influenced by the value of rewards and the probability that rewards depend upon effort. But effort is not enough; there are two other factors which need to be taken into account:

- ability – individual characteristics such as intelligence, manual skills and know-how

- role perception – what individuals want to do or believe they are required to do.

It should also be recognized that there is no linear relationship between motivation and performance, as many people believe. The simplistic view as expressed in Figure 2.2 bears no relation to reality.

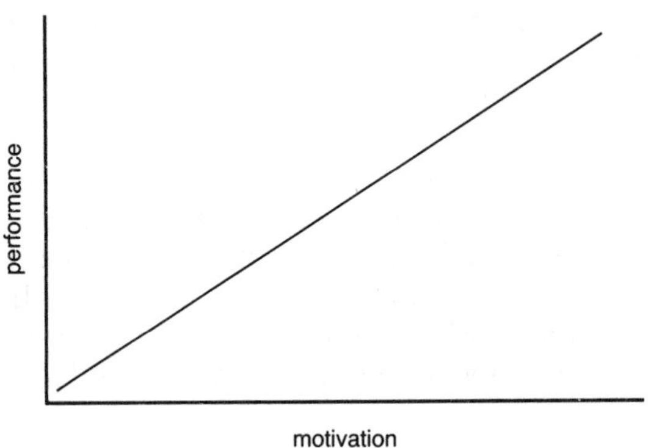

Figure 2.2 *A simplistic view of motivation*

People can also, of course, be over-motivated, which can result in stress and poor performance, as illustrated in Figure 2.3.

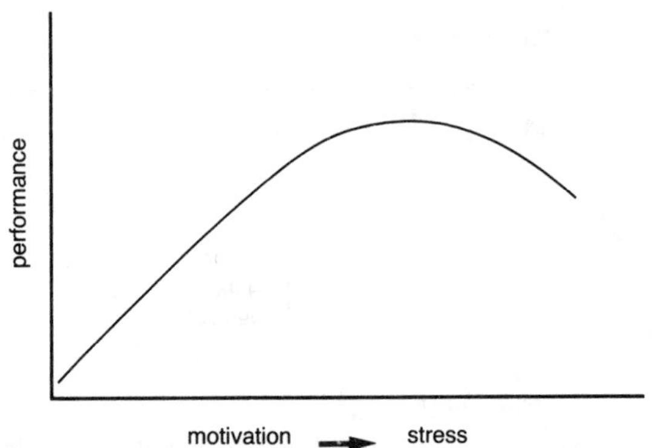

Figure 2.3 *Motivation, performance and stress*

Intrinsic and extrinsic motivation

To relate the concept of motivation to reward management it is necessary to emphasize the importance of goals, the value of rewards and the importance of expectations about getting them. It is also necessary to analyze motivating forces which affect individual behaviour. These can be placed in two categories:

1. *Intrinsic motivation* – the self-generated factors which influence people to behave in particular ways or to move in particular directions. These include self-actualization or self-fulfilment, responsibility, achievement and the work itself.
2. *Extrinsic motivation* – what is done to or for people to motivate them in the shape of financial rewards, fringe benefits, status symbols, recognition of achievement, praise and promotion.

It is generally held that intrinsic rewards may have a longer term and deeper effect in creating and increasing satisfaction, but that extrinsic rewards, including pay, can be important in attracting and retaining employees and, in the short term, increasing effort and minimizing dissatisfaction.

The role of money as a motivator

The overriding consideration in motivation is that the members of an organization contribute to it in return for the inducements that the organization provides. Money is clearly a major inducement but, because of the complexity of the motivation process involving many different needs and goals, it is dangerously simplistic to adopt the old 'economic man' theory, viz that money is the only motivator. Intrinsic rewards are also important.

Money as a motivator for those already in employment will only work if people are in a position to anticipate the rewards they will obtain in return for a certain degree of achievement. In other words, there must be a clear link between effort and reward. People will also be better motivated by money if they can exercise direct control over their rewards. Good incentive and bonus schemes, whose worthwhile and foreseeable rewards are attainable by actions which are under the control of the employee, can be effective motivators.

Motivation theory also supports the case for a fully disclosed pay system. How can money be a motivator if people do not know what they can earn? This applies not only to the amount of bonus they can obtain if they achieve a defined level of performance, but also to how they can progress according to merit, either within their existing salary scale, or through promotion to even more rewarding jobs.

While it is dangerous to place too much reliance on money as a motivator, it is still a powerful force because it is linked directly or indirectly to the satisfaction of all the basic needs. Although money itself has no intrinsic meaning it does acquire significant motivating power when it comes to symbolize intangible goals. Money in itself is a measure of achievement. Reward policies should, therefore, recognize the importance of money as a motivator, but overall human resource management policies should also ensure that the other intrinsic motivators can play their part. Particular attention should be paid to the following non-financial motivators, all of them intrinsic to the work itself:

- opportunity to achieve (enabling)
- job satisfaction
- challenge
- career prospects
- personal growth – ability to pursue academic or professional interests
- status
- ability to provide for family needs and interests
- the quality of working life, not only working conditions but the organizational climate, the core values of the company and the management style adopted by those who run it.

Commitment

While an important aim of reward policies will be to increase motivation and therefore, it is hoped, performance, it is necessary also to consider how the reward system, in conjunction with other human resource management policies in such areas as career development, can increase the commitment of employees to the organization.

The term commitment denotes three areas of feeling or behaviour related to the organization in which someone works:

1. Belief in, and acceptance of, the organization itself and its goals and values.
2. Desire to maintain membership of the organization.
3. Willingness to exert effort on behalf of the organization beyond what is contracted for.

Commitment is a wider concept than motivation and tends to be more stable over a period of time. Committed individuals may go on believing in their organization and wanting to work for it even if they have been demotivated by particular aspects of the way in which they are treated.

Commitment is directly affected by the way in which the organization operates. This will include such matters as:

- its purpose, which might be expressed in a mission statement
- its reputation
- its success
- its values (what is believed to be important) and norms (accepted ways of behaviour)
- the organization climate (working atmosphere)
- management style

- the extent to which the company is a caring and considerate employer

The steps which can be taken to increase commitment are described in Chapter 3.

The influence of culture and organization on reward policies

Reward policies have to take into account the factors affecting performance and commitment mentioned above, but they are also influenced by the corporate culture and values and the type of organization in which the policies are being applied.

Corporate culture

The corporate culture is the set of taken-for-granted assumptions and beliefs developed and learned over the years which determine the core values of the enterprise, its organizational climate and management style. Corporate culture manifests itself as 'the way things are done here'. Its values include beliefs about how well people should be rewarded and the extent to which excellence as a goal can and should be achieved by paying for performance.

The culture of an organization influences and is influenced by the sort of company it is – its products or services, technologies, methods of working, market position, prosperity (growth or decline); and the environment in which it operates: competitive, turbulent, changeable or calm. These factors will all affect the sort of people the organization wants and may indeed attract certain types of people, hopefully those the enterprise needs.

Reward policies must be consistent with corporate culture, although they can be used to engender cultural change.

The policies must also be relevant to the situation in which the organization currently exists and the direction in which it plans to go. In other words, reward policies should be the basis of remuneration strategies which are integrated with the strategic plans of the enterprise.

Type of organization

Reward policies, strategies and procedures will vary according to the type of organization, its culture and its environment. There is no such thing as a 'right' policy. It all depends. For example, a large and bureaucratic company may feel most comfortable with a graded salary structure and highly formalized job evaluation, salary survey, performance review and salary administration procedures. A smaller, more loosely organized company, especially one which is growing and changing rapidly, will not want to overformalize its procedures. It will need flexibility to respond quickly to change. An autocratic style of management will result in control from the top, no participation in formulating policies and as little disclosure of information by the company as possible.

A flattened or de-layered organizational structure will require better team-work amongst managers, and therefore group rather than individual bonus or incentive schemes might be more appropriate. A highly decentralized organization might allow a fair degree of leeway to enable local management to develop their own approaches to the reward system (for example, type of structure or bonus scheme), as long as certain broadly defined corporate policies are followed.

The factors that affect satisfaction with the reward system

The degree to which employees are satisfied with the reward system is related to the following factors:

1. *Fairness* – the extent to which they think the system is fair in that rewards are commensurate with ability, contribution and effort. This is what Elliott Jaques[5] describes as the 'felt-fair' principle. He believes that there is an unrecognized system of norms for fair payment and that individuals are 'unconsciously aware of their own potential capacity for work, as well as the equitable pay level for that work'. To be fair, pay must be felt to match the level of work and the capacity of the individual to do it.
2. *Expectations and value* – satisfaction is highest when rewards meet expectations as to their value and the value of the reward is commensurate with the effort and skill needed to obtain it.
3. *Internal comparisons* – employees are more likely to be satisfied if they feel they are being paid correctly in relation to what other employees who are doing similar jobs at a similar level of competence are receiving. Dissatisfaction may be caused by perceived inequities because people have insufficient information on how salary policy affects them and are therefore not in a position to compare their worth with others; hence the importance of a fair and open job evaluation system and a convincing demonstration that pay is fairly related to performance. Given the problem of achieving effective communication, and the innate suspicion with which many employees view their company's pay policies, this can be very difficult. It is hardly surprising in these circumstances that many

performance-related pay schemes are more successful at demotivating than motivating people.

4. *External comparisons* – satisfaction and commitment to stay with the organization is most probable if people feel that present *and* future rewards are likely to be higher within the organization than elsewhere. This is often a matter of perception, which may be misguided (based on the 'grass is always greener on the other side of the fence' principle). It is therefore sometimes difficult for organizations to reduce feelings of dissatisfaction in this area, especially if promotion prospects are limited.
5. *Self-evaluation* – if rewards are in line with what people feel they are worth, then satisfaction will result. The problem is that, as Michael Beer points out, individuals tend to overrate their own performance: 'It has been found that many employees rate their performance in the eightieth percentile. Given the fact that an organization cannot pay everyone at the eightieth percentile it is not surprising that many employees feel they are being underpaid'.[6]
6. *The total reward package* – overall satisfaction depends on the result of a mix of rewards rather than any single reward. Michael Beer also suggests that: 'The evidence seems to be clear that intrinsic rewards and extrinsic rewards are both important, and that they are not directly substitutable for each other. Employees who are paid well for repetitious, boring work will be dissatisfied with the lack of intrinsic rewards, just as employees paid poorly for interesting, challenging work may be dissatisfied with extrinsic rewards'.

Overall implications for reward policy

This analysis of the factors affecting reward management suggests that the following considerations should be taken into account when formulating reward policies:

1. An appropriate mix of rewards is required which is flexible enough to satisfy, so far as possible, the needs of both the organization and its employees.
2. The reward system should be geared to the attainment of goals but should also recognize the importance of ensuring that there is a clear relationship between effort/ability and reward.
3. Attention has to be given to determining the right levels of financial rewards in relation to the needs of the organization to attract, retain and motivate (or avoid demotivating) staff, the ability of the organization to provide the rewards, and the needs and expectations of employees.

4. In deciding on reward levels, consideration has to be given to external comparisons (market rates) and the achievement of a reasonable degree of internal equity.
5. The type of pay structure and how employees should be rewarded in relation to their performance has to be considered in the light of the culture of the organization and employee expectations. This also affects the degree of freedom managers are allowed with which to manage reward.
6. The degree to which employees are involved in developing reward policies and practices needs to be determined.
7. Employees should be informed about the system and the way it affects them. Also, their expectations should be managed within the bounds of what is realistic in their particular circumstances.

Reward policy areas

The main areas in which policies need to be formulated are:

- the relationship of rewards to business performance
- flexibility
- the level of rewards
- market rates
- equity
- performance-related rewards
- pay structures
- delegation and control
- balancing financial and non-financial motivators
- the reward mix and the total reward system
- the pay determination process.

The relationship of rewards to business performance

A policy needs to be formulated on how pay levels should respond to fluctuations in business performance. Raising basic salaries during profitable times can create problems. The resulting higher salaries could be a serious cost burden in future years if there is a downturn in the business. Furthermore, it implies that the ability to pay is sufficient justification for higher salaries, and this may conflict with other remuneration policies which lay down that individual rates of pay should only be related to performance, competence and responsibility. Business success is best shared with employees either through a profit sharing scheme (see Chapter 15) or by one-off bonus payments which do not have a cost commitment in future years.

Flexibility

Reward policies should allow for flexibility in operating the reward system in response to business fluctuations, the rapidly changing pressures to which the organization and its employees are likely to be subjected, the demand for different types of skills and variations in market rates for different categories of staff.

Flexibility can be achieved by:

- increasing the proportion of variable performance-related pay in the total package
- avoiding the use of rigid, hierarchical pay structures by such means as the use of pay curves, where progression is dependent on competence and performance (see Chapter 7)
- not having a mechanistic system of relating rewards to performance
- relating pay awards entirely to merit and increases in market rates, thus avoiding a separate and explicit link with increases in the cost of living, and giving scope to reward the good performers more and the poor performers less
- allowing greater choice in the range of benefits employees receive
- recognizing that the organization must respond quickly to the problems created by skill shortages and market rate pressures, and flexing the pay arrangements accordingly.

Levels of reward

The policy on reward levels should determine whether or not the company needs to be a high-payer. This is sometimes called its pay posture, which will be the policy on where rates of pay and fringe benefit packages should lie in relation to what comparable companies pay for similar jobs. This policy will be linked to the one on market rates.

Fast-moving profitable companies will want top people and, if they want to stay in front, will pay top rates, or at least in the upper quartile of the range of pay for similar jobs in comparable companies. They will go to great efforts to ensure that they maintain that position. Small concerns, such as advertising agencies working on high margins which depend entirely on the talent of their staff, will pay exceptionally good salaries and provide some magnificent benefits. So much so, that the companies outside this particular 'magic circle' cannot possibly compete.

Other organizations may seek to pay closer to the median – to keep pace with market rates. The authors have rarely come across companies which admit that it is their policy to pay below the median. Obviously, however, that is where half of them are, possibly because they are unaware of the fact, and not through any deliberate actions on their part.

Performance-related rewards

The extent to which performance governs rewards and how the two are linked together depends absolutely on the core values of the organization. Thrusting, thriving and growing companies have to be entrepreneurial. And they must encourage what Gifford Pinchot describes as an *intrapreneurial* spirit.[7] He defines this as taking hands-on responsibility for creating innovation of any kind within an organization. The intrapreneur may not be the creator or inventor but is always the dreamer who figures out how to turn an idea into a profitable reality.

Intrapreneurship within an enterprise should flourish if people believe that the game is worth the candle, ie that potential rewards justify the effort or the risk that have to be put into achieving them. They must *expect* that the value of their contribution to the organization will be rewarded appropriately.

Market rate policy

How far should market rate pressures be allowed to affect or possibly distort a salary structure? They cannot be ignored completely, but there is an element of choice. It might be decided that the salaries for certain jobs have to keep pace with the market. These would be distinguished as special market rates in the salary structure ('red circled') or put into a separate market group. The salaries of other jobs would primarily be fixed by internal comparisons, possibly using as upper and lower limits the chief executive's salary and the salary levels required to maintain a reasonable differential between first-line supervision and the clerical staff or operatives they control. Alternatively, salary levels for all key jobs may be assessed by reference to market rates, which would also indicate differentials between functions and between levels in the hierarchy. The main factor in assessing the influence that external salary levels should be allowed to exercise internally is the degree to which there is open market competition for staff. The less the need to go to the market, the less the need to react to short-term pressures.

In formulating market rate policy it should be remembered that the company is probably operating in several different labour markets. There will be the local market for more junior employees, the national market for managerial, professional and highly technical staff and, possibly, the international market. The increasing importance and relevance of international influences as more and more companies base themselves in Britain, and overseas firms look for talent in the UK, may strongly influence reward policies. Labour markets are becoming increasingly fragmented – between different sections of industry or commerce, for different occupations and in different areas.

Market rate policies have therefore to be flexible and continuously under review so that they can be quickly and easily adjusted to the needs of the organization and changes in the labour markets.

Equity

Equity is a perceived sense that salary policies are just and fair because pay matches individual contribution, capacity and the level of work carried out, pay differentials are related to finite differences in the degree of responsibility, and equal pay is received for equal work. Absolute equity is an unattainable ideal, but the policy should be to achieve as high a degree of equity as possible by adopting a systematic and analytical approach to establishing the value of jobs. It is, however, often difficult to reconcile the two aims of being equitable *and* competitive. It may be hard to avoid paying higher than internal rates for comparable jobs in order to attract the right people. Market forces sometimes have to be allowed to prevail.

This does not imply that elaborate job evaluation schemes are essential. It is possible to be both systematic and analytical, without calling on the aid of an over-complicated job evaluaton scheme. In this context, 'systematic' means a methodical collection of facts about market rates and contents of the jobs, and 'analytical' means the resolution of the data into elements to increase the ease and accuracy with which comparisons can be made between different jobs. The choice of method is wide and the alternatives are discussed in Chapter 5.

Salary structure

The main policy questions to be answered about salary structures are:

- is a formal structure required?
- if a formal structure is necessary, what sort of structure should it have?

Some companies work without a formal structure quite successfully. They decide on a starting rate for a job on some *ad hoc* basis and adjust it as and when required. They can operate flexibly and react quickly to events, and this may be desirable in a fluid situation. The obvious danger is that salaries will be dealt with inconsistently and inequitably unless there is rigid central control, which is not always possible or desirable. By its very name, a salary structure implies a certain amount of rigidity. But this need not be so. A structure can and should be no more than an understood framework within which consistent salary policies can be applied. It is possible to design and operate salary structures which enable a sufficient degree of flexibility to be achieved but allow for an adequate amount of control in order to avoid inequities and excessive costs. The pay curve system, as described in Chapter 7, is a means of achieving this.

Control

The extent to which control can be exercised is partly determined by the choice of salary progression system and salary structure, but it is also a matter of the amount of freedom that is allowed to managers to fix and change the salaries of their staff. This, like so many other aspects of reward management, depends largely on the management style of the company (ie the degree to which decisions are centralized and autocratic or are decentralized and independent). Some central control over the implementation of salary policies and salary costs is necessary, but the aim should be to delegate as much authority as possible to managers. The reward management procedures of the company must, therefore, be designed to achieve a delicate balance between the extremes of rigidity or anarchy.

Balancing financial and non-financial motivators

Reward policy has to strike a balance between the mix of intrinsic (entirely non-financial) and extrinsic (mainly financial) rewards. Neither should be neglected, bearing in mind that financial rewards are important as a means of attracting and retaining staff and achieving short-term motivation, while non-financial rewards are more likely to achieve longer term motivation and commitment.

Total remuneration

There is usually some choice in deciding the best mix of the various elements of remuneration: basic salary, bonus, profit sharing, pensions, life insurance, cars and other fringe benefits. The mix may vary at different levels. For junior clerical staff, the best approach may be to concentrate on straight salary with some scope for progression according to merit, together with the usual pension and life insurance provisions, and either subsidized canteens or luncheon vouchers as the only additional benefit. At senior management and where the market dictates a wider range of benefits, the mix could become more complicated. At this level (or below) it could be a matter of policy to concentrate on paying a competitive salary at a rate high enough to allow individuals to purchase for themselves the benefits they need. This could be preferable to imposing fringe benefits on individuals who may not want them, or providing them on an inequitable basis to a favoured few who happen to become eligible for them. But the tax advantage to the company or the individual may make the provision of a benefit such as a car or a generous pension scheme preferable to an addition to basic salary. In areas of very high pay, tax planning is still important.

The pay determination process

Much will depend on whether determination takes place in a unionized or non-unionized environment. Union negotiations may cover some, but not all, elements of pay or may be comprehensive.

Communication

If money is a motivator, it is right and proper that people should be told what is available to them so that they can be motivated by it. If equity is the first consideration, the fairness of the system has to be seen to be believed.

A company without a formal salary structure is not in a position to communicate details of it to its staff. The need for flexibility in these circumstances may override the need to be open about the system. It is, however, still necessary to keep individuals informed of where they stand in order to persuade them that they are fairly paid. More importantly, they need to be motivated by being given an indication of how their pay can progress, depending on their performance.

Adequate communication is easier when there is a defined salary structure. It should then be possible to tell individuals the grade they are in, the limits of their salary in the present job and the rate at which they might progress to that limit, based on certain assumptions about future performance.

Beyond that point the choice of policy is more difficult. It may do no harm to publish the salary structure, but this is not interesting unless the gradings of jobs in the structure are also revealed. This can and should be done if the company has complete confidence in its ability to justify the gradings to its staff, or if the structure has been developed by means of a joint management and staff job evaluation exercise. Once a salary structure has been fully communicated, withdrawal can be painful and it should be managed very carefully.

Policy statement

It may be useful to produce a statement on salary policies as a guide to management and as a means of communicating to staff the intentions of the company. The problem with such statements is that if they are too specific they can be used by trade unions or staff associations as bargaining points in pay negotiations. Even the use of words such as 'fair', 'just' and 'equitable' in a published statement can produce endless and futile arguments in negotiations as to what these terms mean. On the other hand, a bland statement full of platitudes could be quite meaningless.

There is, however, some value in listing the points considered by the company to be relevant in rewarding staff in a statement such as the following:

'Staff should be appropriately rewarded in relation to:

- the contribution they are expected to make towards achieving the company's objectives
- the results they achieve
- the value placed on comparable jobs within the company
- the value placed on comparable jobs in other companies
- the economic and commercial environment as it affects the company and its staff.'

Note that this statement makes no reference to the cost of living. It is always dangerous to indicate any direct relationship between salary levels and the rate of inflation. In negotiations the company has to be able to resist any claim for the index linking of salaries. Ability to pay must always be the first consideration and it is dangerous to imply that this can be over-ridden by a claim based on the maintenance of the standard of living of staff. No one in employment has the divine right to be protected completely from inflation in all circumstances.

References

1. Top Pay Unit *Putting pay philosophies into practice*, Incomes Data Services, London, 1990.
2. Kanter, Rosabeth *When giants learn to dance*, Simon & Schuster, London, 1989.
3. Peters, Tom *Thriving on chaos*, Macmillan, London, 1988.
4. Porter, L W and Lawler, E E *Managerial attitudes and performance*, Irwin-Dorsey, Homewood, Illinois, 1968.
5. Jaques, Elliott *Equitable payment*, Heinneman, London, 1961.
6. Beer, Michael 'Reward systems', from Michael Beer, Bert Spector, Paul R Laurence and D Quinn Mills *Managing Human Assets*, The Free Press, New York, 1984.
7. Pinchot, Gifford *Intrepreneuring*, Harper & Row, New York.

Chapter 3

The Development and Implementation of Reward Management Strategies and Policies

The development and implementation of reward management strategies and policies is best carried out by reference to a set of basic assessment criteria. This initial study can then be extended into a more detailed diagnostic review.

Basic criteria

From the organization's viewpoint:

- where is it placed in relation to the market place? Is it competitive? (for profit-making organizations). How well is it fulfilling its objectives and serving its clients (non-profit-making organizations)?
- does the current remuneration package represent value for money?
- is the pay policy flexible enough to meet current and future needs?
- is the current mix of base pay, cash performance rewards and benefits appropriate?
- should the present reward structure be changed to provide more incentives for employees?
- is current practice well communicated and are the right messages getting across?

From the employees' viewpoint:

- does the present package adequately reward their contribution?
- are the security needs of individuals and their families properly provided for?
- is the mix of pay and benefits right? Would some element of choice be desirable?

- is the system well understood and are all its components properly valued by individuals?

Diagnostic review

The purpose of the diagnostic review is to assess the extent to which the reward management system is effective in the sense that it is helping the organization to achieve its objectives. The review should cover reward strategies, policies and systems. It will form the basis for action in any area of reward management. The following checklist sets out the points to be covered.

1. *Is there a strategy for reward management which clearly states the intentions of the organization on how the reward system will support the achievement of corporate objectives?*

The strategy should be concerned not only with obtaining, retaining and motivating good-quality staff but also with underpinning the organization's values, conveying to employees the message that the company will satisfy their reward expectations and indicating the type of behaviour that will be rewarded.

2. *Are reward strategies linked to key business and human resource strategies?*

The strategies should be concerned with how the reward system can provide a lever to encourage growth, innovation and improved performance.

3. *Does the strategy provide a good basis for the development of reward policies, systems and procedures?*

The strategy should be flexible and should provide a relevant framework for reasonable equity and proper control.

4. *Is the strategy congruent with the culture of the organization?*

The strategy should not only reflect the culture of the organization but should also be used as necessary to help to change that culture, eg increase the degree to which the company is performance orientated.

5. *What is the policy on levels of rewards?*

The policy on levels of reward should define the 'pay posture' of the company, ie the relationship between internal rates and market rates.

6. *Are reward levels linked to business performance?*

The question should establish how the reward system and structure will respond to fluctuations in business performance and will consider the use of one-off bonus payments in response to business success, rather than basic pay increases which have a cost commitment for future years.

7. *What is the policy on market rates?*

This question covers policy on the extent to which exceptional treatment has to be given to those job categories where market rates are high and which are critical to the future success of the business.

8. *What is the policy on equity?*

This policy should define how the company achieves equity in rates of pay according to levels of responsibility and performance. There is often tension between market rate and equity policies and the answer to this question will be linked to market rate policies.

9. *What is the policy on performance-related rewards?*

This policy should define the extent to which leverage for growth, innovation and improved results is to be provided by performance-related pay. It should consider how far rewards should be related to individual, group or corporate performance and what proportion of total remuneration for different categories of staff should be related to performance.

10. *What is the policy on the pay structure?*

This policy should be concerned with whether or not a formal graded or pay spine structure is required and, if not, what sort of structure is suitable, eg pay curve, job family or spot rate, as described in Chapter 7. The degree to which the structure should be flexible also needs to be considered. The policy should deal with the possibility of different pay structures being installed, as appropriate, for different parts of the organization. This means making decisions on the extent to which uniform pay levels for categories of jobs should be adopted for the whole organization and the scope given to business units to develop their own pay systems in response to local market conditions.

11. *What is the policy on the total reward system?*

The total reward system policy should establish the mix of financial and non-financial or intrinsic rewards. It is necessary to determine whether or not there is too much emphasis on one or the other. Consideration should also be given to the mix of pay and employee benefits and the extent to which employees will be allowed choice in the benefits they receive.

12. *How effective is the reward system in attracting high-quality people to the organization?*

It is necessary to find out if recruitment difficulties are being experienced for any categories of staff. The degree to which these are occurring because the company is paying below the market rate needs to be established. But it should be remembered that problems in getting staff may be a result of the poor image of the company as an employer or the fact that the type of work and prospects in the organization are not attractive.

13. *How effective is the reward system in retaining the people the organization wants to keep?*

Good offers will always attract staff away from the company and, even if pay is ahead of market rates, high-quality staff will leave to develop their careers. The answer to a problem of staff wastage may lie in the areas of improving career development and other employment policies rather than upping rates of pay. Clearly, however, low rates are likely to increase wastage unless the employment conditions and prospects within the organization are significantly better than elsewhere.

14. *How effective is the reward system in motivating employees?*

Paying for performance does provide a means of motivation but this element of the reward system can also demotivate staff if it is not felt to be fair. This is a necessary question to ask, but the link between performance-related pay and results is often obscured by other factors affecting performance and it may be difficult to establish just how effective the reward system is in this respect.

15. *How well are reward policies communicated to employees?*

If reward policies and practices are to motivate employees, they must be told how they benefit. This should start with recruitment advertisements as well as including all the normal processes of communication in employment.

16. *What is the level of employment costs?*

This question should establish how employment costs compare with turnover, profit and value added within the company and with those of other organizations in the same area of activity. If employment costs are increasing at too high a rate or are out of line, it is necessary to determine whether this is due to overall staffing levels or to incorrect reward policies and ineffective remuneration systems.

17. *What information is obtained on market rates as a means of determining what they currently are?*

The information should be obtained by means of systematic studies of published data (not just job advertisements) and the conduct of pay surveys. (Pay surveys are described in Chapter 4.)

18. *Is a formal sytem of job evaluation used to determine internal relativities?*

Any existing scheme should be reviewed to ensure that it is properly constructed, appropriate and correctly administered. Job evaluation schemes can easily 'work loose' ie be eroded, if jobs are upgraded without being adequately evaluated (a process usually referred to as grade drift), and this needs to be checked.

19. *Is sufficient attention given to paying the same for work of equal value?*

The design and implementation of the job evaluation scheme itself and the methods used to fix job grades and pay levels should not discriminate against individual employees or categories of employees in any way.

20. *What type of pay structure or structures exist in the organization?*

There is a choice of structures, including graded salary scales, pay spine, spot rate and pay curves. What needs to be established is the extent to which the structures are relevant to the needs of the organization as a whole or the part of the organization in which they operate. A structure will be appropriate if it:

(a) fits the circumstances and culture of the organization, in that it is flexible in organizations subject to rapid change, or is well-defined and rigorously applied where order and predictability are of paramount importance
(b) provides a logical framework or system for enabling consistent and defensible decisions to be made on the levels of pay and differentials of all the employees to be covered by the structure
(c) makes provision for the reasonable and sometimes inevitable fact that external market rate considerations may have to prevail over the requirements of strict internal equity, especially in areas of skill shortage.

21. *If there is a graded salary structure, is it designed and administered properly?*

This question can be answered by reference to the following sub-questions:

(a) are the grades clearly defined?
(b) are the salary ranges wide enough to allow scope for salary progression in accordance with competence and performance?
(c) is there an adequate differential (say 15 to 20 per cent) between grades?
(d) is there an overlap between grades to provide for some flexibility and to recognize the fact that an experienced individual at the top of one grade may be of more value to the organization than a newcomer in the grade above?
(e) are consistent methods used to allocate jobs into grades, including decisions on recruitment, promotion and upgrading because of greater responsibility?
(f) is there any evidence of inequities in the salary structure because of wrongly graded jobs?
(g) is there any evidence of salary levels falling behind market rates?

22. *Is there a consistent method of progressing salaries according to performance or level of competence?*

This question considers all types of salary progression schemes within a graded structure, up a pay spine or along a pay curve. The methods of determining the rate of progression should be examined to ensure that they are based on fair and consistent methods of reviewing performance or assessing the level of competence achieved.

23. *If a performance related pay system is in use:*
(a) is the amount of the performance-related pay sufficient to act as a motivator not only for high-flyers but also for the reliable 'core' performers on whom most organizations depend?
(b) is the relationship between effort and reward clearly defined?
(c) have employees a reasonable degree of control over the results which determine reward levels?
(d) do bonus earnings fluctuate too much?
(e) is the system easy to understand and administer?

24. *Is there a balanced and cost-effective approach to the provision of employee benefits?*

This question should be answered by examining the whole benefit package to ensure firstly that it provides an appropriate range of benefits at each level and, secondly, that the organization is getting value for money on its benefits expenditure in terms of increased motivation and commitment.

25. *Is there a consistent and fair basis for allocating benefits?*

It is necessary to examine the criteria which govern the allocation of benefits to ensure that they are both logical and equitable. Whether or not the organization has harmonized its benefits sufficiently, ie has provided an equal package for all levels of employees, should be considered in relation to 'good' market practice.

26. *Are individual salary reviews properly controlled to keep within budgets and to be consistent with salary progression guidelines?*

The whole system for setting budgets and controlling increases should be examined to ensure that it is well defined, and properly applied and controlled.

27. *Are there established procedures for fixing salaries on appointment, promotion or transfer?*

The procedures should be well defined and applied consistently.

28. *How are annual reviews handled?*

There is an increasing tendency to provide for more flexibility in relating reward to contribution by not paying separate cost-of-living increases.

29. *How are reviews controlled?*

There should always be a review budget, but managers can still be allowed some discretion within their budgets.

30. *Are managers given a reasonable degree of freedom to make their own pay decisions?*

A reasonable degree of freedom should consist of giving managers scope to decide on pay levels subject to overall policy guidelines.

The outcome of this diagnostic review may be action to correct any specific problems it identifies. It may also indicate actions required in the areas of non-financial rewards to increase motivation and commitment.

Increasing motivation through non-financial rewards

The following ten-point motivation strategy is based on motivation theory and practice as described in Chapter 2, especially the combined message of expectancy and goal theory:

1. Assess the motivation needs of employees by analysing the outcome of individual performance reviews and by the use of attitude surveys.

2. Set and agree demanding goals.
3. Provide feedback on performance.
4. Create expectations that certain behaviours and outputs will produce worthwhile rewards when they succeed but will result in penalties if they fail.
5. Design jobs which enable people to feel a sense of accomplishment, to express and use their abilities and to exercise their own decision-making powers.
6. Provide intangible rewards such as praise for work well done.
7. Communicate to individuals and publicize generally the link between performance and reward, thus enhancing expectations.
8. Select and train managers and supervisors who will exercise effective leadership and have the required motivating skills.
9. Give people the guidance and training which will develop the knowledge, skill and understanding they need to improve their performance.
10. Show individuals what they have to do to satisfy their aspirations through career progression.

Increasing commitment

The following is a ten-point plan for increasing commitment:

1. Define the mission of the organization and ensure that everyone is fully aware of its significance.
2. Develop and implement a set of values and guiding principles which demonstrate that the organization is a caring and considerate employer.
3. Involve employees in decisions on matters which affect them so that they feel they are an important part of the organization.
4. Run change-management programmes in a way which encourages employees to 'own' new procedures and systems which affect their interests.
5. Conduct communication programmes which convey the vision of top management about the future of the organization, and which develop pride in the achievements of the company.
6. Implement personnel policies which emphasize equity, equal opportunity and fair dealing.
7. Organize culture management programmes which develop a positive culture and an attractive organization climate.
8. Run organization development programmes to encourage better team-work and resolve conflict.
9. Foster a prevailing management style which provides for managers to be both visible and approachable.
10. Hold induction programmes for new employees which create

favourable attitudes from the start and ensure that they understand the mission and values of the organization, and how they will benefit from being members of it.

Managing reward to improve results

The following are ten approaches which can be adopted to make sure that in practice, reward management strategies, policies and systems fulfil their promise of improving organizational effectiveness and performance:

1. Relate pay systems to organizational needs and culture.
2. Relate pay to contribution and performance.
3. Establish performance criteria.
4. Assess performance against the criteria.
5. Evaluate jobs systematically to achieve a reasonable degree of equity.
6. Monitor market rates to maintain competitiveness.
7. Segment the pay structure into market groups as required.
8. Ensure that the pay system promotes rather than discourages flexibility.
9. Communicate the message about the system and how and why it benefits employees.
10. Remember the other forms of intrinsic and extrinsic motivation.

Matching pay culture to corporate culture

The way in which pay systems and control mechanisms have been matched to corporate and organizational culture has not always been logical, nor has it helped organizations to respond to change. There is probably a maturity cycle affecting approaches to reward management just as there is a maturity cycle for companies as a whole. The problem is that the cycles do not always move in step and, when they do not, conflicts can occur. Companies then have to decide which phase of the cycle they need to be in and how they are going to tackle moving from here to there.

We summarize below the key stages and typical characteristics of the pay maturity cycle. It is the role of whoever is responsible for reward management strategy, policy and systems to analyze where the organization is on the cycle and decide how appropriate the existing approaches are in the particular circumstances of the company. This may be termed the 'contingency approach' to reward management, where what is done is contingent or dependent on the culture, environment, technology and maturity of the organization.

The pay maturity cycle – key stages and typical characteristics

Start-up and take off

Eg new entrepreneurial businesses and smaller longer established companies:

- spot salary levels
- market driven progression
- high risk/high reward philosophy
- erratic/inconsistent benefits entitlements
- job evaluation – none
- pay is not subject to specialist management – often decided by a director/manager willing to take on the responsibility.

Maturity

Eg longer established businesses and UK subsidiaries of US multinationals:

- evolution of pay progression systems related to competence and performance
- effective performance rewards
- enlightened approach to performance management
- job evaluation – where relevant
- benefit grades
- systematic market monitoring
- rapid response to market pressure
- innovative responses to skill shortages
- a good balance between centralized/decentralized controls in multi-site organizations
- specialist support available.

Old age and stagnation

Eg many parts of the public sector and, until the mid-1980s, some major multinationals:

- comprehensive pay negotiations up to/including management levels
- rigid pay structures
- job evaluation – a 'cottage industry'
- over-centralization of policy development
- complacency in the face of market pressure
- too many pay specialists with too narrow a perspective
- market monitoring over-systematized and mathematical
- fossilized performance rewards which have often long since failed to motivate

- over-emphasis on hierarchical differences
- new policies take forever to get agreed.

Breakout and regeneration – sometimes following massive cut-backs, a merger or a takeover
Eg older businesses after a clean sweep at the top:

- spot salaries in areas of market pressure
- limited market monitoring
- jettisoning of job evaluation
- minimal specialist support (probably brought in from consultants)
- clean cash-minimal benefit bias
- performance rewards only for real added value
- a questioning/cynical attitude to traditional practice.

Note: In describing this cycle we put forward a framework for analysis. We accept that there are many views on what this cycle could look like, but we believe that it provides a helpful framework for assessing at what stage an organization might be, what pitfalls to avoid and what direction to take.

Part 2

Determining Pay Levels and Relativities

Chapter 4

Establishing Market Rates

Competitive pay levels and salary structures can only be developed and maintained if the external market is systematically monitored. This can be done using a range of sources from salary and benefits surveys to job advertisements, companies' annual reports, informal confidential contacts and other forms of market intelligence.

This chapter describes:

- the purpose of making market comparisons
- the process of carrying out analyses of market rates
- the sources of comparative remuneration data
- how to conduct a company or club survey
- how survey data should be used.

The purpose of making market comparisons

Market comparisons aim to compare external relativities, ie:

1. The rates and benefits provided for equivalent jobs in other organizations (market rates) with those provided within the organization, in order to ensure that the latter are fully competitive.
2. The rates at which pay is increasing in other organizations (going rates) in order to provide guidance on pay reviews.

The data from market comparisons help organizations to:

- decide on starting rates
- design and modify salary structures
- determine acceptable rates of salary progression in pay structures and pay curve systems
- review pay, incentives, bonuses and other forms of performance-related pay
- decide on the types and levels of benefits to be provided
- assess the level of increases required to salary levels generally and to individual employees
- identify special cases where market rates have to be paid irrespective of the evaluated position of the job in the grade hierarchy.

The process of carrying out market comparisons

Sources of data

The main sources of data are:

- general published surveys
- specialized occupational, professional, industrial or local surveys
- company surveys – ie those carried out by the company, with or without the help of consultants
- salary survey clubs – ie a group of companies who regularly exchange information
- published data in specialist or other journals, newspapers and the business press
- analyses of job advertisements
- other market intelligence.

We provide a brief description and comparative analysis of each of these later in this chapter, followed by a more detailed examination of company and club surveys. But before looking at these sources, it is necessary to review the basic considerations affecting market comparisons.

Basic considerations

When making market comparisons, the aims as far as possible are to:

- obtain accurate and representative data on market rates
- compare like with like, in terms of data, regional and organizational variations and, importantly, type and size of job
- obtain information which is as up to date as possible
- interpret data in the light of the organization's particular needs
- present data in a way which clearly indicates the action required.

The problem of defining the market rate

People often refer to the 'market rate' but it is a much more elusive concept than it seems. There is no such thing as a definitive market rate for any job, even when comparing identically sized organizations in the same industry and location. There are local markets and there are national markets, and none of them is perfect in the economist's sense. Different surveys of the same types of jobs produce different results because of variations in the sample, timing and job matching.

No survey is designed or, indeed, should be designed to show that one salary level is the 'correct' market rate for any given job. It should give as clear an indication as possible of the current operating or going range for establishing salary levels or setting pay structures, and define which factors affect the distribution of individual salaries within it.

Despite these points, most pay specialists and survey producers will sometimes have to put up with the reader's expectation that their survey will give a 'correct' salary for a job for any given set of conditions. Some top executives, and others needing to make policy decisions but having restricted understanding of the problems of carrying out surveys, still tend to believe that it is possible to find out exactly what the precise market rate is for any given job, in any industry, at any location, for any given age or experience level – preferably to the nearest pound! But this is not a reality and is unlikely to become one. Because survey participation is voluntary, and because decisions about pay levels tend to be pragmatic rather than strictly logical, actual salaries are less predictable than many people would like to believe. Where there is little data available, salary patterns tend to be fairly anarchic. Most salary decisions made in relation to salary surveys are conformist, which can mean that there are more regular and predictable operating ranges for jobs covered regularly by well-established salary surveys than, for instance, for new or rapidly evolving jobs not yet much subject to survey analysis.

This means that, however hard you work at getting accurate results, all you will obtain is an approximation – a range of possibilities. In spite of yourself you may, where data is hard to come by, be forced into averaging averages to obtain an informed view derived market rate. And that is a statistically undesirable process.

It should also be remembered that individuals as well as jobs have market rates. When looking at a range of market rates you have to decide two things – first, what the rate for the job should be, and second, what the range for individuals in the job should be as they enhance their marketability through experience, training and 'track record' or performance. Salary surveys may give some indication of the range of salaries you should offer; for example, you could set the lowest point of the range at the median (the middle point in the distribution of salary rates covered by the survey) and the highest point at the upper quartile (the value above which 25 per cent of the values in the range fall).

The more you can track the actual salaries paid to people in identical jobs in similar areas, the greater the accuracy of the market rate information. But this may require a tremendous amount of effort and you may need to question the cost effectiveness of the process. That is why some people rely on published surveys and other readily available data. Increased accuracy can be provided by company (do-it-yourself) and club surveys, but cost typically limits how far you can go.

However, in spite of these limitations, surveys of market rates are necessary to provide indications, albeit broad ones, of where the company stands in the market-place. Considerable judgement is still required to interpret results, but at least that judgement can be based on data which have been collected and analyzed systematically.

Types of data collected

- *basic (or base) pay*: gross pay before deducting national insurance, tax and pension contributions. It includes merit increments or incremental payments added into salary but excludes performance-related bonuses, overtime pay, fringe benefits and most allowances. In the latter case, the only exception may be a location allowance (eg, a London allowance) which may or may not be incorporated in the base salary, but whether or not it is included should be made clear
- *cash bonuses*: any performance-related bonus or payment under an incentive scheme which is not part of basic pay
- *total earnings* (sometimes called total cash earnings: the sum of the basic annual pay and any cash bonuses received over the previous twelve months. This figure excludes the value of employee benefits
- *employee benefits*: details of the entitlement to benefits such as pensions, company cars, private petrol, mortgage assistance, loans, permanent health insurance, medical insurance, health screening, relocation packages, holidays, other forms of leave, sick pay, etc
- *other allowances*: any cash payments made in special circumstances, such as call-outs, shift or night work payments, car mileage allowances
- *total remuneration*: the total value of all cash payments and benefits received by employees (note that valuing benefits depends on agreed assumptions – these should be scrutinized carefully)
- *salary structure information*: the salary scale or range in the structure for particular jobs.

Regional and company variables

Market comparisons should take account of the following variables which affect the comparability of the data:

- *location*: whether the jobs involved need to be assessed in relation to national, regional or local markets
- *industry*: usually analyzed on the basis of a simplified version of the Standard Industrial Classification (SIC)

- *organization size*: because it can affect job size, there is often some correlation between pay levels (especially salaries for managers) and company size. The following variables are typically taken into account:
  - sales turnover derived from the accounts for the annual accounting period preceding the survey date
  - the total number of employees, analyzed as necessary according to location, company, division or group.

Job matching

Market comparisons are most valid when like is compared with like. This means matching jobs as far as possible in the following respects:

- function, eg general management, marketing, production
- sector – private or public
- industry classification
- location
- size of organization
- range of responsibilities – the tasks or duties carried out by job holders
- level of responsibility – size or weight of the job in terms of its impact on end results, resources controlled, scope for exercising discretion and judgement, and complexity.

The various methods of job matching in ascending order of accuracy are:

- *job title*: this can be completely misleading. Job titles by themselves give no indication of the range of duties or the level of responsibility and are sometimes even used to convey additional status to employees or their customers unrelated to the real level of work done
- *brief description of duties and level or zone of responsibility*: national surveys frequently limit their job-matching definitions to a two- or three-line description of duties and an indication of levels of responsibility in rank order. The latter is also often limited to a one-line definition for each level or zone in a hierarchy. This approach provides some guidance on job matching, which reduces major discrepancies, but it still leaves considerable scope for discretion and can therefore provide only generalized comparisons
- *capsule job description*: club or specialist 'bespoke' surveys frequently use capsule job descriptions which define the job and its duties in approximately 250 words. To increase the refinement of comparisons, modifying statements may be made indicating where responsibilities are higher or lower than the norm.

Capsule job descriptions considerably increase the accuracy of comparisons as long as they are based on a careful analysis of actual jobs and include modifying statements. But they are not always capable of dealing with specialist jobs and the accuracy of the comparisons in relation to levels of responsibility may be limited, even when modifiers are used.

- *full job description*: full job descriptions of individual jobs, sometimes including a factor analysis of the levels of responsibility involved, are sometimes used in special surveys when direct comparisons are made between jobs in different companies. They can be more accurate on a one-for-one basis but their use is limited because of the time and labour involved in preparing job descriptions. A further limitation is that comparator companies may not have available, or be prepared to make available, their own full job descriptions for comparison
- *job evaluation*: job evaluation can be used in support of capsule or full job descriptions and provides a more accurate measure of relative job size or weight. A common method of evaluation is necessary. In the UK, surveys are run on this basis by both Hay and Wyatt. This approach will further increase the accuracy of comparisons but the degree of accuracy will depend on the quality of the job evaluation process. Consistency depends on quality assurance of the evaluation process, both within organizations and across survey participants.

Timing of surveys

The competitiveness of current salaries can only be established by finding out what other organizations are offering and paying now. Pay data can easily become stale when the market is moving erratically, and the time-lag between the collection of the data and its publication is commonly three months. To mitigate this problem, salary surveys sometimes update results. They should always indicate the specific date for which the pay information is applicable and explain the assumptions made if updating has been carried out. Wherever possible, they should set out the pattern of the salary review dates of the companies included in the survey.

Increases from one survey to the next – the importance of matched samples

Market comparisons involve not only assessing current market rates but also trends in pay increases in order to indicate the going rate.

The percentage rise in average pay between successive surveys will be misleading because of changes in the sample of companies and losses, gains or replacements in the sample of job holders.

The problem can be alleviated by matching the sample of companies so that comparisons are only made for companies subscribing to both surveys. But this does not cover changes in job holders, and the most refined matching process will isolate increases for individuals who have remained in the same job between the consecutive surveys. This measure, however, may not distinguish between increases arising from general pay reviews and individual incremental, merit or performance-related payments.

Interpreting average, median and quartile increases

Since many employers review all aspects of salaries only once a year, the increase compared with a year earlier in the average earnings of a group of employees in a sample will usually approximate to the weighted average of the increases granted. The same is true of medians, with some qualifications. But rarely is the increase during a survey year in the upper or lower quartiles of an earnings survey the same as the upper or lower quartile of the increases granted. This is because groups which have lower-than-average increases one year may often secure an above-average increase in the following year to restore their position (which may well be below the median of the market). Organizations which give below average increases continuously over a period of years tend to end up with salaries going right through the market floor. If a firm chooses to place its salaries in the lower quartile of the market and reaches this position by awarding a lower quartile increase for a year or two, what then? To maintain salary levels at the lower quartile of the market (or indeed at any chosen fixed relativity), it may now need to offer near-to-average increases to keep up with others in the market. Otherwise salary levels will fall below even the reduced targets that have been set and will continue to do so indefinitely.

Presentation of data

Data on pay are presented in two ways:

1. *Measures of central tendency*, ie the point about which the several values cluster. These consist of:
   (a) the arithmetic mean or *average* (A), which is the total of the values of the items in the set divided by the number of individual items in the set. The average can, however, be distorted by extreme values on either side of the centre
   (b) the *median* (M), which is the middle item in the distribution of individual items – 50 per cent of the sample fall

above the median, 50 per cent below. This is unaffected by extremes and is generally preferred to the arithmetic mean, as long as there are a sufficient number of individual items (the median of a sample much less than 10 is suspect). Medians are often lower than arithmetic means because of the tendency in the latter case for there to be a number of high values at the top of the range.

2. *Measures of dispersion*, ie the range of values in the set, which provides guidance on the variations in the distribution of the values of items around the median. These consist of:
   (a) *the upper quartile* (UQ): the value above which 25 per cent of the individual values fall
   (b) *the lower quartile* (LQ): the value below which 25 per cent of the individual values fall
   (c) *the interquartile range*: the difference between the upper and lower quartile values; this is a good measure of dispersion
   (d) *upper and lower deciles*: the values above and below which 10 per cent of the individual values fall. This is less frequently used but does provide for greater refinement in the analysis of distribution
   (e) *the total range*: the difference between the highest and lowest values. This can be misleading if there are extreme values at either end, and is less often used than the interquartile range, except where the sample is very small.

Data are usually presented in tabular form but the significance of the information can sometimes be revealed more clearly if the tables are supplemented by graphs.

- *tables* should identify the job, the size of the sample and, where appropriate, may analyze data according to the size and type of organization and its location. For example, see Table 4.1.

An example of a layout of the results of a club survey is given in Table 4.2. This quotes the average gross pay for the job and gives

Table 4.1 *Sample table*

Job title: Marketing Director

	LQ	M	UQ	Sample
Turnover (£m) 1–10				
Base salary	28,420	31,165	34,255	23
Total earnings	30,150	33,643	37,521	
Turnover (£m) 11–50				
Base salary	31,141	33,620	36,591	41
Total earnings	33,409	37,712	39,916	

tabulated details by companies of salary ranges and average salaries and bonuses.

Table 4.2 *Salary survey data*

Job title: Production Manager *Job No*:

Brief job description: To direct the activities of a production department to achieve agreed delivery targets. Monitor costs and profit margins to ensure that agreed prices are met. Deal with day-to-day disciplinary and personnel problems.

Average Salary (Gross) – Min: £18,250 Max: £26,789 Mean: £23,750
Number of Companies – 25

Company code	Sample size	Salary range (min) £	Salary range (max) £	Actual basic average salary £	Average bonus £	Average (gross) £	Rank
12	21	21,860	32,950	26,789	2,100	28,889	01
06	24	21,350	31,350	26,230	1,800	28,030	02
13	19	21,100	30,500	25,650	1,950	27,600	03
09	17	21,250	30,250	25,480	2,000	27,480	04

- *Graphical presentations* can highlight significant data or trends as in the example in Figure 4.1.

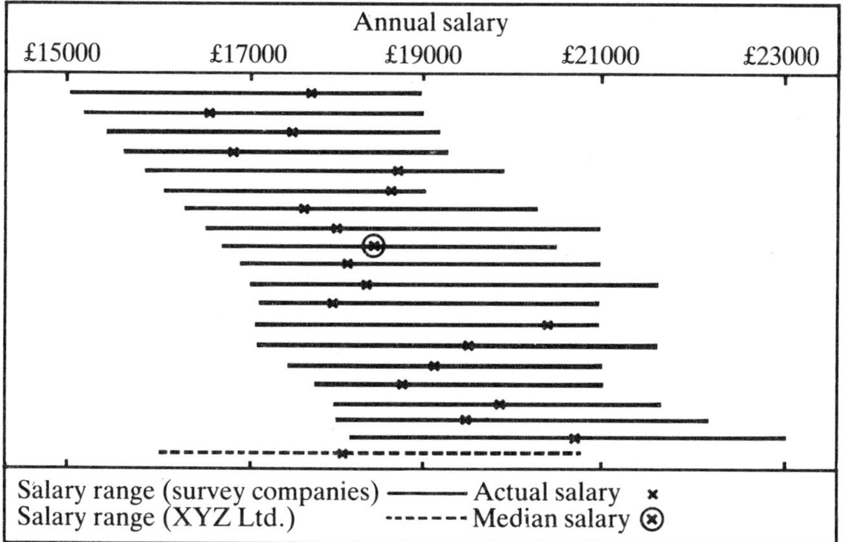

Figure 4.1 *Salary survey data presented graphically*

In practice, there are many variations on these forms of presentation. More are emerging as pay specialists become more creative with the graphics packages available on the computers appearing on their desks. Further information on statistical terms used in pay surveys and analysis is given in Appendix A.

Published surveys

There is a wide range of published surveys which either collect general information about salaries, mainly managerial, or refer to more specialist professional or technical jobs. Many, such as those produced by Hay, Computer Economics, Wyatt and Towers Perrin, are available only to participants but some are available 'over the counter' (eg, Monks/Charterhouse, Remuneration Economics and Reward). In either case, it is advisable to ensure that they will meet your requirements for relevant information. Their potential value as a reliable information source can be evaluated with the help of the following check-list:

1. *Source*
   Who produced the survey?
   (a) a firm of general/specialist management consultants
   (b) a recognized organization specializing in salary and benefits surveys
   (c) recruitment/executive search consultants
   (d) an employment agency
   (e) an employers' association
   (f) a professional body
   (g) a trade union
   (h) the government or one of its agencies
   (i) a company/employer wishing to exchange salary data
   (j) a specialist or other journal.
2. *Database*
   What is the survey based on?
   (a) actual salaries paid to matched jobs or responsibility levels
   (b) average salaries for jobs/grades/levels
   (c) estimated market price given by employers where no direct job match has been made
   (d) recruitment salaries – offered, asked or paid
   (e) annual company report data based on audited earnings for the previous financial year
   (f) informed opinion.
3. *Sample composition*
   Who participated in the survey?
   (a) other organizations similar to or competing directly with the user

(b) individual members of professional bodies or trade unions.

Are there:

(a) enough participants to provide acceptable comparisons assuming that the methods of collection and analysis are effective?

(b) matched samples of participants either on the basis of the same individuals doing the same jobs or the same companies from year to year?

4. *Data collection*

How were the data collected?

(a) personal collection by survey producer to discuss job matching and current salary issues for the jobs in question

(b) postal questionnaire – with what response rate?

(c) from employers or job holders

(d) on a well-designed, clearly explained questionnaire/computer input sheet.

5. *Job matching*

How accurately are survey bench-mark jobs or levels of responsibility matched?

(a) against job titles

(b) against 'capsule' job descriptions or rank definitions with provisions for separating those with more or less responsibility than the core definition

(c) against full job descriptions/definitions of responsibility level

(d) by using an agreed measure of 'job size', eg the same method of job evaluation used by all participants with checks on the consistency of grading and application.

6. *Timing*

How up to date are the salary data?

(a) what is the distribution of salary review dates among participants? Are data on this provided?

(b) are data correct on a given survey date or given over a survey period, eg three months?

(c) how much time has elapsed between data collection and the publication/circulation of results?

7. *Presentation*

How well does the survey illustrate current practice and the reliability of data in individual analysis? Are there:

(a) full details of sample composition and response rate

(b) tables listing average, median, upper and lower quartiles (or other quantiles such as octiles/deciles)

(c) lists or bar charts/scattergrams of the raw data from which the summary analyses are calculated; coded by size/type of organization to allow more detailed analysis;

giving current scales/ranges/actual salaries where not too commercially sensitive
   - (d) analyses by company size, industry, location or other relevant factors
   - (e) regression lines to give a 'feel' for market position; if so is the sample or subsample basis clearly explained?
8. *Increase data*
   How valid is the information provided on pay increases (often hard to interpret)?
   - (a) is it based on matched samples of individuals in the same job year on year/organizations participating in the same survey?
   - (b) do the percentage increases quoted include merit awards, bonuses, cost of living adjustments, or a combination of these, and how well is this explained?
   - (c) is the basis for calculation made clear?
9. *Other data*
   What else does the survey contain?
   - (a) details of major benefits/entitlements
   - (b) amounts/types of incentive/profit sharing payments
   - (c) details of salary administration policy
   - (d) a commentary on current developments including special areas of market pressure or other major influences, written by someone able to interpret the data effectively.
10. *Cost*
   Is it worth its price in terms of:
   - (a) savings in company/personnel resources required to obtain equivalent data?
   - (b) the time/effort involved in participation?
11. *Integrity of survey producers*
   Does the producer maintain consistent and professional standards? Does the survey:
   - (a) state when samples are too small to provide useful analysis and define the point at which this is reached?
   - (b) show ability to adapt/improve in response to changing market demands?
   - (c) include the availability of advice on the interpretation of the data, and is this available free/for a fee?
   - (d) give good value for money?
12. *Purpose*
   Why was the survey produced?
   - (a) as the producer's sole business
   - (b) as an occasional/major part of other business/consultancy activities
   - (c) to provide other organizations/individuals with data on a particular sector of the market

(d) to put forward a point of view
(e) to attract press coverage.

General published surveys

There are many surveys, but the quality of data they provide varies enormously. Both the Top Pay Unit of Incomes Data Services and the *Pay and Benefits Bulletin* published by Industrial Relations Services publish regular reviews of these surveys and analyses of the trend data they contain. The Top Pay Unit also publishes a *Directory of Salary Surveys* every couple of years which is essentially a consumer's guide to the whole of the salary survey market. It gives full information on the jobs covered, sample data, cost and availability, as well as comment on the quality and reliability of the data.

General surveys, such as those produced by Hay Remuneration Economics, Monks/Charterhouse, PE International, Reward and the Executive Compensation Service (now part of the Wyatt Company) are based on data collected from as large a number of participating organizations as they can attract – typically from clients and mailshots to a large number of employers. They cover base salary and total earnings levels paid on a given date and a certain amount of data on benefits entitlements. Most surveys also provide data on annual salary movement.

Survey data are normally grouped by job title and function, and by job size or level of responsibility in relation to company size and type. The most usual company analyses are by industrial sector and size, in terms of annual sales turnover and/or numbers of employees.

Most surveys include some indication of regional variations and can be expected to add to this, given the interest in regional pay differences for jobs where local market influences are more important than national trends. Clerical and shop-floor jobs that are recruited using local sources need local salary analyses to give an acceptable picture of the market – especially among smaller organizations. National data will always be needed, however, for jobs which are recruited on a national basis. It is important to remember that where, for instance, there appear to be regional differences in management pay, this will almost always turn out on deeper analysis to be related to the size of the job and the nature, age and culture of the industry rather than just the location.

Traditional engineering companies tend to pay less than their high-tech counterparts and they tend to be located in different parts of the country. They may often not demand the same academic background and level of skills from the managers they employ. Nor, sadly, are some of them in a position to afford higher salaries for better qualified managers able to improve profitability through innovation and improved financial management, other than in exceptional cases.

Publishers of general surveys can be asked, at a price, to extract data relating to particular firms who participated in the survey. This data is, of course, anonymous, and is only made available if a reasonable number of firms are involved. It can be very helpful if you want more specific information about your own industry.

Specialized professional, industrial or local surveys

There are three basic types:

- analyses of members' salaries conducted by professional institutions
- local or national market surveys of particular industrial groups produced by employers or trade associations
- local or national market studies carried out regularly or on a one-off basis by consultants, either for a single employer or for a group or organizations who may share the cost (a multi-client study).

Professional institute surveys are usually more concerned with providing salary data in relation to age, qualification and membership status than they are with placing members in their organizational context. They therefore provide useful salary profiles and salary movement data, but are often of little help when it comes to looking at an individual's place in the company reporting structure in relation to particular sizes and types of organization. Some are now including analyses by function and level of responsibility within the organization, but the relevance and clarity of the definitions should be looked at carefully. They should, therefore, mainly be used as an additional check on more specific salary survey data from which real job comparisons should be clearly identifiable.

These professional institute surveys are widely read by their members, who may seek to use them either as individuals or through their unions as a negotiating base for salary improvements. If this occurs, it is essential to be familiar with the particular survey quoted and aware of any limitations in the validity of the data. If it does not correlate well with more specific salary market data the reasons should be analysed and explained. There may be distortions caused by the inclusion, for example, of members who are high flyers and have reached director status early in their careers, too large a proportion of members working for highly paid consultancies or multinationals, members who have moved on to more highly/lowly paid areas outside the specialism, or those who are 'blocked' within an organization because performance or an unwillingness to move or take extra responsibility holds them back.

The surveys conducted by employers' and trade associations deal mainly with jobs specific to their industry for which reliable outside salary data often does not exist. They cover a limited market and are useful because they can be very specific about job definitions and organization structures for the staff covered. Often they are only available to participating organizations who may then share the cost of data collection and analysis. They may be local or national and by no means all are produced regularly. It may often be worth checking with the trade association appropriate to the company whether surveys of this kind are likely to be produced before special company market surveys are undertaken.

Employers who have neither the time nor in-house expertise to conduct their own market studies are increasingly opting to commission consultants to carry out this task. The approach used is usually very similar to that outlined in the section on company surveys, and consultants involved in this sort of exercise will need to be briefed accordingly. The choice of appropriate consultants for this type of 'one-off' study should be based on firm evidence of expertise in the field of salary surveys and a good level of understanding of the personnel philosophy and market posture of the commissioning employer.

Company surveys

These are surveys conducted by a company approaching others to exchange comparative salary information on a 'one-off' basis. Company surveys can be held with or without the help of consultants. The use of consultants provides for expertise in the collection and analysis of data and they save time, but they can, of course, be expensive.

Company surveys can be as simple or sophisticated as required. They can be as quick and cheap as simple confidential 'pricings' or exchanges of information over the telephone with established contacts willing to exchange data, or a fully fledged study of pay and benefits which is coded and circulated to all participants.

The principal advantage of the 'one-off' company salary survey is that the company alone decides which jobs it needs to study and which of its local or national competitors should be invited to participate. This should, in theory, produce the best possible comparative data. The main drawback is the time it takes to complete this kind of exercise and the cost and organizational implications of taking staff away from other work while the survey is in progress.

Because of the time, effort and cost of running company surveys, there are advantages in joining or setting up a salary club. The methods used to plan and conduct a company survey are basically

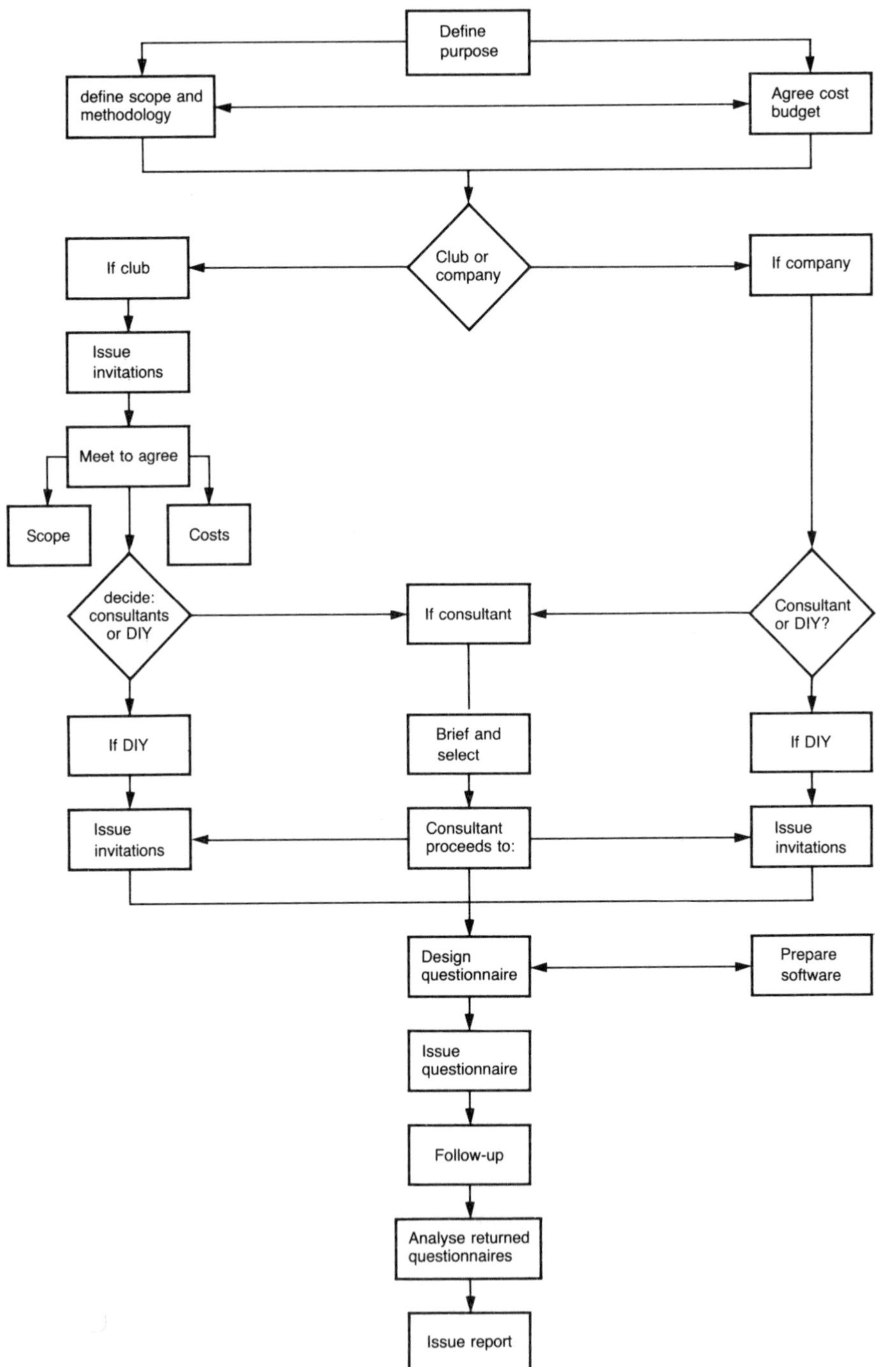

Figure 4.2 *Conducting a club or company survey*

similar to those adopted by salary clubs as described below. The sequence of activities is illustrated in Figure 4.2.

Salary club surveys

Clubs may be administered either by management consultants or by companies themselves. Clubs tend to operate in single industries, although some cover a range of industries – a survey of 'blue chip' companies, for instance. Many cover all managerial and professional grades, although there are those which cover only one employee category – graduates or accountants for example, within one industry. When a single employee category is chosen, this will normally be because there is strong competition for people with skills which are in demand, eg accountants or software engineers.

Club surveys – check-list

Membership criteria

- Which types of company will be eligible for membership? Will they:
  - all be in the same business, ie competitors?
  - all be of similar size and type, eg all 'blue chip'?
  - all be in the same area?
  - all have similar parentage, eg all subsidiaries of US multinationals?
- Will separate parts of the same company be allowed to participate or will only aggregate data be accepted? How will decentralized companies be treated?
- Will there be a pre-set minimum and maximum number of participants?
- Who will decide on requests to join the club from companies who are 'qualified' to do so? Will existing members have a veto?
- Will membership be restricted to companies who are able to provide data on a specified minimum number of jobs?
- Will it be possible to expel a club member if they transgress club rules?

Collecting the data

- Who will collect the data?
  - one of the members
  - a combination of members
  - a consultant
- How frequently will a survey be conducted?
  - annually

  - every six months
  - quarterly
- How will accurate job matching (pricing) be ensured? By:
  - using summary job descriptions
  - personal visits to participants to discuss differences in job scope and other problems
  - a regular 'audit' of job matching
- Will a postal questionnaire be used to collect the data, or a personal visit/interview?
- What data will you collect?
  - basic actual salaries of individuals in post
  - salary ranges
  - incentive/bonus payments
  - other cash additions to pay
  - share options and profit sharing payments
  - fringe benefits including pension, death-in-service provisions, cars, medical insurance, loans, etc.
- Will the survey be 'open' or 'closed', ie will participants be able to identify the salary ranges or the salaries paid by other members?
- Will all grades of employee be included in the same survey, or will separate surveys be conducted for manual, non-manual, professional and managerial grades?
- Is a 100 per cent response rate expected? What sanctions will the club impose if members fail to provide data?

Analyzing and presenting the results

- Will a computer be used to process the data or, will they be analyzed by hand?
- Will actual salaries and salary ranges be listed by company (using a simple number code) in rank order?
- What statistical analyses will be produced from the aggregate data?
  - averages
  - medians
  - quartiles (if large enough sample)
  - interquartile ranges (if large enough sample).
- Should these be related to individuals' salaries, company averages/medians, or salary range mid-points?
- Will any significance regression or correlation tests be made on the statistical results?
- How will the results of the club survey be compared with general data on salaries, from commercial surveys etc?
- Will club members be charged a fee to cover the cost of analyzing the results and producing the survey report?

Setting up the salary club

The establishment of a salary club may start from a more informal exchange of salary information between two or more companies who employ similar types of staff. A club may be the result of individual initiatives by one or two compensation specialists within companies. In some industries, the computer industry for example, there is a more regular exchange of salary information than in others. Some consultants specialize in club survey work in certain industrial groups. If the target group is sufficiently finely defined as, for example, in the international banking sector and the pharmaceutical industry, then not only are a homogeneous group of employees being surveyed, but also a very high proportion of the potential number of participants will probably take part.

Approaching companies

The exchange of accurate, up-to-date salary information depends on mutual trust. This will exist among established contacts but has to be carefully built up when individuals are contacted for the first time. This can be done over the telephone but, unless the person responsible for the survey has a particularly confident and persuasive telephone manner, a carefully drafted letter may be a better approach. Letters may in any case be preferable because the recipient then has time to consider carefully whether it is worth participating and is unlikely to make a snap decision based on an understandable dislike of the use of what may be seen as telephone sales techniques. Letters may be ignored, but this problem is reduced if they are worded properly.

In a letter of invitation to an unknown company the messages that have to be communicated are that:

1. A responsible individual/consultant is conducting the survey.
2. The survey will be carried out competently and in confidence.
3. The information collected and shared will be relevant, up to date and useful.
4. The company will not be put to too much trouble.

Which jobs to include

The major advantage of running a club is that participants to the survey know who the other participants are and that their data are relevant. When members of the same club are in the same industrial sector they may be thought of as competitors for the same type of staff in the same salary market. This is particularly true for managers and specialists whose skills are easily transferable from one company

Table 4.3 *Example of a profile job description used in job matching*

	JOB DESCRIPTION POSITION CODE E27.
POSITION:	PERSONNEL MANAGER (1)
ALTERNATIVE TITLE:	Manager Human Resources, Asst. Vice President, Asst. Director (Personnel), Associate Director
REPORTS TO:	Managing Director, Senior Vice President, Vice President, Branch Manager
SUPERVISES:	Training Officers, Personnel Officers and Staff (4–8 staff)
RESPONSIBILITIES:	Under direction, responsible for the implementation of the bank's policy on personnel, recruitment, training, salary administration, welfare, payroll, pensions and management development. Advises senior management on all matters to do with personnel policies such as legal changes, terms and conditions of employment, pay trends, benefits, etc.
MODIFIER +:	Having more personnel staff or totally responsible for general administration, premises, catering staff, etc.
MODIFIER −:	Having less specialist staff and/or in a small bank or branch of less than 100 people.
EXPERIENCE OR LEVEL:	Possibly a graduate with several years' experience in personnel management or, alternatively, a banker with many years experience and at least five years' personnel management experience in banking.
TYPICAL SITUATION:	Working in his/her own office in close contact with senior management.
NOTE:	The difference between Personnel Management (1) and (2) is the scope of the job and will be a combination of factors such as reporting, supervision given and received and relative position within the overall management structure. Look at both descriptions and decide which most suits your bank. A Personnel Manager reporting to the Financial Controller, Operations Manager, Administration Manager or Company Secretary is unlikely to fall into this category.

Source: London Banks Personnel Management Group Management Salary Survey

to another in a similar line of business. At managerial level, members of the same club typically employ a rather homogeneous group of staff in terms of the experience required, the demands of the job and their qualifications. Some clubs exchange salary information only on managerial and specialist grades, eg from first line to senior management, while others cover technical and professional grades, clerical or indeed only manual employees.

Job matching and pricing

Club surveys offer a potentially better quality of job matching than industry-wide surveys covering very heterogeneous groups. Most salary clubs take great care over this stage of the research.

A typical approach to assist the matching process is to circulate a profile job description for each job to participants. This will contain the job title, a brief description of the job's responsibilities, reporting level, supervisory responsibility (number of subordinates), together with the typical age and/or experience and qualifications an incumbent of such a job might have. An example of a profile job description for a senior personnel manager is shown opposite (taken from the London Banks Personnel Management Group Survey of International Banks). Participants are asked to match as closely as possible, indicating whether their jobs are slightly more or less responsible than the one described, or are about equal. The modifier mechanism is often used as a shorthand way of describing slight differences in job scope – a plus (+) modifier indicates it is more responsible, a minus (−) modifier is less responsible and an equals (=) modifier is used when the participant's job is equal in responsibility to the profile job.

The key to success in any salary club survey lies in accurate job matching, a process demanding painstaking work and eternal vigilance. The wholesale regrading of a set of jobs in one or two companies could potentially throw the results of an otherwise useful survey. The communication of changes in internal relativities is essential to the reliability of survey results. A regular audit is desirable to keep track of company regradings of jobs and to ensure they are still being matched with similar jobs in other companies.

Where individual jobs cannot be matched, organizations may be asked to price them. This involves assessing the relative worth of a job in relation to other jobs carrying similar responsibilities in areas or grades where reasonable comparisons can be made.

Salary data collection

Survey professionals often find that it is worth printing the questionnaire form on coloured paper so that it is less easily lost among the other white papers in the participant's 'in' tray. Colours selected should be light and in no way interfere with the clarity of the printing. Survey questionnaires should always be sent out with a covering letter further encouraging participation and giving a clear final return date. A week or so will have to be allowed after this date for the stragglers to come in. It is always worth telephoning companies who have not yet returned responses a few days before the deadline to check whether the questionnaire has arrived safely or whether there are any problems with job matching which need to be ironed out. In these circumstances the companies may have to be visited to deliver new questionnaires and to collect the comparative data on the spot. However inconvenient this is, it should greatly improve the scope and quality of the data collected.

Club surveys, unlike many commercial surveys, collect information not only on actual salaries, but also on salary ranges. Questionnaires are used and, typically, there are number codes for each company and for each job category covered.

Company and pay data commonly collected/presented

- company name
- number of employees
- annual sales turnover
- data by job:
  - job title/code
  - number of incumbents
  - modifier (+, =, or −)
  - average actual basic salary/total cash
  - median actual basic salary/total cash
  - highest actual basic salary/total cash
  - lowest actual basic salary/total cash
  - salary ranges – minimum/maximum/mid-point
  - salary review dates

All surveys collect salary data, but the information collected on cash additions to basic pay and fringe benefits is very variable. An example of the company information and the detailed fringe benefit data collected by one club survey are listed below:

General company information: number of employees, annual sales turnover

Salary increases: general increases (timing and last percentage increase), and individual increases (criteria and timing)

Graduate starting salaries: basic salary + bonus, projection for the next year

Incentive/bonus schemes: basis of payment, employees qualifying for payment, frequency and amount (%) payment

Overtime premiums: for managers, monthly and professional staff, and weekly paid staff

Shift premiums in relation to shiftwork patterns

Company cars: for business need or status, engine size (bench-mark car), private petrol paid, and charges for private use

Payment for use of employees' own cars: Mileage allowances by car engine size

Regional and occupational allowances: London allowances, telephone and professional institute expenses
Relocation expenses – existing employees: Disturbance, removal, and temporary housing allowances, plus bridging loan facilities
Relocation expenses – new employees: Disturbance, removal, temporary housing allowances, plus bridging loan facilities
Travel and accident insurance: In the UK and overseas
Private medical insurance: Insurer, category covered, proportion paid by the company and type of cover
Redundancy: Payments in addition to statutory minima
Periods of notice: Both from employer and employee
Pension scheme: employer and employee contribution rates, escalation of pensions in payment and ex-gratia supplements
Pension scheme – benefits: Entitlement per year of service (fraction), definition of salary used for pension calculations, contracted in or out, and life assurance provisions
Pension scheme – additional benefits: Death in service: early retirement provisions

Sick pay entitlements
Long term disability absence: salary continuation entitlements

Call out and stand by premiums
Holiday entitlements: Standard entitlement and additional service days
Subsistence allowances: For short and long stays on company business
Overtime pay for travel: Differentials between hourly paid and staff

Share options: entitlements by seniority
Profit sharing: basis, annual percentage paid (including profit-related pay under the 1987 Finance Act provisions)

Analysing and presenting the results

As survey returns come in, they should be checked carefully to ensure that acceptable matching or pricing has been given for each job. Any doubtful figures should be referred back to participants and discussed with them. Where comparisons turn out not to be close enough to be acceptable, the data should be rejected – preferably with the agreement of the participant concerned.

Salary club surveys can generally be processed very quickly and participants typically expect a report within a month of sending in their returns. Strict deadlines usually have to be set and enforced (see above) to ensure this is possible. Whoever is responsible for the survey should also ensure that the analysis of results can begin as soon as the first few returns have come in and been checked.

The methods used in the analysis and presentation of survey results will depend on the number of returns received and the degree of sophistication in salary policy of both the survey producer and the participants. It can therefore vary from simple histograms (bar charts), either set out on graph paper or drawn by computer, showing the salary scales or actual ranges paid by participants and coded company by company, to complex statistical analyses producing computer printouts which present the data in relation to a number of different variables. In selecting which forms of analysis will yield the most meaningful results and present the data in a way which helps the salary policy decision making process, it helps to concentrate on what the data are actually based on and who will use the findings. The use of regression analysis looks very sophisticated and is therefore sometimes seductive. For data based on large samples such techniques have their value and can be used to effect. But the application of sophisticated statistical techniques to rather tentative data collected in a small-scale salary survey is not appropriate. What matters most is presenting a limited amount of directly relevant market data in a way which shows what the actual operating salary range is for any given job – and where the extremes of practice lie as well as the mid-point – backed by a brief commentary on the underlying influences affecting the distribution.

A more detailed set of definitions of the statistical terms used in such analyses is given in Appendix A. In many surveys, the salaries for each job category are typically listed by company code, in rank order of the total cash earnings, actual basic salary or salary range mid-points. In addition, the number of employees in that job category within each company may be printed out as well as the modifier, the minimum, maximum and mid-point of the salary range, the highest and lowest actual salaries, average basic salary and bonus, median basic salary and bonus. Other information which might be provided is the 'compa ratio' in each salary range for each company, matching the company average salary to the mid-point of the salary range.

Confidentiality

Although the company compensation specialist or consultant who processes the survey results will have access to the individual company codes, it is necessary for each club to decide whether all club members should have this facility or not. Knowing which code applies to which company would mean that comprehensive information about participants' salary ranges and actual salaries in payment would be available to each participant. Some clubs think this is a good idea, others do not – commercial sensitivity in the pay area is growing in some sectors!

Response rate

Club surveys usually expect a 100 per cent response rate. Failure to provide data normally means expulsion from the club, except in mitigating circumstances. However, it may also be necessary for the club to set a minimum response rate for each job category – there is little point in a company joining a club collecting data on 60 job categories if they only employ one or two of these, as they are going to lower the general response rate for particular jobs.

Published data in journals

Apart from the summaries of published survey findings that appear at various times in the business press, there are two major sources of company and public sector salary data. Both Incomes Data Services and Industrial Relations Review and Report monitor wage and salary settlements and publish details of agreements as soon as they are made. A great deal of staff and management salary information is available because companies have shown willingness to contribute data in order to benefit from the detailed analysis of trends these organizations provide.

Both sources also comment on economic trends and analyze the effects of any government policy affecting pay. An enquiry service is part of the subscription.

Another useful source of trend information is the *Department of Employment Gazette* which also summarizes the findings of the *New Earnings Survey* as it is produced. It is also worth checking specialist information in journals such as *Taxation* to monitor the changing effects of tax on higher earnings where this might affect management remuneration policy. Newspaper coverage of surveys and major pay awards is also worth monitoring. These days few salary administrators can avoid monitoring the *Financial Times* and the Sunday papers with reputable Business News sections. Where resources permit, it is worth setting up press cuttings files for key jobs or functions and techniques, both to monitor the market and to ensure that those responsible for reward management see the same articles as the executives who may ask questions relating to them and require an immediate response on policy options.

Analysis of job advertisements

Attractive as this approach may be, it is beset with problems. The racily phrased job descriptions used in the hope of attracting high-calibre applicants are not usually precise enough to allow accurate comparisons with real jobs. Salary levels are often 'by negotiation' (often a sign of undeveloped salary policy) or they may be overstated or inflated because the company is desperate. Even where a salary scale is quoted in full this may not be the range within which the vacancy is ultimately filled. A quick check in the main national newspapers will show that the salaries on offer for jobs described as 'finance director' will show an enormous variation. This normally rules out useful application of the data other than as an indication of trends, though it has some value if the prospective employer is named and offers supplementary – if suspect – additions to information derived from more reliable sources.

Similar problems occur in using information provided by employment agencies. Specialist agencies may, however, have a good 'feel' for salaries in the particular areas they cover. They may therefore be worth consulting where the company is already a regular and satisfied client, and when the agencies' expertise in the area is known.

Other market intelligence

Setting salary levels is not, as we have shown, just about the scientific application of survey statistics. Monitoring salary markets also involves gleaning facts and opinions from personal contacts. It means building up a network of reliable people with whom trends and innovations can be discussed and insights shared, and developing a 'nose' for what currently influences pay. Job adverts for salary specialists now often specify that candidates should have a good knowledge of practice in the potential employer's industry. And most effective salary administrators have built up a 'card index' of contacts designed to ensure they know what is going on in their sector and which factors are likely to affect pay levels for all the different types of jobs involved.

Talking to informal contacts, exchanging experience and testing out ideas are valuable supplements to the more formal activities of salary clubs. It happens over the telephone and is a common activity at conferences on pay and related issues, IPM branch meetings and similar gatherings. Over time, the information acquired by this means can considerably sharpen an individual's 'feel' for what is going on in the salary market.

The sort of questions you can ask are:

- what level are you currently paying your junior systems analysts (those with less than two years' experience)?
- what is the increase you believe you will have to pay to your product managers this year to keep pace with the market-place?

- what would you need to offer in the shape of a total remuneration package to attract a really good legal executive?
- what rates of pay are graduate members of your profession getting two years after qualification?
- at what level of salary are you having to offer a company car?
- what do you think the trends in salary levels are likely to be for members of your profession who have executive appointments below board level in industry?
- what is happening to the demand for production managers in your industry sector and what impact is that making on market rates?

One of the reasons why companies employ consultants to carry out salary surveys rather than do the work 'in house' is because a good consultant will have extensive networks of contacts which they will use not just to get a good sample of participants, but to talk to discreetly about market influences. This should enable them to explore, for instance, recruitment pressures, special inducements and incentives, tax strategies and examples of new payment systems which might be of relevance in interpreting survey data and developing remuneration strategy.

Advantages and disadvantages of data sources

The advantages and disadvantages of each source are as follows:

Published general surveys

Advantages: wide coverage, readily available.
Disadvantages: risk of imprecise job matching, quickly out of date.

Published specialist surveys

Advantages: deal with particular categories in depth, quality of job matching better than general surveys.
Disadvantages: job matching not entirely precise, can quickly become out of date.

Club surveys

Advantages: more precise job and company matching, can provide more detail on pay structures and benefits.
Disadvantages: sample size may be too small, relies on goodwill of participants to conduct survey.

Company or 'do-it-yourself' surveys

Advantages: precise job matching.
Disadvantages: time and trouble, problem of building a large enough sample.

Published data in journals

Advantages: readily accessible, good background data.
Disadvantages: not necessarily comprehensive, job matching imprecise.

Analysis of job advertisements

Advantages: readily accessible, highly visible indications of market rates and trends, up to date.
Disadvantages: job matching very imprecise, salary data can be misleading.

Other market intelligence

Advantages: good background.
Disadvantages: imprecise.

Selecting data sources

If time and the budget permit, more than one source should be used to extend the range of data and provide back-up information.

General surveys can be supplemented by specialist surveys covering particular jobs. A company-administered survey or a salary club can provide information on local market rates. If the quality of job matching is important, an individual survey can be conducted or a salary club can be formed. If a salary club already exists it can be joined, if there is room (some clubs are over-subscribed). Published surveys, which are readily accessible and are based on a large sample, can be used to back up individual or club surveys. But the information has to be relevant to the needs of the organization and particular attention should always be paid to the range of data and the quality of job matching.

Market intelligence and published data in journals should always be used as back-up material and for information on going rates and trends. They can provide invaluable help with updating.

Although the analysis of job advertisements has its dangers, it can be used as further back-up, or to give an instant snapshot of current rates, but it is risky to rely on this source alone.

Using survey data

The translation of salary market data into competitive salary levels for individuals, or into an acceptable company salary structure, is a process based on judgement and compromise. The aim is to extract a derived market rate based on informed and effective estimates of the reliability of the data. It means striking a reasonable balance between the competing merits of the different sources used. This is essentially an intuitive process. Once all the data available have been collected and presented in the most accessible manner possible (ie job by job for all the areas the structure is to cover), a proposed scale midpoint or 'spot' salary/rate has to be established for each level based on the place in the market the company wishes to occupy, ie its 'market posture'. The establishment of this midpoint will be based not only on assessment of current and updated salary data, but also on indications of movements in earnings and the cost of living which are likely to affect the life of the whole structure. For organizations needing to stay ahead of the market, this point will often be between the median and the upper quartile (of a significant population). For others, closer alignment with the median is adequate. Once the series of midpoints in relation to the market has been established and assessed, the principles of salary structure construction outlined in Chapter 8 can be applied.

It has to be recognized that salary surveys can rapidly become out of date. To ensure that you stay ahead of the market, or at least do not lag behind, it may be advisable to attempt to forecast how rates will increase over the next year. This can be done by extrapolating trends and analyzing economic forecasts. Inevitably, there is an element of guesswork involved and the forecasts have to be treated with caution. But they at least give you some guidance on where salaries are likely to move and what you should do about it.

Chapter 5

Job Evaluation

Job evaluation is a system of comparing different jobs to provide a basis for grading and determining pay structure. An analysis of market rates will provide the information needed to ensure that a reward management system is competitive, but it is still necessary to maintain a pay structure into which jobs can be slotted according to their relative value. This will be strongly influenced by market forces but it is also necessary to pay attention to internal relativities in order to achieve, as far as possible, both appropriate differentials to reward different levels of contribution and equity in the form of equal pay for work of equal value.

A pay structure consists of a hierarchy, and decisions have to be made on how and where jobs should be fitted into that hierarchy. The aim of this chapter is to assist in making those decisions by:

- defining job evaluation
- describing the main types of evaluation schemes
- in the light of these descriptions, considering the pros and cons of job evaluation
- developing a strategy for selecting a method of evaluation and introducing it
- reviewing in detail the implications of the equal pay for work of equal value legislation in the UK
- outlining the developments taking place in job evaluation following the introduction of new technology, organizational changes and the trend towards the harmonization of the terms and conditions of employment for white- and blue-collared staff.

What is job evaluation?

Job evaluation is a method of establishing the relative position of jobs in a job hierarchy. Job evaluation schemes do not directly determine rates of pay. The rate for the job or the salary bracket for a job grade are influenced by a number of factors outside the scope of most schemes. These include market rate pressures, trade union negotiations and traditional patterns of pay differentials between jobs.

Job evaluation schemes set out to measure the relative value of the job, not that of the job holder. Ideally, the performance of the individual should not enter into job evaluation although, in practice, it may be difficult to dissociate individuals from their jobs where they have been in a position to influence what they do. This applies particularly to senior or specialist jobs where the position has been built round the personal strengths of the job holders.

Job evaluation is concerned with relationships, not absolutes. It cannot measure in definite terms the inherent value of a job to the organization. It is essentially a comparative process: comparisons with other jobs, comparisons against defined standards, or comparisons of the degree to which a common criterion or factor is present in different jobs.

Job evaluation schemes

The main types of job evaluation schemes are:

- *non-analytical or whole job comparison schemes:* ranking, paired comparison (a refined process of ranking) and job classification
- *analytical points rating schemes:* where the jobs are analyzed and compared by reference to different factors
- competency-based schemes

These basic approaches have been developed by management consultants into various types of schemes that they install on behalf of their cients. These may be termed the 'proprietary brands'.

Ranking

Ranking is the simplest form of job evaluation. It is a non-analytical approach which aims to judge each job as a whole and determine its relative place in a hierarchy by comparing one job with another and arranging them in order of importance.

Method of comparison

Jobs may be compared by reference to a single criterion or factor such as responsibility, which might be defined as the particular obligations that have to be assumed by any person who carries out the job; or evaluators may be asked to define several facets of the job, for example:

1. Decisions: difficulty, judgement required, extent to which the tasks are prescribed (amount of discretion allowed).

2. Complexity: range of tasks to be carried out or skills to be used.
3. Knowledge and skills: what the job holder is required to know and be able to do.

A list of factors to be considered may be helpful because it steers thinking towards definable aspects of the content of the job rather than dealing with overgeneralized concepts such as responsibility. But there are dangers. Ranking may be distorted because evaluators will attach different weights to the factors, emphasizing some and not others. But they will do this anyway. Without a defined list, they will, consciously or unconsciously, evaluate by reference to their own choice of factors and weight them according to their own whim or prejudice.

Ranking procedure

The ranking procedure is to:

1. Analyze and describe the jobs, bringing out in the description those aspects which are to be used for comparison purposes.
2. Identify key or bench-mark jobs, the most and least important jobs, a job midway between the two extremes, and others at the higher or lower intermediate points.
3. Rank the other jobs round these jobs until all are placed in their rank order of importance.
4. Divide the ranked jobs into grades. In effect, this means that the grades are now defined by the jobs that have been placed in them. In future, new jobs can be graded or existing ones regraded by reference to the established gradings on a job-to-job basis.

Grading jobs in a ranking exercise

There are no fixed rules for determining grade boundaries or the number of grades required. At this stage, job evaluation becomes less objective and more pragmatic than it has been before. The aim will be to produce grades which are administratively feasible and which conform to broad levels of responsibility in the organization. Their purpose is to collect jobs of comparable responsibility into broad bands before pricing the structure by attaching salary brackets to the bands.

Some guidance on the division of jobs into grades may be provided by a natural promotion ladder: junior clerk to clerk, to section leader, to group leader and so on. The danger of this approach is that the existing hierarchy may simply be reproduced, which could defeat the purpose of the scheme.

Pay structures do not necessarily have to have rigidly defined job grades (see Chapter 8). But grades have their advantages. Grouping jobs together into a grade means that they are considered to be roughly equal and can be priced within the same salary range. This helps to overcome the fundamental problem of ranking, that of placing closely related jobs one above the other on the basis of subjective judgements which cannot be validated.

The process of job grading means that a dividing line has to be placed between adjacent jobs in the rank order. This division can be invidious if, as is often the case, the difference between the importance of the two jobs on either side of the boundary is not significant. This problem is shared by all forms of job evaluation although, in theory at least, points schemes enable divisions to be made where there are natural breaks between bunches of points. This problem can be alleviated by the use of overlap between salary ranges, ie where the maximum salary of a lower range extends beyond the minimum point of the next range above.

Advantages of ranking

Ranking produces a hierarchy without having to analyze the job contents or parts of a particular job individually. This means that the evaluation can be done very quickly and, if the final order is acceptable, the structure can be implemented easily, without excessive cost in terms of cost or resources.

Those who favour ranking claim that the process of assessing the overall importance of the job as a whole to the organization is, in practice, what people do even when they go through the analytical motions of assessing the different facets of a job in a points rating scheme.

Ranking schemes can be used as a check on the results obtained by other more sophisticated schemes to ensure that the hierarchies produced are 'felt-fair'.

Disadvantages

The disadvantages of ranking are:

1. There is no rationale to defend the final rank order if it is challenged. Ranking one job higher or lower than another becomes a matter of opinion. Although, to a degree, even the more sophisticated methods of job evaluation do no more than channel opinions into specified areas. The opinion is confined to one aspect of the job and guidance is given on how to exercise it but, ultimately, it is still an opinion. Ranking systems cannot, for this reason, be used convincingly to deal with equal value problems.

2. Judgements become multi-dimensional when a number of jobs have to be placed in order of importance. Inconsistencies can occur because different individuals will give more weight to one factor than to others because they do not know which complex factors are operating, or what the balance is between them.
3. While it may be easy to establish the extremes in a rank order, it may be difficult to discriminate between the middling jobs. Consensus on the correct rank order may therefore be hard to obtain.
4. Ranking does not provide a clear basis for grading or regrading jobs and a graded salary structure is, after all, often the main reason for having a job evaluation scheme.

To try and overcome these formidable disadvantages, paired comparisons, job classification or points rating schemes can be used.

Paired comparisons

Paired or forced comparisons are a refinement of job ranking. This approach introduces an element of scoring to give an indication of the degree of importance between two jobs. As with job ranking, the method is more appropriate for smaller organizations or where jobs within a similar job family are being assessed.

Specially designed score charts are necessary and the use of a computer to correlate the results will reduce the time an evaluation takes. The method is easily understood and quick. As with job ranking, the approach is hard to defend rationally, even though decisions represent the consensus when an evaluation was done.

How the method is used

As with job ranking, the job evaluation panel analyzes each job as a whole. The panel then goes on to compare it with all other jobs in turn (this may not be necessary with basic job ranking). If a job is considered more demanding it scores two points; if it is as demanding it scores one point; and if it is less demanding it scores nothing. By totalling up the scores, a rank order is produced as illustrated below.

Job	A	B	C	D	E	Total Score	Rank Order
A	–	0	2	0	2	4	2
B	2	–	2	2	2	8	1
C	0	0	–	2	0	2	5
D	2	0	0	–	1	3	3
E	0	0	2	1	–	3	3

Number of calculations

One problem with paired comparisons is that, as the number of jobs increases, the number of paired comparisons rises rapidly so that evaluation of 50 jobs will involve 1,225 comparisons. With the use of a computer, however, this need not be a great drawback.

Advantages

This method combines the advantages of ranking, notably speed and simplicity, with a more efficient way of checking the consistency of the ranking. The number of individual assessments, which may be inconsistent due to bias, is reduced.

The advantages can be summarized as:

- quick and easy to understand
- jobs are assessed as a whole so that more general questions such as creativity or financial responsibilities can be considered without attempting to quantify each particular job factor.

Disadvantages

Paired comparisons may help to eliminate some of the subjectivity and inconsistencies of whole job ranking but it still fails to answer why a job is necessarily more important or more demanding. While analyzing jobs as a whole does give an important 'feel' for the job, paired comparisons assume that everyone reaches the same conclusions about each job – if this consensus does not exist, then it becomes hard to justify where the job should be placed.

The disadvantages can be summarized as:

- difficult to justify why jobs are considered more important
- the number of calculations will be impractical for a large number of jobs unless computer facilities are available
- the evaluation relies on the team's ability to come to a consensus on where a job should be ranked.

The paired comparison method can be applied to all types of jobs. It is well suited to manual jobs where there is already an established feeling about how important jobs are in comparison with one another, ie where an organization does not have to justify why certain jobs are more demanding or considered more important.

An example of a paired comparison scheme is given in Appendix B.

Job classification

Job classification is based on an initial definition of the number and characteristics of the grades into which the jobs will be placed.

The grade definitions attempt to take into account discernible differences in skill and responsibility and may refer to specific criteria, such as level of decisions, knowledge, equipment used and education or training required to do the work. Jobs are allotted to grades by comparing the whole job description with the grade definition.

A job classification scheme for clerical jobs may be based on the Institute of Administrative Management's grading scheme. Examples of systems for clerical and managerial staff are given in Appendices C and D respectively.

Alternatively, a job classification scheme can be built up within a company following a ranking or points evaluation exercise. The number of grades can be determined along the lines suggested earlier when grading procedures in ranking schemes were discussed. The ranking or points system will indicate the grades into which the bench-mark jobs are placed and the descriptions of these jobs provide guidance when writing grade definitions – notably for specific job families. The bench-mark jobs can then be used as reference points to illustrate the necessarily generalized grade descriptions.

Advantages of job classification

The advantages of job classification are that, first, it is simple to operate and, second, standards of judgement are provided in the form of grade definitions. It is often a good system to use in an organization that wants to introduce job evaluation quickly, without elaborate and costly studies, and wants an easy method of slotting new or changed jobs into an established structure.

Disadvantages of job classification

The disadvantage of job classification is that it cannot cope with complex jobs which will not fit neatly into one grade. Like other non-analytical schemes, it is not being accepted for use in equal value cases and it is less suitable for senior positions where grade definitions have to become so generalized that they provide little help in evaluating borderline cases. It also tends to be inflexible in that it is not sensitive to changes in the nature and content of jobs.

The problem with job classification is that, even with clerical jobs where it seems to have more relevance, it is still better in practice to evaluate by comparing jobs with jobs rather than by comparing jobs with job descriptions. Once the initial grades into which the bench-mark jobs have been slotted are established, the system is usually expendable. In addition, like other non-analytical schemes, job classification schemes are proving to be unacceptable in equal value cases.

Points rating

Points rating schemes are based on an analysis of separately defined characteristics or factors which are assumed to be common to all the jobs. It is further assumed that differences in the extent to which the characteristics are found in the jobs will measure differences between the jobs.

The factors selected in points schemes are those considered to be most relevant in assessing the comparative value of jobs. Typical factors include skill (of various kinds), responsibility, decisions, complexity and contacts with other people.

Each factor is given a range of points so that a maximum number of points is available. The relative importance of 'weighting' of a factor is determined by the maximum number of points allotted to it. In each factor, the total range of points is divided into degrees according to the level at which the factor is present in the job. The characteristics of each degree in terms of, say, level of complexity, are defined as yardsticks for comparison purposes. An example of a scheme is given in Appendix E.

Points rating procedure

Jobs are evaluated by studying job descriptions containing analyses of the degree to which the factor is present in the job and comparing them with the factor level definitions. The jobs are graded for each factor and the points for each grading are added to produce a total score. This score can then be related to the scores of other jobs to indicate the rank order. For example, an evaluation of two jobs using the scheme shown in Appendix F could produce the results shown in Table 5.1.

Table 5.1 *Job evaluation results*

Factor	Job A		Job B	
	Level	*Points*	*Level*	*Points*
Resources	4	20	5	25
Decisions	4	60	4	60
Complexity	5	25	3	15
Knowledge and skills	3	15	3	15
		120		115

Grading jobs in a points rating exercise

To develop a grade structure, the points scored are plotted against salaries. Any clustering of scores will help to establish the divisions between job grades, and when the salary ranges have been fixed with the help of information on market rates, the dimensions of each grade can be re-evaluated and slotted into the structure according to their points rating. The procedure for designing a graded salary structure following a points rating exercise is described more fully in Chapter 8.

Developing a points rating scheme

A points rating scheme may be obtained ready-made from management consultants, and the various proprietary brands are described in Appendix F. Alternatively, a tailor-made scheme may be preferred, and the steps needed to design such a scheme are to:

- develop factor plan
- weight the factors
- decide and define the number of levels required for each factor
- test the scheme

Develop factor plan

A factor is a characteristic which occurs to a different degree in the jobs to be evaluated and can be used as a basis for assessing the relative value of the jobs. If, in common parlance, a job is said to be more responsible than another, and therefore worth more, responsibility is being used as a factor, however loosely responsibility is defined. When we evaluate a job, even if there is no formal evaluation scheme, we always have some criterion in mind. It may be some generalized concept of 'responsibility', or may be more specifically related to the size of resources controlled or the contribution to end results.

There are no rules on what are the most appropriate factors or how many there should be. The factors present in most schemes can be grouped under three headings:

1. *Responsibility:* the particular obligations that have to be assumed by any person who carries out the job. Responsibility involves the exercize of discretion in making decisions which commit the use of resources to achieving an objective. It is measured by the degree to which the job holder is accountable for what he does, the scope and size of the job, the impact on end results and the amount of freedom he has to make decisions.
2. *Job characteristics:* the features of the job which help to indicate the demands it makes on the job holder. These include problem solving, complexity, contacts and the conditions under which the job has to be carried out.
3. *Personal characteristics:* the knowledge and skills required to

> do the job. Knowledge is a person's range of information and theoretical or practical understanding of a subject. Skill is his practised ability to do something.

Further examples of factors are given on pages 129–33 of this chapter.

When deciding on the number of factors, the temptation is to multiply them to ensure that every facet of the job is covered. But this apparently valid approach can be self-defeating. The ability of people to discern significant differences between a large number of factors when analyzing and evaluating jobs is limited. The more factors there are, the greater the risk of overlap and duplication.

There is no evidence that increasing the numbers of factors increases the accuracy of results. In fact, the opposite probably applies. It is unnecessary to have more than four to six factors, although some organizations complicate things for themselves and others by having as many as 12 factors, and there are plenty of long-established but increasingly obsolescent schemes with between six and eight factors.

Neither is the choice of factors as significant as it seems to be. They should be drawn from one or more of the categories just mentioned, but it does not greatly matter which are selected. What really counts is that the evaluation should be based first, on systematically collected data which is recorded in the form of job descriptions and, second, on analyses of job characteristics under defined and readily understood headings.

Weighting factors

If a scheme has four factors and, say, the maximum number of points is 100, the decision on how these points should be distributed between the factors (ie how they should be weighted) is a critical one. Overweighting a factor such as resources controlled, for example, could unduly favour managers with large numbers of staff rather than high-powered specialist advisers. Techniques for weighting factors are considered in Appendix G.

Decide and define levels

The number of levels or degrees to each factor depends on the range of jobs to be covered and the amount of sensitivity the scheme is attempting to achieve. It is a matter of choice, like so many other features of points rating schemes; any claim made by any such scheme to be objective or scientific must be greeted with scepticism.

Most schemes seem to have up to six or seven levels. There is no rule that says all factors must have the same number of levels. Points progression is usually arithmetic, eg 20, 40, 60, 80, 100 but can be geometric (eg Hay). Again, this approach cannot be justified scientifically.

The factor levels or degrees are then defined. The aim is to produce a graduated series of definitions which will provide clear guidance on how the factor should be scored. It is an impossible aim to achieve. In practice, the only way to reduce the inevitable subjectivity of judgements is to relate level definitions to bench-mark jobs so that evaluators can compare jobs factor by factor.

Testing the proposed scheme

The proposed scheme is tested by selecting and analyzing a selection of typical 'bench-mark' jobs. These are then ranked overall by the job evaluation committee on a 'felt-fair' basis. The ranking is done by reference to whole jobs (ie the jobs are not analyzed into factors) and the paired comparisons approach, as described in Appendix B, may be used for this purpose.

The same bench-mark jobs are then evaluated by means of the points scheme. The resulting rank order is then compared with the rank order produced by the whole job comparisons. The reasons for differences between the two rank orders are then analyzed. This analysis may suggest that the differences are because the whole job ranking did not take sufficient account of more subtle variations in responsibility levels, which could only be revealed by the analytical evaluation. Alternatively, the differences may arise because inappropriate weightings have been used or because factor or level definitions are misleading. The consequential adjustments to the scheme often involve an iterative process – making amendments, testing, and then making further amendments. Additional information on the selection and use of bench-mark jobs is given on pages 124–6 of this chapter.

Advantages of points schemes

The advantages are listed below.

1. Evaluators are forced to consider a range of factors which, a long as they are present in all the jobs and affect them in different ways, will avoid the oversimplified judgements made when using non-analytical schemes.
2. Points schemes provide evaluators with defined yardsticks which should help them to achieve some degree of objectivity and consistency in making their judgements.
3. They at least appear to be objective, even if they are not, and this quality makes people feel that they are fair.

4. They provide a rationale which, however specious, helps in the design of graded salary structures (see Chapter 8).
5. They are acceptable in equal value cases.
6. They adapt well to computerization (see page 122).

Disadvantages of points schemes

Points schemes have three disadvantages:

1. They are complex to develop, install and maintain.
2. They give a spurious impression of scientific accuracy, though it is still necessary to use judgement in selecting factors, deciding on weightings, defining levels within factors, and interpreting information about the jobs in relation to the definitions of factors and factor levels.
3. They assume that it is possible to quantify different aspects of jobs on the same scale of values and then add them together. But skills cannot always be added together in this way.

Competency analysis

The concept of competence has been given increasing attention in recent years. This has been mainly in the fields of management development and career planning where the debate has centred on what factors, characteristics or 'dimensions' contribute to effective performance at different levels. These can be described as the clusters of behaviours which are necessary to the achievement of job objectives, and these behaviours are a product of knowledge, skill and ability to make things happen.

In any related set of jobs or a job family, such as senior managers, professional staff or scientists, there will be a hierarchy of competences linked to the different levels of demands made on job holders to put to good effect their experience, skills and personal qualities. If, therefore, it is feasible to analyze these different levels it should be possible to derive a form of job evaluation which relates salary levels to a position in a hierarchy of competences.

Methods of analyzing competences are described in Chapter 6, while descriptions of pay curves based on competency analysis are given in Chapters 7 and 10.

This concept is now being applied to the development of pay curves (see Chapter 6). These relate progression to the achievement of defined levels of competency. They are particularly relevant in jobs in the professional and scientific fields, where normal methods of job evaluation may have difficulty with the fact that the contribution individuals make is much more related to their level of competency than to any artificially defined job grade which has been derived from conventional job analysis. Individuals in these situations will be working in a fluid state in which what they are asked to do will be a function of their particular expertise rather than their job title. Relatively junior specialists, with limited experience but unique skills, could be deployed for periods on projects for which they are fitted which are more important than the tasks highly experienced colleagues are currently being asked to handle. But this situation could be reversed at any time. Position in a hierarchy would therefore be dependent on the range and level of competences individuals can deploy, as well as the depth of their experience.

Proprietary brands

A number of management consultancies offer their own 'proprietary brand' of job evaluation, sometimes based broadly on one of the methods just described but offering many refinements based on research and experience. The following approaches are summarized in Appendix F (in alphabetical order).

- Hay Guide Chart-Profile Method
- PA PAGE Method
- PE International Pay Points Method
- PE International Direct Consensus Method
- Price Waterhouse Profile Method
- Saville and Holdsworth SHL method
- Wyatt Employee Points Factor Comparison Method
- Wyatt Multicomp Method
- Ernst and Young Decision Band Method

Many are now supported by computer-assisted processes (see Appendix H). The alternative arguments in favour of using a proprietary brand or developing a tailor-made scheme are discussed on pages 110–14.

Pros and cons of job evaluation

Each of the schemes just described and listed in Appendix E has its advantages and disadvantages and, before choosing between them, it will be useful to consider in general the points for and against formal job evaluation schemes.

Pros

It is sometimes claimed, as a point in favour of the more formal types of job evaluation systems, especially analytical schemes, that they are objective.

Of course this claim, if made, needs to be treated with some caution. No job evaluation scheme can ever be *fully* objective, since it relies upon evaluators making judgements about jobs based upon facts presented to them. Inevitably, individual evaluators' judgements will be coloured by their own background, experience and personality, and even in the presentation of the 'facts' about a job, it may be difficult to separate fully the facts from the opinions of the writer or presenter. In short, job evaluation is not a scientific process, and there are no absolutes against which the validity of a scheme can be scientifically tested.

Once this reality is accepted and understood, the true value of a formal job evaluation scheme can be seen as a means of *improving* objectivity. Indeed the whole nature of most job evaluation methodologies and processes is geared to this end. Thus, job description formats or job questionnaires are designed to collect data about jobs as consistently and objectively as possible. They may not be perfect, but they are substantially better than relying on evaluators' job knowledge which may be patchy, incomplete, out of date or simply wrong.

Similarly the methodology itself, of whatever form, introduces criteria, scales, factors and so on, to provide a more objective means of examining jobs, and forces the evaluators to articulate their judgements rather that simply relying on any preconceived opinions.

Formal processes for job evaluation frequently use groups of evaluators – panels or committees – rather than one individual. Again, this is primarily to improve objectivity, by evaluators challenging the opinions of other members of the group, and forcing them to justify evaluation judgements against the criteria of the scheme.

Probably the acid test of the validity of any scheme is whether it produces results which are acceptable both to jobholders and managers, and which are seen to be fair and reasonable. Formal job evaluation schemes can contribute to this aim in two respects.

First, they can provide a vehicle for genuine participation by managers, employee or trade union representatives in the process. It is difficult to organize such participation without some kind of structured scheme, if the debate is not simply to become a negotiation. This separation of negotiation from joint evaluation is seen by some users of formal schemes as a major benefit, quite apart from the results generated: the evaluation panel may be one of the few opportunities for collaborative effort, outside the traditional negotiating arena. Second, and even if a participative process is not adopted, results from a formal scheme can be communicated and justified to employees much more rationally than in the absence of such a scheme, where they would simply be the product of entirely subjective management opinion.

Cons

Despite their widespread and growing use, as confirmed by recent survey findings, formal job evaluation schemes are the subject of a variety of criticisms. These fall broadly into three different categories.

First, they are criticized for the costs and resources that they absorb, both to implement and to maintain, and the bureaucracy which they tend to gather around them. Second, they are frequently accused of being rigid and inflexible, and of failing to respond to issues of individual and business performance and of market pay, thus not reflecting satisfactorily the realities of pay determination. A third and related criticism is that of failure to respond to the changes in structure which many organizations are experiencing.

Clearly, the implementation of a job evaluation system brings with it a cost, both in terms of internal resources and consultant fees, if external help is used. There is usually an additional cost in terms of the effects on the payroll, since in most cases the pay for jobs which are rated more highly in the new scheme is increased, whereas for jobs rated lower, there is no pay reduction. This last is of course not due to job evaluation *per se*, but is simply a function of pay restructuring; similar restructuring without the use of job evaluation would incur similar payroll costs.

In addition to the initial implementation cost, there will be costs and resources associated with maintaining the system – principally to re-evaluation of new and changed jobs. In designing or selecting an evaluation process, the balance between initial cost and maintenance cost needs careful assessment. A quick initial solution may be appealing, but may generate heavier maintenance costs, whereas higher initial investment may reap benefits in reduced maintenance costs. This is particularly true of the newer computer-assisted processes, where initial costs may be high but maintenance much reduced.

Apart from the pure cost issue, there is little doubt that the criticism of job evaluation generating bureaucracy is in practice often justified. Much of this arises from the way in which job evaluation has been used in many organizations over the last two or three decades. Until relatively recently, job evaluation was seen as the single most important determinant of pay in many organizations, and as such was used very much as a control mechanism. In order to maintain the control, elaborate and bureaucratic procedures have frequently been developed. This has been particularly true when job evaluation was devolved to different businesses, units or locations within an organization, necessitating yet another layer of bureaucracy to maintain standards and comparability between the units.

These features are of course not a function of the particular job evaluation technique used, but much more due to the application process adopted – the committee structures, appraisal processes, appeals mechanisms, steering committees and so on.

In many cases, the role of job evaluation in organizations is changing, as pay structures are developed to respond to issues beyond pure job sizing, such as performance and market variations. In this environment, serious efforts are being made by many organizations to address the criticism of bureaucracy, and more streamlined processes are emerging, particularly those using computer assistance.

The second major area of criticism – that of rigidity, and failure to respond to market forces and/or issues of individual performance and competence – has its roots in similar considerations. Undoubtedly in the past (and in some cases still), job evaluation was seen as the major, if not the only factor on which pay structures were built. Not surprisingly, such structures were therefore insensitive to the market and to individual performance. Realistic pay structures now and in the future take explicit account of these factors as well as pure job size or grade. Thus this is not so much a criticism of job evaluation, but a reflection of the limitations of the process.

Job evaluation only sets out to assess the size or importance of one job against another. It does not purport to take account of market forces or individual performance – indeed most processes take quite careful steps to ensure that these issues do not get mixed up with the job evaluation system. What is required is realism in the expectations from job evaluation; it is not the panacea that some organizations think it may be. Neither is it the total solution to pay structuring questions. Once the job evaluation is completed, many critical questions must still be answered before a workable pay structure results.

A third criticism is failure to respond to the rapid rate of organizational change which most businesses are experiencing. Schemes are frequently criticized for their inability to reflect newer organization structures which are emerging, particularly flatter, more flexible organizations with less emphasis on structure and hierarchy. The degree to which this is justified depends both on the methodology used, and on the assumptions and value judgements which become attached to it. Methodologies in which explicit reference is made in the criteria or factors to specific structural features, position in hierarchy etc, are much more susceptible to this criticism but even those using more flexible and less specific criteria may justify the criticism, because of the rules of thumb and assumptions which may be adopted. To address this, organizations should review their scheme, to ensure that both the explicit criteria and the implicit assumptions, continue to be valid.

Problems of cost and bureaucracy are very much functions of the process by which job evaluation is applied. Criticisms of unreponsiveness to market and performance issues are about the use to which job evaluation is put, and the way pay structures are constructed. Issues of response to organizational change are functions both of the methodology used, and the implicit assumptions which may be built around it.

Each of these can be addressed, but this requires different considerations and approaches, and clarification of the specific problems in each case is an essential first step.

Job evaluation strategy

Is job evaluation necessary?

The pros for job evaluation as given above appear to be self-evident, but the cons are formidable and considering them prompts the question 'Is job evaluation really necessary?' The answer is, of course, yes. You cannot avoid evaluating jobs. That is what you do every time you decide on what one job should be paid in relation to another. Rather, the question needs to be restated as 'Is a formal system of job evaluation necessary?'

Informal or formal?

A completely informal approach means relying on judgement without the benefit of any form of job analysis or a systematic analysis of market rates. Except in the smallest organizations, it is unlikely to work.

A semi-formal system can work for some companies. This involves job analysis so that, even if internal comparisons are fairly crude, they are at least based on fact rather than opinion. Additionally, market rate information is collected regularly and, where the market-place is competitive, these rates will have a dominant influence on the structure. They will largely determine differentials between jobs in different market groups or jobs within a hierarchy where there are well established market rates at different levels. For example, this will apply in marketing organizations where there are clearly defined rates for different grades of product or brand managers.

A semi-formal approach linked to market rate intelligence often works well in loosely structured, dynamic, market-orientated or fairly small companies, and it can form the basis for a 'spot-rate' salary structure as described in Chapter 7. But in larger organizations which are less subject to change and in which equity is a more important consideration, a more formal method is desirable to establish fair and sensible differentials and to achieve consistency in grading jobs. When deciding on what approach is required, the following questions need to be answered:

1. Who should be covered?
2. How many schemes?
3. Should the scheme(s) be specially designed for the company, and if so:
   (a) what type of scheme?
   (b) how should it be introduced?
4. Should one of the standard schemes offered by consultants (the 'proprietary brands') be used and if so, which one?

Who should be covered?
Ideally, every job should be evaluated so that comparisons can be made at best throughout the organization or, at worst between staff in comparable occupations at different levels. Some companies, however, exclude directors and, possibly, senior managers on the grounds that their salary levels are largely determined on a personal basis. Senior jobs are often built round the skills of particular individuals and they can change, sometimes quite radically, when one manager leaves or is promoted and is replaced by another. Where this happens, job evaluation would clearly be about evaluating the individual, not the job.

How many schemes?
The tendency used to be to have different systems for, say, managers, clerical staff and manual workers because of the difficulty of designing a scheme which is equally applicable at all levels of responsibility or for completely different types of work. The factors typically used to evaluate executive jobs were unlikely to be appropriate for manual workers. The attempts to introduce common factors too often resulted in a scheme which did not discriminate effectively at different levels. Even if a 'whole job ranking' system is used (as described on page 95), comparisons at all levels may still be difficult because experience suggests that the criteria that are implicitly used in such schemes are seldom universally applicable.

Although it is not easy, the tendency is increasingly to extend a single scheme to all or at least a wider range of employees. There are two reasons for this. First, the equal value legislation in the UK has made it necessary to compare levels of responsibility across the previously rigidly separated boundaries of clerical and manual staff. The second reason is the drive to harmonize conditions of employment for white-and blue-collar employees. Such extensions are probably most effective when different occupational categories need to be evaluated which are at roughly equivalent levels in the organization structure, although the type of work and conditions of employment are dissimilar. In other words, schemes can be extended horizontally without too much difficulty. Vertical integration demands that the scheme factors are not too geared to any one job category but are more generally expressed. Some large organizations still use the same approach from top to bottom but vary the factors in a tailor-made points rating scheme to meet the evaluation needs at different levels and evaluate with care at the interfaces.

Tailor-made scheme?

The main advantage of a scheme specially designed for the company is that it can easily take into account any unique features of the organization, such as the need to cover different categories of staff. Special factors can be introduced at different levels and appropriate weightings can be applied. Tailor-made schemes can also be designed to fit the salary administration systems of the firm. They are not necessarily less expensive to introduce than a proprietary brand, because account has to be taken of the opportunity costs in the shape of the considerable amount of executive time that has to be spent in designing, developing and introducing a special company scheme. This time can be reduced by getting a firm of management consultants to design a tailor-made scheme. The approach adopted by such firms varies, but essentially, after agreeing the overall objectives for job evaluation they will:

- (a) analyze the existing job and grade structure (if any)
- (b) analyze the existing distribution of salaries
- (c) conduct market rate surveys and/or analyze published market rate data
- (d) set up working parties in conjunction with their client. These will consist of managers only or, preferably, a joint team which includes employee representation – the working parties will probably be involved at each stage of the assignment
- (e) agree with the client methods of informing the staff about the exercise and how it affects them
- (f) determine the factors to be used in analyzing the bench-mark jobs, which are likely to be the factors used in the scheme (the factor plan)
- (g) analyze the bench-mark jobs in terms of the factors
- (h) on the basis of this analysis, they will design a scheme which,

if it is an analytical one (which is most probable), will incorporate factors which will have been weighted by a process such as one of those described in Appendix G

(i) use and test the scheme on the bench-mark jobs

(j) revise the schemes as appropriate in the light of the information derived from stage (i) and, if necessary, re-evaluate the bench-mark jobs

(k) design a pay structure based on the bench-mark job analysis

(l) use the job evaluation scheme to grade all other jobs in the structure

(m) advise clients on how to deal with anomalies thrown up by the grading exercise

(n) advise on methods of progressing salaries in the system and on performance assessment or merit pay systems

(o) help the client to communicate the outcome of the exercise to staff with particular emphasis on its fairness and the benefits it provides

(p) provide a maintenance service if this is required by the client

What type of scheme?

When developing a tailor-made scheme, the choice is between using a 'whole job' ranking, paired comparison or job classifications system, or introducing a more complex points rating scheme. The decision on what type of approach to go for typically depends on:

- the type of organization concerned and the extent to which it wants to mirror local/sector practice
- the number of jobs to be covered
- the scale and diversity of the employee groups involved
- the resources available in terms of time, people and budgets
- the organization's culture – what it wants to keep and what it wants to change
- the employee relations climate
- previous experience of job evaluation – it may be necessary to 're-position' the mapping of internal relativities because an old/decayed or defunct system lost credibility, was subject to manipulation or incurred top management disfavour. Perfectly respectable approaches have been dispensed with because 'process' issues such as the above have rendered them inoperable.

Points schemes have been steadily increasing in popularity, partly because they are thought to be the best way of dealing with equal-value problems, but also because of their 'face validity'. People *feel* that the process is thorough and delivers a more rigorous result. There are certainly question marks over all other approaches on equal value grounds. The critical issue, whatever scheme is chosen, is to ensure that the processes are well designed, defensible and cost effective, as well as being regularly monitored and maintained.

Do it yourself or seek outside help?
A choice is also required on whether to do it yourself or seek outside help from management consultants. Doing it yourself is cheaper, but it can be time-consuming and it may be difficult to convince staff of the fairness of the exercise. Consultants can bring expertise and independent judgement to bear on the problems of introducing job evaluation schemes. If they are responsible for one of the proprietary brands, they will have had a good deal of experience in applying it. Even if it is thought that a tailor-made scheme is preferable to a standard package, consultants can use their experience to help overcome the difficulties of designing a scheme from scratch. The simpler the approach, the less the need for outside help. But even if a basic exercise is being carried out, consultants can still provide extra staff and expertise which may not be available internally. Moreover, they at least may appear to be more objective than people already within the organization.

Introducing job evaluation

The main stages followed in introducing job evaluation are shown in Figure 5.1.
We describe below the processes of:

- project initiation eg setting up the steering committee, which then selects the approach, and project manages the programme
- co-ordinating job analysis
- developing a communications strategy
- clarifying trade union attitudes
- involving staff and trade unions
- setting up the job evaluation committee
- drawing up the project schedule
- use of computers
- selecting bench-mark jobs
- project management
- dealing with anomalies
- setting up an appeals procedure
- informing staff of the results of the exercise

The other aspects of a job evaluation programme described elsewhere in this book are:

- market surveys (Chapter 4)
- job analysis (Chapter 6)

Table 5.2 *Choice of evaluation schemes*

Scheme	Characteristics	Advantages	Disadvantages
1 Ranking	Whole job comparisons made to place them in order of importance	Easy to apply and understand	No defined standards of judgement: differences between jobs are not measured
2 Paired comparisons	Panel members individually compare each job in turn with all the others being evaluated. Points are awarded according to whether the job is more, less or equally demanding than each of the jobs with which it is being compared. These points are added to determine the rank order, usually with the help of a computer. The scores are analyzed and discussed in order to achieve consensus among the members of the panel	Ranking is likely to be more valid on the principle that it is always easy to compare a job with one other job rather than with the whole range of disparate jobs	As with ranking, the system neither explains why one job is more important than another nor assesses differences between them
3 Job classification	Job grades are defined and jobs are slotted into the grades by comparing the whole job description with the grade definition	Simple to operate and standards of judgement are provided in the shape of the grade definitions	Difficult to fit complex jobs into a grade without using elaborate grade definitions
4 Points rating	Separate factors are scored to produce an overall points score for the job	The analytical process of considering separately defined factors reduces subjectivity and helps assess differences in job size. Consistency in judgement is helped by having defined factor levels. In accord with equal value law	Complex to install and maintain. Objectivity is more apparent than real: subjective judgement is still required to rate jobs against different factors and level definitions
5 Competency analysis	Competences are analyzed and arranged in a hierarchy as part of a pay curve system	A good method of dealing with job families where progression is not related to easily defined and measured steps	Difficult to set up and administer

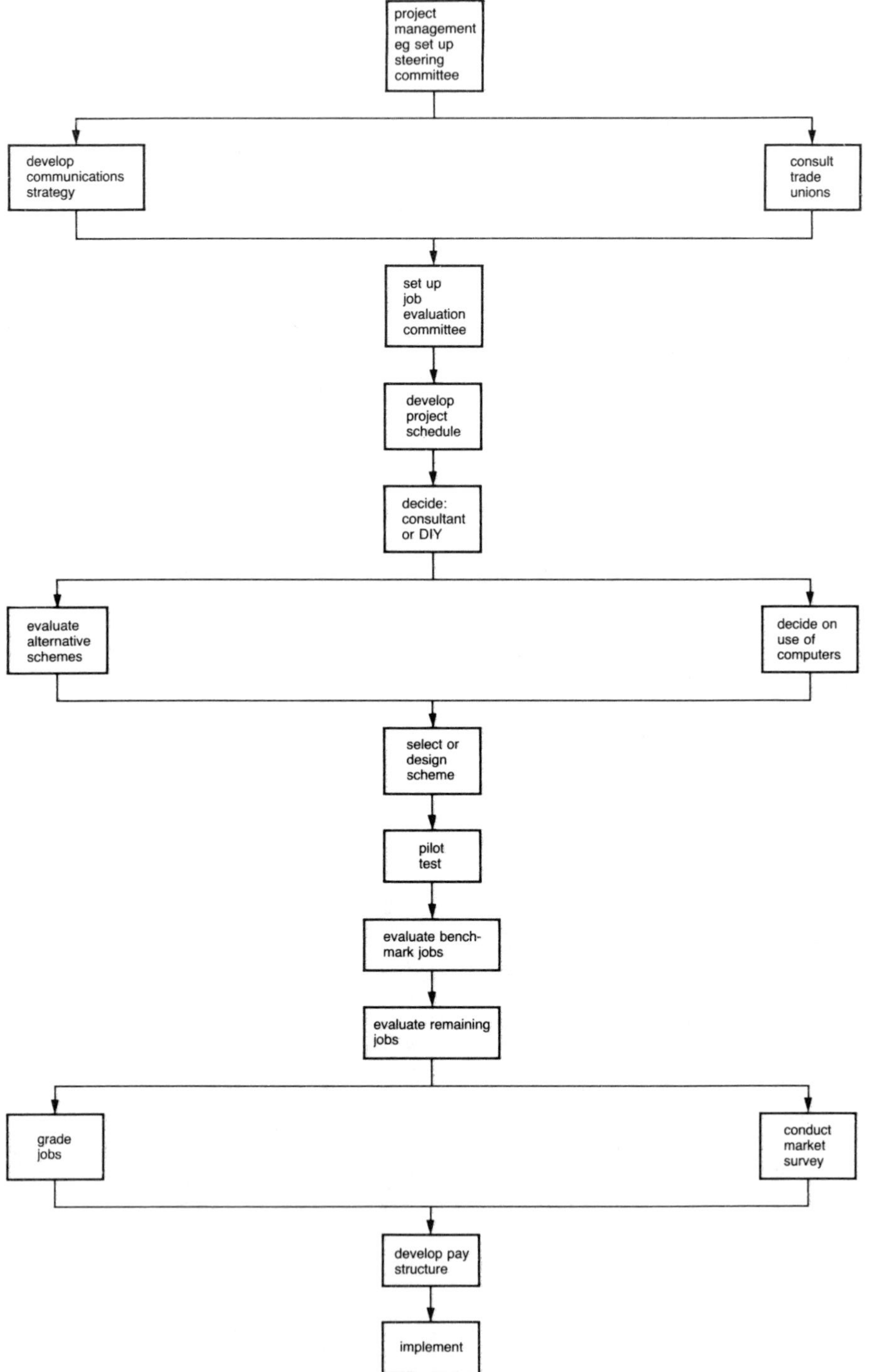

Figure 5.1 *Job evaluation programme*

- designing reward structures (Chapter 8)
- using consultants (Chapter 26)

The particularly important issue of equal pay for equal value is discussed at the end of this chapter.

Project initiation – setting up the steering committee

In a particular environment the steering committee oversees the job evaluation programme from selection of the scheme to communication of the results. It operates within terms of reference agreed by the board or top management. A budget for the cost of installing the scheme, including dealing with anomalies (which can be very expensive), may be allocated to the steering committee. Alternatively, it may be asked to prepare a budget for agreement by the board.

The steering committee is typically composed of a senior executive (often the head of personnel) in the chair with two or three other senior executives. To this may be added a couple of staff/union representatives in a unionized environment. Its function is to:

- select the approach to be used (type of scheme and whether it should be developed internally or with the help of consultants)
- either set up an internal job evaluation team or commission consultants (where relevant) and exercise control over their work
- select the evaluation committee and ensure that it is properly briefed and has workable terms of reference
- monitor the progress of selecting bench-mark jobs, job analysis, job evaluation and market surveys
- assess the results as they emerge and ensure that problems emerging are solved (eg difficulties with factors weightings, relativities between specialist areas and the approach to politically sensitive grading decisions) *before* the results are finalized
- deal with any issues such as market surveys and structure design which are not within the remit of the job evaluation committee
- manage and monitor the effectiveness of the communications process

The purpose of this body is, therefore, principally project management. The membership, which should be kept small (certainly under 10 with 5 to 8 as an optimum size range) should be agreed with this in mind. Where consultants are employed, they should report on progress to the steering committee.

Ideally a steering committee will not have to hold a great many meetings – its purpose is to put the right weight and expertise into the key stages of implementation.

Co-ordinating job analysis

Responsibility for the overall co-ordination of the introduction of job evaluation should be in the hands of a senior executive who can then report on progress to the board and advise it on ensuing salary policy developments.

Where there is a developed personnel function, the personnel director or manager will take control. In larger organizations with a remuneration department, the executive in charge of this function will normally take responsibility for the introduction and maintenance of the scheme. The practice of using armies of job analysts has largely gone. By the early 1990s job descriptions/questionnaires are normally completed by job holders and countersigned by their manager. The role of the job analyst has moved on to providing quality assurance and helping the job holders where difficulties arise. It is as often a line management role as a personnel role. Where used analysts will need to be taught the basic skills of interviewing and the elements of a concise descriptive style for writing job descriptions (see Chapter 6).

The use of analysts either to write job descriptions or check on those written by job holders and their managers often greatly improves the quality of job descriptions submitted for evaluation.

Developing a communications strategy

Staff must obviously be informed about the exercise and the effectiveness of communications to staff on job evaluation can have a major influence on the potential success and acceptability of the scheme. It is best done face-to-face in a series of staff meetings. Everyone affected should know that a scheme is to be introduced at the same time. The strategy for these should be meticulously planned to ensure that positive messages about job evaluation are given and understood.

Initial meeting

The first meeting will need to cover the basic ground required to ensure that the concept of job evaluation is properly understood. The key concepts to get across at this stage are that:

- job evaluation is about measuring the relative value of jobs – it is not concerned with the assessment of any one individual's performance

- its objective is to provide a fair and factual basis for assessing internal relativities
- the facts will be collected in job descriptions/questionnaires completed to a high and consistent standard
- both the company and its staff should benefit from having a more rational, consistent and defensible basis for grading jobs
- job evaluation is not a one-off exercise but a process, with useful spin-offs, which will need to be monitored and maintained

A good way of dealing with the many questions which employees (and their managers) are likely to ask is to prepare a simple question-and-answer sheet for distribution at the first meeting. This will need to answer the following typical questions in language familiar to the staff concerned:

- what is job evaluation?
- why do organizations use it?
- why does this organization need job evaluation?
- how will it work?
  - who will complete the job descriptions?
  - what will they cover?
  - how will evaluation take place?
- how will the scheme affect promotion policy?
- does job evaluation mean that everyone in the same grade will be paid the same?
  - if not, what will happen?
- how will the system be kept up to date to cater for additions or changes to jobs?
- what happens if individuals are unhappy about their grading?
  - will there be an appeal procedure?
  - how quickly will appeals be dealt with?
- how will the company cater for reorganization, restructuring and/or the addition of new jobs that results?

Questions and answers will, of course, have to be written, amended and adapted to suit individual company needs and circumstances.

Where consultants are being employed, they can be expected to take much of the burden of the first series of meetings. In these circumstances they will usually ask a senior executive, such as the head of personnel (but it could be the chief executive), to introduce the meeting. They will then describe how the system will be introduced and explain (with visual aids) exactly how it works. Questions at the end of this presentation should be taken by both company representatives and consultants. Staff/union representatives should be closely involved in these meetings and be invited to contribute.

Clarifying trade union attitudes

When developing a job evaluation scheme, trade union attitudes must be considered. They may want to get involved in the job evaluation programme, although they might not be prepared to commit themselves in advance to accept its findings. The guidelines on job evaluation issued by one major union are:

1. A preliminary meeting should be held between management and union to establish the need for job evaluation and the method to be used.
2. A job evaluation committee should be set up to define the scheme's terms of reference and the extent and method of communication between management and union.
3. A decision should be made as to which union members should take an active part in the scheme.
4. An appeals procedure should be set up.
5. Revision of the scheme should be carried out at regular intervals in order to identify changes both in individual jobs and in company objectives.

One union has stated very firmly that no job evaluation scheme should be allowed to undermine the traditional role of collective bargaining in determining pay. The function of job evaluation, according to this union, is to deal with the job structure. The pay structure is a matter for negotiation.

Another union produced the following list of reservations about job evaluation:

1. Error-prone management judgements will replace negotiations and weaken the joint determination of wage rates and structures.
2. The wage system arrived at can be rigid, whereas wage systems should be dynamic and part of a continuous process.
3. Job evaluation can emphasize 'the rate for the job' and overlook the importance of 'the rate for the ability to do the job'.
4. At the time of introduction there is the possibility that the new pay structure will involve no more than a rearrangement of the old structure and not include any increase or benefit for employees as a whole.

These guidelines and attitudes are typical. They should be taken into account in any organization where staff are represented by unions or by staff associations with negotiating rights.

Involving staff and trade unions

In any job evaluation scheme worthy of the name staff should know exactly how the scheme affects them. When planning the introduction of a new job evaluation scheme, the nature and scope of staff involvement should be planned at the outset. Full co-operation and involvement should be the objective. It should go without saying that if staff have been properly informed and consulted about the scheme's approach and the process of implementation then they are more likely to accept and 'own' the results, and feel that the grading scheme that emerges produces fair grade and, eventually, salary differentials. These principles apply, of course, in both unionized and non-unionized environments.

The typical areas where staff/union representatives can be involved and are typically needed are:

- as members of the steering committee
- as part of the communications process
- as job analysts
- as members of the evaluation panel
- as members of the appeals panel (if different from the evaluation panel).

Where unions accept or insist on full participation in job evaluation this could well involve:

- a meeting between the union and management to establish and agree the need for job evaluation and the most suitable approach to adopt
- participation in the steering committee to work with management in:
  - defining the scheme's terms of reference
  - selecting consultants, if they are to be used
  - agreeing the factors and weightings in tailor made points factor schemes monitoring progress
  - planning and implementing communications strategy
- negotiating on the resulting grade and salary structures
- negotiating/agreeing the basis on which the scheme is monitored and updated.

Although trade unions typically expect to be fully involved in job evaluation from the outset, they may not be willing to commit themselves to accepting the results ahead of time. It is not unusual for grade structures to be the subject of further negotiations. If, however, union representatives have been fully involved in the development of the grade structure at the end of the evaluation process, then they are more likely to be able to recommend the results without reservations.

The research departments of most major trade unions are well able to provide advice and support to their members on job evaluation. They are familiar with all the major approaches in use and the 'off-the-peg' schemes and the typical *modus operandi* of the consultants who implement them. It is therefore important to take account of this and, where necessary, to check what experience consultants have of introducing and implementing job evaluation in a unionized environment, and to assess whether they have responded positively before commissioning them to start work.

Setting up the job evaluation panel

Job evaluation can be achieved by individuals (typically in personnel – sometimes assisted by consultants). But panel evaluation is often preferable and certainly more participative. Job evaluation panels typically supervise the detailed work of selecting bench-mark jobs, job analysis and job evaluation. It is activity rather than policy based in operation. Terms of reference and budget are defined by the steering committee which has the right to approve or reject recommendations made by the job evaluation panel and may reserve to itself the management of market rate surveys and the design of the pay structure. The steering committee would most probably deal with implementation problems and anomalies, where necessary delegating the work required to deal with them to members of the personnel or remuneration department.

Staffing the job evaluation panel is a fairly delicate exercise. A balance has to be struck between the different divisions or departments in the organization and the different levels of staff covered by the scheme. Again the process of job evaluation is an excellent training ground because it exposes panel members to a detailed analysis of the kinds of work done elsewhere in the organization, and to an extended period of discussion and negotiation with other staff of different levels. Where trade unions are involved it is usual for them to nominate an agreed number of representatives balanced by management nominees and a mutually acceptable chairperson, often the personnel director or manager.

Briefing the job evaluation panel

Much of the success of a job evaluation panel depends on how it is briefed and the way in which an *esprit de corps* is developed. The first meeting should discuss the collective responsibilities of the panel, answer members' questions, and perhaps try a few 'practice runs' before formal grading gets under way.

Briefing is usually the chairman's responsibility or that of the personnel manager if he or she is not chairman. The main points that need to be covered at the first meeting are:

- restatement of the purpose of job evaluation.

- detailed briefing on every aspect of the company's own scheme
- reminders that the committee has the right to go back to the individual or supervisor for further details and clarification as often as necessary, and the right not to evaluate any job until they are completely satisfied that the job description is adequate.

Panel proceedings are usually confidential but minutes summarizing the reasons for grading each job should be kept.

Drawing up the project schedule

The job evaluation panel draws up its project schedule (or, if appropriate, approves the schedule submitted by the consultant). Careful consideration will have to be given to the time required. A bar chart such as the one illustrated in Figure 5.2 is a good method of setting out the schedule; it also provides a basis for monitoring progress. This example includes market rate surveys and developing the pay structure, which may be the concern of the steering committee and would not necessarily involve the job evaluation panel directly. It indicates when 'milestone' meetings should be held by the steering committee to review progress.

The committee may also prepare detailed cost estimates to ensure that the cost budget determined by management is not exceeded.

How much time is involved?

However much the company may want to get the scheme fully implemented, it is unwise to rush job evaluation. Even the keenest evaluation committee can only grade a limited number of jobs in a day: eight is probably a realistic average maximum. After this, the quality of evaluation tends to drop and more time has to be spent later in checking and assessing the validity of grading. The final review of all the grades allocated to check that no inconsistencies have occurred should be done meticulously and with enough time allowed for re-evaluation if necessary. Extra time devoted at this stage will help reduce appeals to the inevitable few. Careful preparation for the communication of job grades and of the handbooks or other documents describing the scheme and its operation will also assist acceptance.

Use of computers

A job evaluation exercise can generate a lot of paper and take considerable time. The use of knowledge-based software systems, usually referred to as expert systems, can organize the analytical processes in a way which makes the best use of the database, assists

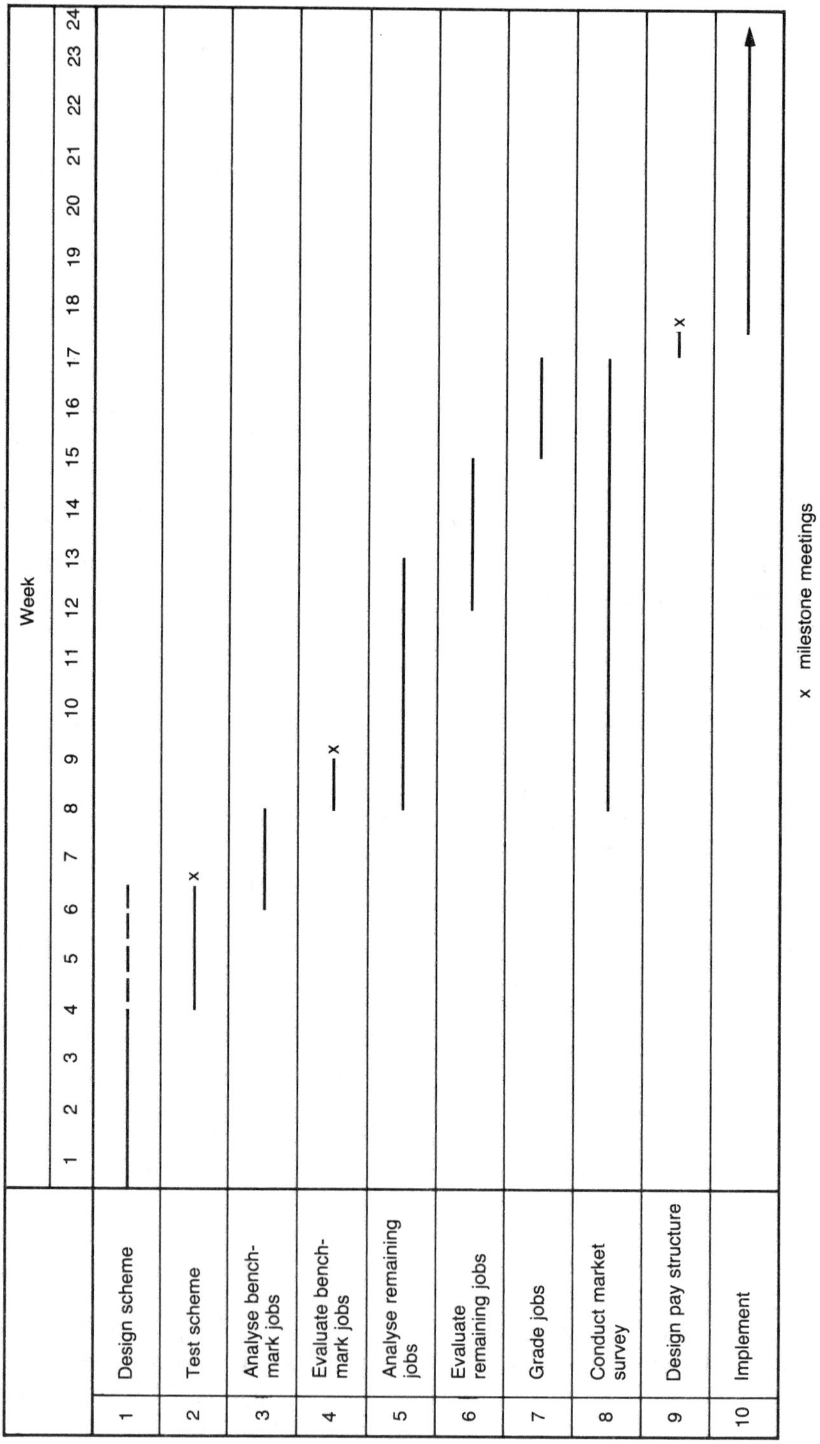

		Week																							
		1	2	3	4	5	6	7	8	9	10	11	12	13	14	15	16	17	18	19	20	21	22	23	24
1	Design scheme																								
2	Test scheme																								
3	Analyse bench-mark jobs																								
4	Evaluate bench-mark jobs																								
5	Analyse remaining jobs																								
6	Evaluate remaining jobs																								
7	Grade jobs																								
8	Conduct market survey																								
9	Design pay structure																								
10	Implement																								

x milestone meetings

Figure. 5.2 *Job evaluation project schedule*

in making consistent judgements and records decisions to be added to the database. An expert system will do this by:

- defining the evaluation rules relating to the weighting of factors, the points, levels or degrees attached to each factor and the assessment standards which guide evaluators to the correct rating of jobs – these may take the form of bench-mark jobs and/ or level definitions
- programming the computer to ask appropriate questions concerning each factor in a job to enable it to apply the evaluation rules
- applying the rules consistently and determining the factor score for the job
- grading the job
- sorting the job into position in the rank order
- storing the job information entered in the form of a factor analysis into the computer's memory so that it can be called to the screen or printed at any time.

Use of such systems is increasing fast – examples of computerised job evaluation systems are given in Appendix H.

Selecting bench-mark jobs

Bench-mark jobs are jobs selected at each level in the organization because they are well structured and recognized as being unambiguous and representative of that level. Bench-mark jobs are evaluated first in any job evaluation exercise because they can be relied upon to give the evaluation panel the signposts it needs across the organization against which to assess the rest of the jobs involved – noticeably the difficult or contentious ones – of which there are always a few.

The preliminary evaluation of bench-mark jobs is used to pilot-test the scheme. It will indicate whether or not the ranking of the bench-mark jobs is felt to be fair. It may also reveal ambiguities in factor or level definitions and distortions in the factor weightings. On this basis, necessary modifications can be made to factor and level definitions or weightings. If major changes have to be made (which should not be necessary if the scheme was well conceived), it may be necessary to conduct another pilot-scheme bench-mark exercise. If it has only been necessary to fine-tune the scheme, the full exercise (including the bench-marks) can be carried out.

The typical process for selecting bench-mark jobs is as follows:

- list all discrete jobs to be covered by the scheme by department
- select from this list a sample of well-known/easily recognized jobs which reflect the range of responsibilities in the

organization, both vertically and horizontally across departments/divisions/sites
- ensure that equal value considerations are taken into account (these are discussed later in this chapter).

The size of this sample will obviously vary from organization to organization, but it ought to include around 25 per cent of the distinct jobs. A good way of ensuring effective coverage is to draw a matrix (see Figure 5.3). This covers the ground both in terms of division/department and discrete job levels. It gives a useful visual check as to whether bench-mark job selection is thorough enough and truly representative of all the employee groups to be covered.

Project management

The steering committee (where used) is responsible for the detailed management of the project (see page 123 and Figure 5.2). The normal rules for managing any type of project should be applied as follows:

1. Prepare a list of the major operations in sequence.
2. Break down each major activity into the sequence of subsidiary tasks.
3. Analyze the interrelationships and interdependencies of major and subsidiary tasks.
4. Estimate the time required to complete each activity and task.
5. Allocate the appropriate resources for each stage.
6. Set up a feedback and control system to enable progress to be monitored by reference to the satisfactory completion of specified tasks and to ensure that costs are controlled within budget.

The initial preparation of the project schedule (steps 1 to 4 in Figure) should be done by the steering committee, but the job evaluation panel is closer to the action and should subject this plan to detailed scrutiny, and recommend amendments if necessary. The continuous process of monitoring progress may require the job evaluation panel to propose and justify further amendments.

It should be emphasized that project management is not just about getting things done on time. It is also very much concerned with the effective allocation and use of resources to deliver acceptable results which meet the required standards.

Dealing with anomalies

All job evaluation exercises throw up anomalies – jobs which are clearly over- or under-graded for historical or other reasons. It is

	Corporate	Marketing	Manufacturing	Distribution	Finance	Human resources	Development	Mgt. services
Senior management								
Management								
Junior management								
Senior professional								
Professional								
Junior professional								
Supervision								
Senior administrator/ operative								
Administrator/ operative								
Junior administrator/ operative								

Figure 5.3 *Bench-mark job matrix*

always wise to be prepared to make difficult decisions about when and how to regrade jobs. Even if it is decided to 'red circle' a job (ie register it as an anomaly and make no immediate alteration to the rate of pay), it will still be necessary to consider with great care the implications of telling people that they are wrongly graded, or informing them that, although they will not lose money now, their salary ceiling may be restricted.

It is advisable to develop ground rules on how to deal with anomalies. It is also necessary to calculate the cost of dealing with them, immediately or in the future, if it is decided to phase salary increases for staff who are underpaid following regrading. This cost should be related to the budget for the job evaluation exercise and, if the budget is exceeded, it may be necessary to reconsider methods of dealing with anomalies, possibly by extending the period over which increases are phased. Decisions on dealing with anomalies and the costs thereof would be dealt with at steering committee level.

Setting up an appeals procedure

Even the most committed and highly trained job evaluation committees make mistakes. Add to this 'political' considerations such as managers who expect the people they supervise to be more highly graded as a reflection of departmental status and individuals who feel the importance of their job has been undervalued, and the need for an appeals procedure is inevitable. Unions will want to negotiate the basis for appeals when the introduction of job evaluation is agreed. A fairly typical appeal sequence covering unionized and non-unionized staff would be:

1. Appeal goes to supervisor.
2. Supervisor and employee appeal to grading committee.
3. If the decision is not acceptable:
   (a) unionized staff involve branch officials
   (b) non-unionized staff go through their own grievance procedure to higher authority.
4. Ultimately the appeal goes to a top management committee for final decision.

Informing staff of the results of the exercise

Communicating the results of evaluation and grading needs to be handled with great care. Despite a continuing flow of positive communication throughout the job analysis/evaluation phase, many employees will be nervous of the outcome. Their primary questions when the results are published will be:

- what does the new grade structure look like?
- where do I come in the pecking order?
- how does this relate to the jobs around me?
- how does/will the whole process link to pay?
- what can I do if I believe my job/the jobs of people reporting to me have been wrongly evaluated?

Once agreed, the new grade structure should ideally be communicated in a series of meetings. The structure and individual gradings should be communicated to employees individually. Again, this should be done in person by the individual's immediate superior who should be able to explain:

- how the new structure works
- where the individual fits
- how they have been allocated their place in the new pay scales attached to the new grade structure
- how to appeal if the individual seriously believes that the evaluation is wrong.

Once the scheme is in place and bedded down, there should continue to be communication on the scheme. The key communication needs from then on are likely to be:

- ensuring that new employees are properly briefed on the scheme and how it affects their job
- reporting the results of appeals – to demonstrate both that fair hearings have been given and that appeals have been speedily heard
- reporting how the scheme is applying to new jobs resulting from reorganization or restructuring
- periodic reminders to staff on the way the scheme works – typically as part of the process of auditing jobs to ensure that descriptions are kept up to date and major changes on scope re-evaluated
- communicating, where relevant, how some of the 'spin-offs' from job evaluation have proved useful.

Developing your own job evaluation scheme

The stages of developing your own job evaluation scheme are identical to the ones described above for introducing job evaluation, but you will probably have to design your own factor plan (unless you take one 'off the shelf', which is not advisable).

If you decided to introduce a points scheme (the most typical approach), there is a lot to be said for doing this with a team comprising managers, staff and, where appropriate, trade union representatives. This could later form the job evaluation panel.

A case-study

A large voluntary organization recently developed a scheme by getting a team of managers and staff representatives together in a 'workshop' for a week.

The workshop started with a brief description of the purpose and techniques of job evaluation, and its members were then plunged into the process of designing the factor plan. This was done by brainstorming – any suggestions were accepted in accordance with brainstorming rules. About 50 possible factors were listed on flip charts and these were distilled into the following list of 30 factors:

accountability
communication skills
complexity
contacts
creativity
decisions
discretion exercised
education and training
effect of errors
effort
environmental conditions
experience
financial responsibility
impact on end results
judgement
know-how
mental skills
physical demands
problem solving
resources controlled
responsibility (general)
responsibility for cash and materials
responsibility for confidential data
responsibility for people
responsibility for records and reports
scope
social skills
supervision exercised
supervision received
working conditions

These were further analyzed into five key factors:

1. Knowledge and skills.
2. Responsibility.
3. Complexity.
4. Resources controlled.
5. Contacts.

The workshop then went on to define the factors and levels and agree weightings. These were evolved by testing the scheme on bench-mark job descriptions which were prepared during the workshop. Paired comparisons were used to produce a verification of the rank order produced by the points scheme. The scheme was then tested in the field on additional bench-mark jobs which resulted in a number of refinements to factor and level definitions and some adjustments to weightings.

The scheme produced by this process is described in Appendix D.

Equal pay and job evaluation

The impact of equal pay legislation

The Equal Pay Act of 1970 provided that a woman was entitled to equal pay with a man (or vice versa) working for the same employer at the same establishment where her work was 'like' to his, or where their work had been rated equivalent on a job evaluation study.

The Act was amended with effect from 1 January 1984, following a European Court ruling which found the provisions insufficient to meet the requirements of the European Economic Community's Directive on Equal Pay.

Under the Equal Value Amendment, women are entitled to equal pay with men (and vice versa) where the work is of equal value in terms of the demands made under various headings, to quote: 'for instance, effort, skill, decision'. Claims can cut across job families, occupational groups and bargaining units. Women can claim equal pay with men employed on work quite dissimilar in nature – and they have. The legal provisions are especially important in instances where there is separation of men's jobs and women's jobs, and where methods of pay determination vary within the organizations. The legislation forces comparison of the content of jobs where neither employers nor union pressure would have demanded it.

The implications for job evaluation

Job evaluation has become central to equal value because the jobs concerned must, by definition, be evaluated by some method in order to determine their relative value. Employees can base claims on the results of a job evaluation scheme. Employers can seek to have a claim set aside at an early stage if the work of both the applicant and comparator has been rated differently under a common job evaluation scheme.

Claims for equal pay can be made whether or not a job evaluation scheme is in existence in the organization concerned. If a defence to a claim is based on an existing scheme, the onus is on the employer to prove that this scheme is analytical in nature and free from sex bias both in design and implementation.

Unless the tribunal can dismiss a claim at this early stage, it must commission a report by an 'independent expert'. The independent expert is drawn from a list appointed by the Advisory Conciliation and Arbitration Service (ACAS) and is required to assess the equality of value between the applicant and comparator. The method and basis of assessment is decided by each individual independent expert although, again, it must be an analytical approach.

Case law affecting job evaluation

Case law affecting job evaluation is limited, but there have been three major decisions, which are summarized below.

Hayward v. Cammell Laird (House of Lords 1988)

The first successful case under the Equal Value Amendment was that of a cook, Julie Hayward, claiming equal value with three male comparators – a painter, a joiner, and a thermal insulation engineer.

An independent expert was appointed to examine the relative 'value' of the work and concluded that the cook's work was of equal value to the male comparators. The tribunal accepted this conclusion and ordered the employers to raise Hayward's pay in line with the pay of the comparators.

The company argued that a variety of benefits to which Hayward was entitled should be offset in the difference in base pay levels. When the case reached the House of Lords, it was ruled that the proper interpretation of the law, as written, was that 'term' meant any specific element of the remuneration package. Hayward therefore gained equal basic pay and retained the additional benefits which were applicable to her job, but not to the jobs of the male comparators.

Pickstone v. Freemans (House of Lords 1988)

The significant ruling of this case was that the female applicants were not precluded from claiming Equal Pay for Work of Equal Value with higher paid men performing different work just because a small percentage of those performing the same work as the applicants were men.

Bromley and others v. H & J Quick (Court of Appeal 1988)
Although the detailed anatomy of the job evaluation system was not the issue on which this case turned, it did serve to establish that a job evaluation system can only provide a defence if it is analytical in nature.

This case also established that the onus rests with the employer to demonstrate absence of sex bias in any common job evaluation system which is to be relied on as a defence.

The need was indicated for careful attention to procedures for slotting jobs against bench-marks. Since the jobs of applicant and comparators had neither been fully evaluated using the factors, nor were identical to the bench-mark jobs, it was ruled that they were not, for the purposes of law, 'covered' by the job evaluation system common to all. The system could, therefore, not be relied upon to set aside the claim and the report of an independent expert had to be obtained.

Example of discriminatory job factors

Factors	*Maintenance fitter*	*Company nurse*
(each factor is scored on a scale from 1 to 10) (for simplicity no weights have been applied)		
Skill		
Experience in job	10	1
Training	5	7
Responsibility		
For money	0	0
For equipment and machinery	8	3
For safety	3	6
For work done by others	3	0
Effort		
Lifting requirement	4	2
Strength required	7	2
Sustained physical effort	5	1
Conditions		
Physical environment	6	0
Working position	6	0
Hazards	7	0
TOTAL	64	22

This set of factors is discriminatory because it contains many aspects of the male job and very few relating to the female job. There is also double counting, for example 'strength required' and 'lifting required' would frequently have similar scores, either high or low. The example below shows what in the opinion of the Equal Opportunities' Commission are less biased job evaluation factors.

Example of non-discriminatory job factors

Factors	*Maintenance fitter*	*Company nurse*
(each factor is scored on a scale from 1 to 10) (for simplicity no weights have been applied)		
Basic knowledge	6	8
Complexity of task	6	7
Training	5	7
Responsibility for people	3	8
Responsibility for materials and equipment	8	6
Mental effort	5	6
Visual attention	6	6
Physical activity	8	5
Working conditions	6	1
TOTAL	53	54

Factor weighting

A scheme may also discriminate in the factor weightings used. Bias will creep in if the factors on which a male job scores highly are given higher weights than the factors on which a female job scores highest (or vice versa).

The EOC example opposite shows how discriminatory factor weights produce a biased evaluation of the two jobs.

A single integrated scheme is advisable

The most effective method of ensuring a remuneration structure is unbiased is to evaluate all jobs using a common approach. This should provide vertical coverage from the largest to the smallest job and horizontal coverage across all occupational groups.

Indeed, the *relative* value of jobs throughout the organization

Table 5.3 *The EOC's example of discriminatory factor weighting*

Factors	Unweighted scores		Biased weights	Weighted scores		Unbiased weights	Weighted scores	
	Fitter	Nurse		Fitter	Nurse		Fitter	Nurse
Basic knowledge	6	8	7%	0.42	0.56	5%	0.30	0.40
Complexity of task	6	7	8%	0.48	0.56	15%	0.90	1.05
Training	5	7	7%	0.35	0.49	15%	0.75	1.05
Responsibility for people	3	8	15%	0.45	1.20	15%	0.45	1.20
Responsibility for materials and equipment	8	6	15%	1.20	0.90	15%	1.20	0.90
Mental effort	5	6	8%	0.40	0.48	10%	0.50	0.60
Visual attention	6	6	10%	0.60	0.60	10%	0.60	0.60
Physical activity	8	5	15%	1.20	0.75	10%	0.80	0.50
Working conditions	6	1	15%	0.90	0.15	5%	0.30	0.05

cannot be fully understood unless the measurement is by a single analytical method of job evaluation.

Where there are different methods of job evaluation covering different jobs, it is important that the 'read across' of the functions and jobs is understood. This can best be achieved by selecting a sample of jobs covered by different methods and evaluating them using a single analytical method which is appropriate to all jobs.

Administration of the scheme

Once factors are selected and weightings applied so that sex bias is avoided, the administration of the scheme should be in line with good personnel practice. Hay Management Consultants have published a useful code of practice, the main points of which are summarized below:

- the formation of steering and review panels should have regard to the distribution of men and women across the organization
- where it may not always be easy to persuade women to be involved, appropriate education should be provided in order to bring home the importance of active participation
- individuals involved should be thoroughly trained in the techniques and approaches which they are required to assess and monitor and should be briefed to avoid sex bias (both direct and unintentional)
- allocation of jobs across more than one evaluation panel should avoid adherence to any traditional occupational/grading or historical difference in the sex of job holders
- an appointed chairperson should monitor panel operation and encourage active involvement of all panel members in the process
- evaluators should possess the qualities of open-mindedness and fair judgement and, in addition to being thoroughly trained in the job evaluation method, they should be specifically briefed on guarding against sex bias in their interpretation of job descriptions and subsequent evaluation
- evaluation of jobs should be the result of panel consensus based purely on job content without reference to job holders or historical position in the pecking order
- evaluations should be updated to reflect changes in jobs, and results should be regularly audited to ensure sex bias does not creep in over time
- where a series of 'bench-mark' jobs is fully evaluated and other jobs subsequently positioned within that framework, the

bench-mark sample should be equally representative of typically female- and typically male-dominated jobs and, where possible, should include jobs populated by both sexes
- evaluation and appeals panels should comprise a cross-section of individuals representative of the range of job groups/occupations to be evaluated and should reflect the distribution of men and women
- detailed descriptions of all jobs should be prepared using a uniform format
- where job analysts are involved in the preparation of job descriptions, both men and women should be selected with reference to their distribution across the range of jobs
- all individuals involved in the preparation of job descriptions should, in addition to receiving appropriate training in the approach to collection and presentation of information, be briefed to avoid sex bias in discussion, interpretation and choice of words used to describe jobs
- job descriptions should be agreed as representative of the job by job holders, line management and, where appropriate, the job analyst and union/staff association representative
- job titles appearing on job descriptions should avoid any indication of sex of job holder (eg not 'manageress')
- the name and gender of the job holder should be avoided on copies of descriptions put forward for panel evaluation.

Developments in job evaluation

Job evaluation in transition

Job evaluation is in a state of transition. The main reasons for this are:

1. The equal value legislation referred to earlier which has necessitated the re-examination of schemes to ensure that they are free of bias and are sufficiently analytical.
2. The introduction of new technology is changing roles and eliminating job differences that existed previously. New skills are being introduced and these are spread over a wider range of jobs by the process of multi-skilling.
3. There is more flexibility in working arrangements.
4. Information technology has helped to reduce the numbers of layers in organizations. Decisions which were previously reserved for senior managers are now being made by people at lower levels in the hierarchy.
5. Market rate pressures resulting from skills shortages mean that

precedence is being given to external relativities at the expense of the internal relativities established by job evaluation.

6. The pressure for performance related pay emphasizes individual contribution which is not recognized by job evaluation.

The impact of these changes on job evaluation is considerable, and the main areas in which evaluation schemes will be affected are discussed below.

Obsolescence

Changes in long-established relativities mean that jobs will have to be re-evaluated and new pay structures designed. An existing job evaluation scheme, however, may not be sensitive to the new and amalgamated pattern of skills across the organization as a whole, the changes in the balance of skills within jobs, and the redistribution of decision-making authorities in the organization. The scheme may have become obsolescent, if not obsolete, because it was originally designed and (if a points scheme) weighted to fit a now outdated range of jobs.

Requirement for increased flexibility

Multi-skilling may mean that workers are undertaking a much wider range of responsibilities, and that therefore the scheme may not be able to slot the jobs neatly into ranges. More and more, the tasks carried out by individuals will be related to their personal skills and abilities rather than constrained by the parameters of the tasks allocated to job holders. It will no longer be possible to say that you must evaluate the job, not the person. For this reason, there will be a greater emphasis on salary progression or competency curve systems (see Chapters 7 and 10), which are designed to accommodate people whose contribution develops over a longish period and across several conventional salary grades as they gain experience. 'Spot rate' pay structures (which can, of course, be underpinned by job evaluation) (see Chapter 7) may also become more important where the rate for the job is largely determined by market rates, and where bonus schemes cater for extra special contributions.

Chapter 6

Job and Competency Analysis

Job analysis

Job analysis is the process of defining the purpose of a job, identifying the principal accountabilities of job holders, listing the main tasks or duties they carry out and assessing the demands made by the job on job holders in order to produce a job description.

Job analysis is the foundation of job evaluation. The better it is done, the more valid the results, irrespective of the type of scheme used. The process of job analysis can be divided into three stages:

1. Information is collected about job content and responsibilities.
2. The information is recorded in the form of a job description or as responses to a specifically designed questionnaire.
3. The content and responsibilities of the job are further analyzed in terms of the factors to be used for job evaluation.

These stages are described in full below.

Collecting information

Information about jobs can, as we have said, be collected both by means of questionnaires and by interviews. Observation is a possible method, but it is too time consuming to be of much practical value.

Questionnaires

Questionnaires to be completed by job holders and approved by the job holder's superior are useful when a large number of jobs are to be covered. They are widely used for computer assisted job evaluation. They also save interviewing time by recording purely factual information and by helping the analyst to structure questions to cover areas which may need to be explored in greater depth.

Questionnaires should provide the following basic information:

- the job title of the job holder
- the job title of the job holder's superior

- the job titles and numbers of staff reporting to the job holder (best recorded by means of an organization chart)
- a brief description (one or two sentences) of the overall role or purpose of the job
- a list of the main tasks or duties that the job holder has to carry out; as appropriate, these should specify the resources controlled, the equipment used, the contacts made and the frequency with which the tasks are carried out.

These basic details can be supplemented by questions designed to elicit from the job holders some information about the level of their responsibilities and the demands made upon them by the job. Such questions are difficult to phrase and answer in a meaningful way. The replies may be too vague or misleading and usually have to be checked with the job holder's superior and in subsequent interviews. But they at least give job holders an opportunity to express their feelings about the job and they can provide useful leads for development in discussion. These questions can cover such aspects of the job as the:

- amount of supervision received and the degree of discretion allowed in making decisions
- typical problems to be solved and the amount of guidance available when solving the problems
- relative difficulty of the tasks to be performed
- qualifications and skills required to carry out the work.

Interviewing

With a new and/or complex job it is necessary to interview job holders and to check the findings with their superiors. The aim of the interview should be to obtain all the relevant facts about the job, covering the areas listed above in the section on questionnaires.

To achieve this aim, job analysts should:

1. Work to a logical sequence of questions which help interviewees to order their thoughts about the job.
2. Pin people down on what they actually do. Answers to questions are often vague and information is given by means of untypical instances.
3. Ensure that the job holders are not allowed to get away with vague or inflated descriptions of their work. They will know that the interview is part of a job evaluation exercise and they would not be human if they did not present the job in the best possible light.
4. Sort out the wheat from the chaff: answers to questions may

produce a lot of irrelevant data which must be sifted before preparing the job description.

5. Obtain a clear statement from job holders about their authority to make decisions and the amount of guidance they receive from their superiors. This is not easy. If asked what decisions they are authorized to make, most people look blank because they think about their job in terms of duties and tasks rather than abstract decisions.
6. Avoid leading questions which make the expected answer obvious.
7. Allow job holders ample opportunity to talk by creating an atmosphere of trust.

It is helpful to plan interviews with the help of a questionnaire or checklist, and examples are given in Appendices I and J respectively.

Writing job descriptions

Job descriptions, or job statements as they are sometimes called, should be based on a detailed job analysis and should be as brief and as factual as possible. The headings under which the job description should be written and notes for guidance on completing each section are set out below.

Job title

The existing or proposed job title should indicate as clearly as possible the function in which the job is carried out and the level of the job within that function. The use of terms such as 'manager', 'assistant manager' or 'senior' to describe job levels should be reasonably consistent between functions with regard to gradings of the jobs. But this does not mean that all posts described, say, as manager, should be in the same grade. It is quite possible for someone correctly described as a manager in one function to have a less responsible job than a manager in another function.

Reporting to

The job title of the manager or supervisor to whom the job holder is directly responsible should be given under this heading. No attempt should be made to indicate here any functional relationships the job holder might have to other managers.

Reporting to the job holder

The job titles of all the posts directly reporting to the job holder should be given under this heading. Again, no attempt should be made here to indicate any functional relationships that might exist between the job holder and other staff.

Overall responsibilities

The section should describe as concisely as possible the overall purpose of the job. The aim should be to convey in no more than two or three sentences a broad picture of the job, which will clearly identify it from other jobs and establish the role of the job holder and the contribution made towards achieving the objectives of the company and the individual's function or unit.

The activities carried out should not be described under this heading, but the overall summary should lead naturally to the analysis of activities in the next section.

When preparing the job description, is it often better to defer writing down the definition of overall responsibilities until the activities have been analyzed and described.

Main tasks/accountabilities

The steps required to define the main tasks of the job are as follows:

1. Identify and list the tasks that have to be carried out. No attempt should be made to describe how they are carried out, but some indication should be given of the purpose or objectives of each task.
2. Analyze the initial list of tasks and, so far as possible, simplify the list by grouping related tasks together so that no more than, say, seven or eight main activity areas remain.
3. Decide on the order in which tasks should be described. The alternatives include:
   (a) frequency with which they are carried out (continually, hourly, daily, weekly, monthly, intermittently)
   (b) chronological order
   (c) order of importance
   (d) the main processes of management that are carried out; for example, setting objectives, planning, organizing, co-ordinating, operating, directing, motivating and controlling staff.
4. Describe each main task separately in short numbered paragraphs. No more than one or, at most, two sentences should be used for the description, but, if necessary, any separate tasks

carried out within the task should be tabulated (a,b,c, etc) under the overall description of the activity. A typical sentence describing a task should:

(a) start with an active verb to eliminate all unnecessary wording. Use verbs which express the actual responsibility to recommend, to do, to ensure that someone else does something, or to collaborate with someone; for example, prepares, completes, recommends, supervises, ensures that, liaises with
(b) state what is done as succinctly as possible
(c) state why it is done: this indicates the purpose of the job and gives a lead to setting targets or performance standards.

5. Amplify as appropriate with examples and details of any quantitative measures of the amount of work involved. The frequency with which the work is carried out and, when it can be estimated, the proportion of time involved should also be stated wherever possible
6. Group related tasks under descriptive headings to enable a quick appreciation to be obtained of the range of activities. For example, all the work a manager does in connection with manpower and facilities planning could be placed under the heading 'planning'.

Factor analysis

The final step is, in 'tailor made' schemes, frequently to analyze the job in terms of the factors that will be used to evaluate it. For example, in an analytical scheme or in questionnaire-based computer assisted schemes the factors and the points to be covered under each heading may be any of those listed below.

Resources controlled

The resources controlled should include details of any aspect of the job which will indicate its relative size, importance and contribution. For example:

- total number of staff analyzed into managerial, higher grade and other staff
- annual budget
- value of assets
- floor space
- turnover
- throughput.

Decisions

The job should be analyzed and described in terms of:

- The amount of authority the job holder has to make decisions.
- The importance of decisions with regard to their impact on the results achieved by the company and function or unit.
- The difficulty of making decisions taking account of:
  (a) the amount of guidance received from superiors
  (b) the existence of clearly defined procedures or precedents
  (c) problems in obtaining the information required to make the decisions
  (d) problems in forecasting the outcome of decisions
- The extent to which originality or creativity is required in solving problems or making decisions.
- The time-span over which the decisions are made, ie the length of time that will elapse between making a decision and obtaining information on the results achieved.

Complexity

The complexity of the job should be analyzed in terms of:

- The number of units, functions or separate management positions directly controlled by the job holder.
- The variety of tasks that have to be carried out or problems that have to be solved.

So far as possible, supporting details should be given to indicate the degree of complexity.

Knowledge and skills

The knowledge and skills required by the job holder should be analyzed with regard to:

- professional or technical aspects of the work
- people management
- administration
- commercial activities
- contacts with other people
- communications – written or spoken
- the analytical requirements of the work.

Where appropriate, indicate the level of professional or technical skill required or the type of experience or training needed to meet the demands of the job.

Contacts

The type, level and frequency of contacts inside and outside the organization.

An example of a job analysis form which can be used to produce a job description is given in Appendix K.

Even if a whole job ranking or classification scheme is used, it may still be useful to analyze the job under the sort of headings listed above. The discipline of having to write down these comments ensures that the job is subjected to suitably rigorous analysis.

Again, the aim should be to be as succinct as possible. No one is going to absorb or even read lengthy and discursive narratives. But it is not easy to summarize impressions about jobs. However detailed the analytical process has been up to this stage, subjectivity inevitably creeps in. Job analysis is still more art than science and there is always a danger of the job evaluation structure being built on sand. Job descriptions can too easily set out what is supposed to be happening or what people think is happening rather than what actually happens, and an analysis based on an interpretation of doubtful facts cannot be reliable. An example of a job description is given in Appendix L.

Competency analysis

Competency in its broadest sense consists of the knowledge, skills and qualities applied by managers to the successful achievement of their objectives. As we mentioned in Chapter 5, competency analysis has evolved recently mainly as a technique for use in management and career development. But the level of competency demanded for the effective performance of different jobs is a measure of the relative value of those jobs. The concept of competency can therefore be used as a form of job evaluation and, as we shall see when we discuss reward structures (Chapters 7 and 8) and performance-related pay (Chapter 10), an approach to determining the rate of pay appropriate for different levels of contribution or performance. We therefore discuss in the last section of this chapter methods of analyzing competence.

Techniques of competency analysis

Competences can be defined as behavioural dimensions affecting job performance.

A competency analysis will almost certainly be based on interviews, although a 'workshop' approach can be adopted in which a number of people who are in the jobs being analyzed, or have extensive knowledge of them, get together as a group to analyze the job.

During the interview or workshop, the questions would concentrate on what people do, the situations they face and, importantly, what distinguishes performers at different levels of competence in terms of behaviours. This information can then be developed to assess what particular knowledge, skills and abilities are needed to behave appropriately at these levels and thereby deliver the required results.

The following check list includes the main questions that should be asked in analyzing competences.

1. What is the job holder expected to accomplish overall?
2. What are the actual objectives the job holder has to achieve?
3. What are the positive or negative indicators of behaviour which are conducive or non-conducive to achieving objectives? Consider these under the headings of:
   (a) personal drive
   (b) impact
   (c) ability to communicate
   (d) team management and leadership
   (e) interpersonal skills
   (f) analytical power
   (g) ability to innovate (creative thinking)
   (h) strategic thinking
   (i) commercial judgement
   (j) ability to adapt and cope with change and pressure
   (k) ability to plan and control projects.
4. Can you illustrate any of these with specific instances of effective or less effective behaviour?
5. What type of experience and how much of it is required to achieve a reasonable level of competence?
6. What types of education and training and level of qualifications are required to meet job objectives?

Although the straightforward interview or group discussion using a check-list like the one given above is the normal method of defining competences, there are two analytical techniques that can be used to provide data which help to probe more deeply into competency requirements. These are the critical incident technique and repertory grid analysis.

Critical incident technique

The critical incident technique involves asking a number of individuals, a job holder or a manager to recall critical incidents relating to the performance of a job which had a noticeably successful or unsuccessful outcome. Information is collected on a number of incidents, covering a range of responsibilities.

The questions to be asked are:

- what were the circumstances?
- what did the individual do?
- what was the result of the individual's actions?

The incidents are analyzed under a series of headings, eg systems, behaviour and outcome and, if a group is taking part, the main features of each incident are written on cards.

The cards are then sorted out into similar categories and a rating scale is used to sort out each behaviour according to its effectiveness.

A similar approach can be used for project managers and members of project teams who can be asked to describe critical incidents in sequence during a project.

Repertory grid analysis

Repertory grid analysis is a method for finding out how people look at things – their perceptions of the social system in the organization, ie the way in which people interact and work together, and also the factors or criteria they use to make judgements about significant differences between aspects of how this system works. These judgements are called 'constructs', and the aspects of the system to which they are applied are called 'elements'.

The technique uses individual or group discussions which involve the selection of three dimensions or characteristics which might be related to a job, such as ability to communicate in writing, ability to plan and ability to solve problems. The individual or group is then asked to identify which is the odd one out and specify the quality which puts it into this category. This process is repeated until 10 to 12 qualities have been elicited. The qualities are then rated on a scale of, say, seven points, and using the statistical technique of principal component analysis to identify the key characteristics, these are listed in rank order.

Other uses for job analysis

Job analysis is a process for providing information which describes what people do at work. It is therefore not only an essential element in job evaluation, but also a fundamental tool for obtaining data relating to many other aspects of personnel and training administration, namely:

- *recruitment* – to help in the preparation of job specifications and advertisements and to provide criteria for assessing candidates

- *training* – as a basis for skills analysis and therefore for the preparation of systematic and relevant training programmes
- *performance management* – to provide the criteria in the shape of principal accountabilities which will be used to assess performance and thereby identify training needs and the scale of merit awards
- *career management* – to specify the requirements for more senior or responsible jobs so that potential can be assessed against the demands of the jobs to which individuals may be promoted, and management development programmes devised which will help those individuals to acquire the skills they need to advance their careers
- *organization design* – to provide the basic information needed to define structures and to define the roles and responsibilities of each position in the structure
- *job design* – to decide on the content of jobs in terms of their duties and responsibilities, the methods to be used to carry out the work, and the relationships that exist between job holders and their superiors, subordinates and colleagues.

Part 3

Developing Reward Structures

Chapter 7

Reward Structures

A reward structure consists of a company's salary levels or scales for single jobs or groups or grades. In a graded structure, these will be defined by the minimum and maximum salaries in each grade payable to the jobs placed in the grade. But a system of individual job rates without any defined grades could equally be construed as a salary structure, as long as a logical method is used for fixing salary levels.

Types of reward structures

There are seven main types of reward structure:

1. Graded salary structure.
2. Individual job range.
3. Progression or pay curves related to competency levels.
4. Job family system.
5. Spot rates.
6. Pay spine.
7. Rate for age.

These are described in turn in this chapter. The criteria for selecting reward structures and the considerations affecting the number of structures are discussed at the end of the chapter. Methods of designing reward structures are described in Chapter 8.

Criteria for reward structures

The criteria that should be used when selecting or modifying a reward structure are that it should:

1. Be appropriate to the needs of the organization, in terms of its culture, its size, the degree to which it is subject to change, the need for mobility of staff and the type and level of staff to be covered.
2. Be flexible in response to internal and external pressures, especially those related to market rates and skills shortages.

3. Give scope for rewarding high flyers while still providing appropriate rewards for the bulk of employees.
4. Facilitate rewards for performance and achievement.
5. Provide a basis for career planning which will motivate ambitious staff.
6. Facilitate consistency in the treatment of varying levels of responsibility and performance.

Graded salary structures

Definition

A graded salary structure consists of a sequence of salary ranges or grades, each of which has a defined minimum and maximum. It is assumed that all the jobs allocated into a range are broadly of equal value, although the actual salaries earned by the individuals in a range will depend on their performance or length of service.

Main features

The main features of a graded salary structure are:

1. All jobs are allocated into a salary grade within the structure on the basis of an assessment of their internal and external value to the organization.
2. Each salary grade consists of a salary range or band. No individual holding a job in the grade can go beyond the maximum of the salary range unless he or she is promoted.
3. The jobs allocated to a salary grade are assumed to be broadly of the same level. In other words, they normally have the same minimum and maximum rates, which correspond with the grade boundaries.
4. The range may be defined in terms of the percentage increase between the lowest and highest points in the range, for example:

minimum £	*midpoint* £	*maximum* £	*range* %
20,000	23,000	26,000	30
20,000	24,000	28,000	40
20,000	25,000	30,000	50

Alternatively, the range may be defined as a percentage of the midpoint, for example:

minimum %	*midpoint* %	*maximum* %	*range* %
90 (£22,500)	100 (£25,000)	110 (£27,500)	(22)
85 (£21,250)	100 (£25,000)	115 (£28,750)	(35)
80 (£20,000)	100 (£25,000)	120 (£30,000)	(50)

5. The midpoint of the range is the salary level which represents the value to the organization of any job in that grade in which the performance of the job holder is fully acceptable. It may be regarded as the 'target salary' for the grade, which would be the average salary of the staff in the grade, assuming a steady movement of people through the range.
6. The midpoint of the range is aligned to the market rates for the jobs in the grade. The salary policy or 'posture' of the organization will determine whether the midpoint is equated to the median market rate or whether it is related to another point, for example, the upper quartile market rate or 10 per cent above the median market rate.
7. The rate of salary progression through a range would be determined by performance (variable increments) or by time (fixed increments). Fixed incremental scales are rapidly disappearing in the private sector since their introduction in the 1970s to combat the impact of incomes policies. They still exist in the public sector, mainly in the form of 'pay spines' as described below, although a certain amount of flexibility has been introduced through accelerated increments or 'range points' which are used to reward high performance in the Civil Service and other agencies and local authorities.

   All staff in a performance-related system may eventually progress to the top of the range but at varying rates depending on performance, as illustrated in Figure 7.1. Alternatively, there may be a range of 'target' salaries for staff according to their level of performance, as illustrated in Figure 7.2. Salary progression systems are considered in more detail in Chapter 10.
8. The number of salary ranges or grades will depend on:
   (a) the salary levels of the highest and lowest paid jobs to be covered by the structure, which give the overall range of salaries within which the individual salary ranges have to be fitted
   (b) the differentials between grades
   (c) the width of the salary ranges.

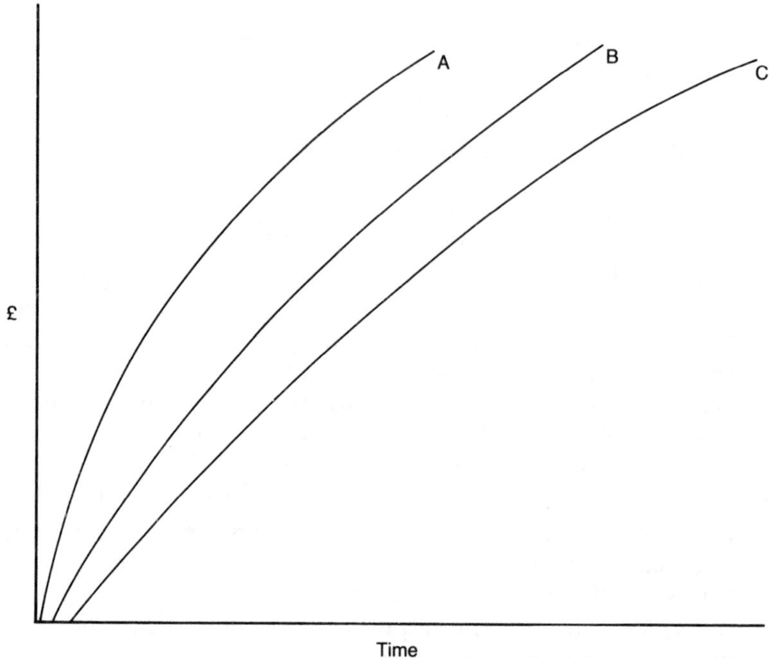

Figure 7.1 *Progression to the top of a range at rates varying according to performance*

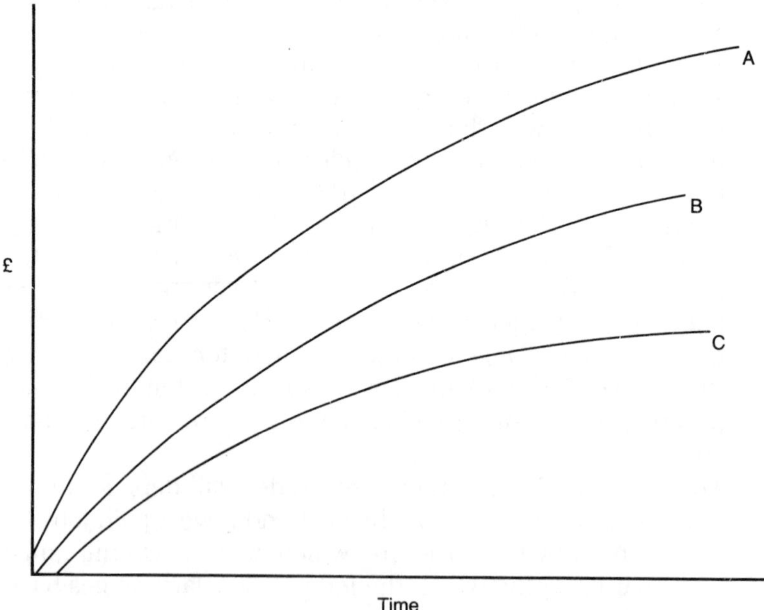

Figure 7.2 *Progression to varying target salaries according to performance*

9. There is a differential between the midpoints of each salary range which provides adequate scope for rewarding increased responsibility on promotion to the next higher grade, but does not create too wide a gap between adjacent grades or reduce the amount of flexibility available for grading jobs. This differential should normally be 15–25 per cent, but 20 per cent of the midpoint of the lower grade is a typical differential.
10. The salary ranges are sufficiently wide to allow recognition of the fact that people in jobs graded at the same level can perform differently, and should be rewarded in accordance with their performance. To allow room for progression, the ranges at junior clerical level need be no wider than 15–20 per cent of the minima for the grade. At senior levels, however, where there is more scope for improvements and variations in performance, the ranges could be 35–60 per cent, although the most typical width is about 50 per cent, or plus or minus 20 per cent of the midpoint of the range.
11. There is an overlap between salary grades which acknowledges that an experienced person doing a good job can be of more value to the company than a newcomer to a job in the grade above. Overlap, as measured by the proportion of a grade which is covered by the next lower grade, is usually 25–50 per cent. A large overlap of 40–50 per cent is typical in companies with a wide variety of jobs, where a reasonable degree of flexibility is required in grading them. It results in a larger number of grades than is required for a typical promotion ladder within a department, and implies that in some circumstances a grade can be jumped following promotion.

General increases in salary levels, following pay negotiations or changes in market rates or the cost of living (usually expressed in percentage terms), are dealt with by proportionate increases to the midpoints of each salary range. Assuming that the policy is to maintain range widths, this would result in proportionate increases to the maxima and minima of each grade.

Jobs can be regraded within the structure when it is decided that their value has altered because of a change in responsibilities, the level of competences required, or a pronounced movement in market rates. In the latter case, it is necessary to note that this is a special market rate or premium for the job imposed by external circumstances and that this does not imply that jobs previously placed by job evaluation at the same level should also be regraded. Increasingly, in the fragmenting UK salary market, market premia of various kinds are having to be paid. At their peril, however, do organizations allow jobs to be 're-graded' to match the market – so destroying the integrity of internal relativities and embarking on the reward management 'sin' of grade drift.

Variables to consider in designing or modifying a graded structure

The advantages of order, consistency and control in a graded salary structure may outweigh the disadvantages. In this case, the following design and maintenance variables need to be considered:

1. The number of salary ranges or grades.
2. The differentials between salary ranges, as measured by the percentage difference between the midpoint salaries of adjacent grades.
3. The width of the salary ranges, which can be measured either by expressing the whole width or span of the range as a percentage of the lower limit, or by expressing the difference between the midpoint salary and the upper and lower limits of a range as a percentage of the midpoint.
4. The degree of overlap, if any, between adjacent ranges, expressed as the proportion of a range which is covered by the next lower range.

These variables interact. Given a structure which has to cover jobs within defined upper and lower salary limits, the greater the number of ranges, the lower the differentials between them and vice versa. The amount of overlap between ranges is a function of the width of the salary ranges and the differentials between them. With constant range widths, the lower the differential, the greater the overlap. With constant differentials, the narrower the range width, the smaller the overlap. This is illustrated in Table 7.1.

Table 7.1 *Relationship between range width differential and overlap*

Grade	Salary range			Range width %	Differential %	Overlap* %
	Minimum £	Midpoint £	Maximum £			
A_1	20,000	24,000	28,000	40	–	–
B_1	24,000	28,800	33,600	40	20	42
A_2	20,000	24,000	28,000	40	–	–
B_2	23,000	27,600	32,200	40	15	54
A_3	20,000	23,000	26,000	30	–	–
B_3	23,000	26,450	29,900	30	15	44

* As measured by the proportion of a grade which is covered by the next lower grade.

Number of salary ranges or grades
The number of salary ranges required will depend on:

1. The upper and lower salary levels of the jobs to be covered by the structure, which give the overall range of salaries within which the individual salary ranges have to be fitted.
2. The number of distinct levels of responsibility in the hierarchy which need to be catered for by separate grades.
3. The size of the differentials between each range (see below).

While the grade structure should take account of the main promotion ladders, it should pay more attention to the distinct levels of responsibility in the organization as established by job evaluation. It is necessary to ensure that specialist jobs outside the promotion ladder are accommodated at appropriate levels, sometimes through separate technical or professional 'dual ladder' scales. It is also necessary to distinguish between jobs in different functions which, although broadly at the same level as other jobs, exhibit special features which require them to be graded slightly above or below them. The grade structure must allow for some flexibility in grading and this is achieved by adjusting differentials and range widths (and, consequently, overlaps) to meet the needs of the company.

A structure to cover jobs whose midpoint salaries range from £10,000 to £30,000 would require seven grades if differentials were 20 per cent. Research has shown that the average number of grades for managerial, executive and professional staff in the 1970s used to be ten but, as differentials widen at upper limits to allow more scope to attract top people or to reward high performers, and as organizations embark on the necessary process of de-layering, the number of grades is diminishing – sometimes to no more than three.

Differentials
The salary structure has to provide for appropriate differentials to reward additional responsibility. If differentials between ranges are too close – less than 10 per cent – many jobs become borderline cases and frequent reassessments are required. There may be endless arguments about gradings which could not be resolved by job evaluation, which is too blunt an instrument for making marginal decisions. Staff will be upgraded without adequate increases in responsibility, and this tendency towards 'grade drift' erodes the salary structure. It was, however, a ploy used under the incomes policies of the 1970s to engineer promotion increases on regrading.

If differentials for junior staff and middle management are too wide – more than 25 per cent – injustices may be done when jobs are considered to be on the borderline between ranges, and it would not be easy to allow for the finer gradations that exist between salaried jobs in most organizations, except at the highest levels.

Experience has shown that in most companies a differential of from 15 to 20 per cent between salary ranges is appropriate for the bulk of staff. This is large enough to provide an adequate increase for promotion between grades. It also avoids an excessive number of grades and reduces the endless arguments about marginal cases. These arguments inevitably result in grade drift when pressure is applied for upgrading rather than a specific market response and, in such cases, this can be difficult to resist because of the small variation in responsibility between grades.

There is a good case for wider differentials at higher levels when increases in responsibility are more significant. A structure can start with 15 per cent differentials for junior staff and then have 20 and 40 per cent or more for middle and senior managers, respectively.

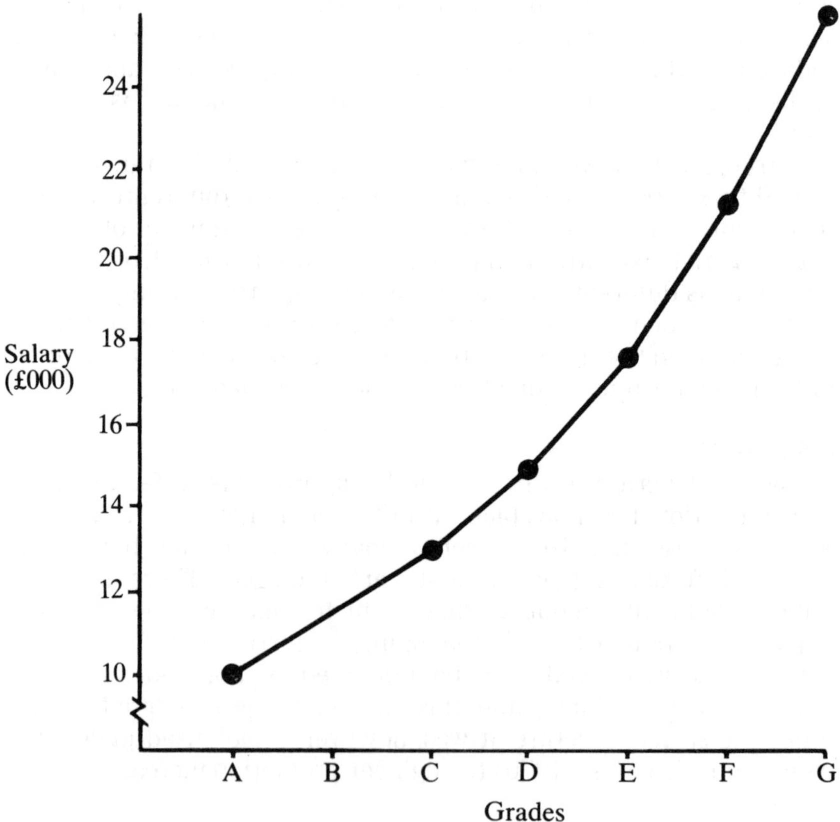

Figure. 7.3 *Example of a concave salary curve*

Above that level, differentials can widen dramatically as rewards are related directly to personal market value as well as to achievement. This is stimulated by the need to attract talent at the highest levels where the competition for high flyers is intense. It is unlikely that anyone with any ambition would move for an increase of less than 20 per cent, and the increasing use of head hunters to find top managers or specialists can help inflate this. Rigid salary structures cannot cope with this phenomenon. Differentials have to expand dramatically, and this often means the abandonment of salary ranges and the introduction of job ranges or spot rate systems which are much more flexible and can absorb external pressures.

Where a constant differential is used, the result is a salary curve as illustrated in Figure 7.3 where the differentials between the midpoint for each range are 20 per cent.

Range width

The width of the salary ranges should allow sufficient scope to reward improved performance in a job according to company policy. Reasonably wide ranges – at least plus or minus 15 per cent around the midpoint, giving a 35 per cent spread of salary – provide some flexibility in fitting jobs into a grade where their evaluations or market rates are slightly different. Wide ranges also allow flexibility in fixing salaries for new or promoted staff. If market rates or the salary earned in the previous job mean that the starting salary in a new grade has to be above the minimum, there can still be room for advancement within the grade.

Broad-banded structures (35 per cent plus) emphasize the performance of the individual within the grade; narrow-banded structures place more emphasis on the job level and promotion. In practice, the concept of moving through a single wide grade or through a hierarchy of narrow grades can be applied so as to produce very similar effects for the organization and the individuals concerned. But the controls required in a narrow-banded structure to prevent grade drift may cause some inflexibility.

Surveys of salary structures have indicated that the average width of salary ranges is about 40 per cent but the actual width varies considerably. The usual policy is to vary the widths according to the employee's category: 15–20 per cent for junior staff; 25–40 per cent at middle management level; and, perhaps, 40–60 per cent at senior levels. Wider ranges for senior jobs acknowledge that, at these levels, individual merit assumes greater importance. The scope for improving performance in routine jobs is limited and there is no need to have wide bands. High flyers can be catered for by promotion, rather than by steady salary progression within a grade.

Overlap
Overlap provides flexibility because it is associated with range widths which, in percentage terms, are greater than differentials (see Table 7.2).

Table 7.2 *Examples of overlap between grades*

Range width (span as a % of minimum)	Differentials between ranges	Salary range £						Overlap %
%	%	Grade A		Grade B		Grade C		
		Min	Max	Min	Max	Min	Max	
50	20	12,000	18,000	14,400	21,600	17,280	25,920	50
35	20	12,000	16,200	14,400	19,440	17,280	23,328	36
20	20	12,000	14,400	14,400	17,280	17,280	20,736	0
10	20	12,000	13,200	14,400	15,840	17,280	19,008	Gap of £1,200/1,440

In the example illustrated in Table 7.2, an overlap of 50 per cent between grade A and grade B means that grade A also overlaps with grade C. A double overlap of this nature can cause confusion when people in one grade are paid the same as, or more than, people in grades two steps higher. In this case, the double overlap could be avoided by reducing the overlap between adjacent grades to 45 per cent or less, which would be achieved if range widths were reduced to less than 44 per cent.

Alignment with market data

A critical factor to be considered when designing or modifying salary structures is how they should be aligned to market rates. The most appropriate reference point is the midpoint of the salary range. This is the salary level which represents the value to the organization of any job in that grade in which the performance of the job holder is fully acceptable. Recruitment salaries, although normally at the bottom of the range, may have to go as far as this level to obtain a fully qualified and experienced individual. The midpoint salary should therefore not be below the average of the market rates for the jobs in the grade.

The salary policy or 'market posture' (sometimes called 'salary posture') of the company will determine the relationship between market rates and the midpoint of salary ranges. If, for example, the policy is to pay at the 'upper quartile' (ie the salary level above which the top 25 per cent of the jobs in the survey are paid), the salary curve or salary policy line joining the midpoint of the salary ranges would correspond broadly to the upper quartile of the range of market rates for the jobs in each grade. An 'upper quartile' posture, although it may be desirable in a company wanting to attract and retain above-average quality staff (eg one in a start-up position) could be expensive and inherently inflationary. It is however a perfectly viable place to be in a business start-up dependent on high flyers or where leading-edge, ie upper-quartile people, have to be recruited and kept.

If the company is prepared to accept that it should do no more than keep pace with the market by paying average market rates, the policy line might be set to correspond with the median market rates (ie the middle item in the distribution of all the comparable jobs for which survey data is available). Fifty per cent of the jobs will be paid more than the median and 50 per cent of the jobs will be paid less. An intermediate position between the median and upper quartile might be established by a policy of paying, say, 10 per cent above the median rate. This is illustrated in Figure 7.4.

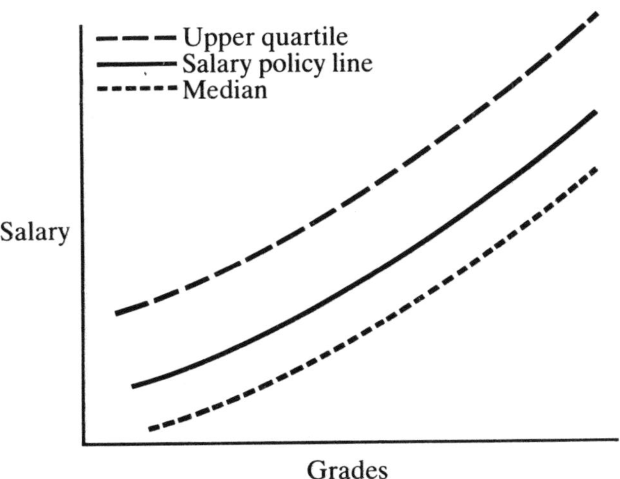

Figure. 7.4 *Relationship of salary structure to market rates*

Types of graded structures

Graded structures appear in a wide variety of forms depending on how the design variables are treated. The main types are:

1. *Narrow-banded structures* without overlaps between ranges (Figure 7.5). These unduly restrict movements within ranges except for routine jobs.
2. *Broad-banded, non-overlapping structures* (Figure 7.6).

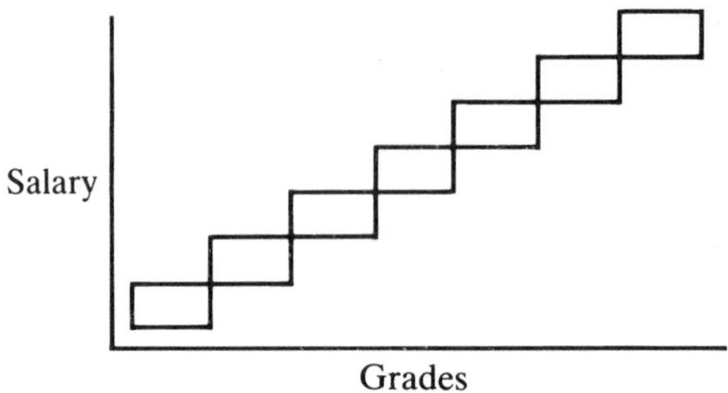

Figure. 7.5 *A narrow-banded structure*

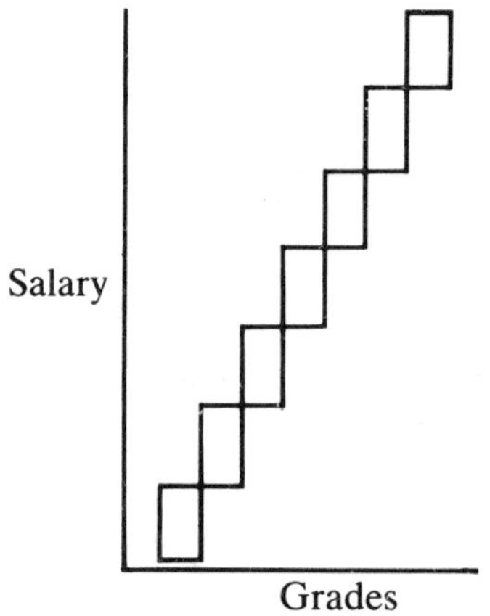

Figure 7.6 *A broad-banded, non-overlapping structure*

These produce so coarse a step from range to range that borderline decisions on gradings become overcritical.

3. *Finely graded structures* (Figure 7.7) where a large number of very wide ranges exist with low differentials and considerable overlaps between them. These can result in serious administrative problems arising from borderline disputes, grade drift and the probability of staff receiving identical salaries in a number of grades.
4. *Broad-banded, overlapping structures* (Figure 7.8) which will typically have differentials of 15–20 per cent between salary ranges, the widths of which vary from 15–20 per cent, depending on level and which overlap by up to 50 per cent. This is the most typical structure as it provides the best basis for a flexible approach without prejudicing the scope for controlling the system, or creating too many administrative problems.

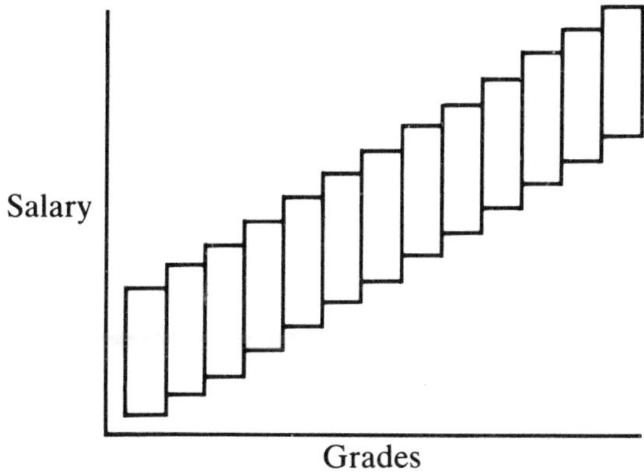

Figure 7.7 *A finely graded structure*

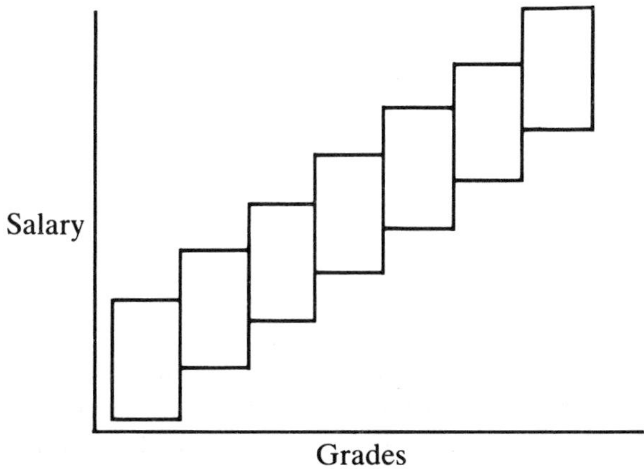

Figure 7.8 *A broad-banded, overlapping structure*

Make-up of a salary range

The areas into which a salary range is divided should reflect the typical stages through which an individual might go if he or she starts at the bottom of the scale and moves to the top. It is safe to assume that most people starting a new job will take some time to settle down and learn the tricks of the trade before they are fully competent. This is the learning curve, and the length of time required to go through a learning zone will depend on the job and the previous experience and capacity of the job holder.

The second area covers the period during which the job holder continues to increase his or her capacity to do the work and to improve performance. The average individual should move on through this zone to the midpoint of the salary band, which could be regarded as the target salary for the grade to be achieved by all job holders. But there will be some people who will do better, and there should be further scope above the target salary for a very competent, if not exceptional, individual to progress to a higher salary; which could be regarded as the normal maximum. Most people would remain in this zone unless they are promoted or leave, but there would always be some individuals, especially in the higher grade jobs, who achieve exceptional results but are not ready for promotion or for whom suitable promotion opportunities do not exist. For these individuals, a third zone is required which will enable outstanding staff to be given additional rewards and encouragement.

A 40 per cent salary band made-up according to these principles is illustrated in Figure 7.9.

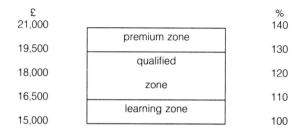

£		%
21,000		140
	premium zone	
19,500		130
	qualified	
18,000		120
	zone	
16,500		110
	learning zone	
15,000		100

Figure 7.9 *Make-up of a salary range*

The learning zone begins at the minimum salary for the band, which is the starting rate for an inexperienced individual. The upper limit of this zone is set at ten per cent above the minimum rate for the band and newly appointed or promoted staff who start at the bottom of the band would be expected to progress to the top of the learning zone in not more than, say, two years.

The qualified zone for experienced staff starts at 10 per cent above the minimum salary for the band and the top of the zone is 30 per cent above the minimum. The width of this zone is, therefore, 20 per cent of the minimum salary for the band and the midpoint of the band or target salary falls in the middle of the zone. Staff might progress at different rates through this zone according to merit, stopping at the midpoint if average performers, but going on to the maximum of the zone if they are above average.

The premium zone is reserved for staff whose performance is exceptional but for whom promotion opportunities do not exist. It extends in this example to a level 40 per cent above the minimum for the band and its width is, therefore, 10 per cent. This zone could also be used to accommodate staff who have special responsibilities, which are higher than those carried by other staff in the same grade but are not high enough to justify allocating the job into the next highest grade.

Advantages of graded structures

The advantages of this type of structure are that:

1. The relative levels of jobs in different functions can be readily assessed and recognized.
2. Consistent methods of grading jobs and establishing differentials between them can be maintained.
3. A well-defined and comprehensible framework exists within which salary and career progression can be planned and controlled.
4. Better control can be exercised over salaries for new starters, merit increments and promotion increases.

Disadvantages of graded structures

The main disadvantage of graded structures is that they are inflexible. Many organizations believe that this is more of a virtue than a defect because graded structures facilitate order, consistency and control. Others find that fixed grades make it more difficult to accommodate the many changes to which reward structures are subject because of internal or external (market rate) pressures. They would also argue that the sort of people they employ cannot be confined within rigid range boundaries – their progression may depend on an increase in competence over a time continuum rather than a series of predetermined steps. Flexible organizations and flexible people need flexible pay structures.

Graded structures bring people to top-of-the-range barriers where they stick if there are no opportunities for promotion to the next grade. This problem can be alleviated by granting lump sum bonuses to the highly rated staff in this category on an annual or sometimes less frequent basis (sometimes called continuing good performance bonuses). But these barriers may be largely artificial for those whose market rate is steadily increasing and who are making a real added value contribution to the company.

Individual job range

Where the content of jobs is widely different, or where flexibility in response to rapid organizational changes or market rate pressures is vital, an individual job range system may be preferable to a graded structure. In these circumstances, differences should not be blurred by the procrustean process of forcing a number of dissimilar jobs within the rigid confines of a salary grade.

Individual job range systems as illustrated in Figure 7.10 simply define a salary bracket for each job. The midpoint of the range is related to market rates and the limits are expressed as plus or minus a percentage of the midpoint salary, typically, at senior levels, plus or minus 20 per cent.

The advantages of individual job ranges are that they are more flexible and avoid the inevitable problems which occur when positions are evaluated just below grade boundaries. But they are more difficult to control and require more administrative time and effort.

Individual job ranges are probably best for senior jobs or for rapidly growing companies where a conventional grade structure would be too stultifying. They are often associated with points-based job evaluation schemes which provide a basis for assessing relativities between jobs and fixing benefits. They are obviously easier to manage in the context of a well-designed computer-based salary management system.

It may be necessary to superimpose a benefit grade structure on top of a job range system. Each benefit grade will define the benefits that can be obtained, such as a company car or an improved pension scheme. Jobs can be slotted into benefit grades by means of job evaluation or by a more subjective assessment of what benefits are required to provide increased rewards for greater responsibility or to compete with market rates. A benefit grade structure is shown in Table 7.3.

Table 7.3 *Benefit grade structure*

Management grade	Salary range (midpoint) £	Company car £	Petrol	Pension scheme	Medical insurance
A	35,000–50,000	19,000	Yes	Senior fund ⅔ of final salary after 20 years' service	Yes
B	25,000 35,000	15,000	Yes	Senior fund ⅔ of final salary after 30 years' service	Yes
C	19,500 25,000	9,500	No	Normal fund ⅔ of final salary after 40 years' service	Yes

A benefit grade structure superimposed on an individual job range structure is illustrated in Figure 7.10.

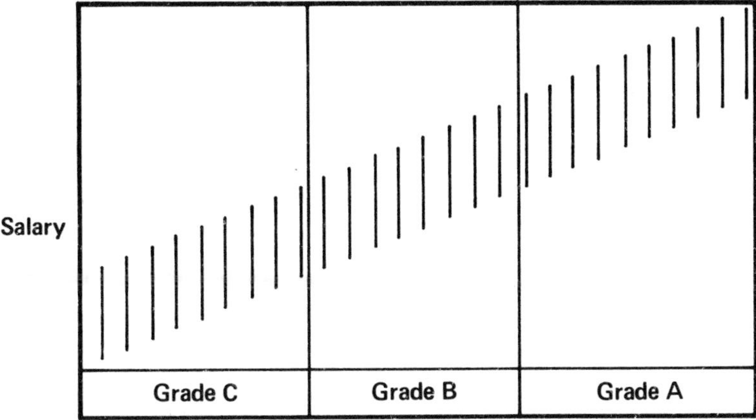

Figure 7.10 *Individual job ranges and benefit grades*

Progression or pay curves

The types of salary structure we have just described work well when market rates and/or the process of job analysis and evaluation can clearly discriminate between different levels of responsibility in terms of the work people are doing, rather than their capacity to do the work. They may not, however, be as appropriate in companies or departments where the work is predominantly carried out by young professional staff, engineers, scientists or technologists. It may be more difficult to grade jobs, especially in research and development departments, and staff in these categories often have more opportunities to compare their prospects with those employed elsewhere.

In these circumstances, the critical factors determining salary levels and progression are, firstly, the extent to which individuals can contribute whatever they are expected to do in terms of meeting objectives and performance standards and, secondly, the market rates for those individuals.

The ability to deliver desirable results can be described as the level of competence individuals have attained. Market rates will govern what individuals should be paid now and in the future as their competence, and hence their marketability, increase.

A competence progression curve as illustrated in Figure 7.11 will relate salaries for people in a particular family of jobs, such as scientists or computer staff, to levels of competence defined as points to be attained (as in this example) or as bands, on the assumption that competence develops progressively rather than between a number of fixed points. The rate of pay for each level or band of competency is determined by reference to market rate data, which may have to be collected specially from comparable firms

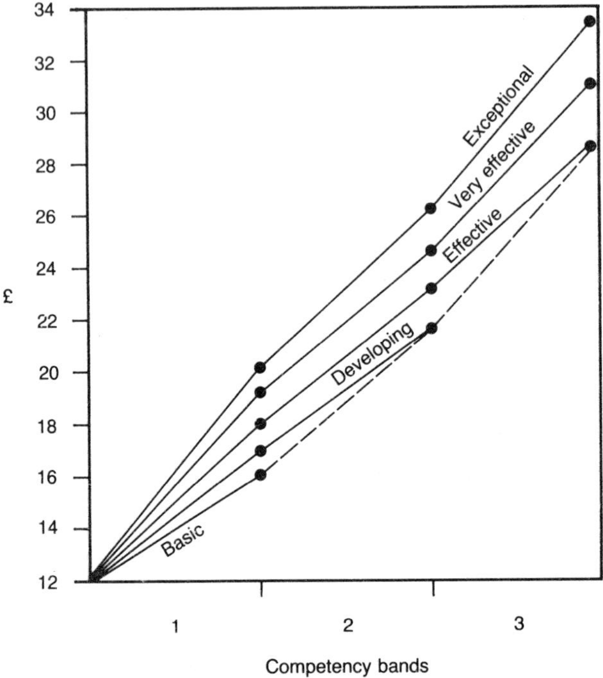

Figure. 7.11 *A pay curve system*

when comparisons between competency levels and payments can be made.

In a competency progression curve, the assumption is made that salaries will not increase beyond certain points unless individuals have attained the right level of competency. The pay curve system may, however, be refined by allowing for different rates of progression up the salary scale according to performance. Competency and performance pay curve systems are described in more detail in Chapter 10 and the Glaxo approach to operating a pay curve system is summarized in Appendix M.

Job family system

The advantages of operating one pay structure for all jobs in terms of achieving consistency and facilitating control seem to be obvious. But it becomes progressively more difficult to do this in situations when market rate pressures impinge so strongly on particular categories of employees that the existing grade structure can no longer accommodate them. An over-rigid structure can make it difficult to reward individuals according to their levels of competence and contribution.

A job family system recognizes that there will be different market rates for different categories of staff in the organization. It will also recognize that rates of progression may have to vary according to individuals and the jobs they are in.

Job families or market groups might, for example, be created to cover research and development engineers, marketing and sales staff, IT specialists, production managers and engineers, personnel professionals, lawyers, accountants and other categories of administrative or support staff. Separate job families could be linked within the same discipline to distinguish, for example, between those with professional and those with managerial competences. This might involve accepting the principle that top professionals or specialists in a field could progress to a higher salary band than managers in the same area, thus recognizing that, although professionals and managers use different skills, they can, in their own way, make equally important contributions which could be reflected in their relative market rates.

This type of structure is strongly orientated towards market rates and individual competences. Strict considerations of equity may not be so prominent and, unless great care is taken to justify differences in terms of competences and market rates, it could be difficult to ensure that the principle of equal pay for work of equal value is maintained.

Spot rate structures

In its simplest form, a spot rate or individual job rate system allocates a specific rate for a job. There are no salary brackets. There may, however, be what might be termed 'salary zones', which define the benefits that employees receive and may also indicate the basis upon which salaries are fixed and progressed within the zone. Rates are fixed by reference to market rates or by negotiation with trade unions – spot rate structures remain almost universal for manual workers. Job evaluation can be used to establish the hierarchy but this may not be the case if rates are negotiated in relation to traditional craft demarcations, or if there are considerable market pressures.

Modifications to the spot rate system

The basic system can be modified in one or more of the following ways:

1. Performance-related bonuses can be earned on top of the basic rate.

2. Additional payments can be made to the spot rate for special skills or responsibilities. This is common in structures for manual workers.
3. Scope may be allowed for some discretion to pay people below the spot rate if they are not fully qualified to do the job. The assumption is that if the spot rate is the market rate then the company has to pay to attract and retain someone who is fully capable of meeting the standards expected by the company. If those standards are higher than its competitors, then the company spot rate would be higher than the external market rate; for example, it would be located at the upper quartile of the distribution of market rates. People appointed or promoted to a job for which they are not yet suitably qualified could be paid up to, say, 10 per cent less than the spot rate and progressed towards that rate as quickly or as slowly as their progress warrants. This salary would remain below the rate if they did not progress, in which case their continued retention by the company would be in question.

Example of a spot rate system

The following is an example of a spot rate system used by a firm for its 200 marketing, buying and advertising staff at its London headquarters. The company is very marketing-orientated and subject to considerable market rate pressures from competitors, including high-paying advertising agencies. Recognizing that it cannot compete with the £35,000 plus Porsche' that top agencies offer to bright young graduates with, say, two years' experience (at 1990 values), the company still has to maintain a competitive pay structure at the median to upper quartile market rate level. It also has to be prepared to adjust these rates quickly in response to change. Spot rates are therefore set at or about this level; for example, in mid-1990 the rates in the marketing department for jobs below marketing management level were:

Senior product manager	£21,000 (plus car)
Product manager	£18,000
Assistant product manager	£14,000

The Hay guide chart method of job evaluation is used to check on internal relativities, but differentials established by this system may be overridden by market rates.

Bonuses based upon results as assessed under what is called a 'system of accountable management' (SAM for short, a type of management by objectives) are payable above the spot rates up to, in exceptional cases, 20 per cent.

Staff can be appointed or promoted to a job at around 10 per cent below the spot rate. Thus, someone who started as a senior product manager at £20,000 could progress to the top rate, if all goes well, within 12 months and would still be eligible for an additional bonus.

No general salary reviews take place. Market rates are kept under constant review and individual spot rates adjusted accordingly. The structure could therefore be described as organic, responding rapidly to the needs of the organization as affected by its own dynamics and by its external environment. For this company, and for the type of people employed there, a rigid graded structure with fixed increments and across-the-board cost-of-living increases simply would not work.

Pay spines

Pay spines are mainly used in the public sector, or in agencies and organizations which have adopted a pubic sector approach to reward management.

They consist of a series of incremental points extending from the lowest to the highest paid jobs covered by the system. Pay scales or ranges for the various grades are then superimposed on the pay spine as illustrated in Figure 7.12 (this only represents part of a typical pay spine).

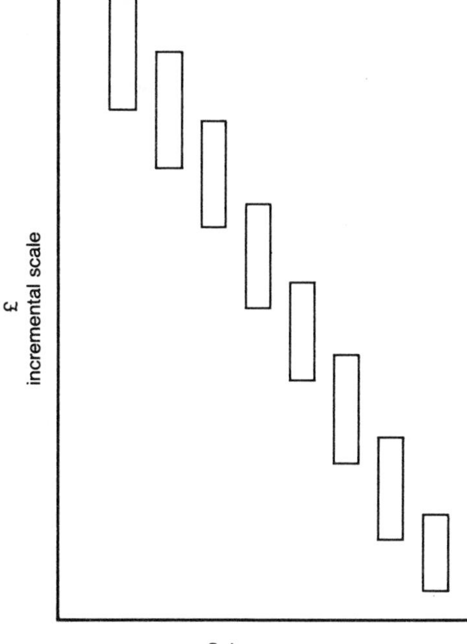

Figure. 7.12 *A pay spine system*

Pay spines are essentially incremental scales but, if performance related or flexible pay is introduced (see Chapter 10), individuals can be given accelerated increments. The Civil Service adds range points on top of the normal scale which enable staff who achieve very high or consistently high performance ratings to advance above the scale maximum for their grade.

Rate for age scales

A rate for age system is an incremental scale in which a specific rate of pay or a defined pay bracket is linked to each age for staff in certain jobs. Rate for age scales are usually reserved for young employees under training or for junior clerical or laboratory staff carrying out routine work. The assumption behind rate for age scales is that the staff are on a learning curve which means that their value to the company is directly linked to increased experience and maturity.

The simplest structure consists of one rate for each age as shown in Figure 7.13.

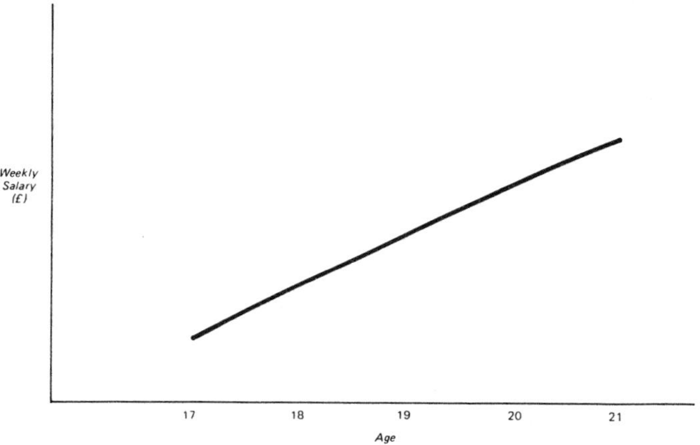

Figure 7.13 *Basic rate for age structure*

A more complex structure to accommodate three different job grades is shown in Figure 7.14.

It may be thought desirable to allow some scope for merit at each age and Figure 7.15 shows how merit can be catered for in a rate for age scale. Organizations using this approach in the 1990s tend only to use it for school-leavers and at most for three to four years. At this stage, and because frequent recognition of progress is important to young employees, pay increases may be given every six months rather than annually.

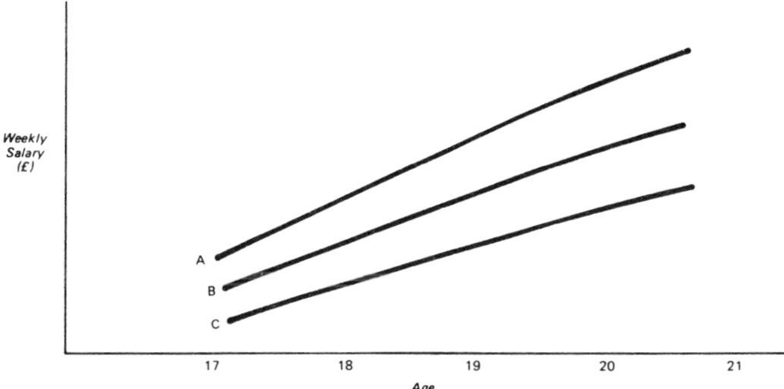

Figure. 7.14 *Rate for age structure for three job grades*

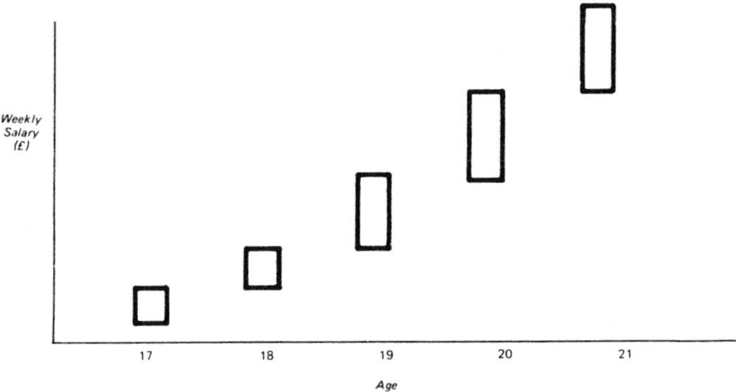

Figure. 7.15 *Rate for age structure with merit bands*

Rate for age scales of the basic type illustrated in Figure 7.9 are inflexible, but they may have to be used because they are traditional in the local labour market and, with a highly mobile form of labour, it is essential to keep pace with market rates. Their great advantage is that they are easy to administer: invidious decisions about the relative merit of people under training do not have to be made and the scales, in a sense, achieve complete equity. They may be worth retaining for these reasons, but there is a lot to be said for relating pay to age *and* performance as in Figure 7.15 rather than just to the arbitrary criterion of age.

Many companies, however, have abandoned this somewhat out-of-date concept and simply have grades or spot rates in the structure which cater for employees who are starting out more or less at the bottom and are on a learning curve. Progression is according to merit and the faster the learning period is completed, the sooner they get paid the full rate for the job alongside other staff who are doing the same job. At this stage, age is no longer material. For staff on prolonged training courses, a salary progression curve system can be used.

Choice of structure

Larger enterprizes and institutions which have formal organization structures still tend to prefer graded salary systems. They will be less subject to acute market pressures or to rapid change, and they will believe in orderly administration systems. Managing internal relativities remains of critical importance. They need to demonstrate to themselves, their staff and the trade unions, that internal equity is a prime consideration. Incremental scales may be retained at least at the bottom end of ranges where 'performance bars' are used, but are increasingly being replaced by performance-based progression.

Individual job ranges may be favoured by companies which feel that a degree of formality is necessary, for example, in progressing salaries through a range, but do not wish to put a number of 'one-off' jobs in the strait-jacket of a graded salary structure.

Smaller organizations, those whose environment induces a more flexible approach to administration, companies which are market rate driven, and fast-moving entrepreneurial concerns which demand very high performance, may prefer a spot rate system, which is organic in the sense that its form is determined by the nature of the organization.

Organizations who wish to operate flexibly in response to market rate changes and the needs of managerial, professional, scientific and technical staff, may prefer a pay curve and/or a job family system.

Chapter 8

Designing and Implementing Reward Structures

To design and implement a new or modified reward structure, it is necessary to:

1. Analyze existing arrangements – reward strategies, policies, pay levels, procedures and problems. This should be based on the diagnostic review checklist given in Chapter 3.
2. Obtain market rate information on bench-mark jobs (see Chapter 4).
3. Analyze and evaluate bench-mark and related jobs (see Chapters 5 and 6).
4. Decide on the type and main features of the structure or structures required. Criteria for selection were given in Chapter 7 and the choice will be between the following types of structure:
   (a) graded
   (b) job range
   (c) progression or pay curve
   (d) job family
   (e) spot rate
   (f) pay spine.

Structure design should be based on the general principles set out below. The particular approaches to designing each type of structure are described in turn later in this chapter.

Principles of reward structure design

The design of reward structures tends to be an empirical process. There is no one right way of doing it. The information on internal relativities and market rates seldom points to an inevitable design conclusion. Alternatives usually have to be considered and adjustments made to the various solutions to produce a result with which on balance one can feel reasonably happy.

The aim should be to produce a structure which:

1. Is in accordance with the company's pay philosophy and policies concerning differentials and the scope for salary progression in jobs.
2. Is designed on a logical basis and helps in the application of consistent and equitable salary administration procedures.
3. Assists in the maintenance of appropriate internal and external relativities.
4. Is flexible enough to enable the company to respond to change and reward performance effectively.
5. Can be implemented with the minimum amount of disruption and the maximum degree of acceptance from management and staff alike.

Graded structure design

There are three basic methods of graded structure design, each of which has the same basic aim – to integrate data on external and internal relativities within a logical framework.

1. *Points evaluation scheme method* which follows through the results of a points scheme evaluation. This is described in detail below.
2. *Ranking/market rate method* which combines an internal ranking exercise with market rate information.

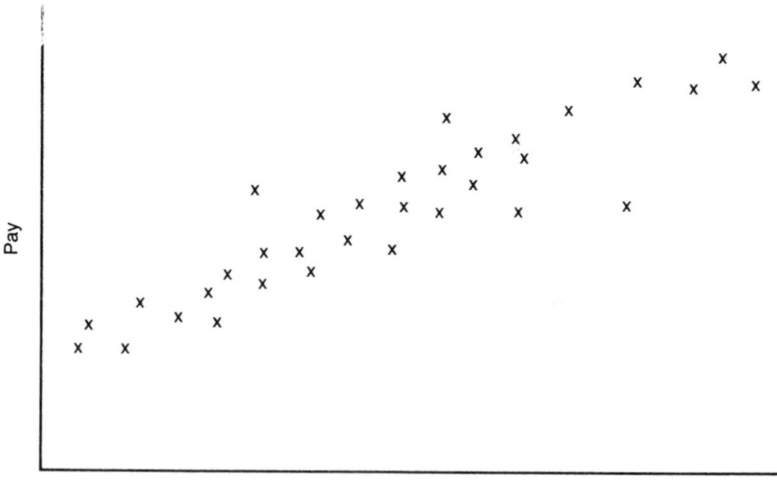

Figure 8.1 *Scattergraph of job evaluation scores and current salaries.*

3. *Range structure method* which reverses the process in methods one and two by starting with a pre-designed salary range structure into which jobs are slotted by reference to their internal ranking and to market rate data.

Points evaluation scheme method

This method consists of six steps, which are outlined below.

Step 1
Plot point scores against current salaries. The resulting scattergraph will normally reveal a positive correlation between actual rates of pay and points as shown in Figure 8.1.

Step 2
Draw a trend line through the scatter points to produce the salary practice line, as shown in Figure 8.2. The line of best fit can usually be drawn by visual inspection, the object being to have roughly the same number of points above and below the line. This line can be drawn more accurately by the statistical technique of least squares, but such a degree of accuracy is inappropriate in a process which is based on largely unscientific judgements.

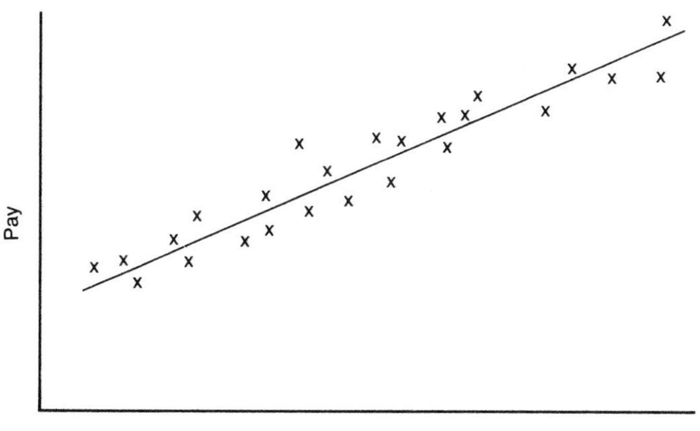

Figure 8.2 *Trend line through scattergraph to produce salary practice line*

Step 3
Obtain information on the market rates (median and upper quartile) for the bench-mark jobs and, if sufficient data is available, plot the median and upper quartile trend lines, as shown in Figure 8.3.

If the salary practice line is drawn on the same chart, the

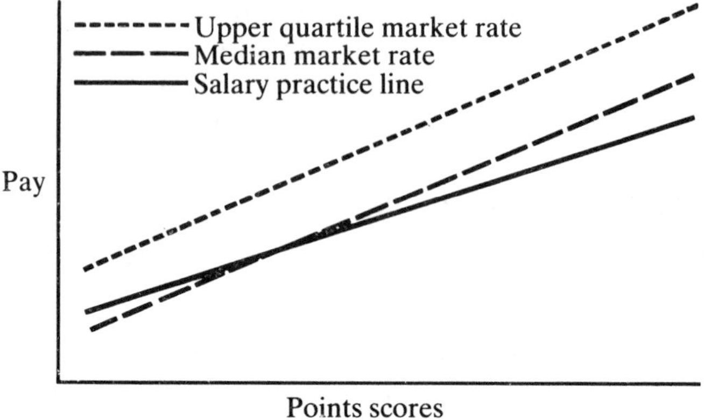

Figure 8.3 *Comparison of market rates and salary practice line*

relationship between actual salaries and market rates will be shown. Figure 8.3 shows a salary practice line which is slipping behind market rates for more highly rated jobs; clearly an unsatisfactory state of affairs. The value of this exercise clearly depends upon the number of accurate comparisons that can be made between actual and market rates. Most of the Hay surveys adopt the common method of points evaluation as a useful basis for comparison.

Step 4
Decide on the salary policy line that the company wants to adopt in relation to the market rate and salary practice lines. This can then be plotted on a graph in addition to the market rate and salary practice lines as shown in Figure 8.4, which clearly indicates the gap between policy and practice. The slope of the salary policy line represents the policy of the company on the rate at which it wants salary and career progression to take place through the job hierarchy. The salary posture of the company will also be shown by the relationship between the policy and market rate lines.

Step 5
Decide on the overall design of the structure in relation to the salary policy line. This requires decisions on the number of grades, the midpoint salaries of each grade (ie the differentials between them) and the boundaries of each grade in terms of point scores and salaries. This is the critical design stage and, because of the number of interacting variables, an empirical approach is essential, testing out alternatives in the light of the general principles which underlie graded structures. To summarize, these general principles cover the need to:

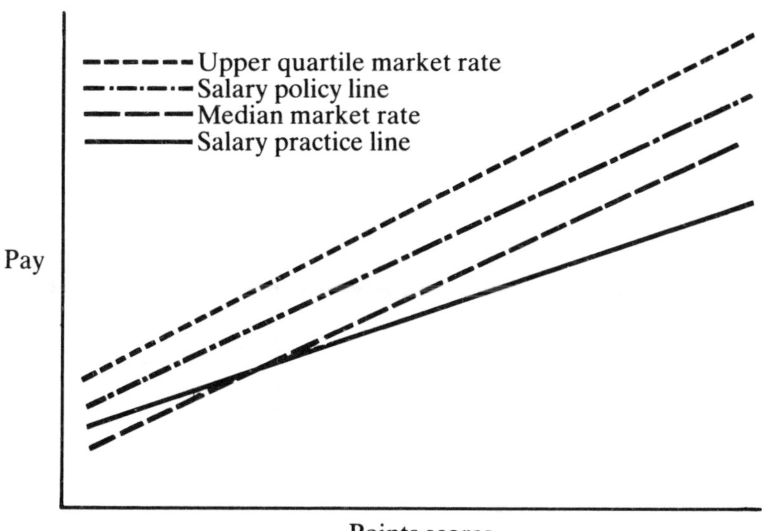

Figure 8.4 *A salary policy line in relation to the salary practice line and market rates*

1. Have grades a reasonable distance apart so that a typical promotion results in a grade change rather than a movement within a grade.
2. Provide the number of grades required to reflect the differences between jobs in the hierarchical structures of different departments.
3. Provide appropriate differentials between grades and scope for progression within grades.
4. Ensure that, as far as possible, grade boundaries occur at points where there are relatively few jobs.

It may be decided that, for the more senior jobs, an individual job range structure should be used, but, on the assumption that a more conventional graded structure is adopted, it would be necessary to proceed by breaking down this step into a number of interconnected sub-stages as outlined below:

1. Take the preferred differential of, say, 20 per cent between grades and test its impact on the number of grades. The number will clearly depend on the design constants – the slope of the salary policy line and the upper and lower levels of the salaries for the jobs to be included in the structure.
2. Consider whether the number of grades produced by this means satisfies the general design principles listed above. If it does not, and the salary curve remains unchanged, the differential

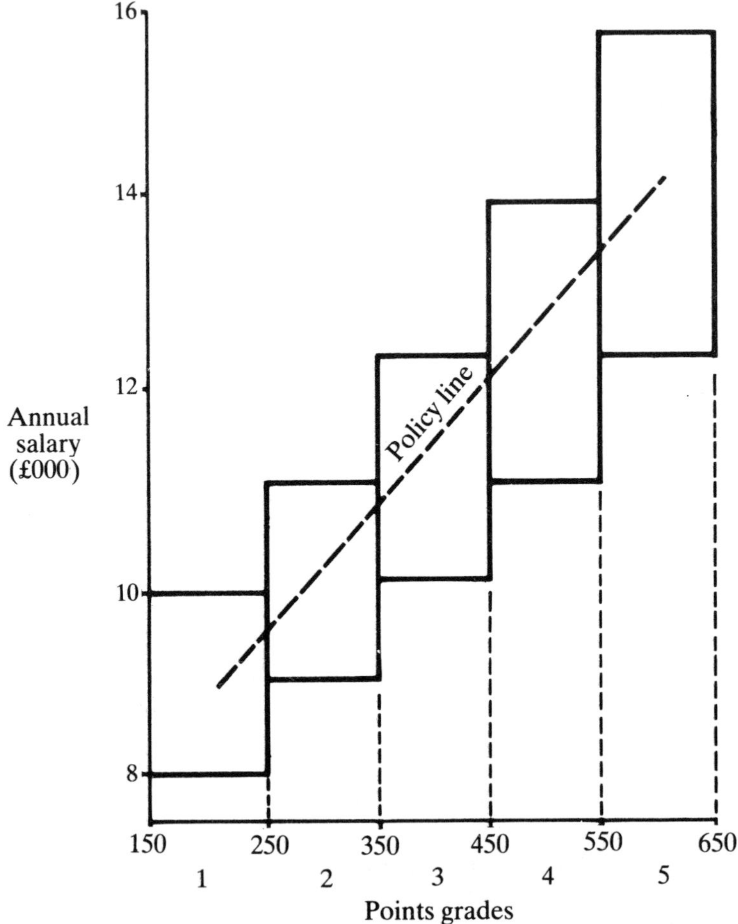

Figure 8.5 *A points scheme grade structure*

would have to be varied to produce the number of grades required.

3. Having decided on the differentials and thus on the number of grades and the midpoint salaries of each grade, plot the midpoints on the policy line as shown in Figure 8.5.
4. Define the grade demarcation lines in terms of points scores. This has largely been predetermined by the previous decisions on differentials and the salary line, but it would be necessary to select appropriate boundaries and, therefore, the range of points for each grade. The aim would be to have a logical relationship between grades – either an equal range for each grade or a suitable progression towards wider spans at the top of the range. To avoid confusions in grading, the points ranges

should not normally overlap. The flexibility required between grades can be provided by having overlapping salary ranges. The aim should be to place grade boundaries at points in the hierarchy where there is a gap in the scores. If, for example, a set of jobs produced the following points scores: 342, 344, 346, 347, 352, 353, 355, 356, then the grade boundary should fall roughly in the middle of the two clusters at, say, 350. The grade demarcation lines should be tested to find out if too many jobs are bunched around grade boundaries. If this is the case, some improvement may be achieved by adjusting the demarcation lines. Should the problem still be serious, it may be necessary to alter the number of grades and/or the differentials between them. The grade demarcation lines are shown in Figure 8.5.

Step 6
Define the salary ranges for each grade, taking into account policies on differentials and overlap. An example of salary structure for jobs paid between about £8,000 and £35,000 is given in Table 8.1 and illustrated in Figure 8.6 overleaf.

In this structure:

1. Differentials between midpoints are 15 per cent from grades 1 to 3 and 20 per cent from grades 4 to 8.
2. Range widths are 30 per cent in grades 1 to 3 and 40 per cent in grades 4 to 8.

Table 8.1 *A graded salary structure*

Grade	Salary range (£)			Points range	
	Minimum	Midpoint	Maximum	Minimum	Maximum
1	8,050	9,257	10,465	150	249
2	9,257	10,646	12,034	250	349
3	10,646	12,243	13,839	350	449
4	12,243	14,692	17,140	450	549
5	14,692	17,630	20,568	550	649
6	17,630	21,156	24,682	650	749
7	21,156	25,387	29,618	750	849
8	25,387	30,464	35,542	850	949

Ranking/market rate method

This method consists of five steps, which are outlined below.

Step 1
Rank the bench-mark jobs and plot their actual salaries to show salary practice line (Figure 8.7 overleaf).

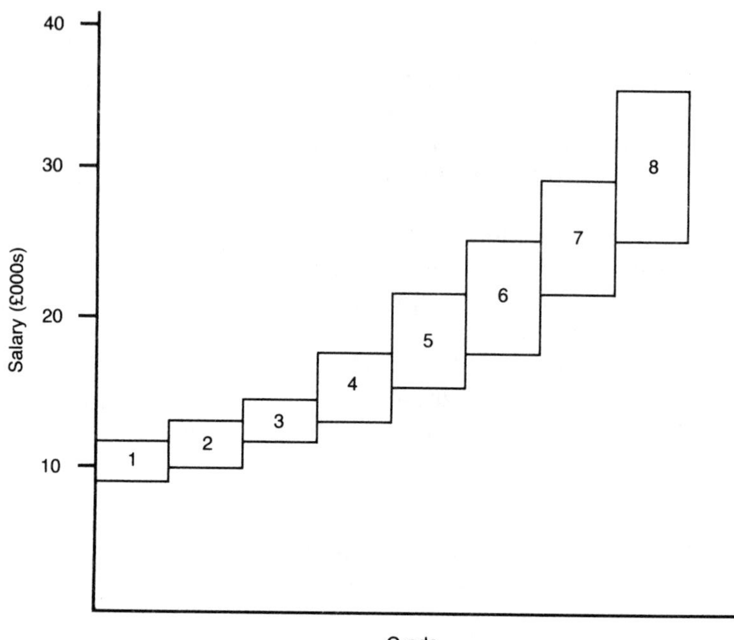

Figure 8.6 *A graded salary structure*

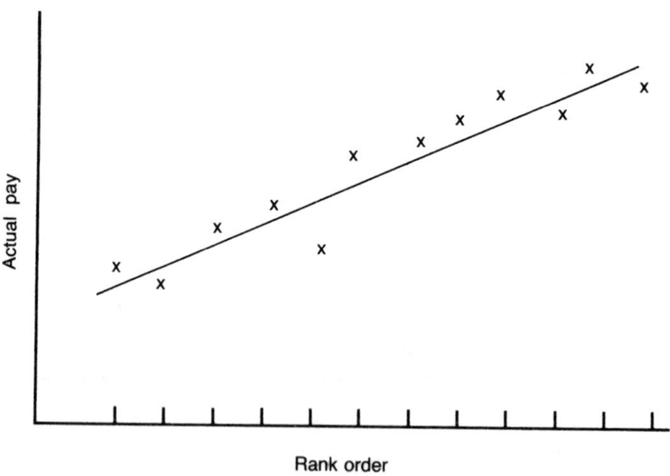

Figure 8.7 *Ranking salary practice line*

Step 2
Obtain market rate information on the bench-mark jobs, plot on chart and derive salary policy line (Figure 8.8)

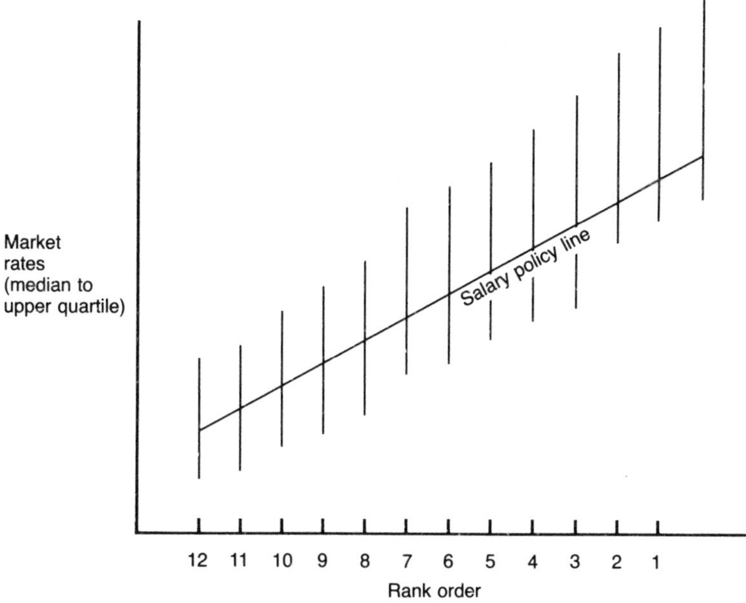

Figure 8.8 *Ranking salary policy line*

Step 3
Using the salary policy curve as the midpoint guideline, plot the upper and lower limits of the salary range for each bench-mark job in accordance with range width policy, eg ± 15 per cent of midpoint (Figure 8.9 overleaf).

Step 4
Develop grade structure using the parameters established in step three as the guidelines. The number of grades, differentials between them, and demarcation lines would have to be determined in accordance with the general principles which underlie grade structures as listed. Experimentation to get the right balance between possibly conflicting principles might be required at this stage. If a satisfactory grade structure cannot be evolved, consideration could be given to adopting an individual job range structure, especially at more senior levels.

Step 5
Slot the non-bench-mark jobs into the grades by reference to the gradings of the bench-mark posts.

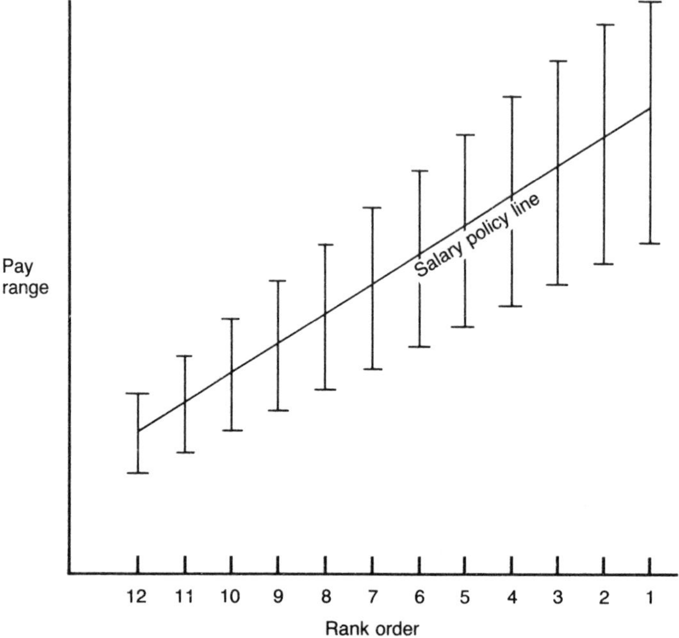

Figure 8.9 *Bench-mark job range widths*

Range structure method

The range structure method consists simply of the following four steps.

Step 1
Establish by means of market rate surveys and studies of existing structures and differentials the salary levels of the most senior and most junior jobs to be covered by the structure.

Step 2
Draw up a salary range structure between the parameters established in Step 1 according to design policies for differentials, the width of salary ranges and the size of overlaps between ranges.

Step 3
Conduct a job ranking evaluation exercise and obtain market rate data for the bench-mark jobs.

Step 4
Slot the bench-mark jobs into the predetermined range structure in accordance with their rank order and the relevant market rate

comparisons. Alternative solutions to these borderline problems will have to be tested, and it is helpful to seek the aid of a planning board as illustrated in Figure 8.10. This sets out the salary ranges down the left-hand side and has separate columns for each function. Cards for the bench-mark jobs are prepared which can be moved to alternative positions until what is felt to be the right set of vertical and horizontal relationships is achieved. The ranking and market rate data is available to provide guidance on relativities and positioning in the structure, but the final decisions depend on the judgement of the design team based on this information, their knowledge of the jobs and their understanding of what they feel to be fair.

Grade	Salary range		Functions				
	Min £	*Max* £	*Corporate*	*Production*	*Marketing*	*Finance*	*Other*
1	8,000	10,000					
2	9,200	11,500					
3	10,580	13,225					
4	12,167	15,208					
5	13,992	17,490					
6	16,090	20,917					
7	19,309	25,101					
8	23,170	30,121					
9	27,804	36,145					
10	33,365	43,374					

Figure 8.10 *Salary structure planning matrix – by function/family*

Choice of method

The points scheme method is the obvious means of using the results of a points based job evaluation scheme. Despite the concerns raised in Chapter 5 about the subjectivity of some points schemes, they undoubtedly provide a rationale for designing a graded structure and for maintaining it once it has been set up.

The ranking/market method is similar in many ways to the points scheme approach, but can be used without having to go through the elaborate ritual of points evaluation.

The range structure method is the most empirical and, it might be argued, the crudest method of the three. The judgements made in allocating jobs to ranges are subjective, but so are all judgements on the relative values of jobs, even when points schemes are used. This method at least enables the judgements to be marshalled within a logical framework and, if a systematic analysis of job content and market rate data is available, it can produce results which are just as effective and acceptable as the apparently more scientific, but certainly more time-consuming, alternative approaches.

Job range structure design

To design a job range structure, the first step is to fix the midpoint of the salary range, which represents what is considered to be the value of the job to a company when it is performed by a job holder who is fully competent. This rate may be fixed by reference to market rates or be determined by the points score in a job evaluation scheme, where the points have been translated into financial values. Thus, one point may be given a value in terms of annual salary of £25 so that the midpoint rate for a job valued at 1,000 points would be £25,000. This value would be revised whenever general uplifts of the salary structure took place in response to increases in the cost of living or in market rates.

A salary range for the job would then be calculated by adding and subtracting, say, 20 per cent to the midpoint salary. Thus the range for the job where the midpoint is £20,000 would be £16,000 to £24,000.

Pay curve design

The design of a pay or progression curve requires the following steps:

1. Decide on the jobs or job family to be covered by the curve.
2. Define each level or band of competency for the job or job family. This process is also described in Chapter 10, but essentially involves:
   (a) deciding in broad terms what different levels of competence exist for the job family – it is usual to start with three or four stages but these may be extended later and it is most unlikely that there would be less than three levels
   (b) giving provisional names to each level; for example, development engineer, senior development engineer, principal development engineer
   (c) analyzing and defining in some detail the competences at each level as described in Chapter 6
   (d) as necessary, reconsidering the number of levels in the light of the analysis – it is sometimes appropriate to divide a broad competency band into two or three sub-levels.

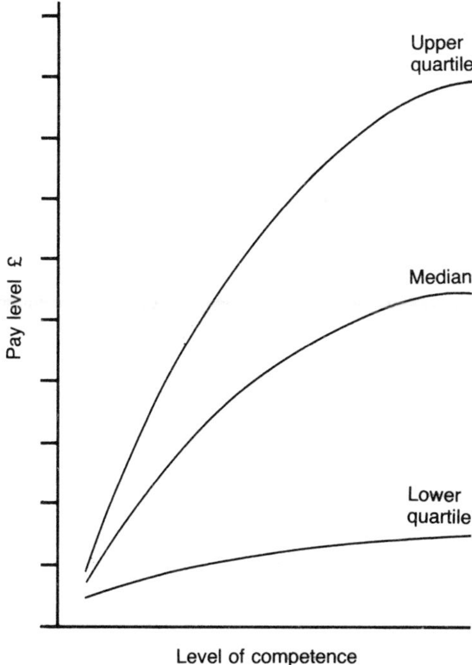

Figure 8.11 *Market rates for levels of competence*

3. Obtain market rate data for jobs in the different competency bands to show the market rates of progression (see figure 8.11).
4. Decide on the basis of the salary policy or posture of the company how salary levels should be related to the median and quartile rates as shown in figure 8.12 overleaf.
5. Define the progression rates and maximum salaries for each competency band and performance rating. For example, the range for an effective individual in a job family with three competence bands could be:

Table 8.2 *Competence band progression for an effective individual*

		£	% increase	years*
Competency band 1	Minimum Maximum	12,000 18,000	– 50	0 3
Competency band 2	Minimum Maximum	18,000 23,000	28	2
Competency band 3	Minimum Maximum	23,000 30,000	30	2
Overall			150	7

* *years to progress through the bands assuming a total increase of approximately 15% covering both the increase in market rates and a merit payment*

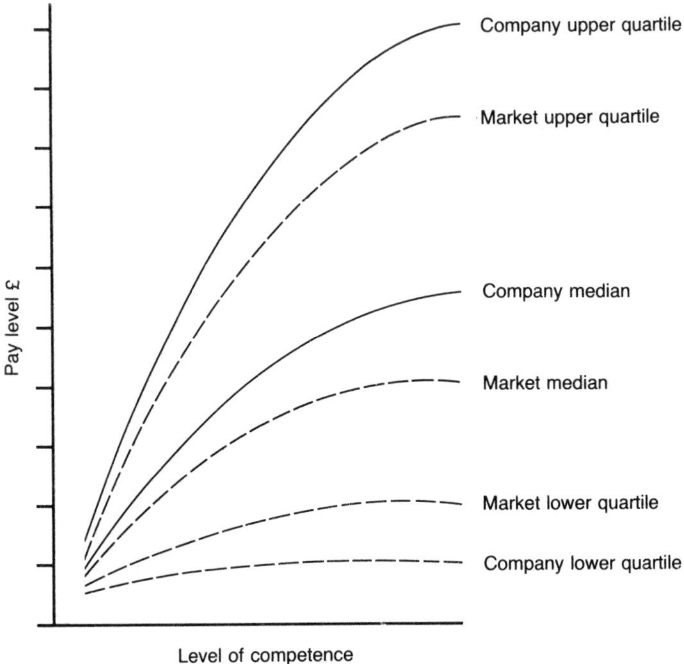

Figure 8.12 *Relationship between competency-based company salaries and market rates*

The total structure for the job family could then be developed as follows:

Table 8.3 *Pay curve matrix*

Competency level		Performance Level B	D	E	VE	EX
Band 1	Min	12,000	12,000	12,000	12,000	12,000
	Max	16,000	17,000	18,000	19,000	20,000
Band 2	Min	–	17,000	18,000	19,000	20,000
	Max	–	21,500	23,000	24,500	27,000
Band 3	Min	–	–	23,000	25,000	27,000
	Max	–	–	30,000	32,500	35,000

Key: B = basic D = developing E = effective VE = very effective EX = excellent

Job family structure design

Designing a job family structure is a matter of identifying the different job families which constitute either a market group or represent a discrete area of competence. The aim is to establish distinct families, but they may be linked together, as described in Chapter 7.

The number of families will, of course, depend on the complexity, size and structure of the organization. Judgement is required in deciding on the number to be created – too many could lead to administrative complications and difficulties in distinguishing between categories; too few might defeat the purpose of the system by not differentiating sufficiently between different levels and skills.

Each job family could have its own grade structure which would be designed as described above. Alternatively, separate families could each have their own pay curve, and this approach is being increasingly adopted by organizations who like the progressive, individually orientated and flexible characteristics of the pay curve system, and whose market monitoring is sufficiently well developed and sensitive to support the process.

Spot rate structure design

The spot rates for each job are usually initially determined by reference to bench-mark market rates. The salary posture of the company will determine how the spot rates should compare with market rates, either matching them or paying a market premium. The rates for non bench-mark jobs are then determined by comparisons, preferably using a job evaluation method, although smaller or highly flexible companies may dispense with this formality. More rarely, spot rates are fixed according to points score values as for job grade structures.

Pay spine design

A pay spine, as described in Chapter 7, is in effect a series of incremental scales stood on end. Pay spines are more often re-designed rather than designed from scratch and they are usually used where pay is negotiated with trade unions which often means that the scope for major innovation is restricted.

The points to be considered when re-designing or negotiating pay spines are:

- the range of pay in the market place and jobs to be covered
- the size of the increments needed at different points in the scale
- the job grades as defined by scale points which will be superimposed on the pay spine
- the market rates for individual jobs covered by the spine
- the extent to which job grade scales currently, and should, overlap
- whether or not 'range points' at the top of each job range should be included to enable highly rated individuals to receive additional performance pay.

Implementation

The outcome of a salary system design study should be presented in the form of:

1. An analysis of the job evaluation results (where relevant).
2. An analysis of the market survey results.
3. Proposals on the grade and pay structure; as there is always some choice of method, it may well be desirable to present alternative structures with an assessment of their pros and cons.
4. A programme for repositioning staff in the structure.
5. Proposals on how anomalies should be treated.
6. Costings of the implications of the new or revised structure.
7. Proposals on how staff should be informed.

Treating anomalies

The repositioning of staff in the new structure will reveal anomalies in the shape of staff who are either overgraded or undergraded. It has to be accepted that a re-design programme is going to be costly because, while undergraded staff must be upgraded with an appropriate salary increase, overgraded staff will have to remain in their same grade, as no one should suffer a reduction in salary.

When dealing with undergraded staff, the choice is between bringing them up to the minimum of their new grade in one jump or phasing the increases over a period of time. Before deciding on a policy it is necessary to measure the cost implications of putting everyone on the minimum. If the costs of full regrading are too high, consideration should be given to a policy of limiting regrading increases to a maximum of, say, 10 per cent of present salary at one time. Increases above that level would be phased at a minimum of 10 per cent a year. Where a pay structure is negotiated, the union may ask for staff who are regraded to be placed at the same point of the new range as they were in the old one. This request would be based on the argument that, if staff are placed on the minimum of the new grade, they would lose the benefit of the merit or service increments they received in their previous grade. This argument has a sort of logic, especially when fixed incremental scales are in operation but, if accepted, the costs would be considerable.

Overgraded staff could have their salaries frozen or 'red circled' at their present levels, apart from any future across-the-board pay increases. But this might be regarded as inequitable if in their previous grade they could reasonably have expected merit or service increments above their existing salary to the top of the range or a fixed higher point within the range. In these cases the just approach may be to give a 'personal-to-job-holder' grade which allows the individual to progress to the maximum expected in the old grade.

Informing staff about new pay systems – a critical success factor

It is important to plan communications to staff about the new structure carefully. If the structure is fully disclosed, its rationale should be explained. Individual members of the staff should be told explicitly how the new arrangements affect them, whether or not pay policies and structures are communicated generally.

When communicating the results to staff, trade unions and management, it should be remembered that in each area there will be different expectations about the new structure, some of which may be disappointed unless special care is taken over the way in which information is presented. Some, perhaps many, staff will be unhappy because they disagree with their new gradings. The trade union or staff association may feel annoyed because it has not attained what it wanted. Management may feel disappointed because after all their hard work they think that the changes have been inappropriate and the reaction of the staff has been indifferent.

All these reactions are common after a major salary design exercise. To the extent that they are predictable, they can be minimized, if not avoided completely. But their possibility makes it essential to think hard before implementing a new or revised salary structure and to present the details in terms of:

- why the exercise has been undertaken
- how it should better suit what the organization is trying to achieve
- what the overall benefits are
- how individuals/groups/job families will be affected
- who to talk to in order to find out more or clarify misunderstandings.

Major changes typically need to be supported by an information pack which explains the changes in clear and simple language – often backed up with graphics.

Part 4

Paying for Performance

Chapter 9

Performance Management

As a key business concept, performance management took shape over the 1980s, growing out of the realization that a more integrated process than just performance-related pay is needed to manage and reward performance.

Definition

Performance management is a means of getting better results from the organization, teams and individuals by understanding and managing performance within an agreed framework of planned goals, objectives and standards.

Performance management therefore consists of a systematic approach to the management of people, using performance, goals, measurement, feedback and recognition as a means of motivating them to realize their maximum potential. It embraces all formal or informal methods adopted by an organization and its managers to increase commitment and individual and corporate effectiveness. It is a broader concept than performance appraisal or performance-related pay (PRP). These can indeed be important elements in a performance management system (PMS). But they will be part of an integrated approach, which consists of an interlocking series of processes, attitudes and behaviours which together produce a coherent strategy for adding value and improving results.

Perhaps the most important thing to remember about performance management is that it is a continuous process shared between managers and the people for whom they are responsible. It is about improving both results and the quality of working relationships. Good performance management means that people are clear about what their priorities are, what they should be doing currently, what they should be aiming for and how well this contributes to both team and company performance. It grows from open, positive and constructive discussion between managers, individuals and teams to produce agreement on how to focus on doing the job better.

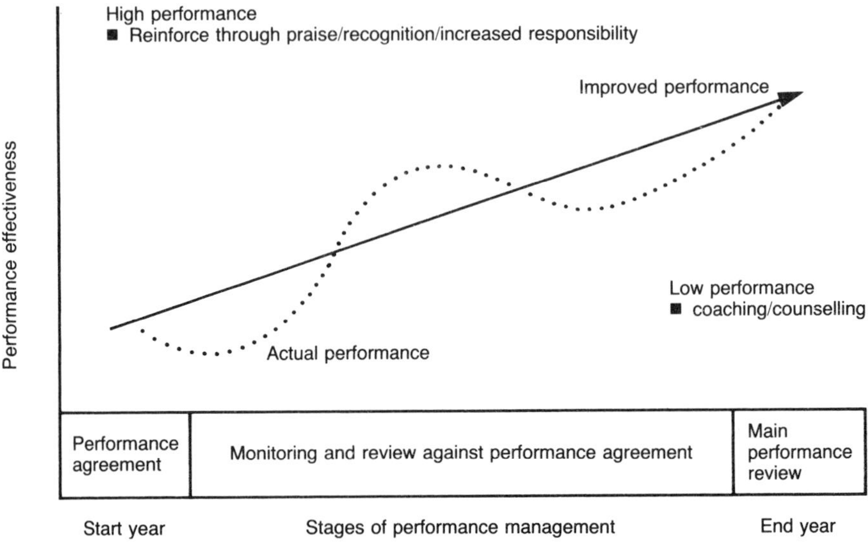

Figure 9.1 *How performance management works*

How performance management works

How performance management works is illustrated in Figure 9.1. The process of performance management starts with a performance agreement between individual and manager which sets out objectives and development needs. During the ensuing year, performance is continually monitored and assessed. High performance is reinforced with praise, recognition and the opportunity to take on more responsible work. Low performance is dealt with by coaching and counselling, which takes place at the time – it is not deferred until the formal review at the end of the year when it will have lost its immediacy and where the relative formality of the proceedings will militate against a constructive discussion. The main performance review is, to a degree, a stocktaking exercise but its emphasis is on looking forward to next year and formulating a performance agreement rather than raking over past events.

It will be noted that PRP is not mentioned as part of this process. This is because performance management is essentially a system for setting and reviewing objectives and development needs. PRP, as described in Chapter 10, is an addition which, in the right circumstances and for the right people, can reinforce the messages provided by the sequence of activities illustrated in Figure 9.1. Some organizations, however, have introduced performance management successfully without any element of PRP, and others have found that PRP has not delivered the results they expected when it has been

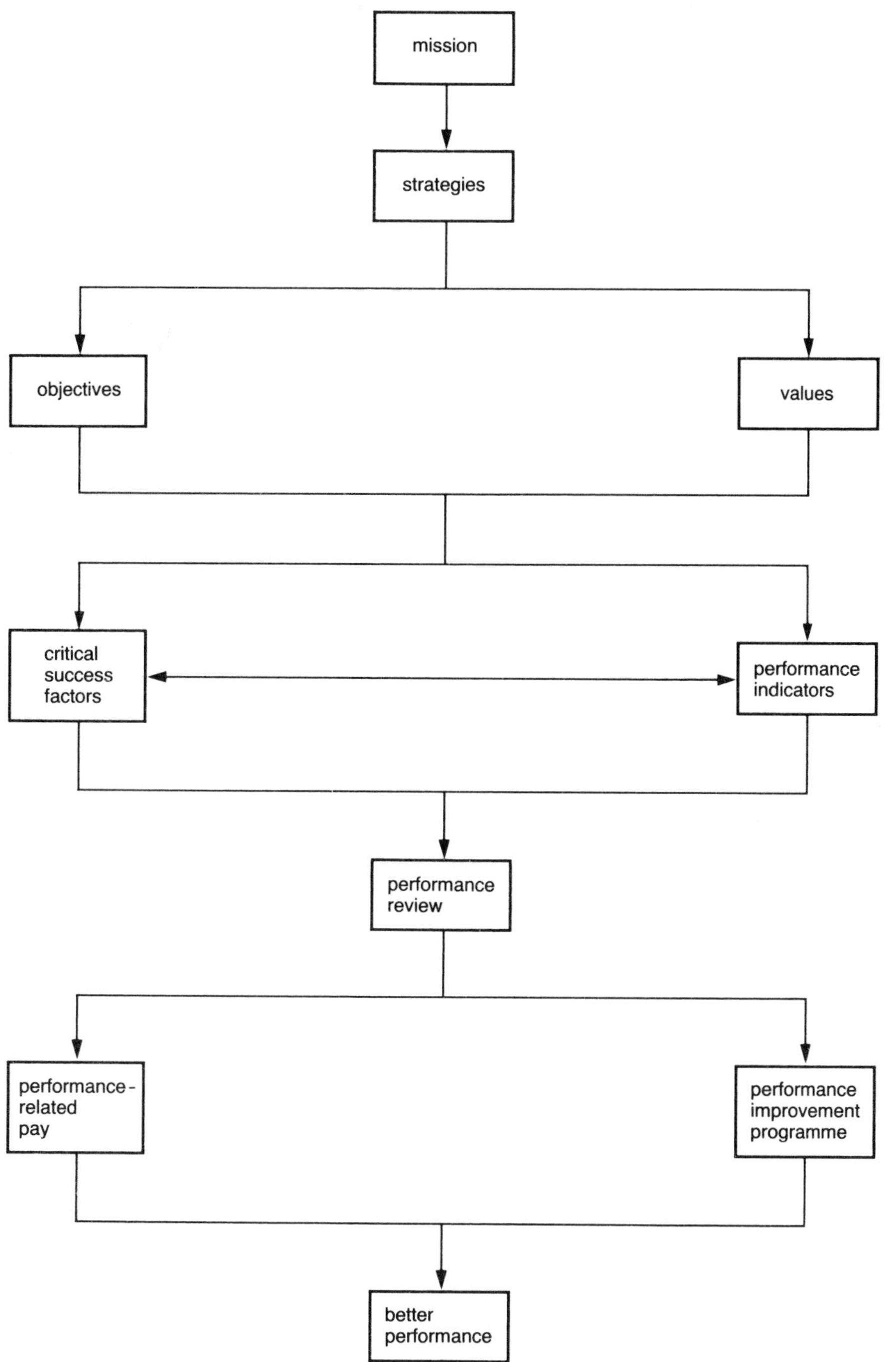

Figure 9.2 *A performance management system*

grafted without sufficient thought on to a performance appraisal scheme ill fitted for the purpose.

Performance management systems

Performance management is now sufficiently well established to have its own vocabulary and set of processes. It is founded on activities that are at the heart of the business; those concerned with mission, strategies, objectives, core values and critical success factors. These lead to the definition of performance indicators and the interrelated systems for performance review and, in some organizations, performance-related pay. At the core of the performance management system, however, is the joint agreement or contract on which commitment to performance improvement is based.

Main features

The main features of PMS are illustrated in Figure 9.2. They consist of:

- *the mission statement*, which defines in broad terms the business the organization is in (its purpose) and the direction in which it is going. This provides the inspiration for the formulation of strategies, objectives, values and performance requirements
- *strategies* – statements of intent which provide explicit guidance on the future behaviour and performance required to achieve the mission of the enterprise
- *objectives*, which state in precise terms the performance goals of the organization
- *values* – what is regarded as important by the organization with regard to how it conducts its affairs. Values will be concerned, amongst other things, with performance, excellence, teamwork, innovation and the development of people
- *critical success factors*, which spell out the factors contributing to successful performance and the standards to be met
- *performance indicators*, which are worked out in association with the critical success factors and enable progress towards achieving objectives and implementing values to be monitored and the final results to be evaluated
- *performance review*, which by reference to objectives, values, and performance indicators measures achievements and identifies development needs
- *performance-related pay*, which links rewards explicitly to performance and can take the form of merit pay, individual bonuses, group bonuses and other variable payments related to corporate or group performance (eg profit sharing schemes)

- *performance agreements or contracts* – action plans, plans for the future which look forward to planned achievements and form the basis of performance improvement programmes.
- *performance improvement programmes*, which are concerned with:
  - improving motivation and commitment by means other than financial rewards
  - training
  - career development
  - coaching
  - counselling
  - communications on the benefits of the approach.

Performance management systems – main characteristics

The main characteristics of an effective performance management system are that it:

- is congruent with the existing culture of the organization but will help to change or re-shape that culture if necessary
- plays an integral part in implementing the overall strategies of the organization, achieving its mission and objectives and upholding its value system, especially those values concerned with the achievement of high standards of performance
- is a continuous process, not an annual event – it should be seen as an essential part of the everyday lives of managers which they practise because they are good managers and not just because they are told to by the personnel department
- constitutes a fundamental approach (it is not an optional technique) which concentrates the minds of everyone on principal accountabilities (key result areas), objectives, critical success factors and development needs
- relates, where possible, to quantifiable outputs which contribute directly to achieving corporate or departmental objectives, but does not neglect more qualitative assessments of the contribution individuals make to upholding core values
- is realistic about the setting of objectives or the agreement of performance standards appropriate to different levels within the organization, recognizing that what works well at senior management level needs modification to fit the work patterns of junior staff
- relies upon consensus rather than coercion – managers and their staff discuss and agree objectives, standards, assessments of performance and action plans, ie the system is open and recognizes the mutual dependence of managers and their subordinates in achieving results

- looks forward and not back, ie it is dedicated to deciding what can be done to improve performance in the future rather than indulging in post-mortems about the past
- provides opportunities, not constraints, emphasizing self-control rather than control from above, ie it adopts a 'can do, will do' stance which helps people to achieve more through self-determination rather than tying them down
- concentrates on strengths to be developed more than weaknesses to be overcome, ie adopts a positive rather than a negative approach
- leads to action plans designed to obtain even better performance and to develop competences and careers
- recognizes that objective setting, appraisal and counselling are skilled processes and therefore provides thorough training and continuing training in the approaches and techniques involved
- does not impose a bureaucratic burden on managers
- is accepted as a key part of a manager's role – in fact managers themselves will typically be assessed on their effectiveness in conducting performance reviews.

Design considerations

To design a performance management system, it is first necessary to:

- define its purpose
- decide the factors that are going to be covered by the system in terms of what is to be assessed, eg the achievement of objectives, upholding core values, meeting development needs or potential
- agree policies on 'transparency' (the degree to which employees are informed of the results of their appraisals) and on the link between performance reviews and rewards.

Purpose

The extent to which the system has to cater for some or all of the following requirements has to be made clear from the outset:

- review of performance for training and development purposes – this is perhaps the most important reason for conducting reviews
- potential assessment for career development and management succession planning purposes – this tends to be given less prominence in current schemes and is often omitted completely because of the difficulties managers have in making realistic forecasts
- rating to determine eligibility for performance-related pay.

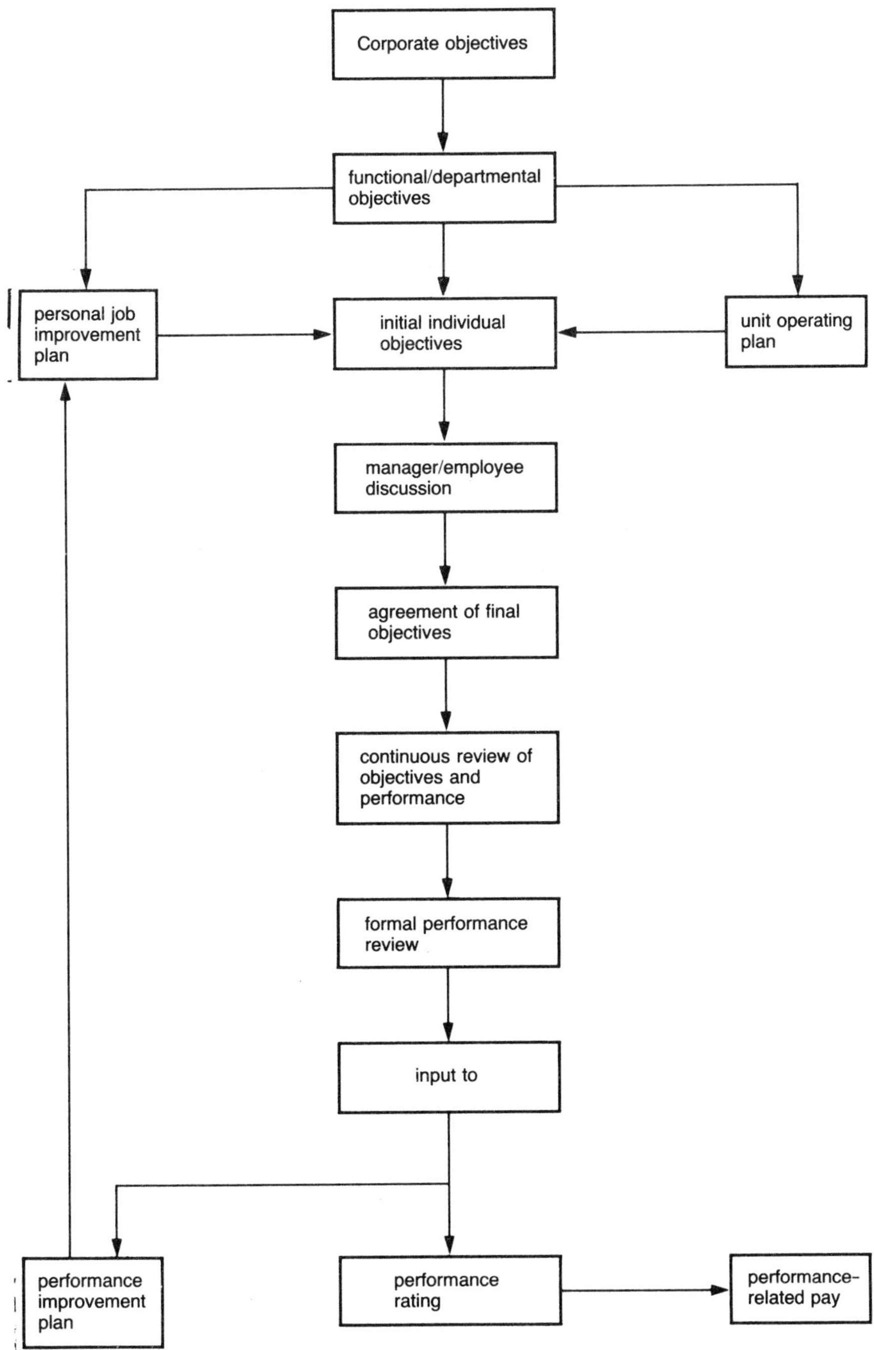

Figure 9.3 *The objective setting and review process*

Factors to be covered by the scheme

The main factors that can be assessed in a performance management system are:

- *the achievement of objectives:* performance management systems assess performance by reference to agreed objectives and include a performance agreement which spells out future objectives. Objectives may be expressed in terms of targets, standards of performance or tasks to be accomplished within a period of time and to an agreed specification. A distinction is made between continuing objectives which, as it were, are built into the job description, and short-term (less than one year) objectives. Continuing objectives, however, can change as the job holder's responsibilities evolve. The process of setting objectives is illustrated in Figure 9.3
- *observing core values:* performance management systems are increasingly recognizing that performance is not just about achieving objectives. It is also about behaving in a way which makes the core values of the organization a reality, not just a string of pious platitudes. One example we encountered in a major multinational assessed managers on the extent to which they observed core values under the headings of:

  - contribution in the job beyond normal expectations
  - contribution to the work of others (this organization had problems with team-work!)
  - contribution to change (the organization was trying to create a more flexible culture)
- *personal qualities:* some performance appraisal schemes still ask managers to assess the personal qualities of staff under such headings as drive, judgement, communication skills, interpersonal skills and creativity. Performance management systems, however, seldom include such headings. The argument against assessing personal qualities is that managers are thereby asked to measure abstract personality traits, which they are seldom qualified to do. Such approaches mean that individuals are in danger of becoming passive objects, receiving judgements from on high.

  A joint review of how well individuals have achieved objectives will be rooted in the reality of their performance. It is concrete, not abstract, and it enables managers and individuals to take a positive look together at how performance can become even better in the future and how any problems in achieving objectives can be resolved. Individuals become active agents in improving their results and managers adopt their proper enabling role

- *potential:* performance management systems generally concentrate on the identification of development needs rather than attempting to rate potential. Unless managers have a very clear understanding of the competences required at higher levels of responsibility, such ratings are likely to be guesswork, and such understanding is rare. In any case, although it can be said that people generally have to perform well in the present to succeed in the future, good performance at one level does not guarantee success at the next or succeeding levels, hence the 'Peter principle' (promotion to the level of incompetence).

  The measurement of potential is increasingly taking place at performance assessment centres where the assessment criteria are related to well-researched and clearly defined core competences which are indicators of successful performance at higher levels in the organization.

Policy on openness

There is no point in a performance management system in which the review process is not shared between the reviewer and the person being reviewed. The review's most important purpose is to be developmental – to assist in the improvement of performance. Unless employees are fully involved through self-assessment in the pre-review stage, and in the joint analysis of achievements and development needs during the actual review, they will not 'own' any of the performance improvement steps which should form part of the performance agreement or contract.

Policy on performance-related pay

The other major policy issue concerns the link between the performance review and performance-related pay. Some people object to any link because they say that a preoccupation with the existence and size of an award during the review will seriously contaminate the developmental purposes of the appraisal. These opponents of such a link are usually doubtful about the value of relating a reward to what they believe to be a largely subjective performance rating. Their views will also be coloured by the fact that they have fundamental doubts about the motivational value of extrinsic rewards.

Those who support performance-related pay say that, logically enough, you must have a performance rating to determine the reward and, if that is not going to be produced at the performance review, where is it going to come from? Given a belief in PRP, this argument is unanswerable.

One way to reconcile these opposed views is to conduct the

assessment at a different time from the pay review. This enables those involved to concentrate on its developmental aspects. When the pay review is carried out, a 'read across' can take place between the assessment to provide the basis for the performance-related pay decision. It may be necessary to update the ratings in these circumstances, depending on the length of time between the reviews and the existence of any new factors. This can have motivational value in managing performance at the margins. Given a three or four month gap between a poor performance assessment and a pay review, an immediate response and improvement can be recognized and rewarded accordingly.

Designing the performance management system

The performance management system operates as a continuous cycle, as illustrated in Figure 9.4, and this should be reflected in the design of each of its main components as described below.

- *the performance agreement:* this sets out the key objectives for next year and the main development needs (areas where existing skills can be enhanced or performance improved). This

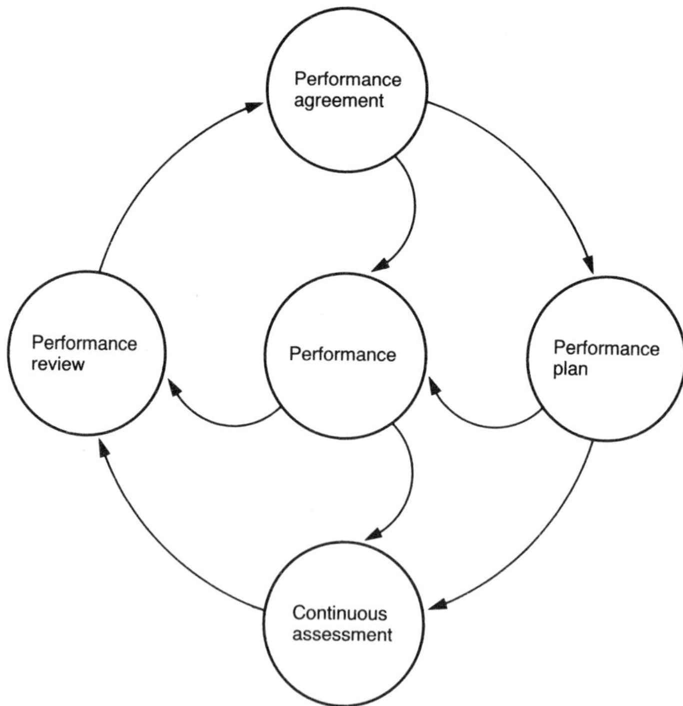

Figure 9.4 *The performance management cycle*

agreement is concluded between the manager and the individual during the performance review. It leads to the preparation of the performance plan and is a constant point of reference when implementing the plan and achieving performance targets and standards. The emphasis in the performance agreement is on self-direction and self-control

- *the performance plan:* this describes how the objectives and development needs established in the performance agreement are going to be achieved or satisfied by individuals with whatever guidance they need. It directly impacts on performance and, together with the performance agreement, provides the basis for the continuous monitoring and assessment of performance
- *continuous assessment:* both the manager and the individual continually assess performance in relation to the performance agreement and plan. As necessary, objectives are added or raised. New development needs may emerge and are also added to the plan. At the end of the assessment period immediately prior to the performance review, individuals assess their own performance using a personal preparation form designed for that purpose. Managers also prepare for the review by referring to the agreement and plan, and the outcome of the continuous performance management process throughout the year. Managers record their initial impressions on the performance review form for discussion with individuals
- *the performance review:* in which managers and individuals refer to their continuous assessment and the personal preparation form. They jointly review achievements and progress, comments and ratings are made as required and a new performance agreement is concluded. Most importantly, these meetings provide the opportunity for a full and frank discussion between managers and the individuals whose performance they are reviewing.

There should be no surprises if performance issues have been dealt with as they should have been – during the continuous assessment process. In one sense the review is a stock-taking exercise, but this is no more than an analysis of where those involved are now, and where they have come from. This static and historical process is not what performance management is about. The true role of performance management is to look forward to what needs to be done by people to achieve the overall purpose of the job, to meet new challenges, to make even better use of their knowledge, skills and abilities and to help them to develop their competences and improve their performance. This process also helps managers to improve their ability to lead, guide and develop their staff, as individuals or as a team.

Performance management system forms

Performance management forms vary widely but, typically, the systems being developed today include four forms:

1. Personal preparations form.
2. Performance review form.
3. Performance agreement.
4. Performance and development plan.

An example of each type of form is given in Appendix N. These are not intended as models – every organization has to develop systems and procedures to suit itself. But the examples do illustrate how the various activities during the performance management cycle as described above can be recorded. Too much importance, however, should not be attached to these forms. Performance management is a continuous process which is about managers and individuals getting together and discussing and agreeing forward plans and actions, having assessed progress in achieving current objectives. It is not a paperwork exercise.

The performance review records illustrated in Appendix M concentrate on the agreement and review of objectives and development needs. They do not include any assessments of personal qualities or potential. This example includes rating scales for the achievement of objectives and overall performance. But some organizations, especially those who do not believe in performance-related pay, omit such scales on the grounds that they prejudice the constructive discussions, which are the prime purpose of the scheme, by forcing managers to make arbitrary and sometimes indefensible judgements.

Performance rating

A performance rating is an overall assessment of the performance of individuals which managers make by reference to the achievement of objectives, which may themselves have been rated, as shown in the example of a performance review form in Appendix M.

As mentioned above, and despite their widespread use, there can be strong arguments against the use of such scales unless it has been decided that they should form the basis for determining performance-related pay awards. If they are used, the rating classifications need to be defined with care and managers have to be given explicit guidance on the approach they should use in making this assessment. The most typical arrangement is for there to be five levels, for example:

A Outstanding performance in all respects.

B Superior performance, significantly above normal job requirements.
C Good all round performance which meets the normal requirements of the job.
D Performance not fully up to requirements. Clear weaknesses requiring improvement have been identified.
E Unacceptable; constant guidance is required and performance of many aspects of the job is well below a reasonable standard.

There is, however, also a strong case for having six levels on the grounds that this gives a wider range and eliminates the inevitable tendency in five-level schemes to pick the central rating. In the following example, the six levels are defined as:

XC Exceptional performance: meeting all objectives and requirements and contributing outstanding achievements which significantly extend the impact and influence of the total job.
EX Excellent performance: meeting all objectives and requirements and contributing some notable achievements beyond normal expectations for the job.
W A well-balanced performance: meeting objectives and requirements of the job, consistently performing in a thoroughly proficient manner.
R Reasonable performance: a contribution which is stronger in some aspects of the job than others and where most objectives are met, but with varying degrees of effectiveness.
BE Barely effective performance: meeting few objectives or requirements of the job – significant performance improvements are needed.
U Unacceptable performance: failing to meet most objectives or requirements of the job and demonstrating a lack of commitment to performance improvement, or a lack of ability which has been discussed prior to the performance review.

This approach means that the 'core' of competent performers who are given a third level 'W' rating are aware that there are three levels below them. This will have a greater motivational value than being placed in the third of five grades with only two lower categories. In this system, A to F or 1 to 6 ratings have deliberately been avoided – to dispel associations with old systems (which often go back as far as school reports!).

Another approach which is increasingly being adopted is to design a rating scale which provides positive reinforcement at every level. This means that employees cannot be damned out of hand. If their performance is totally unacceptable, this fact should have been identified during the continuous process of assessing results and action taken at the time; this is not something that can wait several months until the next review. This scale has five levels.

Excellent	Exceeds all objectives and requirements. Achievements are notable and outstanding and are far beyond the normal expectations of the job.
Very effective	Meets all the objectives of the job. Exceeds required standards and consistently performs in a thoroughly proficient manner beyond normal expectations.
Effective	Achieves required objectives and standards of performance and meets the normal expectations of the job.
Developing	A contribution which is stronger in some aspects of the job than others, where most objectives are met but where performance improvements should still take place.
Basic	A contribution which on the whole meets the basic standards required although a number of objectives are not met and there is clearly room for improvement in several definable areas.

The problem with rating scales is that it is very difficult, if not impossible, to ensure that a consistent approach is adopted by raters. It is almost inevitable that some people will be more generous than others (the 'swan effect'), while others will be harder on their staff (the 'goose effect'). Ratings can, of course, be monitored and challenged if their distribution is significantly out of line, and computer-based systems have been introduced for this purpose in some organizations. But many managers want to do the best for their staff, either because they genuinely believe that they are better or because they are trying to curry favour. It can be very difficult in these circumstances to challenge them. The only solution may be to tackle the problem on a group basis by running workshops every year to reinforce the values of the scheme and the basis upon which ratings should be given. Ultimately, however, such judgements will always be subjective, and this is an argument which can be used against using such scales and relating pay to performance assessed in this way.

Ranking systems

An alternative approach, which has been adopted by Marks and Spencer, The Alliance and Leicester Building Society and others, is to rank staff in order of merit and then distribute gradings through the rank order, for example, by giving the top 10 per cent an A rating, the next 15 per cent a B rating, the next 60 per cent a C rating and the remaining 15 per cent a D rating. This is, in effect, a forced distribution, which eliminates a skewed allocation of ratings but still depends on the accuracy of the rankings. The rank order may be produced by scoring various merit factors for each member of a group of staff and adding them to produce a total score. Even this approach cannot eliminate inequitable ratings if the basic assessment is unfair.

Introducing the performance management system

To make any impact at all, top management must put its whole weight behind the performance management system. The chief executive must demonstrate his or her total commitment to it and must make plain that all managers must be equally committed.

'Packaging' is important! Well-designed forms, which are simple and straightforward to fill up, will be completed better. At all costs, avoid designing forms which smack too much of 'officialdom' and bureaucracy. People will respond best to well-printed forms on good-quality paper.

It is well worth issuing the description of the scheme and the notes for guidance in an elegantly designed and well-produced folder which in itself demonstrates the importance attached to performance management. This documentation needs to reflect the organization's culture and be of a quality which suggests that employees are valued as much as customers and shareholders, to whom prestige publications are sent as a matter of course.

The performance management system should be introduced with a reminder of the purposes of the scheme and its benefits. The roles of reviewers and those being reviewed should be spelled out in a way which emphasises their joint responsibility for the success of the system and explains how they should conduct the preparatory work, the meetings and the continuous process of appraisal.

The information about the scheme should include:

- a statement of its objectives
- guidance to managers on objective setting, how to conduct reviews and how to counsel and coach the individual members of their team
- guidance to individuals on the part they play in completing the pre-review form, agreeing objectives and development needs and preparing and implementing the performance and development plan
- brief descriptions of how the documents are to be filled in with examples of what a well-completed form should look like

- a statement emphasizing that the system should be regarded as a fundamental aspect of management throughout the organization.

Launching the system

The system should be launched by the chief executive, who should personally brief the management team. In smaller organizations this briefing should be extended to all employees. In larger concerns, the brief should be cascaded down the organization using a team briefing approach. A video can be used to good effect. Experience suggests that training in the concepts and practice of performance management appraisal should precede detailed briefing on the procedure to be used. This briefing and training process will be greatly enhanced if it is based on good material. This is why it is so important to make the procedures and documentation user-friendly and to present the material well.

Training

The effectiveness of performance management systems depends ultimately on the quality of the reviews carried out by managers and the attitudes of the staff to the system. An essential part of the implementation of a system is therefore a training programme for all managers. Ideally, this should take the form of a workshop, and both managers and their staff should be involved. The workshop should last at least one day (preferably two) and should include sessions concerned with:

- describing the system and the role of managers and their staff
- analyzing the skills required to set and review objectives, review and rate performance, identify development needs, prepare performance agreements and plans and provide guidance to individuals by means of counselling and coaching
- practising the skills – this should comprise 75 per cent of the programme.

Use should be made of case-study material drawn from the organization referring to typical performance problems, role plays and video. The aim would be to enable both managers and their staff to try out each other's roles in a safe environment where important lessons can be learned.

Chapter 10

Performance-Related Pay

Definition

Performance-related pay (PRP) explicitly links financial rewards to individual, group or corporate performance, or to any combination of these three.

This approach to salary progression is now probably the dominant force in the UK, having replaced many of the fixed incremental systems that were a legacy of the incomes policies of the 1970s.

Objectives

The overall objective of PRP is to improve the performance of the organization and the individuals and groups who are members of it. To achieve this objective PRP aims to:

- motivate all employees, not just the high flyers who probably do not need motivating by this means anyway, although it is essential to avoid demotivating high flyers by under-rewarding their achievements
- increase the commitment of employees to the organization by encouraging them to identify with its mission, values, strategies and objectives
- reinforce existing cultures and values where these foster high levels of performance, innovation and team-work
- help to change cultures where they need to become more performance- and results-orientated, or where the adoption of other new and key values should be rewarded
- discriminate consistently and equitably on the distribution of rewards to employees according to their contribution – rewarding the better people more highly and paying for achievement, not just effort
- deliver a positive message about the performance expectations of the organization – one of the main merits of PRP is that it does focus attention on key performance issues
- direct attention and endeavour where the organization wants them by specifying performance goals and standards

- emphasize individual performance or team-work as appropriate – personal schemes focus on individual contribution and group schemes foster co-operation – although, as many UK employees have learned, it is wise to ensure that individual schemes also reward good team performance as a 'core' value
- improve the recruitment and retention of high-quality staff – many employees expect PRP to be part of a well-managed working environment
- flex pay costs in line with company performance.

Factors to be taken into account in achieving these aims

The gap between the simple idea of paying for performance and the successful implementation of performance-related pay systems is wide. PRP is not a panacea which will cure all your problems by instantly motivating staff to achieve significantly higher levels of performance. Introducing performance-related pay is an act of faith based on the assumption that people will perform more effectively if offered financial incentives to do so. Most people act implicitly on that assumption, but no convincing research evidence has yet been produced to prove that it is true – principally because, as we know, a multiplicity of factors is involved in most performance improvements and most of these factors are interdependent. What recent research has taught us is that badly designed and poorly implemented PRP schemes will demotivate staff probably more successfully than well-designed and implemented schemes will motivate them. And inadequate schemes will be produced if:

- they do not match the culture and value systems of the organization
- managers and those who implement systems are not committed to making them work and are not properly prepared and trained to do so
- performance rewards are not closely linked to the business, do not support overall strategy and are not flexible enough to respond to changes in strategic direction
- the key performance indicators and critical success factors are not clearly identified
- the system is unfair in that rewards are arbitrary and not linked clearly to competences and achievements through an effective appraisal system which is preferably in place *before* PRP is introduced
- performance targets are too mechanistic – qualitative targets and standards can be just as important to success as quantitative ones

- provision is not made for monitoring, evaluating and reviewing the system to ensure that it can develop and respond to changing needs. Systems 'set in stone' are dishonest and fail to reflect the need for organizations to learn from and build on experience gained from year to year.

These are difficult criteria to satisfy and, even if they are met, account has to be taken of the arguments that can be advanced against PRP when designing a scheme. These may be voiced by managers fearful of the new responsibilities PRP brings, just as often as by trade unions and individual employees who doubt management ability to conduct the performance review process openly and fairly.

Arguments against PRP

The criticisms most frequently levelled at PRP are that:

- it is difficult to measure individual performance objectively, and subjectivity may lead to unfair assessments
- it can encourage people to focus narrowly on the tasks which will earn them 'brownie points' fast, to do them as quickly as possible, to be less concerned about quality and longer term issues and to take fewer risks
- extrinsic rewards can erode intrinsic interest – people who work just for money may find their tasks less pleasurable and may therefore not do them so well
- financial rewards may work for some people because their expectations that they will receive them are high. But these people will tend to be well-motivated anyway, and less confident employees may not respond to incentives which they do not expect to receive
- if there is undue influence and emphasis on individual performance, essential team-work and co-operation may suffer
- it can lead to pay rising faster than performance if the control systems are not strong enough – experience shows that there is a strong tendency for performance-related pay to drift upwards.

Counter-arguments

The counter-arguments to these criticisms are that:

- an analytical and systematic approach to developing PRP as described below should minimize the risk of producing an inadequate scheme
- while it has not been proved that PRP guarantees better motivation, neither has it been disproved. The concept that people react positively to financial incentives has considerable

face validity – as long as you do not simplistically imply that money is *all* they work for
- controls can successfully be built into a scheme which will minimize the danger of pay drift – cost iterations on computerized payroll systems greatly assist achievement of this
- PRP may be necessary simply because of market pressures and employee expectations that it will be part of competitive practice
- while it may be argued that PRP can have a limited effect as a motivator, in some circumstances it can still play an important role in focusing effort, defining the performance expectations of the company and increasing commitment – many organizations have found that the joint discussions managers and employees have in this area are proving to have significant value on their own
- it is not suggested that PRP is the only, even the best, long-term motivator – attention should also be given to the development of non-financial approaches to motivation and recognition as described in Chapter 2. The total approach to performance management, as advocated in Chapter 9, involves using the right mix of non-financial and financial motivators.

Introducing PRP – key considerations

As we have already made clear, PRP in any form – be it performance-related salary increases, bonuses or incentives, is not an easy option. Before embarking on a policy development programme it is essential to take the following factors into account:

- *matching the culture:* PRP schemes cannot be taken off the shelf. There is no magic scale of performance measures and simple set of rules waiting for adoption on a universal basis. Successful PRP schemes need to match the culture and core values of the organization. It is only by understanding and working with the culture that it is possible to develop systems which underpin a bias to action
- *linking PRP to the performance management process:* if PRP is to be an effective strategic tool it must be linked to business strategy. The focus needs to be on issues which emerge from the business planning process, such as profitability, research initiatives, product development, market penetration and shareholder value
- *rules for successful PRP:* Mike Langley, past Vice President of the Institute of Personnel Management's National Committee for Pay and Employment Conditions and first Chairman of the IPM

Compensation Forum, has defined the following five golden rules for successful PRP schemes:

- individuals need to be clear about the targets and standards of performance required, whatever they may be
- they should be able to track performance against those targets and standards throughout the period over which performance is being assessed
- they must be in a position to influence the performance by changing their behaviour or decisions
- they should be clear about the rewards they will receive for achieving the required end results
- the rewards should be meaningful enough to make the efforts required worthwhile – and the communication of the rewards should be positively handled

The same principles should, as far as possible, apply to group schemes, although these are necessarily more diffused. Company-wide profit sharing schemes (see Chapter 15) are more about providing general rewards, increasing commitment and sharing in success than providing specific incentives

- *balancing quantitative and qualitative measures:* while most PRP schemes rely on quantitative measures of performance, there is a strong case for introducing qualitative factors which may be related to the degree to which individuals behave in line with corporate values in such areas as innovation, team-work, customer service and delivery
- *the need for flexibility:* many PRP schemes at top management level tend only to pay out if a profit or other quantified target has been completely achieved. But, in some circumstances, there is a case for flexibility in making 'milestone' payments which convey the right messages for the future (see Chapter 23 on start-ups)
- *the need to promote team-work:* bad PRP schemes can produce a lot of single-minded individualists. The importance of team-work should be recognized in structuring the scheme and defining critical success factors and performance indicators. Individuals should be told that achieving their targets at the expense of others is not considered competent performance
- *the need to avoid short-term thinking:* poor PRP schemes can focus attention on short-term results at the expense of other more important longer term objectives. This must be avoided by setting long-term as well as short-term goals and by discussing short-term objectives in their overall context
- *involvement in the design process:*designing PRP schemes should be, and usually is, an iterative process – trying and testing ideas on measures and structure with those who will eventually be involved in a scheme. It is also a valuable learning process

which can throw up fundamental strategic and business issues. Those due to benefit from the scheme should have an input into agreeing critical success factors and performance indicators both for themselves and for the organization

- *getting the message across:* all types of PRP are very powerful forms of communication. To get the right messages across for any scheme, key decisions will need to be made on:
  - how can the scheme achieve the best possible launch?
  - is it better to give no payout than low payout?
  - what is the best psychological moment for payout?
  - what communications should be used to gain maximum motivational impact from payments?
  - how should communications be handled when the scheme requires change?

Development programme

PRP schemes need careful implementation over a period of time to achieve maximum effectiveness and acceptability. Many boards of directors do not appreciate this when they first decide to introduce PRP. They need to be persuaded that undue haste will prejudice the successful introduction of a scheme. The foundations have to be in place first and the organization must be ready for the introduction of a process which has to be managed with great sensitivity and which can made a significant impact on the culture, for better or, if not handled well, for worse.

The sequence of activities in a PRP development programme is illustrated in Figure 10.1. Our experience in introducing PRP to many organizations over the last few years indicates that the following questions must be answered at each stage:

1. Why and how do we want to do it?
   - why does the organization want to introduce PRP?
   - what does it want to get out of it?
   - how much money and effort should be put into designing and operating the scheme?
   - to whom should the scheme apply?

2. Are we ready?

Analyze the readiness of the organization to introduce PRP and the cultural, attitudinal and systems factors which will have to be taken into account. The PRP check list at the end of this chapter lists the analytical points to be covered. It could be very helpful to conduct an employee attitude survey.

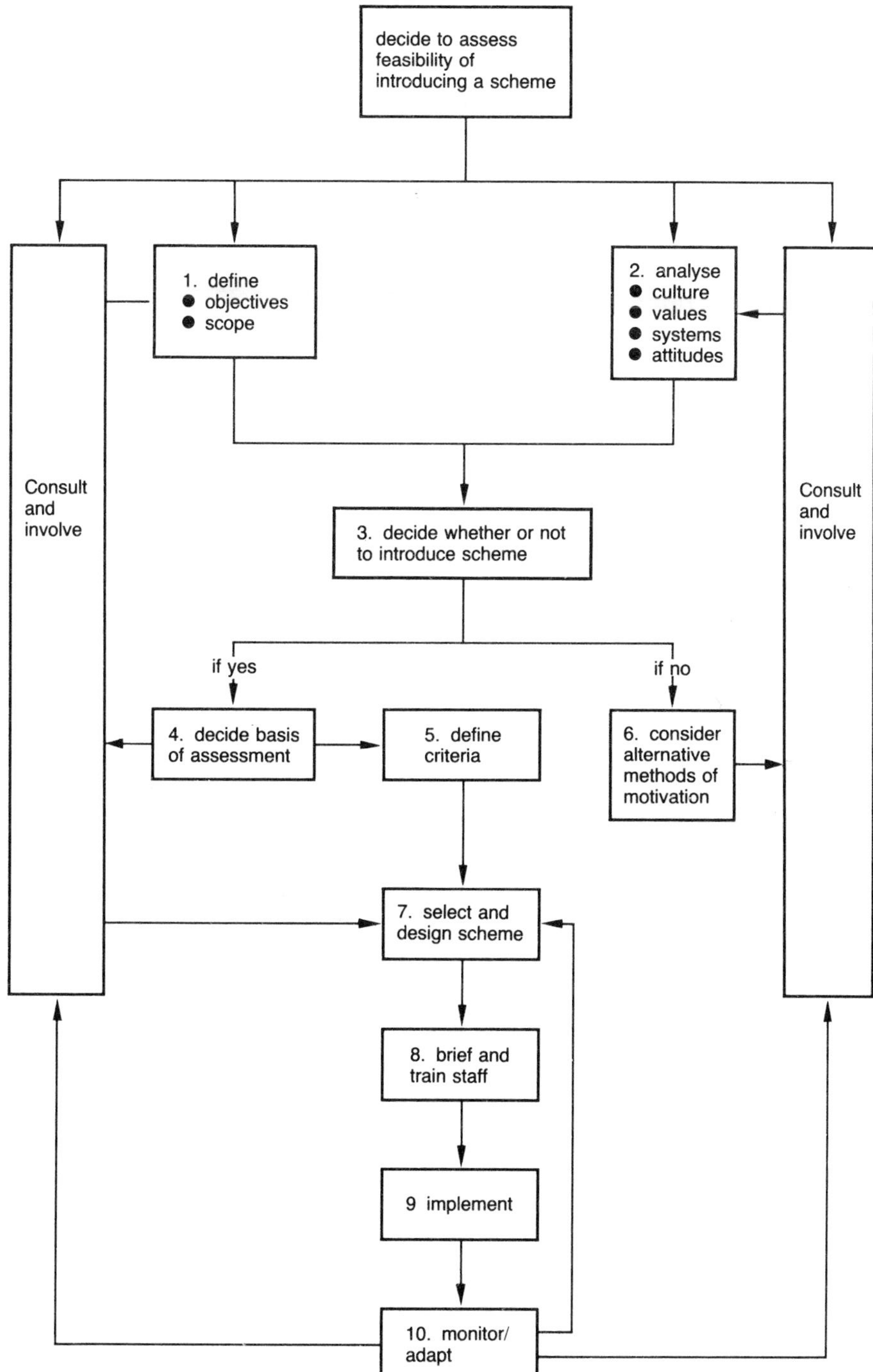

Figure 10.1 *Introducing performance-related pay*

3. Should we go ahead?

Decide on the basis of the results of the stages 1 and 2 analyses whether or not to go ahead with PRP. The PRP check list in Appendix N sets out the points to be covered.

4. What are our criteria concerning performance?

Decide in principle on the basis of assessment. This involves considering the extent to which the criteria will be:

- outputs in the form of quantifiable results
- outputs in the form of qualitative contributions to implementing and developing core values
- inputs in the form of competences and behaviours which influence outputs
- an appropriate mix of the above.

Decisions on criteria will be affected by the extent to which it is possible to assess and measure them and will both be influenced by and influence the format of performance reviews.

5. How will we identify the elements of performance that matter?

Identify the main objectives, critical success factors and performance indicators applicable to the organization as a whole and to the key jobs for which performance-related pay would apply. In each case, assess the extent to which:

- objectives can be defined clearly
- the critical success factors do indicate when objectives will have been achieved and are necessary and sufficient for their accomplishment
- performance indicators are available which will enable achievements to be measured.

6. If we decide against PRP, what else can we do?

If the decision is not to go ahead with PRP, consider other forms of motivation and recognition which the organization could provide, for example:

- improved training
- better succession planning
- sympathetic career development counselling
- non-cash individual or team awards to mark special and identifiable achievements.

7. How do we synthesize our findings?

Decide in the light of the previous analysis:

- which scheme or schemes are going to be introduced – merit, individual, group or company bonus
- what corporate values it is going to be based on
- who will participate in the scheme
- what the features of each scheme will be
- who will be involved in the development, implementation, monitoring and future evolution of the scheme
- when the scheme is to be introduced.

8. How do we achieve 'buy in' from all concerned?

It is important that all concerned know exactly how the scheme will operate and how they can benefit.

9. How do we start the process off?

It is necessary to introduce the scheme with great care. However carefully it has been planned, some unforeseeable problems will almost inevitably arise. It is usually advisable to start with a pilot scheme, often at senior levels of management so that they understand the principles, benefits and difficulties before applying PRP to the staff for whom they are responsible.

10. How do we learn from what we are doing?

It is essential to monitor the introduction of the scheme closely, especially during the trial period, so that the scheme can be amended as necessary. The rules of the scheme should allow for such revisions.

The staff affected by the scheme should be involved as much as possible in analysis, design and review at each stage. This is critical for executive incentives but will take different forms in merit payment schemes for more junior staff.

A PRP check-list is given in Appendix O.

Types of schemes

For most employees, the choice of schemes lies between individual merit payments, individual lump sum bonuses or team bonuses. We deal with these in turn below. Executive incentive schemes and profit sharing are considered, respectively, in Chapters 11 and 15.

Individual merit payment schemes

The main types of individual merit payment schemes are described below.

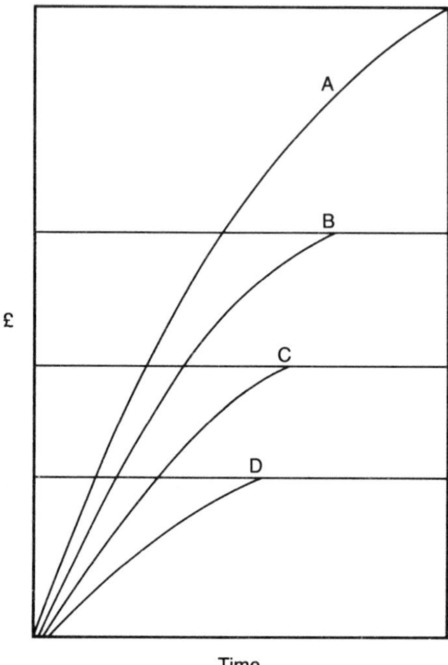

Figure 10.2 *Variable rates of progression within a salary range*

Salary range schemes

Basic features

Salary range schemes are commonly found in the private sector. Their basic feature is that salary progresses within a salary range according to performance. The differential between the minimum and maximum of the range is specified and the midpoint represents the rate for a fully competent person in the job (the relationship of this rate to the market rate is determined by the market posture of the company). Typical ranges are 90 per cent to 110 per cent, 85 per cent to 115 per cent, 80 per cent to 120 per cent.

A typical individual merit scheme will provide for progression through the range to be governed by performance ratings, (eg A–D) as illustrated in Figure 10.2. There will be different rates of progression over time and limits (merit bars) beyond which employees with certain ratings cannot progress.

Dealing with those reaching the top of their scale

Some organizations, when faced with the problem of good employees reaching the top of their scale without any immediate prospects of promotion (one of the implications of the flatter organization structures of today), are prepared to ignore scale ceilings and pay above the range for truly exceptional performance. Others deal with this situation by paying lump sum bonuses which avoids distorting the salary structure, if this is strictly defined. It is, however, dangerous to adopt this practice in response to market rate pressures because this can give entirely the wrong messages to the individuals concerned. These should be dealt with by separately identified market premia. It is a hard reality that market premia sometimes have to be paid to rather average performers in short supply.

Rating scales

Examples of rating scales for use in determining performance-related pay were given in Chapter 9. As we explained there, the rating classifications need to be defined with great care and managers should be given explicit guidance on the approach they use in making this assessment. The whole purpose of performance-related pay could be undermined if such ratings were biased or unduly subjective. One of the strongest arguments against PRP is that it is very difficult to avoid these problems unless continuous effort is directed to monitoring ratings to ensure that they are distributed fairly and are based on well-balanced judgements.

One method of dealing with biased ratings is to adopt a ranking system as described in Chapter 9.

Relationship between ratings and the size of merit increases

The ratings determine the size of the merit increase expressed as a percentage of base salary; for example, guidelines could be issued as follows:

- exceptional performance 10 per cent plus
- excellent performance 7 to 10 per cent
- well-balanced performance 5 to 7 per cent.

These increases could be in addition to an across the board cost-of-living award. But many companies are now combining merit and cost-of-living increases in one payment which, although it makes allowance for underlying inflation, is geared entirely to merit. This provides for more flexibility – there is more scope to discriminate between different levels and give really significant increases to outstanding staff – 25 per cent or more. It also enables companies effectively to reduce the real salary of poor performers by giving them an increase which is less than inflation.

Size of increases

The size of increases will be affected by the following factors:

- the organization's ability or willingness to pay. Ability may often be the first consideration, but there could be a case in a start-up or turn-round situation where an organization should be willing to pay more than it can strictly afford to provide motivation in particularly demanding circumstances, and as an investment in the future
- increases in market rates
- the rate of inflation may also have to be taken into account although not in addition to market rate increases. If an attempt has to be made to protect employees from high rates of inflation, it may be felt that merit increases have to be restricted until the rate of RPI increase drops. This is a pity because such temporary 'fire-fighting' can undo months or even years of work in getting the performance-related pay message across
- what is regarded as a worthwile increase for different levels of performance? There are no absolute standards for what is 'worthwhile'. It will depend partly on the type of organization and its culture. A performance-orientated organization will offer high rewards in line with its high expectations. A company which is more prepared to jog along (and, sadly, they do exist) will restrict the size of merit payments. It will also depend on the type of employees and their marketability. If the organization wants to retain high-quality staff whose skills are much in demand, it will have to take account of the market rates of progression for those people. A meaningful increase in one organization for a particular individual may be significantly higher or lower than in other organizations for different people. One company may feel it has to pay its top performers 15 to 20 per cent plus inflation, while another would be content with 8 to 10 per cent. As a rule of thumb it would be difficult to justify a merit increase of less than 5 per cent for an average performer or 8 per cent plus for an above-average employee – in addition to market movement.

Guidance on the market rates of progression can be obtained by studying market surveys which provide data on the increase in pay of matched samples of individuals over a period of time. If such a survey indicates that the average total increase has been, say, 12.4 per cent, this is a good starting point for a decision on the average increase (merit plus inflation) that the company should consider awarding.

Flexibility and control

In some schemes there is a fair amount of flexibility with regard to the size of merit payments and the rates at which individuals can move through a salary bracket. There may be an overall budget of X per cent of payroll, but managers may be allowed to exercise discretion on how they distribute their budget. This inevitably means that distributions and rates of progression vary between departments.

But it can be argued that, if you are going to hold managers totally responsible for achieving their objectives by making the best use of their human resources, then, within a financial budget, you ought to allow them to stand or fall on their ability to distribute rewards fairly and to motivate their staff in ways which they believe will work. This approach assumes that you have competent and well-trained managers, but it may still be necessary to provide advice to those managers who need it on the distribution of payments. Heads of remuneration in companies which adopt this policy of delegation support it because it is in accordance with the belief that more authority should be devolved to line managers, especially in today's flatter, decentralized, flexible and more responsive organizations. But they know that they may still have to engage in a lot of 'hand-holding' while managers are learning how to exercise their newly granted authority.

Some companies, however, do not feel that they can trust their managers to act responsibly and adopt a more rigidly controlled, even mechanistic approach (although it may be asked that if you never trust anyone to be responsible, how can they ever *be* responsible?). And low trust organizations can be unpleasant and demotivating to work in.

Rate of progression

The size of the merit payment obviously determines the rate of progression through a salary range, which will vary according to ratings. For example, in an 80 per cent to 120 per cent range, say £16,000 to £24,000, an 'A' rating may result in an increase of 10 per cent of the bottom of the scale. Someone who consistently received an 'A' would therefore progress through the range in five years. A 'C' rating might result in a 5 per cent increase, which would mean that it would take ten years to move through the range.

There is choice on the size of increments as people progress through a grade. The most typical approach is illustrated in Figure 10.3(a) where the rate of increase declines as salary progresses. This is in accord with the most frequently met pattern of market rate progression where salaries for occupations such as accountants, IT specialists and scientists tend to advance more quickly in their earlier careers when they are able to apply their professional expertise relatively quickly. But they begin to 'plateau out' when they get to their thirties and there are fewer opportunities for promotion, or to be deployed on more advanced projects.

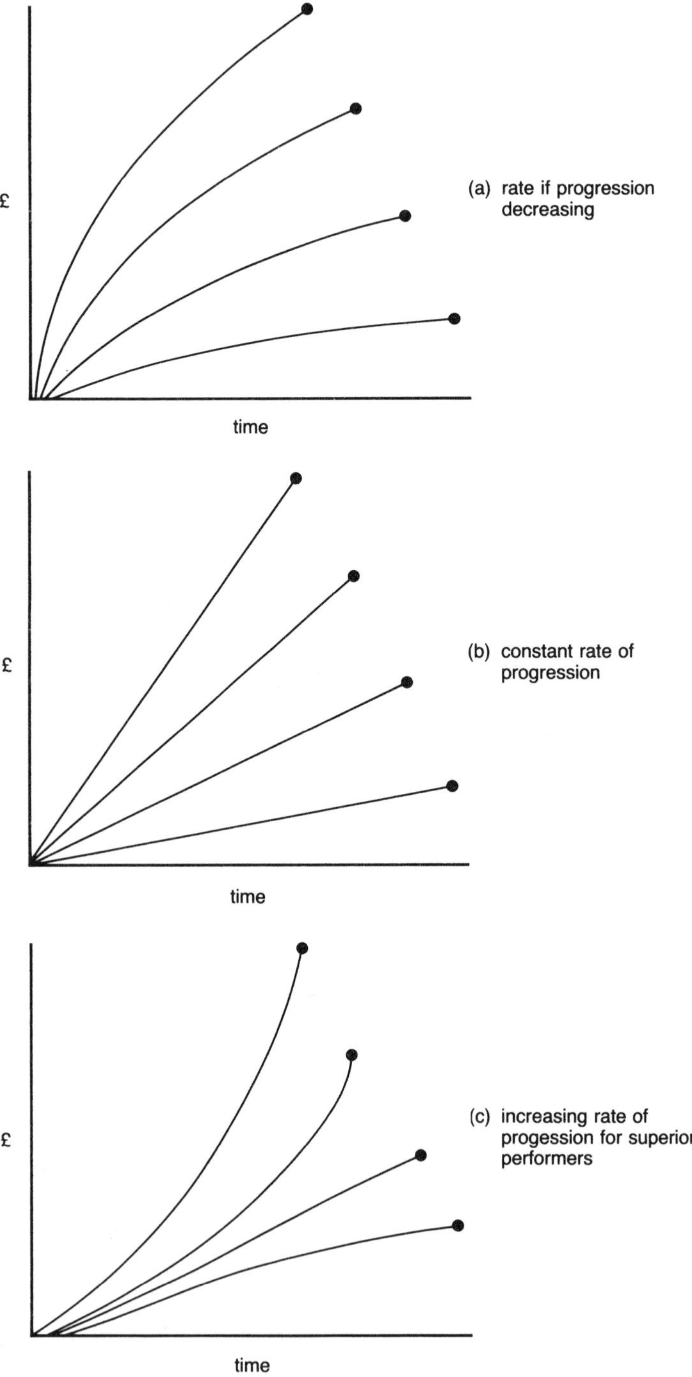

Figure 10.3 *Alternative patterns of salary progression*

Another argument in favour of this 'learning curve' approach is that the earlier period in a job makes the greatest demands on job holders and they should be rewarded accordingly. At later stages it is easier for them to maintain standards so that the reward need not be so high. They are also well paid compared with what they could earn elsewhere, and there must be a limit to how much you want to pay people. If they are overpaid, apart from being costly, you may be locking them in by making it difficult to find jobs elsewhere. Many people would applaud this 'golden handcuff' approach. But it has its dangers. Do you really want to tie someone down with money? Is it not possible that they will become increasingly frustrated because they feel that they are missing out on career opportunities? In other words, the extrinsic motivator of money will almost certainly fail to operate when intrinsic motivation has been seriously reduced.

Some people question this pattern, arguing conversely that demands do not diminish over time, especially in situations subjected to rapid change, and that employees still need motivating at the same rate. To offer an experienced individual who is maintaining a high level of performance under pressure a lower merit payment will deliver a conflicting message about what the organization is expecting. Adopting a reducing scale can result in the ludicrous situation of high-level performers moving towards the top of the scale getting less than an inferior performer at the beginning of the range (this has been a feature of some misconceived schemes). It is, of course, easy to avoid this happening, but the case for not reducing increments remains a strong one. This is illustrated in Figure 10.3(b).

A third and rare approach is to carry the argument in favour of a straight line progression even further and increase increments at the upper end of the range for superior performers as illustrated in Figure 10.3(c). This, however, could only be justified if some way were found of making it more difficult to merit a higher rating as experience is gained in a job by setting more taxing objectives or standards. And this could be difficult. The best way to provide extra rewards for continuing high achievers is to give them lump sum bonuses for meeting a particularly demanding requirement.

Performance matrices

Curves such as those illustrated in Figure 10.3 show the different shapes of progression but may not indicate precisely the increment that should be awarded at any point in the salary range. Many organizations are quite happy to retain these curves as guidelines because they want to allow a fair degree of flexibility in the system. Others, the majority, prefer to be explicit about the size of increases on the grounds that consistency and therefore equity in the distribution

performance assessment \ position in salary band	90–94%	95–99%	100%	101–105%	105–110%
	% increase	% increase	% increase	% increase	% increase
Excellent	12	12	11	11	10
Very effective	10	10	9	9	8
Effective	7	6	5	5	0
Developing	4	4	3	3	0
Basic	3	3	3	0	0

Figure 10.4 *Performance matrix – increases in addition to market movement*

of merit payments will only occur if managers are given explicit rules to follow rather than broad guidelines.

A frequently used method of controlling the distribution of rewards and the rate of progression is to have a performance matrix like that illustrated in Figure 10.4. This provides for increases to be related to both performance and the position of the individual in the salary range. Such systems also spell out the limits (merit bars) within a salary range beyond which salaries for people rated at lower levels cannot progress.

The performance matrix will be constructed by reference to the remuneration policies of the organization, with particular reference to its views on the size of increments and the shape of progression curves, as discussed above. It will also be related to market rates of progression.

A performance matrix will have to be reconstructed annually (assuming an annual merit review) to allow for inflation, market rates and the organization's ability to pay. Many organizations flex the merit payment 'pool' according to overall performance by setting an overall percentage limit to the payroll increase and then deciding how that pool should be divided. The division may be determined by an analysis of the distribution of performance ratings. A computerized system is very helpful and, in large organizations, essential in conducting this analysis.

To summarize, the following factors have to be taken into account in designing a performance matrix:

1. The number of progression curves, ie the number of points on the rating scale.
2. The shape of the curves, ie diminishing, linear or increasing.
3. Market rates of progression.
4. The policy on combining inflation or market rate increases (not both, because market increases incorporate inflation) with merit payments.
5. The size of the increases, which will be related to the factors listed above.
6. The fact that the majority of staff will be covered by the central group of increases (shaded in the example in Figure 10.4). Particular care will therefore have to be taken in deciding on the rates in this area and they may have to be flexed more often.
7. The risk of management taking fright at exceptionally high merit increments for top performers. But they can be assured that great care will be taken to ensure that only truly deserving cases will get these awards and that they will be in a distinct minority.

8. The positioning of the merit bars will have to be determined. This could be done by reference to market rates. If, for example, the organization's market 'posture' policy is to pay on average between the median and upper quartile market rates, then this would define the maximum level to which the averagely competent performer could advance. The next higher level could advance to the upper quartile rate and top level staff could progress to the upper decile rate. Following these market rate indicators could, however, lead you into difficulties if you reward people much more highly for excellent performance in some job families or market groups than others. While it may be advisable to ensure that the average rate of progression reflects the market rates for different job categories, it may introduce an unacceptable degree of inequity if highly rated individuals benefiting from market pressures at this level gain even more than the top performers elsewhere in the organization.

Pay spine scheme

This is a typical approach in the public sector. The 'box' rating given in the assessment determines whether or not an individual should get accelerated increments on the pay spine or 'range points' above the top of their scale. One 'box A' rating, for example, would automatically entitle an eligible employee to a range point or increment. The use of merit bars and range points means that relatively few staff can progress at a faster rate, or above the normal scale, and then only to a limited extent. These schemes may provide for a modicum of flexibility but are not powerful motivators.

Variable increment scheme

Although fixed incremental scales, in which people progress through a salary grade for 'being there' rather than in relation to their competence, are now much less common in the private sector, they do still exist in parts of the public sector and in the more bureaucratic or trade union-dominated organizations (trade unions can and do still fight against merit pay because they believe it is fundamentally unfair). Some companies have, however, wanted to provide a measure of performance-related pay, on the grounds that it is more inequitable *not* to reward people according to their contribution than to pay everyone the same irrespective of their performance. To cater for this need, these firms have provided for extra increments to be paid, or increments to be withheld according to performance, much as in pay spine schemes.

Competency related schemes

These are relatively new in the spectrum of approaches to PRP and, although they are not strictly merit schemes, they are most conveniently listed under this heading. They are sometimes referred to as skill-based schemes. Competence is defined as the ability in a person which leads to desirable results. It is concerned with doing and action, rather than the mere possession of knowledge. It is, however, a broader concept than skill and can usefully be thought of as encompassing knowledge, skill, understanding and will.

The analysis of competences is playing an increasing part in management and career development, and it is logical to extend its application to reward. Linking pay to levels of competence embraces the fundamental belief that rewards should be related to a demonstrable ability to apply know-how to deliver results.

A competency scheme typically divides the range of competency requirements in an organization or for a category of employee, for example scientists, into a series of career bands. Each band is defined in terms of its objectives, associated competences and any formal education or training required. For example, a competency band for professional staff in a research and development organization could be defined as follows:

- *Objectives* – ability to work independently on well-defined assignments or shorter-term projects
- *Associated competences*
  - apply basic theory to practical problems
  - set priorities
  - develop and execute an individual work plan
  - deliver results in accordance with agreed assignment or project specification
  - ability to direct small project teams of junior professional staff or technicians to complete work assignments
- *Formal education and training*
  - minimum B. Tech or equivalent
  - *project management*
  - application training relevant to technical area (discipline)
    human resource management programme
  - effective communication programme.

Each competency band has a broad pay range and progression within each band depends on performance assessed by reference to the competency requirements.

These schemes can be linked to competency approaches to

management development. But it may be difficult to define a hierarcy of competences with sufficient accuracy.

Performance and competency pay curves
A competency and performance-related scheme adds more explicit guidelines in the shape of pay curves as illustrated in Figure 10.5. This is a relatively new approach which is still being tested but it promises well, although difficulties do occur in the definition of competences.

These schemes recognize that the rate of pay of individuals is determined by three factors:

1. Their level of competence – ie their ability to apply knowledge and skills to reach a satisfactory level of performance.
2. The level of performance they achieve in whatever competence band they are in.
3. The market rate for the levels of competence and performance they have achieved.

The main features of a competency and performance-based scheme are as follows:

- the horizontal axis on the chart (Figure 10.5) represents the level of competence individuals achieve. In this example, three competence bands have been established, although the competence development line along this axis represents a continuum of progression rather than three finite steps. There is no limit to the number of steps but, if there are too many, it might be difficult to differentiate between them. No times would be set for moving through these bands – this would depend on the level of performance. It could be assumed, however, that a continuing effective level of performance would take individuals through the bands at a certain rate, thus indicating the length of time, on average, it might take to reach each competence band
- The curves represent different levels of performance. In this example, there are five rates, 'effective' being regarded as the normal level. Six or four level scales could be used. The curves govern pay progression, although this could be limited if an individual cannot advance to a higher competence band. Pay within each competence band would vary according to performance. The progression of individuals through the competency bands might be restricted if they receive only 'basic' or 'developing' ratings. Improvement would result in a higher rating and the opportunity to advance to the next band. Individuals in the highest band who get a less than effective rating might not receive a merit increase and could even be given a negative increase in real terms by being awarded less than the rate of inflation

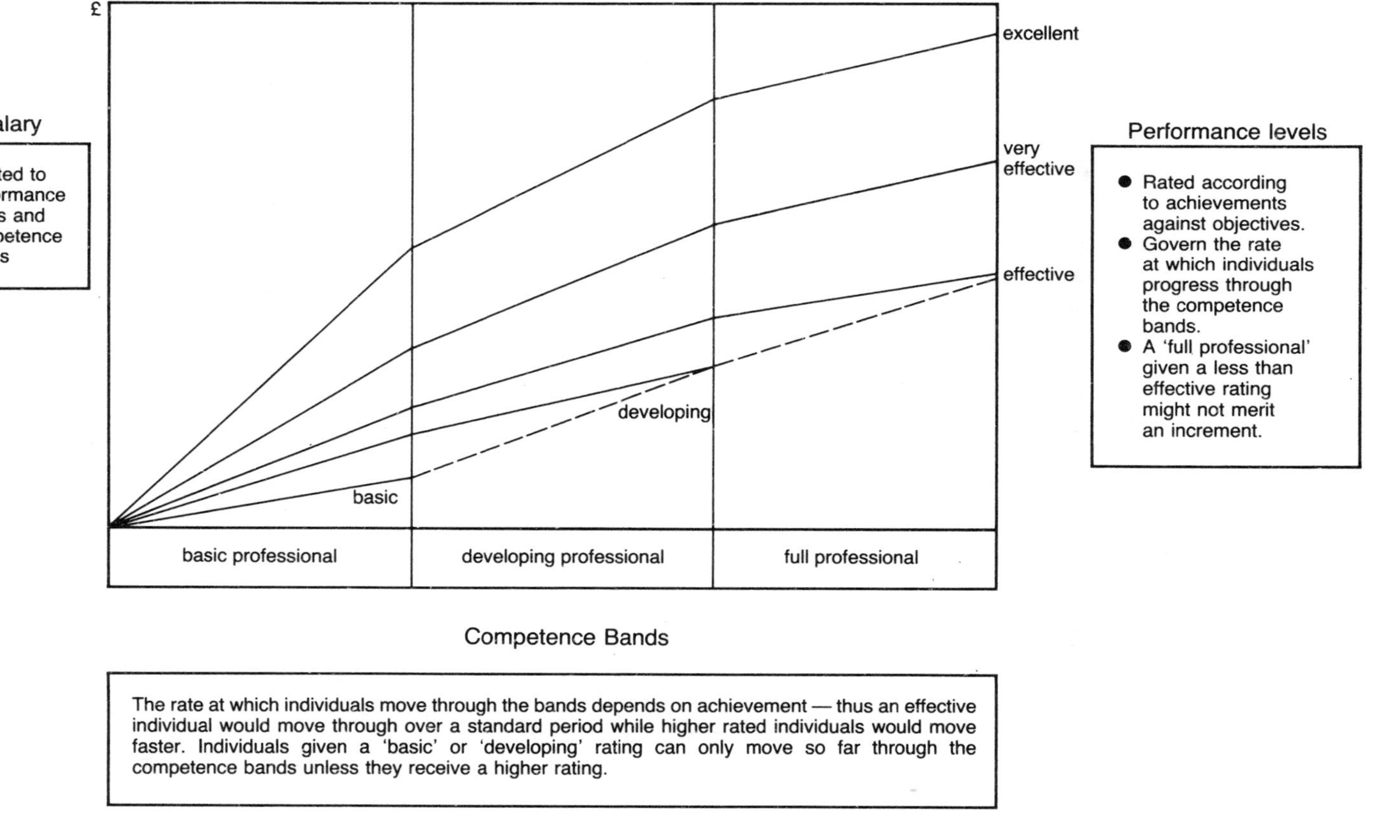

Figure 10.5 *Pay curves*

- the vertical axis represents the rate of pay appropriate for different levels of competence and performance. These would be linked to market rates
- the rate of increase in pay according to performance would have to be determined. Clearly, increases have to be meaningful. The example indicates a reduction in the rate of pay progression at higher levels, but it might well be considered that percentage increases should continue at the same rate
- there would be scope to give a lump sum (typically non-pensionable) bonus equivalent to the normal pay increment for high-level performers who have reached the limits of their salary bands. Lump sum bonuses could also be awarded in special cases where, for historical reasons, someone is paid more than his or her competence level or performance rating warrants. In these circumstances it might be felt that it is best not to demotivate someone by not giving any award at all, but that a bonus would provide a measure of recognition without continuing to perpetuate the anomaly
- although the system would be designed to relate pay to competence and performance, it would also provide the basis for career planning and development. Individuals could be made aware of career 'aiming points' expressed in terms of what they must be able to do and, as appropriate, the qualifications, training and experience they need to reach a defined level of competence. This provides additional motivation and, when the company supports the development programme, a means of increasing commitment and retaining valued staff.

To develop this system it would be necessary to:

- define the competence bands – this is a demanding and time-consuming task and is best achieved by means of a workshop where those who are going to be affected by the scheme are given the opportunity to make their contribution in the design stage
- decide by reference to market rates the salary limits for each level of competence and performance – it might be assumed that the rate paid for an effective performer should be between the median and upper quartile of the market rate, while the upper quartile, upper decile or even the top rate would be paid for outstanding individuals
- define the rates of increase applicable to each curve
- define the rating scale
- decide how ratings should be made – the performance review system
- define methods of budgeting for and controlling merit increases.

Advantages of individual merit payment schemes

The advantages of an individual merit scheme are that it:

- directly links performance and salary progression
- provides individualized progression rates
- recognizes increasing competence gained through experience.

Disadvantages of individual merit payment schemes

The potential disadvantages of a merit scheme are that:

- it is dependent on the quality of appraisal, which can be arbitrary, subjective or inconsistent, especially when the appraisers have been inadequately trained in the process and its core values
- unless it is very carefully conceived and managed, it can demotivate a lot of people who, although they may not be delivering spectacular results (and therefore receiving spectacular rewards) are still essential ingredients in the achievement of organizational success
- merit payments, as distinct from bonuses, create extra payroll costs when benefits such as pensions are related to base pay; they also, of course, increase National Insurance payments
- a merit payment is, in effect, a permanent increase in salary, yet the quality of performance in future years may not justify this payment
- because it results in increases in base salary, merit pay can result in an upward drift in payroll costs without a commensurate improvement in organizational performance
- it is only effective as a motivator if rewards are clearly related to performance and are of a significant value, but it is difficult for conventional schemes to discriminate properly and the size of the award may have to be controlled to offset the cost factors mentioned above.

Design of individual merit payment schemes

The points to be considered are:

- the critical success factors which govern performance for the group to be covered by the scheme
- the performance indicators to be used and their rationale
- the amount of money available for distribution expressed as a percentage of the payroll (the merit payment pool)
- how the merit payment pool will or can be flexed in relation to company performance

- the range of payments to be made, expressed as a percentage either of base salary or the lowest part of the salary range
- the distribution of rewards so that the scheme contributes to the motivation of the core of competent performers upon whom the organization largely depends as well as the high flyers
- the width of salary ranges expressed as a percentage of the lowest point (this width may be expressed as a percentage on either side of the mid-point of the range – it may increase for senior jobs where there is more scope for variations in performance)
- the amount of freedom to be given to managers within their budgets to determine merit increases
- the shape of the progression curves or the design of the performance matrix, if it is decided to control the distribution of merit increases
- what happens to highly rated staff who have reached the top of their scale and for whom there are no immediate prospects of promotion (consideration may have to be given to bonus payments in these circumstances)
- how the quality of assessments and ratings will be monitored and controlled
- how budgets for merit increases and payroll costs will be controlled
- how staff are going to be convinced that the scheme is fair, equitable and provides reasonable rewards, not only for the super-achievers but also for the more modest but essential contributors to success.

Individual bonus payments

Definition

Individual performance bonuses are payments made in addition to base salary which are related to the achievement of specified targets, the completion of a project or a stage of a project to a specified standard, the receipt of an appropriate performance rating, or a combination of any of these.

An individual bonus for those at the top of their salary scale could be the normal merit payment, according to performance, converted into a lump sum.

Bonuses can, however, be more explicitly linked to performance if they are related to the degree to which targets have been achieved. For example, three levels of bonus may be paid according to whether individuals have:

- only just achieved the target – the threshold bonus
- completely achieved the target – the full bonus
- significantly exceeded the target – the exceptional bonus.

Individual bonuses were at one time only paid to senior management and sales representatives and others whose performance could be targeted with precision. Their use is now spreading generally to more junior levels and jobs where targets are more difficult to quantify as organizations seek to contain consolidated payroll costs and benefit from the reality that bonuses can, if well implemented, give very strong performance messages. One reason for the effectiveness of bonuses as part of a reward system is the simple fact that people often spend bonus money differently from a 'drip feed' pay increase. They remember and appreciate the extra luxury or weekend in Paris on which they spent the award.

Executive bonus and incentive schemes can differ in a number of ways and are considered separately in Chapter 11.

Advantages of individual bonus payments

The advantages of bonuses related to individual targets or ratings are that:

- the reward is immediately payable for work well done
- the bonus can be linked to specific achievements and future targets, and this constitutes both a reward and an incentive
- the payment is not perpetuated as part of base salary irrespective of future performance
- lump sum payments appeal to some people
- additional rewards can be given to people at the top of their salary scale without damaging the integrity of the salary structure
- the arrangements can be flexible
- the system can be designed for easy administration

Disadvantages of individual bonus payments

The disadvantages of bonus related to individual targets are that:

- it is more difficult to apply to people whose jobs have less tangible outputs
- an individualistic rather than a team approach may be encouraged
- people may be diverted away from the innovative and developmental aspects of their work because they are concentrating on the task in hand
- it could be difficult to establish a fair and consistent relationship

between the results achieved and the level of the reward, which could be seen as arbitrary and inequitable
- it might be hard to discriminate fairly between those on long-term projects, who could wait for some time before they are rewarded, and those with shorter-term and more visible objectives, who could be rewarded more rapidly.

Design of individual bonus schemes

The points to be considered are:

- the constituents of the bonus in terms of the mix of the payments related to target achievement, ratings or company results
- the method of defining targets and standards of performance for tasks to be completed; and/or
- the basis upon which performance ratings could be translated into bonus payments (including the range of payments that can be made)
- how agreement should be reached with individuals on their targets or tasks
- how performance should be measured and who measures it
- the amount of money to be made available for bonuses, and how and when bonuses should be paid
- how to make the scheme differentiate rewards in relation to performance in a fair, consistent and relevant way, having regard to the disadvantages listed above.

Group bonus scheme

Definition

Group or team bonus schemes relate the reward to the satisfactory completion of a project or stage of a project, or the achievement of a group target.

Advantages of group bonus schemes

Group bonuses are increasingly being used by organizations who want to underpin and reward collective effort. They are particularly helpful in areas such as research and development and information technology where work is strongly project based. Group bonuses can:

- promote the value and successful operation of team-work
- facilitate the setting of group targets where results depend on joint effort

- be less invidious than individual payments, especially when these are affected by the work of other people in the team which is outside the employee's control.

Disadvantages of group bonus schemes

Group bonuses:

- are only feasible where it is possible to identify teams who are working together to achieve defined tasks
- can diffuse individual motivation because the relationship between individual effort and reward may be remote
- can cause ill-directed peer group pressure which effectively punishes weaker performers.

Design of group bonus schemes

The points to be covered are:

- the identification and definition of the groups to be included in the scheme
- methods of defining targets
- how agreement should be reached with groups on their targets
- how the performance of groups should be measured
- the formula for deciding on bonus payments (including minima and maxima) and the extent to which a discretionary element is required
- the amount of money available for group bonus payments and how and when bonuses should be paid
- the procedure for monitoring the scheme.

Company-wide schemes

Company-wide schemes are discussed in Chapter 15 (profit sharing).

Choice of PRP scheme

The matrix illustrated in Figure 10.6 is designed to help in the choice of scheme or mix of schemes by summarizing the impact of different approaches in terms of motivation, commitment, retention and time-scale.

It is advisable, however, to reinforce the impact of the selected scheme or schemes by taking additional steps to increase longer-term motivation by the use of such non-financial incentives and rewards as:

Type of Scheme / Time Scale	Instrumental Schemes		Schemes creating a sense of participation and involvement
	individual motivation	team motivation	commitment/ retention
immediate	individual bonus	group bonus	—
short-term	merit pay	—	—
medium-term	deferred pay/ bonus	gain-sharing	profit-sharing
long-term	—	—	share option phantom option

Figure 10.6 *PRP choice matrix*

- recognition of achievement
- additional responsibility
- greater autonomy
- involvement
- enhancement of skills and knowledge
- career development.

Chapter 11

Incentive and Bonus Schemes

Incentives and bonuses are two of the principal ways in which performance can be rewarded. Research has shown that their use has grown rapidly in the UK over the last few years. The proportion of major UK employers operating such schemes has risen from under one-third to well over two-thirds since 1980. Free of the constraints of incomes policy, organizations have sought either to re-establish, or to introduce for the first time, schemes which reinforce the messages required to produce improved performance and increased productivity. Private sector employers in particular now increasingly believe that they are not providing an appropriate or competitive package for their directors and senior executives, unless there is some element of risk money to add on to basic salary and reward the achievement of company growth, profitability and success. At the same time, companies have been re-examining the use of bonus schemes for more junior employees in order to increase motivation and to reward them for their contribution.

Incentive and bonus schemes are dealt with in this chapter under the following headings:

Overall considerations

- the role of incentive and bonus schemes
- advantages and disadvantages
- the difference between incentives and bonuses
- the principles that should be taken into account when selecting and designing schemes
- the importance of communications
- the need to balance rewards for corporate, team and individual performance.

Executive incentive schemes

- the nature of the strategic decision that has to be made when introducing a scheme
- aims of an executive incentive scheme
- relationships with other components of the reward package

- the target group – who should be included in the scheme
- the main features of incentive schemes
- tax planning considerations
- administration of schemes.

Executive bonus schemes

- the profit pool approach
- the discretionary approach
- the personal target approach.

Incentive and bonus scheme for less senior staff

- target-based incentives
- merit bonuses
- productivity payments

Sales incentive schemes have a number of special characteristics and are therefore dealt with separately in Chapter 12.

Overall considerations

Role of incentive and bonus schemes

The role of incentive and bonus schemes in a reward management system is to provide a basis for paying for performance which is related to the achievement of defined objectives, targets and standards of performance.

Advantages

The advantages of incentive and bonus schemes are that they can:

- establish a clear relationship between performance and pay
- provide the most direct form of financial motivation available by linking rewards to achievements
- reinforce and develop a corporate culture which is biased to action and permeated by the spirit of enterprise, and where success is the watchword
- encourage entrepreneurial behaviour
- concentrate effort in priority areas
- clarify the key issues with which executives should be concerned
- attract people who are confident in their own abilities to deliver results
- retain people who are hungry for success and the rewards which go with it
- improve salary competitiveness for high-quality executives
- enable staff to share in the organization's prosperity.

Disadvantages

The disadvantages of incentive and bonus schemes are that they can:

- be divisive and inequitable
- encourage concentration on short-term issues linked to annual incentive and bonus payments and thus detract from the achievement of longer-term plans
- over focus on financial results, to the detriment of other initiatives, such as training, management development, quality, brand building, R and D etc
- be open to manipulation by unscrupulous executives
- be demotivating when corporate performance is adversely affected by outside influences such as exchange rate fluctuations
- appear to conflict with the belief that executives should be rewarded by competitive, pensionable basic salaries which they receive because they are expected to give their utmost as senior professionals
- be treated as just another remuneration fashion or fad and will be dropped the moment there is a major downturn in the economy and the prospect of substantial payments evaporates
- add to remuneration costs without delivering real performance improvements.

These disadvantages can be formidable and should be weighed very carefully against the advantages set out earlier when introducing a new scheme or reviewing an existing one. However, the advantages are considerable in the right environment and when the criteria listed in the next section are satisfied. The design and administration of any plan must take account of the potential drawbacks. The goal of a successful scheme should be to:

- reward the right people (incentives are paid only to high achievers)
- motivate all the people (all participants have the opportunity to earn bonus and are motivated if targets are fair)
- focus attention on business objectives (specified in incentive targets)
- create a performance results culture (pay for results not effort)
- make pay a variable cost, not a fixed cost (paybill decreases if business targets not achieved: increases if targets exceeded)
- add credibility to the budgeting/targeting process (targets only acceptable to incentive participants if felt fair, since their pay is dependent on them)
- emphasize team-work or individual effort as appropriate (team-based incentives foster team co-operation: personal targets with significant sums of money attached to them emphasize individual performance)

- pay only for performance when it occurs (one-off non-consolidated payments are made rather than adjustments to salary, which may have a higher cost in the longer term and after year 1 are not related to performance).

The difference between incentives and bonuses

The terms incentive and bonus are often juxtaposed. In this book, the terms are used with specific meaning. They resemble one another in that they are both lump sum payments which are related in some defined way to performance. But there the similarity ends.

Incentives: are payments linked to the achievement of previously set and agreed targets. They aim to encourage better performance and then reward it, usually in fixed proportion to the extent to which the target has been reached. Incentive schemes are found from the shopfloor to the boardroom and can be applied to individuals or groups. They vary principally in the type and range of targets applied.

Bonuses: are essentially rewards for success and are paid either at the time the individual or group achieves something oustanding, or at a given point in the year. By their very nature, bonuses tend to be discretionary. The amount paid out depends upon the recommendations or decisions of the employee's boss, the chief executive or the board, and is constrained only by budgetary limits. Bonus schemes are therefore often less structured than incentive schemes and can also be useful in smaller and cyclical businesses to help control fixed costs.

Selecting a scheme – guiding principles

Although there are individual factors that affect each of the incentive or bonus schemes described in this chapter, there are a number of guiding principles, as set out below, which relate to all schemes and should always be taken into account when selecting one.

Competitive base rates

Basic pay should be competitive, perhaps close to the median market rate for the job. Research into a wide range of UK schemes shows that incentive or bonus paying companies typically pay slightly higher basic salaries than non-incentive or bonus paying firms. They appear to believe that fluctuations in earnings should not threaten an individual's basic living standards although, in good years, an incentive or bonus payment could improve them substantially. The exception to this rule is often provided by salesforce incentive schemes where the commission or bonus element may form a much higher proportion of remuneration.

Significant payment
The reward should be commensurate with the achievement. It is often better to pay nothing and say why, rather than give a derisory amount. To some people, even seemingly quite small amounts of variable pay opportunity can have significant impact. In general, however, small payments of, say, less than five per cent or even ten per cent have little motivational value. If this is all a scheme can pay out, it may be better to reward performance through a sharper merit payment system.

Agreed and quantified targets
Where incentives are based on targets, these should be discussed and agreed with each individual or group. The targets should as far as possible, be quantified and should include financial criteria.

Tough but achievable targets
Targets should be achievable, but not too easily. Nowadays many companies use budgets as the basis of their targets. Others regard it as heresy to link schemes to budget.

Simple and clear
A simple design and a clear explanation of how the scheme works are needed to allow individuals to calculate what their payments will be, easily and quickly. Complex systems do not motivate well.

Appropriate to business needs
Incentive and bonus schemes should be designed to meet the needs of the business and to reflect and encourage the culture appropriate for performance improvement within it.

Acceptable
The schemes should be acceptable to the employees they cover, bearing in mind the need for careful and persistent communication to achieve this.

Policy for dealing with 'windfall bonuses'
A policy on how unplanned and excessive 'windfall bonuses' will be dealt with should be formulated when designing the scheme. This could be linked to any limits or 'caps' placed on the maximum percentage payable, or it could be dealt with separately.

Provision for review
Schemes should be introduced with a proviso that they will be reviewed regularly. After two or three years, sometimes less, but rarely more, all schemes will need fine-tuning, and many will need more fundamental changes. The areas that will need review are:

- has the strategy changed? If so the scheme should change too
- whether or not the factors affecting the amount of payments will reflect operational realities and needs, and whether they are still pointing in the same direction as the business
- the extent to which employees take the scheme for granted, so causing it to lose motivational value
- whether or not the balance between pensionable pay and unconsolidated bonus is still correct in relation to market practice
- the extent to which the scheme needs re-packaging and re-communicating to rekindle interest and improve performance.

Where it is clear that a scheme has decayed to the point that continuing with it is a waste of time, consideration will have to be given to what type of scheme, if any, should replace it. This should be based on a review of the place of incentives in the organization's overall approach to rewarding performance.

The importance of communications

The success of any scheme depends on how well it is communicated. The message that must be got across to all concerned is that these are the targets and improved performance will result in a worthwile reward. The subject of communications is dealt with in Chapter 26.

The need to balance rewards

The need to reward individual performance should be balanced against corporate needs. Incentive schemes are counter-productive if they encourage staff to get results which are in their own interests but not in those of the organization. The classic example is the sales director rewarded only for sales turnover who loses the company business and customers because more items are sold than could be produced, delivered or serviced. This problem can be avoided by taking care over the choice of targets and by introducing a team performance element. The latter approach is particularly important if there are disparate individuals in the group for whom a sense of common purpose needs to be developed. A group incentive scheme can therefore help to enhance team spirit.

It is also necessary to balance the rewards for individuals against the expectations of shareholders on what level of return they will get from their investment. The company's profits must be large enough to provide a meaningful benefit to all concerned.

Executive incentive schemes

A strategic decision

The introduction of an executive incentive scheme should be closely tied to a searching review of corporate plans and objectives. It is essential to know where the enterprise is planning to go and what constitutes success before deciding how executives should be rewarded for their performance. The main question to be answered when making this strategic decision is – what do executives have to do and achieve for the company to be more successful? A good scheme will ensure that executives concentrate on business priorities.

Aims

The primary aim of an executive incentive scheme is to increase executive motivation in order to improve company performance. The other aims are to:

- make executives more aware of the key measures of company performances;
- provide executives with a share in the company's prosperity;
- reward personal commitment and success;
- ensure competitive, total compensation linked to company performance and so help to recruit and retain good calibre executives.

Relationship with other components of the reward package

It is essential to relate the incentive scheme to other elements of the reward package. This means reviewing basic salary and benefit packages to ensure that they are competitive. It also means deciding what the incentive scheme is expected to contribute in addition to existing merit payment systems, share option schemes and profit sharing arrangements.

Defining the target group

Only executives who can exert personal control over the selected performance measures as individuals or members of a team should be included in the scheme. These will certainly consist of members of the board, who may need different criteria with individual performance triggers, although incentive schemes for directors often incorporate a common measure based on overall company profitability.

Incentives for executives below this level are often more difficult to design.

The main features of executive incentive schemes

When designing an incentive scheme the following features of it will need to be considered:

1. The choice of performance measures, which lies between financial or non-financial measures or a combination of the two.
2. The extent to which the scheme should be tied down to a formula or should allow an element of discretion when making awards.
3. The link that should exist between the scheme and the performance appraisal system.
4. The level of payments that should be made according to performance, which will take account of the target level, the starting point and any limits or 'caps' that will be placed on incentive earnings.
5. The action that should be taken over any 'windfall' profits.
6. The frequency with which payments should be made.

These considerations are dealt with in the following sections of this chapter. Examples of incentive schemes are given in Appendix P.

Financial performance measures

The principal financial performance measures are:

- profit before tax (pre-tax profit)
- profit after tax (post-tax profit)
- earnings per share
- return on capital or assets employed
- cash flow
- others specific to individual businesses.

The factors governing the choice between these measures are discussed below. The main criteria are first, relevance to organization requirements, second, the extent to which the individual or group can influence results, and, third, the existence of reliable methods of measurement – a credible and sophisticated management information system is a prerequisite for any scheme using financial measures.

Profit before tax
This is the key indicator of corporate success and is therefore frequently used as the sole criterion.

Incentives are based on a percentage of profit, typically paid after the achievement of a threshold figure, the level of which is set to protect the interests of shareholders. The threshold may need adjustment after an acquisition or change in the capital structure. Both interest and management charges are taken into account if they are within management control. This, however, may not be the case when interest rates are fluctuating widely or where the situation is complicated by overseas activities.

Profit after tax
This measure aligns more closely with shareholders' interests because it gives a clearer indication of the funds available for reinvestment and for payment of dividends. However, it can be significantly affected by changes in national and international tax laws and by the way in which those laws are interpreted. Profit after tax is rarely used as the chief measure in executive incentive schemes below main Board level, although it is sometimes included as one of a set of criteria. The criteria for choosing before or after tax depends upon the degree to which managers are expected to take account of tax considerations when making business decisions.

Earnings per share
This measure relates post-tax profits to the average weighted number of ordinary shares in issue during the financial year. It is used by the City to judge company performance, and is being increasingly adopted as the main measure in Directors' incentive schemes. It is, however, subject to changes in corporate taxation in the same way as post-tax profits. It can also be difficult to measure within the year. Before selecting this measure, the possible impact of mergers, takeovers and changes in accounting policy should be considered.

Return on capital or assets employed
This is another key measure of company performance. It can, however, be manipulated by management who could improve the ratio dramatically by the sale of assets. This criterion is, therefore, generally used in conjunction with others.

Cash flow
This measure is also focused on by the City, who will value the company by estimating the Net Present Value of future cash flow. Shareholder Value techniques also put a greater emphasis on cash flow.

The importance of managing cash can be emphasized by using this criterion as one of the factors in an incentive scheme, but it is not really suitable as the sole measure of performance because it only relates to one aspect of management responsibility.

Use of criteria
The measures used for incentives vary by job level. The 1989 Monks Guide to performance related incentives shows how these are used for directors and senior managers:

Measure	*Board Directors* %	*Senior Managers* %
Pre-tax profit	72	73
Post-tax profit	6	6
Earnings per share	30	15
Return on capital	28	32
Cash flow	9	9
Job-related targets		
– quantifiable	26	40
– qualitative	21	33

Non-financial targets

Although it is always desirable to relate incentives to financial targets they may not be applicable to all aspects of an executive's job, especially in service departments such as personnel. To cover each key result area it may be necessary to set job-related targets which indicate what needs to be achieved to earn a specified level of reward. For example, the target may be to complete a project which meets agreed objectives within a time limit. The objectives would be defined in such terms as cost reduction, increase in productivity, or improvement in quality or customer service levels. Some schemes set a 100 per cent level for full achievement of the objectives, but provide for a partial payment if the results are less than 100 per cent.

The target mix

The mix of performance criteria between financial and non-financial measures will depend on the requirements of the business and the particular demands made on the executives in the scheme. At board level, the mix may be dominated by measures of corporate performance such as earnings per share, to which all directors contribute. But a proportion of the incentive payment may be related to individual targets, which could be defined in financial or non-financial terms and would cover each of the key result areas of the job in accordance with the contribution of job holders to overall performance. To concentrate the minds of executives on these areas and to avoid over-complicating the scheme, it is best not to have more than three or four factors.

Discretionary element

Many schemes which have a mixture of targets also allow for a discretionary element in incentive payments. This may be used by the chief executive or the remuneration committee of the board to reward a manager for exceptional performance 'beyond the line of duty', which would not be adequately recognized by the normal measures.

Link with performance appraisal

Discussion on the setting and achievement of targets should take place as part of the normal performance appraisal procedure. An important feature of this appraisal will be the review of all aspects of the results achieved by the executive so that those factors not covered specifically by the incentive scheme are also dealt with. There is always the risk in any incentive scheme that an important aspect of the job such as development, leadership or teambuilding is neglected because the executive concentrates only on those areas where short-term rewards can be achieved. Discussions during appraisals can help to put these matters into perspective.

At board level it is advisable to have special meetings to discuss the operation of the incentive scheme. The compensation/remuneration committee of the main board, consisting wholly or mainly of non-executive directors, is often used for this purpose.

Level of payments

Three decisions are required on the level of incentive payments:

1. The target level expressed as a percentage of base salary.
2. The starting point for incentive payments.
3. The limit, if any, to the maximum payment that can be made.

Target level: The level of incentive which is paid if the performance targets are reached must be meaningful. As mentioned earlier, payments of less than 10 per cent can have little motivational effect. In the case of senior executives, target figures of 20–30 per cent are typical. For this level of incentive payment, however, the target, although achievable, should be tough.

The payment for reaching the target level of performance should also be self-financing. It should be based on the assumption that the company as well as the individual will benefit. Payments should be regarded as serious money, not to be handed over lightly.

Starting point: The starting point will depend upon the extent to which demanding levels of target performance are set. If the target is reasonably difficult to attain, as it should be, then a trigger point of 90 per cent achievement of the target level of performance would be appropriate.

It is necessary, however, to provide a significant incentive to achieve the target. This can be done by gearing the incentive payment as a percentage of base salary so that its increase between the starting point and the target figure is greater than the percentage improvement in performance needed to reach the target. For example:

Performance level as a percentage of target		Incentive payment as a percentage of base salary
Start	90%	10%
Target	100%	30%

Upper limit: Many schemes 'cap' incentives by setting an upper limit to payments to avoid them getting out of hand and in the belief, which may or may not be correct, that above a certain level, executives are unlikely to be able to achieve anything more by their own efforts. Some companies are also wary about offering glittering prizes that are over-enticing and therefore misdirect executives into concentrating so much on exceeding their personal targets that the needs of the business are neglected. This happened quite often in the City in the heady days before 'Black Monday' (18 October 1987). Other companies worry, perhaps unnecessarily, about the detrimental effects on executives of wide fluctuations in earnings if there is no upper limit.

A further factor which has led to capping is the incidence of high rates of taxation. The 1988 budget, however, largely removed this factor and companies are becoming more willing to de-limit their incentive schemes.

Where the limit, if any, is fixed depends on the circumstances, especially the level of performance that an executive could achieve. The gap between the target level and the limit may be the same as the difference between the target and the starting point, say 10 per cent on either side of the target. In some schemes, however, the range from the target to the limit is wider at, say, 15 per cent, than the range from the starting point to the target of, say 10 per cent. This very much depends on the nature of the business and the ability of the management to lever results. Examples of alternative approaches are given in Table 11.1.

Table 11.1 *Incentive payment levels – alternative approaches*

Scheme	Performance range	levels %	Payment as a % of base salary	
			Alternative A	Alternative B
	Start	90	10	15
1	Target	100	20	30
	Upper limit	110	30	45
	Start	90	10	15
2	Target	100	20	30
	Upper limit	120	40	60

Some companies would regard the upper limits shown in Table 11.1 as being rather modest and limits as high as 200 per cent can be found.

The 1989 Monks Survey showed that the maximum payment made to board directors in the parent companies covered by the survey varied as follows:

Table 11.2 *Distribution of maximum bonus payments for board directors in parent companies*

	%
Under 20% of salary	5
20% and under 30%	17
30% and under 50%	22
50% or more	20
Other limit in IE	2
No formal limit	34

(*Source*: Monks Guide to performance related incentives for senior management 1989)

It is interesting to note that 34 per cent of these companies have no upper limit, and aggressive commercial organizations which set demanding performance targets for their executives are increasingly taking the view that incentive payments should not be capped. This is based on the conviction that the benefits to shareholders more than compensate for the high payments made, which would not in any case be given unless they were deserved. What, they ask, is the justification for an arbitrary limit on rewards for real achievements? But, in these circumstances, what has to be made absolutely clear to the executives concerned is that what they can earn from the scheme is risk money. The credibility of any scheme where payments are potentially high to shareholders, the public and other employees, depends on the strict application of the no profit – no payout principle.

Treatment of windfall profits

Even when a 'no limit' approach is adopted it may still be necessary to make provisos in the scheme for the treatment of any windfall profits arising from circumstances outside the control of executives, such as the sale of company assets or favourable changes in foreign exchange or interest rates. The decision on whether or not these 'acts of God' should generate incentive payments depends on the nature of the business and the likelihood of such windfalls occurring. This is a matter upon which a remuneration sub-committee of the board may be expected to adjudicate. The perceived need to curb excessive gains in these circumstances should be balanced against the demotivating effect of denying executives the incentive payment they believe they have earned. And it can be argued that extra payments for windfall gains are entirely justified if the system works both ways and executives have their payments reduced in line with unexpected or uncontrollable profit losses. Another argument is that if the circumstance was not covered in the original plans when the incentive targets were set, then they deserve their 'windfall' for making it happen.

If it is decided that earnings should be 'capped' when windfall profits arise, steps should be taken to reduce possible demotivating effects by spelling out in the rules of the scheme the circumstances in which this could happen.

Relationship between performance improvements and payments

The choice is between a straight line relationship between performance improvements and incentive payments, as shown in scheme 1 in Table 11.1, or an arrangement in which payments accelerate over a given threshold. Clearly, if targets become even more demanding above the level that executives can reasonably be expected to reach, then incentive payments should accelerate. Thus, if achieving 10 per cent above the target performance level were twice as difficult as raising performance from 90 per cent to 100 per cent, the gap between the target payment and the maximum should be twice the size of that between the target and the starting point so long as the shareholders benefit to the same extent.

Frequency of payments

Most executives incentive schemes pay out annually, after the annual results have been published. There are an increasing number of long-term incentives in the UK. Most of these are three-year plans, designed to reflect the reality that one year is often too short to reflect the success or not of a business strategy.

Tax planning

The main choices of payment vehicle are shares, share options and cash. Since 1988 – when highest rates of capital gains and income tax were set at 40 per cent – the scope for tax planning has reduced.

The timing of incentive or bonus payments can affect how much tax is paid on them. To minimize (but not avoid, which is, of course, illegal) the tax liabilities of executives who are in the higher tax bracket, tax advice should be sought (see also Chapter 18 which deals more fully with tax considerations).

Administering an incentive plan

The incentive plan should be set up by the Board. To ensure its integrity, its operation should be supervised by a remuneration committee which should be composed of non-executive directors, if they exist. They are there to ensure that the plan is run properly and that the shareholders' interests are protected.

The rules and procedures governing the plan should be set out in a short document given to all participants. From this they should be able to work out how their incentives are calculated and what they have to do to achieve certain payment levels.

The following points should be covered in the rule book:

- scheme objectives in relation to the corporate plan
- eligibility to join the scheme
- timing of payments
- treatment of leavers, voluntary and otherwise
- accounting standards used, indicating whether the scheme is related to the audited or to the management accounts
- a caveat which states that the scheme will be reviewed at regular intervals by the board and/or the remuneration committee to ensure that it is operating effectively and achieving its objectives.

(Examples of executive incentive schemes are given in Appendix P.)

Executive bonus schemes

As an alternative to a formal, highly structured and complicated incentive plan many companies, especially smaller ones, prefer to use the more flexible approach of an executive bonus scheme. The three main types of scheme are:

1. Profit pool.
2. Discretionary.
3. Personal target.

Profit pool bonus schemes

A profit pool plan sets aside a given percentage of pre-tax profit over an annually defined threshold. This is distributed pro-rata as a percentage of salary, as in the following example:

1. *Bonus pool*: set at five per cent of pre-tax profits over a 1988/9 threshold of £6m. Its total pre-tax profits are £8.8m, the pool is therefore £140,000.
2. *Salary cost*: the total cost of the basic salaries paid to executives in the scheme is £500,000.
3. *Basis for distribution*: the proportion of the bonus pool to total salary cost applied as a percentage of basic salary.
4. *Calculation*: Bonus pool (£140,000) × 100 ÷ Total salary cost (£500,000) = 28 per cent of salary for each participant.

This approach has the merit of simplicity. It can also be controlled from year to year by adjusting the threshold. But agreement on the formula or process to adjust the threshold can be difficult to achieve.

Discretionary bonus schemes

Some companies, expecially private ones, prefer to adopt a completely discretionary approach. This involves awarding bonuses simply on the basis of the opinion of the chief executive or the board, which may or may not be related to objective criteria. If there are no such criteria, there is a danger of favouritism creeping in – the link between achievement and reward is no longer clear and the scheme can have a positively demotivating effect, particularly in an autocratic culture. It can be difficult to justify large payments in such a scheme, and the danger is that the total pay package becomes uncompetitive. On the other hand, large payments for unclear reasons tend to be discounted by employees when they calculate the total value of their package.

Personal targets

Discretionary bonuses are often paid where companies do not want to be tied to an overall criteria and prefer an individual approach. To avoid the dangers of an entirely subjective scheme, some companies relate bonuses, especially for executives below board level, to the achievement of agreed personal targets.

Some schemes may operate on a purely individual basis with the overall limits of a bonus pool determined by the board, the size of which would be determined by the results obtained by the company. Guidelines are produced on how bonuses should be distributed, for example, to no more than X percentage of executives, and on a scale from Y to Z percentage depending on performance. These guidelines would be worked out by reference to the total fund available and control would be exercised to ensure that the guidelines were adhered to and that the total pay-out was not above the limit.

A more structured approach is to allocate units to executives which reflect performance in relation to targets or, in some schemes, in relation to age, service and seniority as well as 'value' to the firm. The total number of units allocated is divided into a bonus pool to give a unit value which is then distributed according to the number of units allocated to each individual. For example:

1. Size of bonus fund – £850,000.
2. Total number of units allocated – 1000 between 250 executives.
3. Value of unit – £850.
4. Allocation – an individual who earns three units for, say, achieving sales targets, would receive a bonus payment of 3 × £850 = £2550.

Long-term incentives

Incentives over periods of greater than one year were relatively rare but are becoming much more common. 1990 salary surveys show about 10 per cent of companies had cash long-term incentive schemes. The pressure for developing such schemes is the concern that annual schemes overfocus on the short term.

The traditional long-term incentive was the executive share option, but there has been increasing questioning of the incentive value these really have. The new long-term schemes are usually cash based, paying out over three years or longer. There are two main types:

- schemes for main board directors and possibly a limited number of top executives where direct measures of performance are felt to be more motivational than use of the share price
- schemes for subsidiary directors, who only have a limited impact on the group share price. Here schemes can be designed which reward long-term performance of the subsidiary. Schemes can be designed to mimic what an option scheme in the subsidiary would look like. This type of scheme can be highly motivational as the executives see the opportunity of significant capital accumulation based on the part of the business they impact upon.

The design process of long-term incentives follows a similar process to that of executive incentives discussed earlier in this chapter. The major addional decision is the choice between a one-off scheme or rolling cycles of schemes. Concern must also be given to the size of payment. This should be larger than – or at least comparable to – the annual scheme. The emphasis of the payment size and the incentive package must be on the long term, not short term. An example of a long-term incentive plan is given in Appendix P.

Incentives and bonuses for less senior staff

The merit payment systems described in Chapter 9 are still the most frequently used methods of relating pay to performance for less senior staff. There are, however, three other ways of providing incentives for these employees which are described below.

Target-based incentives

Target-based incentive schemes link the reward to the achievement of agreed targets within the employee's department over which the individual has real control: for example, completing a systems design project, achieving a quality improvement target, test launching a new product, developing a new product or service, finalizing a company training needs analysis. Incentives would only be paid if defined quality standards are achieved within a laid-down timescale.

Target-based incentive schemes may be applied to teams or individuals. The choice depends on whether the need is to promote and reward effective team-work or whether the emphasis in the firm is on motivating individual achievement.

An example of a target-based incentive plan for middle-managers is given in Appendix P.

Merit bonuses (see also Chapter 9)

Merit bonuses are lump sum, non-consolidated payments given to individuals to reward special achievements. They may be based on the overall rating given in a performance assessment. For example, those rated as 'outstanding' would be eligible for a bonus of, usually, somewhere between 5 and 10 per cent. Some companies allow for graduated payments so that on a five-point scale, those rated as A would get, say, a 10 per cent bonus while those rated B would get 5 per cent. It is advisable to incorporate control mechanisms in such schemes to ensure that rewards are truly related to merit and that the total cost is within pre-determined limits. Forced distribution guidelines are sometimes used in large companies which restrict A level bonuses to, say, 5 per cent of the total population and B level bonuses to, say, 10 per cent of the population.

Another use for the merit bonus is to provide rewards for people who are still performing well but who have reached the top of their salary scale and for whom little or no promotion opportunities exist. Such individuals can be very valuable, not only in performing their job reliably and well, but also in a mentoring or training role. The bonus therefore recognizes both their value and their loyalty to the company and the extra contribution they can make because of their experience.

But merit bonuses can demotivate if they are awarded arbitrarily or if they only go to the favoured few, leaving those who do not benefit with the not unreasonable feeling that the organization is dependent on ordinary mortals too, so why should they be left out?

Productivity payments

Shopfloor incentive and bonus schemes are outside the scope of this book but, because of changes in technology and the growth of single-status terms and conditions of employment (harmonization), the old distinction between white and blue collared worker is blurring and, in some organizations, is disappearing completely. For many of their employees, pay increases and incentives are being linked to the acceptance of increased flexibility (multi-skilling), adoption of new technology, and other moves designed to allow employers to respond to market and technological changes. The difference between these schemes and the so-called productivity deals of the 1970s is that they reward achievement when it has happened rather than offering payment up-front for productivity which may or may not materialize. As such, they are effectively target-based incentives, given to groups of employees in the same way as the target-related incentives for managers described earlier in this chapter.

The biggest danger of these schemes is that they institutionalize existing working practices and standards, and target only a small increase in productivity. It can be argued that they have contributed to the UK becoming internationally uncompetitive both in productivity and rates of pay. Well-designed schemes need to produce:

- high levels of productivity compared to the major national and international competitors
- high levels of value added per employee
- high levels of pay for real productivity improvements.

Branch incentive schemes

A growing number of retailers, banks and building societies have introduced branch incentive schemes. These organizations can have several hundred or even thousands of similar outlets, which all exist to deliver roughly the same organizational objectives and strategies.

Branch schemes should focus on the key measures that branch managers and staff can really influence and that relate to overall organization objectives, both short and long term. They should reinforce team/individual roles; they can also support interdependencies between service outlets and support centres. Many organizations are finding these schemes a useful tool through which to communicate the direction in which the organization is moving.

It is imperative that schemes are consistent with all the other performance messages at branch level, eg appraisal processes, promotion criteria, training. This is necessary to support clarity about what performance is in the branch.

To work effectively, schemes need targets that are realistic and accurate measurement systems. The timescale to implementation must accommodate the necessary changes to Management Information Systems and branch budgeting processes.

Schemes that capture real interest and motivate participants tend to have short time frames, for providing information about performances against target and for making payments, ie quarterly or half-yearly (not annual). They typically pay out to around 75 per cent of branches if the total organization has performed.

Profit related pay schemes

Details of the Government-sponsored profit related pay scheme are given in Appendix R.

Chapter 12

Salesforce Incentives

Payment systems for sales staff often differ fundamentally from other staff because of the behavioural assumptions about salesforce motivation. This is the area of 'ego-driven' individuals who, conventional wisdom has it, will only deliver acceptable performance if offered the 'carrot and stick' of substantial financial involvement. Recent research by the IPM's National Committee for Pay and Employment Conditions (to which one of the authors was a contributor – see bibliography) questioned some of these assumptions. It admitted however that, dubious as the stereotypes of the salesforce are, they are believed implicitly by most of the sales managers who devise sales incentive schemes, by the salesforce, and often by the salary administrators responsible for remuneration practice in this area.

Not surprisingly, this research found that this is one area where the top sales executive will have far more power over incentive scheme design and operation than the personnel department. Often the latter is forced, because it is less powerful in corporate terms, to accept and administer schemes which sit ill with remuneration policy for the rest of the staff and which have to be kept separate from them.

Basic design issues

In designing a suitable sales incentive scheme the following questions have to be answered:

- Are the performance measures appropriate?
- Are the territories or targets properly equalized so that staff with 'easy' sales patches or product lines do not have an unfair advantage over those working in areas or with merchandise where the going is tougher?
- Is the plan equitable between people performing at the same level and managed consistently?

Links with remuneration policy for other employees

For many employers it makes more sense to have a separate salary structure for sales staff. This should be designed to be competitive in relation to salesforce remuneration in the industry or sector. It will need to reflect the local, regional and hierarchical breakdowns required to run the sales operation effectively. These may or may not fit sensibly into existing company grading and pay structures. It is often difficult to match sales jobs with job evaluation schemes which have value factors that are irrelevant to the sales function. Where analysis of this relationship with the company job evaluation scheme shows a poor fit, as for example in areas such as data processing, it is better to establish a notional relationship or accept that there need not be one at all.

Merit reviews and annual progression may also need to be on a different basis. The organization may feel it is paying twice for the same performance if it operates both a merit payment scheme and a sales incentive plan. Or, it may decide that the incentive covers only the sales performance and that the merit review looks at wider issues than the bottom line. Whichever way this decision is determined, annual, or in a tight market, more frequent market-related adjustments should be made to keep basic salary levels competitive.

Types of salesforce remuneration plan

There are seven basic forms of salesforce remuneration:

1. *Salary only*: generally used either where the product being sold does not lend itself to incentive payments. For example, in some forms of capital equipment sales where identifying the 'seller' can be difficult; or where the use of incentives could be construed as unethical (eg pharmaceuticals); or where the company makes a decision that it will recruit and pay high basic salaries to exceptional salespeople, whose performance is subject to regular scrutiny and reward through the merit payment system. Where the 'salary only' approach is used, organizations may, nevertheless, award non-cash incentives to reward success in short-term sales campaigns. They may also have other rewards, such as all-employee profit sharing schemes to reinforce the messages of success.
2. *Salary and standard bonus*: this is basic salary plus a target-related bonus to be paid out at set levels in relation to the achievement of company sales targets. Bonus targets can be based on a formula related to sales or a range of agreed objectives and they might contain a discretionary element.
3. *Salary and individual bonus*: as above, but geared to the

achievement of individual targets. They can be a mixture of sales and other factors such as retaining customers, achieving a given percentage of new business, numbers of sales visits made in relation to a plan etc.

4. *Salary with standard bonus and commission*: where there is a bonus in relation to overall sales levels and other targets plus commission paid as a percentage of sales revenue. As with executive and other incentives, commission payments can be subject to 'accelerators'. That is, higher percentage payments are made once a given sales threshold has been met or 'decelerators' to control maximum earnings levels.
5. *Salary with individual bonus and commission*: as above, but where the bonus element is related to the achievement of individual targets – sales and non-sales.
6. *Salary plus commission*: where basic salary is set in relation to the market, and commission as a percentage of sales is paid in addition. In some cases basic salary can be set very low as an incentive to stay on the road and generate sales. As with the commission only approach described below, these schemes tend rapidly to sort out good sales staff from poor sales staff and cause the latter to resign and leave this type of work.
7. *Commission only*: the really tough end of the sales remuneration spectrum. This means that, typically, after a brief training and induction phase, the individual is out on his or her own – dependent on maintaining a high level of sales for survival. This approach has been commonly used in the selling of insurance and double glazing for example, but organizations who use it expect, and get, a very high drop-out rate with new sales people. A salesforce paid commission only is typically self-employed.

Sales bonus or commission schemes – advantages and disadvantages

Bonus schemes related to targets, or commission schemes where the payment is calculated as a percentage of sales, each have their advantages and disadvantages as described below.

Bonus schemes

Advantages

According to the IPM's research, the main advantages of bonuses over commission schemes are that they:

- permit flexible design – so enabling management to encourage and reward various types of individual or group behaviour

- provide for a basic salary element to cover basic needs thus, in accordance with Maslow's theory of motivation, freeing the representative to attain higher recognition needs through the bonus scheme
- enable payments to be timed to suit the business and its need to retain good staff
- provide some protection against fluctuations in third-party demand levels
- make the equalization of reward easier.

Disadvantages
The main disadvantages of bonus schemes are:

- the link between effort and reward can be weakened
- objectives may be unattainable or difficult to appraise
- where a group bonus pays at the average, it rewards good and poor performers equally
- they can be more complicated than commission schemes
- there can be a confusion between bonus and merit payments
- replacing one with the other can be demotivating unless the rationale of the change is properly communicated.

Many of these problems can be removed by careful planning and monitoring of whichever type of scheme is chosen.

Commission schemes

Advantages
The IPM research also found that commission schemes had certain advantages:

- pay is linked solely to sales volumes or profitability
- there is the maximum financial incentive
- only successful sales representatives will stay
- sales costs related to salaries vary with the measure of performance chosen
- where there is more than one product, they can offer greater flexibility by paying different commission rates to promote different products
- they are generally easy to understand and monitor
- payments can be closely linked to income received and so avoid the problem of tying up money in salaries in advance of receipts
- from the sales representative's point of view, commission schemes keep up with inflation because payments generally increase in line with product price rises
- they can allow the salesforce to be truly self-employed.

Disadvantages
Despite these advantages, the IPM researchers go on to point out some quite severe disadvantages:

- uncertain and fluctuating earnings can be a demotivator
- sales representatives can be tempted to act unethically by overloading customers with stock and pushing goods they may not need – this is potentially damaging to customer relations and the long-term stability of the business
- management has little financial control over earnings
- management has little disciplinary control
- loyalty to the organization can easily take second place to individual self-interest. Self-employed representatives have been known to use the sales area set out by one company to sell the products of another to supplement their income
- schemes may emphasize sales at any price rather than profitable sales
- non-selling services (merchandizing, stocking-up, maintenance, etc) are discouraged because they cost the individual money in terms of lost sales time
- incomes from commission schemes can exceed those of other, higher graded employees – if income exceeds that of sales managers, the problem can be compounded by promotion difficulties
- the greater the commission element, the more likely are sales representatives to be inflexible about sales territory divisions, calls to be made, non-selling services, etc
- lack of pay security can cause recruitment and retention problems, especially during an economic downturn when, ironically, companies need a high calibre sales team
- where commission is linked to sales turnover, price rises are automatically built into salesforce remuneration – internal relativity problems can ensue where price increases exceed pay rises.

The use of decelerators

Although, as we have shown, accelerators are used in commission schemes to reward additional sales, decelerators are also used. These produce a 'regressive' commission line, ie one which pays out a lower percentage once a given sales threshold is reached. The reasons are as follows:

(a) to avoid 'windfall' pay-outs;
(b) in circumstances where high sales are not directly attributable to extra sales effort;

(c) where the correlation between 'selling' the product to the customer and the size of the eventual order is low;
(d) if a maximum earnings level is thought necessary;
(e) to encourage new orders by reducing the commission value of repeat business;
(f) where there is a danger of sales exceeding productive capacity.

Adminstering sales incentives

Policy in the following areas needs to be set up at the start of a sales incentive scheme to ensure that it has the best chance of working effectively. Once the type of scheme has been selected it is necessary to:

1. Allocate sales territories and product lines carefully and formulate a policy on inter-area crediting.
2. Decide on the timing of payments which are designed to maximize staff retention by only paying out if staff are still in employment after a given period, say, six months.
3. Communicate the objectives of the scheme – with provision for regular reinforcement of these through meetings, newsletters, etc.
4. Establish a system for monitoring the scheme's operation and reviewing the rules if they are not meeting business needs.
5. Develop a policy on short-term incentives designed to reward achievement at the end of seasonal or other sales campaigns.

Non-cash incentives

The provision of various kinds of non-cash incentives to meet the needs of sales campaigns and other reward policies is now a multimillion pound business operation in the UK. It delivers everything from specially produced lapel badges and pens to holidays in the Bahamas.

The principal types of non-cash incentives available are:

1. *Luxury consumer goods*: available either directly or through catalogues catering for tastes from windsurfing to cut glass.
2. *Holidays*: of varying length and location depending on the size of reward required, so that employees can find somewhere that suits them.
3. *Car schemes*: recognizing exceptional performance by allowing top sales representatives to have, say, a more prestigious car such as a white BMW.
4. *Premium clubs*: set up to provide special rewards for top sales

representatives or a given number of high achievers at the end of a sales contest. Membership can be marked by anything from a special tie to a 'conference' on the Riviera.

Use of non-cash incentives for other staff

Severe market pressure and the search to find new reward systems for staff outside the salesforce now means that non-cash incentives are finding a wider use. They can, for instance, be used to reward project completion in the data-processing area, meeting a very tough production schedule, or, in the personnel area, to reward staff who have ensured that a sensitive redundancy exercise went according to plan.

When and how to use non-cash incentives

To get the maximum benefit from non-cash incentives, the following points may be useful:

1. *Beneficiaries*: decide whether it is better in terms of company practice and business needs to reward just the top performers or distribute rewards more evenly to recognize general achievement and reinforce the message that everyone is in with a chance.
2. *Publicity*: right from the outset, publicize the rewards and the means of achieving them and, at the end, give wide publicity to the 'winners'.
3. *The award ceremony*: make an occasion of it, say, a formal occasion where the chairman or managing director makes the presentation in front of the winners' colleagues. Local press coverage can be helpful as well as coverage in company magazines. The prize winners should be given as much personal recognition as possible and be made to feel the centre of things.

Problems

Where non-cash incentives reward short-term effort, care is needed to ensure that the 'prize-hunters' do not pursue the rewards to the detriment of longer-term objectives. Research in this area also suggests that it is unwise to let this approach overshadow the continuing need to have competitive basic salaries and cash incentives. Consumer goods should not replace pay to any serious extent. Their role should be just to provide additional recognition – a 'fillip' in the hope that this will increase performance. Poor administration of schemes and unwise selection of prizes and options can also cause problems, as can tactless handling of those unable to reach the standards required to get a prize. Finally, and more importantly, the tax implications of all non-cash incentives should be considered. There is little motivation to be had from being awarded, say, a video machine and then finding that tax is due on its purchase value with no company provision to cover the liability – see Chapter 19 (tax considerations).

Chapter 13

Other Cash Payments

To ensure a balanced set of remuneration policies, organizations often have to use one or more of a number of different additional payments to meet market needs. These can be divided into two categories:

1. Payments in response to market pressure.
2. Payments to reward special circumstances or working practices.

In times when there is a formal incomes policy, or to get special, subtle, market advantage, payments in the latter category can be, and certainly have been, used as responses to the market.

Market pressure responses

These are essentially lump sum payments or continuing allowances used to obtain competitive advantage in a tight labour market. They are used on recruitment and as 'top-ups', often called 'market premia', to basic salary – paid only to employees in scarce categories, whose basic salary will otherwise be contained within the organization's normal salary structure. They are now in widespread use in the UK both in the private and the public sector, but most of the thinking behind them has come from the United States.

The following are the most common forms of payment in this category:

1. *Golden hellos*: also called recruitment bonuses, 'up-front' or 'front-end' bonuses. These are payments to entice sought after individuals to join a particular employer. They can be paid as a lump sum on joining or as a phased bonus, sometimes over as much as a couple of years. Such payments have been used for graduates with rare specialisms: computer specialists, researchers, financial specialists and top executives likely to make an exceptional contribution to the business.

   These are no set formulae for determining these payments – they can run from quite large amounts, say, a year's salary, down to a few hundred pounds. At senior executive level, the offer of shares, usually using a 1984 Finance Act share option scheme to obtain maximum tax benefits, is also common.

Market premium payments can also be given as benefits: perhaps a larger or more exotic company car than is normal for the grade, a second car, special personal pension arrangements, housing assistance, additional relocation assistance etc. In conceding to demands for additional benefits, organizations need to think hard about the effects this may have on others who have the same rare specialisms, but have been in the job well before market pressure built up. Some adjustment to their reward package may have to be considered, therefore, to keep the team together. In addition, the tax implications of golden hellos should always be explored.

2. *Golden handcuffs*: these are payments given to staff to lock them in to the organization and prevent them being 'attracted away' by the competition. Again, they are being used in both the public and the private sector in the UK. They are used both as 'retention payments' for staff subject to severe market pressure and, more rarely, for keeping staff in departments that have been cut back by redundancy – to ensure that a core of the best people stays. 'Golden handcuffs' can take the form of phased lump sum payments, sometimes in the form of guaranteed bonuses, which may then be phased out if the market eases or circumstances change. They also commonly take the form of shares – especially at executive level – on the basis that equity participation breeds additional commitment to the business. Again, the tax implications of these provisions should be fully explored.
3. *London and large town allowances*: these are paid because of housing and other cost-of-living differentials. Most London employers either have a separate London allowance which is reviewed annually and paid as an addition to basic salary or, alternatively, they expect to pay extra on basic salary in response to local market pressure. Both Incomes Data Services and Industrial Relations Services report regularly on changing company practice in this area. Reward Regional Surveys report in detail – through local cost-of-living surveys – on the effects of changes in living costs including house prices.

Rewards for special circumstances or working practices

Golden handshakes

Golden handshakes are also discussed in the context of redundancy (see Chapter 17), and are essentially termination payments – usually substantial ones – paid typically to top executives to ensure that they leave with a financial cushion and without making any fuss. In size they tend to bear some notional relation to the unexpired period of the executive's contract where there is one. But for tax reasons this must never be stated in the contract. Where there is no fixed term contract, or where the company feels that, in addition to its statutory redundancy obligations it only needs to tide the individual over until a new job is found (enshrined in the legal concept of obligation to mitigate loss) – then a year's salary tends to be the maximum. But again there are no set rules. Lawyers are quite often involved in top executive 'separations' and the good ones are familiar with current practice as it is likely to apply to the case in question. Such payments are generally, for tax purposes, defined as compensation for loss of office. Payments to directors show up eventually in the accounts of public companies – something in which the press usually takes great interest. This should be borne in mind at the time the details of a separation are negotiated – a case for making any large payment the size it is should be prepared and it should be one that holds water for shareholders as well as curious journalists. Part of the separation 'handshake' package may also involve outplacement counselling to enable executives to decide what to do next with professional assistance and support.

Overtime payments

Overtime payments are made wherever the standard working week is exceeded on a regular basis for employees at supervisory level and below. In some union negotiated environments and in other special circumstances it may be extended to the lower levels of management. But it is usually implicit if not explicit in most management contracts that managers will work whatever hours can be reasonably required to ensure the fulfilment of their responsibilities. Sometimes exceptional management overtime (eg in business start-ups or during special projects) is rewarded by one-off bonuses.

For staff working overtime and being paid for it, the levels of payment vary in relation to whether the work is done on weekdays, at the weekends or on National Holidays. Payments currently vary from time to time-and-a-half (sometimes after a minimum threshold of overtime working, say, eight hours a month) on weekdays to time-and-a-half on Saturdays and higher multiples for Sundays and National Holidays. People who maintain essential services on Christmas Day expect very high rewards – as high as four times the normal rate – as compensation for being away from their families and sometimes in addition to time off in lieu.

The payment of overtime pay is generally held to be reasonable as long as the nature and amount of overtime working is strictly controlled. People do not work well and consistently if excessive overtime is worked and they should never be allowed to take on too much to supplement what may be, or perceived to be, an inadequate basic salary.

Shift pay and unsocial hours payments

These are given where the pattern of working hours differs from the typical working day. They are typically given to computer staff, production employees, various medical staff, broadcasting employees and others where 24-hour cover for services is essential. Payments relate to the shift patterns worked, to associated time-off arrangements and to market practice in the sector in question. As with overtime, care should be taken to ensure that working practices are sensible and not geared to propping up otherwise uncompetitive pay rates. Buying out practices that have got out of hand is both difficult and expensive.

Attendance bonuses

Attendance bonuses are generally paid to categories of staff where absenteeism is a problem and the organization wishes to encourage more consistent attendance. They can be useful where the work itself or the environment is unpleasant and it is not within the employer's power to improve this. Many employers reject the idea because they consider it is a payment for what is already a contractual obligation which merely gives employees the opportunity to earn a bit more 'by getting out of bed earlier'. Such employers have not always been so scathing however, in the face of severe market pressure during times of national incomes policy; or indeed in the face of a very tight local market where they need to resort to payments of this mind to get the edge.

Clothing allowances

Clothing allowances are paid to staff who need to buy special clothing for work where the company does not provide uniforms. Such payments are market-related and should be reviewed for tax implications. Dry cleaning vouchers are sometimes also provided as part of the policy.

Christmas bonuses and thirteenth-month payments

These are normally paid as a matter of tradition in some sectors. Christmas bonuses tend to be relatively small unless they contain a performance element. The essential purpose is generally to reward loyalty and recognize this by helping with the extra costs of the season. Thirteenth- or even fourteenth-month payments have come to the UK from Europe. They are found among organizations with European parents where home country policy has been translated into local practice. Such payments tend to be given as 'double month' salaries paid either at Christmas or in the summer or sometimes divided between the two. A UK variation is the payment of an annual salary on a four-weekly basis, giving thirteen equal payments in the year.

Payments for qualifications

These are used by companies to reward success such as passing accounting, actuarial, legal, managerial or other professional and technical examinations to recognize their added value to the organization. Such payments are generally given as lump sum payments, but can be given as pay increases – sometimes as part of a reward system linked to competency development. Where these payments are made to people who have recently left full-time education, they can fill a useful motivational 'gap'. The wait between annual reviews can seem a long time to someone in their teens (which is one of the reasons why increases for junior staff are often paid on a six-monthly basis).

Chapter 14

Executive Share Ownership Schemes

A stake in the company

One of the major ways of increasing executive identification with the aims of a business is to give executives shares or share options. As shareholders or potential shareholders, with the chance to benefit from the organization's success and achieve capital accrual beyond the scope of pay alone, their perception of their role can change. They can become 'owners' rather than just paid employees and this can have a beneficial effect on their commitment to the long-term future of the business. So goes the argument for executive share schemes, backed by the experience of the many organizations who have adopted this approach as a key element in executive remuneration.

Executive share schemes normally take the form of share options. Essentially the rules of these schemes provide for executives to be given an option to buy shares at a future date for their market price at the time the option was granted. Provided that the share price appreciates, the individual makes a profit when the option is exercised and the shares sold. The profit is the difference between the purchase price when the option was granted and the new market price for which shares can be sold at the end of the option period less any tax due on the capital sum. The prevailing tax regime can have a major effect on the attractiveness of share options.

Why entitlements have grown

In the years that have passed since the 1984 Finance Act provided a favourable tax climate for Inland Revenue approved executive share option schemes, an overwhelming majority of major UK public companies have introduced such schemes. They have done so because, like the Chancellor of the Exchequer who introduced the legislation, they believe in the value of these schemes as motivators. In his budget speech in 1984, the Chancellor said: 'I am convinced that we need to do more to attract top calibre company management and to increase the incentives and motivation of existing executives and key personnel by linking their reward to performance.' Boards of directors are, not unnaturally, attracted by the prospect of doing well personally out of their company's success; but they have also gone for share options because they saw their competitors introducing them and felt that these should also be part of their company's remuneration package. For those few who got in early after the legislation and exercised their options ahead of 'Black Monday' in October 1987, substantial capital gains have been possible, and widely reported in the press.

In the bear market that followed 'Black Monday', views on share options were more mixed and perhaps more realistic about the ups and downs in the system. There is however, no sign of option schemes going out of favour or being abandoned and new forms of share option are being developed based mainly on US models to meet particular needs. Tax-approved share options have been available in the US since 1945 and in the UK since 1984. With the widespread operation of these plans, a number of serious shortcomings have emerged. These shortcomings have been identified by compensation experts on both sides of the Atlantic, and variations are emerging that attempt to match shareholder requirements more closely to the extensive reward package.

Building executive commitment and loyalty

Most companies coming to the market for the first time include details of an executive share option scheme in their prospectus, usually alongside an all-employee share scheme. This is a sign to potential shareholders that the organization is a well-managed company where executives have a stake in the future success of the business with a remuneration package structured accordingly. It also shows that the top management team should be 'locked in' by the handcuffs of the share scheme as the company goes for growth. Directors are also, it is thought, more likely to stay loyal to a company in which they have options in difficult times in the hope that things will come right by the time they come to exercise their options. Share schemes should make beneficiaries less vulnerable to approaches from executive search consultants – or at least make them very expensive to lure away. Potential employers may baulk at having to buy out existing share options by paying substantial 'golden hellos' to compensate for the lost benefit – probably in addition to granting new options to the executive in question who will negotiate for them as an expected part of the remuneration package.

Types of executive share ownership scheme

In many organizations, directors have shares as part-owners of the business. The Sainsbury family, Lord Weinstock, Lord Hanson, and 'Tiny' Rowland, to name but a few high-profile UK businessmen at the top of public companies, all gain far more income from their dividends as shareholders than they do from the earnings figures which appear in their companies' annual reports. This is also true of many smaller organizations where the income deriving from ownership merges with income from employment. Apart from executive shareholdings which exist as the result of part-ownership, directors and senior managers may also be granted shares under various forms of option scheme.

There are three principal forms of executive share option schemes in the UK:

1. *Inland Revenue approved schemes* – taking full advantage of the 1984 Finance Act provisions and making up the vast majority of current UK schemes (see also Chapter 18 on tax considerations).
2. *Unapproved share options* – either those introduced prior to 1984 or running in addition to an approved scheme to provide additional potential shareholdings.
3. *Phantom stock plans* – set up in organizations where no shares or no further shares are available for distribution, now or in the future. These are essentially a form of deferred incentive based on a notional share issue and linked to the share price of the company.

The shortcomings that have been identified with option plans are that:

- the options as currently issued are not true long-term incentives
- the options pay no regard to long-term interest rates or inflation
- the options are not affected by dividends or demergers and therefore do not reflect total shareholder return.

To deal effectively with these shortcomings and to produce plans that reward executives in line with long-term shareholder returns, is a challenge that has been taken up by US and UK compensation experts. Professor 'Bud' Crystal of UC Berkeley has proposed a sophisticated phantom plan linking to long-term share values and dividend payments in what is known as the 'Crystal Plan'. Perhaps more practically, in the UK we have newly developed approaches such as the 'Cockman Combined Plan' which combines options that can only be exercised after a seven-year period to a restricted share plan that accumulates the 'dividends' on the option shares. Both approaches are specially designed to overcome the shortcomings of conventional option plans.

Apart from the technicalities of tax management, for which specialist advice is usually necessary, the administration of all forms of executive share schemes tends to run along similar lines.

External controls

The final entitlements granted under approved executive share option schemes are closely affected by Inland Revenue requirements for tax relief and, in the case of quoted Public Limited Companies (PLCs) with institutional shareholders, by the guidelines of the Investment Protection Committees (IPCs). All share schemes for directors and employees, other than phantom stock plans (which are, as we have explained, really deferred incentives) must, in the UK, be approved by shareholders in accordance with Stock Exchange rules for listed and USM companies. The IPCs represent the institutional shareholders, but also speak for the interests of shareholders as a whole. Their shareholding is normally sufficient in most PLCs to secure observance of their guidelines. The two main IPCs are the British Insurance Association and the National Association of Pension Funds. Their guidelines apply to both approved and unapproved schemes, and the principal objective is to limit the extent to which the shareholders' equity is diluted. The guidelines have not always been welcomed and have already been modified twice since 1984 (notably in response to proposed changes by the Burton Group) to reflect changing company practice. It is also clear that individual companies, usually with the help of specialist advisers, have successfully negotiated modifications to suit special circumstances – as long as they could convince the IPCs that this remained in the shareholders' interests.

Factors to be taken into account when introducing a scheme

Employers considering the introduction of an executive share option scheme will therefore need to be sure they obtain a full understanding of:

1. The tax position and requirements for gaining Inland Revenue approval.
2. Stock Exchange rules.
3. The effect of current IPC guidelines on potential entitlements.
4. Market practice in their industry or sector.
5. Which issues they will need to monitor to ensure that practice remains competitive.

Executive share options – key policy decisions on entitlements

The place of options in the remuneration package

For as long as share options are given to executives because they have reached the board rather than on a performance-related basis, there will always be a difference of opinion as to whether they are a benefit or an incentive. Like company cars provided on the basis of status rather than job need, share options can create a major distortion in remuneration differentials. The total earnings potential of those with options is substantially greater – and therefore results in a higher differential than a simple difference in salary scale would produce.

Options are certainly perceived by executives as a sign of success – in the same way as a luxurious company car. Share options are thus also a form of recognition for achievement, and well worth having if such recognition breeds commitment.

Deciding entitlements

For approved schemes, the Inland Revenue rules set a maximum multiple of earnings that can be granted in the form of share options; unapproved or phantom stock plans are, of course, free of these rules. But the Investment Protection Committee rules also affect potential entitlements by limiting the amount of the organization's share capital that can be allocated to options. These will, of course, not just affect the first grant of options under a new scheme, but will have to be complied with when schemes are extended. Companies need to ensure that they will have shares available to grant under option when new top executives are appointed.

Within these constraints companies therefore have to decide:

1. Whether to give the same entitlement to all directors.
2. Whether to differentiate on the basis of status, the need to retain key individuals or to recognize particular achievements or, indeed, length of service.
3. How large a differential to make between the chief executive and the rest of the board or others picked out for special recognition.
4. Whether to grant options or permit their exercise only when agreed individual or corporate performance targets have been met.
5. Whether to extend the scheme to other key executives outside the board whose services are highly valued and whose long-

Outline of Executive Share Option Scheme

SCOPE	Non-transferable options to acquire shares, granted and exercised within ten years.
GRANT OF OPTIONS	
Whom Invited	Full-time directors and executives selected by board.
When	Within N weeks of announcing annual or half-yearly results.
Option Price	Middle market price at date of grant (or nominal value, if higher) – not payable until option is exercised – subject to adjustment on fair and reasonable terms if capital is varied, eg by a scrip issue.
Fee For Grant	Nominal (£1) or nil.
Individual Limit	Aggregated share values, at market price at time of grant, not to exceed four times the individual's annual emoluments. (The individual's quota of options under this scheme to be reduced if options exercised under an earlier scheme and vice versa).
Company Limited	The aggregated value of shares as above, for all options granted under this and earlier executive schemes not to exceed five per cent of the company's total equity, or, together with company-wide share schemes, ten per cent.
EXERCISE OF OPTION	
General Rule[1]	Not before three years or after ten years from date of grant.
Death[1]	Within a year of death by deceased's nominated representative but not after ten years from date of grant.
Severance[1]	
(a) Redundancy, incapacity, retirement, take-over, liquidation	Within X months (normally less than a year) and before ten years.
(b) Otherwise	At board's discretion. In the event of option lapsing on loss of office, no compensation payable for loss of option rights.

SHARES

Company to keep available unissued shares to permit exercise of options. These shares to rank *pari passu* with other shares issued by company at time of allotment. Adjustments to be made as necessary on variation of company's capital.

ADMINISTRATION

The main features of the scheme cannot be amended in main outlines without shareholders' approval. Administration in hands of board (aided by Compensation Committee in some cases).

[1] Options exercised outside these time limits would not attract tax relief under the Finance Act, 1984.

Figure 14.1 *A typical Public Limited Company approved scheme*
Source: Incomes Data Services Top Pay Unit

term commitment to the company ought to be secured in some way.

6. The policy on death of scheme participants or severance by redundancy, retirement, take-over, liquidation or misconduct.
7. Whether the new approaches, such as those being developed in the US and UK initiatives, eg the Cockman Combined Plan, should be used instead of conventional option plans.

These decisions will normally be the task of the non-executive remuneration committee of the board – part of its role in supervising share option arrangements and safeguarding shareholders' interests. This committee will need to take advice from the organization's financial, legal and tax advisers to ensure that scheme rules comply with any regulations affecting them, are tax-efficient, and reflect best practice in this complex area.

An outline of the main rules to be covered by an approved share option scheme is given in Figure 14.1.

It was always the intention of the 1984 Finance Act that share options be used on a discretionary basis. There is nothing in its provisions which prevent the grant of options to, say, a brilliant research and development manager, a key sales executive or other specialists making a major contribution to company success. In reality, however, survey evidence from a number of reputable sources (Monks Publications, Hay, IDS Top Pay Unit) shows that the first post-1984 options were granted by boards of directors to themselves on a non-performance-related basis. By the late 1980s, however, this pattern was beginning to change, and performance measures were being used such as growth in earnings per share, a place in *The Times* Top 1000 companies and other signs of profitability and success.

Communicating the benefits

In common with other remuneration policies, the motivational effect of share options can be strongly affected by the way in which the new policy is communicated. Bear in mind that any share options granted to directors will be shown in the company accounts so that secrecy is impossible. This could cause problems if any directors are excluded, so steps should be taken in advance to ensure that there are no unpleasant surprises.

Options are valuable to executives, even though they may incur no costs in the books of the employing company. Current practice in the US is to quantify the value of options using the well-known 'Black–Scholes' option pricing model, and to treat this as part of remuneration together with basic pay and bonus. This approach has not been adopted in the UK, but many companies want to communicate the value of options to employees so that they appreciate the worth of the grant. The 'Judes' option pricing model was published in *Accountancy Age* in August 1990, taking account of tax rates and option granting practice (something that Black-Scholes ignores). It is expected that organizations will increasingly use the Judes model as a basis for communicating with employees (see Appendix R).

Corporate PEPs

Personal Equity Plans (PEPs) were first introduced in 1986 to foster wider shareholding by small investors on a tax-effective basis. Sold by high street banks, building societies, insurance companies and other financial institutions, they were not initially a great success. They have, however, grown in popularity as the permitted investment in them has increased (to £6000 pa in 1990) and the rules surrounding them have simplified and relaxed. PEPs are based on the following principles:

- contributions to a plan can be monthly or annual within the current prescribed limits;
- contributions are invested by the plan managers in shares in listed companies held for members;
- dividends are exempt from income tax and can either be reinvested to buy more shares or paid out;
- share disposals are exempt from capital gains tax – gains can be used to buy more shares or paid out;
- there is no minimum holding period other than the 'Plan Year' for obtaining tax benefits.

Corporate PEPs confine shareholdings to a single specified share and can be used to offer both employees and outside shareholders the tax-effective benefits of such plans. Within the organization, corporate PEPs are effectively employee share purchase plans. Their numbers are growing and include companies such as ASDA Group, Bass, Glaxo, Reed International, South West Water and Lonrho. By October 1990 there were over 40 major UK-listed companies with plans, typically those with a firm belief in the value of wider employee share ownership as well as an eye to providing extra tax-effective components to the remuneration package – albeit a component to which employees contribute themselves. Plan managers such as CC&P Trustees (who were first in the field), Bradford and Bingley and a growing number of others have been able to offer real savings over the administration cost of PEPs available to individual shareholders from high street sources.

Corporate PEPs cannot be introduced without professional advice from a reputable source. If they are to create the increased identification with shareholders' interests, which must be a major motivation for introducing them, the timing and communication of implementation will be critical to success.

Corporate TESSAs?

From January 1991 the Tax Exempt Special Savings Account (TESSA) route can be used to help employees finance share purchase in a tax effective manner. Such schemes are inevitably in their infancy, but could be set up to help fund share purchase in the range of employee share ownership plans currently available. Again reputable professional advice should be sought when considering implementation.

SAYE share option schemes

Following the 1980 Finance Act and sometimes called 'Sharesave' schemes, 'save as you earn' share option schemes enable employees to purchase shares in their employer through a treasury nominated savings authority within defined limits. Such schemes are a form of financial participation commonly implemented when executive share options are introduced and, perhaps for this reason, their use is widespread. Professional advice is normally required for implementation.

ESOPs

An ESOP (Employee Share Ownership Plan) is an employee benefit trust linked to a share participation scheme. The trust receives contributions from the company or borrows money, and then buys shares in the company which are allocated to employees. In 1989 the UK government introduced legislation which gave statutory recognition to ESOPs, and in 1990 a rollover relief for capital gains tax was added. Statutory ESOPs are subject to quite onerous conditions and so far most UK ESOPs have been set up on a non-statutory basis. This seems set to change. Again, ESOPs are an area where professional advice is needed for implementation.

Chapter 15

Profit Sharing

Profit sharing is a plan under which an employer pays to eligible employees, as an addition to their normal remuneration, special sums in the form of cash or shares in the employer related to the profits of the business. The amount shared is determined either by an established formula, which may be published, or entirely at the discretion of management. Profit sharing schemes are generally extended to all employees of the company.

Objectives of profit sharing

Most companies which operate profit sharing schemes have one or more of the following objectives in mind:

- to encourage employees to identify themselves more closely with the company by developing a common concern for its progress
- to stimulate a greater interest among employees in the affairs of the company as a whole
- to encourage better co-operation between management and employees
- to recognize that employees of the company have a moral right to share in the profits they have helped to produce
- to demonstrate in practical terms the goodwill of the company towards its employees
- to reward success in businesses where profitability is cyclical.

It is generally recognized that schemes which share profits according to some universal formula among all or most employees will not provide any real incentive because they fail to satisfy the three basic requirements of an incentive scheme, namely:

(a) that the reward should bear a direct relation to the effort;
(b) that the payment should follow immediately or soon after the effort;
(c) that the method of calculation should be simple and easily understood.

Types of schemes

The main types of profit sharing schemes are:

1. *Cash* – a proportion of profits is paid in cash direct to employees. This is the traditional and still the most popular approach.
2. *Stock* – a proportion of profits is paid in shares. This is much less popular, especially since the advent of the approved deferred share trust scheme with its considerable tax advantages.
3. *Approved deferred share trust (ADST)* – the company allocates profit to a trust fund which acquires shares in the company on behalf of employees.
4. *Mixed schemes* – an ADST scheme is sometimes offered in addition to a cash scheme, or the latter is made available to staff before they are eligible for ADST shares, or as an alternative to ADST shares.

In addition, the British government introduced in 1987 its profit-related pay (PRP) scheme which provides income tax relief for approved schemes (details of this are given in Appendix N). However, despite flexibility introduced in 1989, this scheme has not so far been greeted with great enthusiasm because of its rather rigid nature. It has been adopted mainly by smaller organizations. A survey of profit sharing in 356 firms published by the Glasgow University Centre for Research into Industrial Democracy and Participation revealed that in two-thirds of the survey firms which operated profit sharing, the most popular scheme, especially among the smaller firms, was the simple cash-based option. The ADST type scheme is, however, gaining in popularity. Profit sharing was much more common among US-based companies (64 per cent) than their European counterparts (29 per cent), and the schemes were more prevalent in London and the South than in the Midlands and the North.

Cash schemes

The main characteristics of typical cash schemes can be analyzed under the following headings, which are discussed below:

(a) eligibility;
(b) formula for calculating profit shares;
(c) method of distributing profit shares;
(d) amount distributed;
(e) timing of distribution.

Eligibility
In most schemes all employees except directors are eligible. The normal practice is to require one year's service to be completed before a share in profits can be received. Profit shares are then usually paid in relation to the pay earned or the time served between the date on which one year's service was completed and the date on which the profit shares are paid.

Formulae for calculating profit shares
There are three basic approaches to calculating profit shares. The first is to use a predetermined formula for distributing a fixed percentage of profits. This formula may be published to staff so that the company is committed to using it. The advantages of this approach are that it clarifies the relationship between company profits and the amount distributed and demonstrates the good faith of management. The disadvantages are that it lacks flexibility and the amount paid out may fluctuate widely in response to temporary changes in profitability.

The second approach is for the board to determine profit shares entirely at its own discretion without the use of any predetermined or published formula. The decision is based on a number of considerations, including the profitability of the company, the proportion of profits that it is felt should reasonably be distributed to employees, estimates of the expectations of employees about the amount of cash they are going to receive and the general climate of industrial relations in the company. This is the more common approach and its advantages are that it allows the board some flexibility in deciding the amount to be distributed and does not commit it to expenditure over which it has no control. Random fluctuations can be smoothed out and the profit sharing element of remuneration can be adjusted easily in relation to other movements in pay within the company. The disadvantage is that a secret formula or the absence of a formula appears to contradict one of the basic reasons for profit sharing: the development among employees of a firmer commitment to the company because they can identify themselves more clearly with its successes and appreciate the reasons for its set-backs. The scheme is no longer a completely realistic profit sharing device if employees feel that they are insufficiently rewarded for improved performance or insulated from reverses. These arguments against flexibility are powerful ones but, on balance, a flexible approach is to be preferred because it does not commit the company to distributing unrealistically high sums when profits are shared out.

The third approach is a combination of the first and second methods. A formula exists in the sense that a company profit threshold is set below which no profits will be distributed. A maximum limit is set on the proportion of profits that will be distributed, for example, five per cent and/or that percentage of salary that will be distributed as a profit share, for example, ten per cent.

Methods of distributing profit shares

The main ways of distributing profit shares in cash schemes are to:

(a) distribute profits as a percentage of basic pay with no increments for service. This is a fairly common arrangement and those who adopt it do so because they feel that profit shares should be related to the individual contribution of the employee, which is best measured by pay. Service increments are rejected because the level of pay received by an individual should already take into account the experience he or she has gained in the company;

(b) distribute profits as a percentage of earnings with payments related to length of service. This approach is also frequently used and its advocates argue that it will ensure that loyalty to the company will be suitably encouraged and rewarded. They claim that to rely on pay as the sole arbiter of profit shares would be unjust because many valuable employees have, through no fault of their own, limited opportunities to move out of their present occupation or grade;

(c) distribute profits in proportion to pay and some measure of individual performance. This approach is rare below board level because of the difficulty of measuring the relationship between profits and performance and because it is considered that individual effort should be rewarded directly by performance-related pay or promotion;

(d) distribute profits as a fixed sum irrespective of earnings or service. This is completely egalitarian but rare.

The choice of approach is usually between distributing profit shares either in relation to pay or in relation to pay and service. The arguments for and against each approach are finely balanced but there is a good case for providing some uplift for longer service staff in any situation where a company relies on its experienced staff to contribute their specialized skills and knowledge to its success, and cannot ensure that its normal policies for paying merit increments or promoting staff will adequately reward their loyalty to the organization.

Amount distributed

A survey conducted by Incomes Data Services in 1986 revealed that rather more than half of the companies surveyed leave the amount to be distributed to 'directors' discretion'. Others provide limits within which the directors decide. A maximum of five per cent of profits is typical, but this may only be paid if it is triggered by profits reaching a defined level. At British Home Stores, for example, there is a maximum of five per cent of profit, providing profits exceed £23 million.

Other surveys into the amounts distributed in British profit sharing schemes have indicated that the proportion of pay shared out can vary from as little as two per cent to 20 per cent or more. The Glasgow University survey showed that in 60 per cent of the firms surveyed which had profit sharing schemes, the share amounted to less than six per cent of pay. Ideally, however, the share should be somewhere between five and ten per cent of pay in order to be meaningful without building up too much reliance on the amount to be distributed.

Timing of distribution

Most schemes distribute profits annually, although a few share out profits twice a year. Distribution is usually arranged to fall in good time for either the summer holidays or Christmas.

Approved deferred share trust (ADST) schemes

The basic rule for an ADST scheme, which must be followed to obtain the tax concessions in the 1978 (as amended) Finance Act are as follows:

1. Schemes must operate through a trust set up for this purpose, and trustees must be appointed to run it. Where there is a group of companies, a single scheme can be set up by the controlling company to cover all the employees of the group.
2. The company must make cash payments to the trustees, who use this money to buy shares in the company. The shares are held by the trustees but are set aside for the individual employees taking part in the scheme.
3. The shares must be part of the ordinary share capital of the company which has set up the scheme, or of its controlling company. They must have the same rights to dividends and bonus issues and so on as other ordinary shares, but the company is allowed to make its own arrangements about voting rights.
4. Employees must agree to leave their shares in the scheme with the trustees for at least two years.
5. The value of the shares set aside for any employee in any one tax year must not exceed a certain limit. At present the limit is

£2,000 or ten per cent of an employee's earnings, whichever is the greater, subject to a ceiling of £6,000.

6. Anyone who has been a full-time employee of the company for five years must be allowed to join the scheme. In addition the company can allow part-time employees and those with less than five years' service to join the scheme.
7. All employees within a scheme must take part on similar terms – the scheme cannot exclude or favour particular individuals or certain groups of employees.
8. Shares cannot be set aside for an employee more than 18 months after he or she has left the company. There are also restrictions on employees taking part in more than one scheme.
9. Employees receive the dividends from shares which are held on their behalf. The dividends are taxed in the normal way, the final amount of tax depending on the employee's total income.
10. Employees cannot normally sell their shares during the first two years they are held in trust. Subsequently, if the rules of the particular scheme permit, they can be sold, but there may be income tax payable on the proceeds.
11. If the shares are held for over five years, there is no tax to pay. If the shares are sold early, tax is payable on either their value at the date they were set aside, or on the proceeds of the sale, whichever is lower.
12. When an employee sells shares he or she may be liable to capital gains tax on the difference between the sale of proceeds and the value of the shares at the time they were set aside for him. But tax will not be payable unless net gains in any year exceed the exempt amount for that year.
13. If an employee dies, the shares may be sold and there will be no income tax payable, irrespective of how long the shares have been held.
14. If employees lose their jobs because of injury, disability or redundancy, or if they reach state pensionable age, their shares may be sold immediately, however long they have been held. If the shares have been held for less than five years, income tax is paid as if the five-year period had been completed.
15. If employees leave for any other reason, their shares cannot be sold until they have been held for two years. Whatever the reason for the employees' departure, they can choose to leave their shares within the scheme.
16. The scheme has to be cleared with the Inland Revenue and the company's shareholders in advance.

Employees' attitudes

The Industrial Participation Association (IPA) recently questioned 2,700 employees in 12 companies about their attitudes to profit sharing. The following are extracts from the survey:

Table 15.1 *Attitudes to profit sharing – Industrial Participation Association*

	Agree strongly	Agree	Don't know	Disagree	Disagree strongly
	%	%	%	%	%
1 Profit sharing created a better attitude in the firm	10	55	16	18	1
2 It is popular because people like to have the bonus	24	69	4	3	–
3 It strengthens people's loyalty to the firm	6	41	12	34	2
4 It makes people try to work more effectively so as to help the firm to be more successful	6	45	15	31	3
5 It is good for the company and its employees	14	72	11	3	–

The IPA believes that the survey 'suggests that profit sharing does significantly improve employee attitudes and employee views of their company'. They reach this view essentially by adding together the percentages recorded under 'Agree Strongly' and 'Agree'.

However, in the Incomes Data Services 1986 study of profit sharing, the comment was made that:

> 'another interpretation would be to add up all the responses except those under 'Agree Strongly', the one clear positive statement. This would suggest that most employees do not have a particularly positive attitude.'

Of course, employees like the cash, but their gratitude to the company is probably short-lived. Company profits are remote figures to people in the offices and on the shop-floor. They will express some interest in their size, because it affects the hand-out, but the idea of working harder to generate more profit for someone else will not necessarily appeal to them.

Profit-related pay

Details of the Government's profit-related pay scheme are given in Appendix Q. Introduced in 1987, by December 1990 there were 1,270 schemes covering only 267,000 employees. An important reason for this lack of interest is that employees find it difficult to relate their efforts to the relatively remote concept of profitability.

Benefits of profit sharing

Profit sharing and profitability

A survey carried out by Wallace Bell and Charles Hanson in 1985–1986 sought to establish a correlation between profit sharing and profitability. 113 profit sharing companies and 301 non-profit sharing companies were surveyed and their performance compared on the basis of nine economic ratios over a period of eight years. Taking the composite results of all 414 companies, the average performance of the profit sharers over the eight years was better than that of the non-profit sharers on every one of the nine economic ratios used. And taking an average of averages, the average of ratios of the profit sharers was 27 per cent higher than those of the non-profit sharers. Of course, as Bell and Hanson say, the profit sharing companies were not better just because they had profit sharing. It was because they were good companies that they introduced profit sharing.

The particular features of how these companies achieved success were that managers:

- had clear and defined objectives and the ability to harness the resources needed to achieve them
- recognized that their most important resource is people
- saw employees not in terms of 'them and us', as adversaries, but as part of a team that should be working together for the success of the enterprise and sharing in its success
- were able to generate a reciprocal attitude among the employees and thus overcome the 'them and us' feelings that are found equally, and sometimes more strongly, among employees towards management
- were able to generate a commitment to success.

Profit sharing and industrial relations

The Glasgow University survey referred to earlier expressed the more pessimistic view that the influence of profit sharing on industrial relations is marginal. The researchers concluded that profit sharing was used by employers as an effort-reward operation and not as an attempt to involve employees more closely in the decision-making apparatus. Yet, the evidence that profit sharing does increase effort hardly exists at all and that is simply because, as was mentioned earlier, the link between effort and reward is so tenuous. What, therefore, is the point of having a profit sharing scheme if it is not used to increase productivity by means of involving employees and mounting a communications campaign pointing out how *they* benefit from increased output and profitability?

Conclusions

It is worth noting that a number of companies have introduced profit sharing primarily because they feel that it is their duty to share their prosperity with their employees. If this view is held, then any uncertainty about the benefits arising from profit sharing is not an argument against its introduction. It is, of course, possible to take the opposite view: that profits are the wages of capital and that a company is not under any moral obligation to share profits with its employees, although it has the duty of treating them fairly and providing them with the rewards, benefits and conditions of employment that are appropriate to the contribution they make.

For anyone contemplating the introduction of profit sharing, or wondering whether to continue an existing scheme, the fundamental question is, 'do you consider that, in addition to all the benefits already provided by the company to its employees, it has a moral obligation to share its prosperity with them?' If the answer to this question is 'yes', a profit sharing scheme is what you want. If the answer is 'no', there may still be good reasons for considering profit sharing. But alternative means of rewarding employees and increasing their identification with the company (as described elsewhere in this book) may well deserve attention.

Part 5

Employee Benefits and Total Remuneration

Chapter 16

Employee Benefits

Definition

Employee benefits are elements of remuneration given in addition to the various forms of cash pay. They provide a quantifiable value for individual employees, which may be deferred or contingent like a pension scheme, insurance cover or sick pay, or may provide an immediate benefit like a company car. Employee benefits also include elements which are not strictly remuneration, such as annual holidays.

The term 'fringe benefits' and 'perks' (perquisites) are sometimes used derogatively, but should be reserved for those employee benefits which are not fundamentally catering for personal security and personal needs.

Objectives

The objectives of the employee benefits policies and practices of an organization should be:

- to increase the commitment of employees to the organization
- to provide for the actual or perceived personal needs of employees, including those concerning security, financial assistance and the provision of assets in addition to pay, such as company cars and petrol
- to demonstrate that the company cares for the needs of its employees
- to ensure that an attractive and competitive total remuneration package is provided which both attracts and retains high-quality staff.
- to provide a tax-efficient method of remuneration which reduces tax liabilities compared with those related to equivalent cash payments.

Note that these objectives do not include 'to motivate employees'. This is because benefits seldom have a direct and immediate effect on performance unless they are awarded as an incentive; for example, presenting a sales representative with a superior car (eg a BMW) for a year if he or she meets a particularly demanding target. Benefits can, however, create more favourable attitudes toward the company, leading to increased long-term commitment and better performance.

Benefits policies

Policies on employee benefits need to be formulated in the following areas:

- *range of benefits provided*: some benefits, such as pensions and holidays, are expected, others, such as permanent health insurance, are optional extras
- *scale of benefits provided*: the size of each benefit, taking into account its cost to the company and its perceived value to employees. Note that the perceived value of some benefits such as company cars, or pension schemes (particularly in the case of older employees), can be much greater than their actual cash value
- *proportion of benefits to total remuneration*: in cash terms, a benefit such as a pension scheme can cost the company between approximately 5 and 10 per cent of an employee's total remuneration. A decision has to be made on the proportion of total remuneration to be allocated to other benefits which incur expenditure of cash by the company. This policy decision is, of course, related to decisions on the range and scale of benefits provided, and it can be affected by decisions on allowing choice of benefits and on the distribution of benefits. Many companies are trying to move towards a 'clean cash' policy which minimizes the number and scale of fringe benefits. It is a policy supported by the UK Government but not one that has found much favour in terms of competitive practice
- *allowing choice*: benefits will be most effective in the process of attracting and retaining employees if they satisfy individual needs. But individual needs vary so much that no benefits package or single item within the package will satisfy all employees equally. Younger employees may be more interested in housing assistance than a company pension plan. Some employees have ethical or political objections to medical insurance schemes. Not everyone wants a company car – especially if they live in an Inner City area and have a spouse with a better car entitlement. Many people may prefer cash to an automatic benefit which is not precisely what they want. Methods of providing employees with choice are discussed in Chapter 19

- *allocation of benefits*: policy on the allocation of benefits determines the extent to which it is decided that a single status organization should be created. If the policy is to have a hierarchy of benefits, then the allocation of these at different levels has to be determined, usually in terms of broad bands of entitlements – typically called benefit grades
- *harmonization*: in the new flatter organizations, where multi-skilling is prevalent and new technology is eliminating the old distinction between white- and blue-collared workers, harmonization of benefit packages is increasingly taking place. The objective is to increase unity of purpose and improve team-work by abolishing invidious distinctions between benefits, rewarding different levels of responsibility and contribution by pay alone. Single status companies are becoming much more common. Full harmonization means that there are no distinctions at any level in the hierarchy between the benefits provided, which may vary only with length of service.

  Partial harmonization may provide the same basic benefits in some areas such as pensions, holidays, sick pay and redundancy for white- and blue-collared staff, but have a hierarchy of benefits above this base according to job grades. These benefits could include company cars, topped-up pension schemes or medical treatment insurance
- *market considerations*: whatever degree of choice or harmonization is decided upon, the precise arrangements will always be affected by market considerations. It may only be possible to attract and retain some key staff by, for example, offering a company car in line with what other organizations are doing for similar jobs. To attract a senior executive, it may be necessary to offer him or her a special pension arrangement – especially if they are earning over the £64,800 (1990) tax treatment threshold. As in all aspects of pay, market considerations and the need to offer competitive packages may have to override the principle of equity
- *government policy*: the main current impact made by government policy is in the field of personal taxation, but changes are afoot. It is essential, when reviewing benefit policies, to monitor tax legislation in order to assess the relative tax efficiency of benefits and to keep employees informed of the implications for them. As we move into the skills shortages of the 1990s we can expect the development of policies enabling the more effective recruitment and retention of women returners, older workers and the like who will be needed in the UK labour force
- *trade unions*: trade unions are increasingly concerned with the whole remuneration package and therefore may be involved or

ask to be involved in negotiating the provision and level of benefits. Many companies, however, resist negotiating such items as pensions although they will be prepared to consult unions or staff associations on benefit arrangements and do sometimes have trade unionists as trustees of the pension scheme.

Benefits practice

All employers provide benefits in some form or another to employees, but practice varies according to:

- employee status: typically, the more senior the employee, the more benefits provided. But this is not always the picture. A growing number of organizations, especially in high technology and other sectors requiring rapid growth and employee flexibility, are opting for harmonized benefits and conditions for core benefits
- local 'national' sector practice: there are marked differences in benefits entitlements between the finance sector and the rest of the private sector, between organizations where manpower costs form a small part of corporate expenditure and those which are labour intensive, and between profitable and progressive organizations and those which have to keep a tight control on manpower costs to survive. Differences by job function may not exist.
- private or public sector status: differences were much greater in the early 1980s than by 1990. Apart from generous, index-linked pension schemes and longer holidays, the public sector enjoyed comparatively few fringe benefits and they certainly did not have company cars – market competition for scarce skills has changed that for many public servants, notably in local authorities, non-departmental public bodies and the new agencies being hived off from the core of the Civil Service
- employers' views on the advisability of providing benefits: the extent to which they wish to use benefits to attract and retain staff – some organizations take a much more generous line than others or simply prefer to pay more in 'clean cash' than in benefits.

So the emphasis now in the UK is on cash payments rather than benefits. Most employers have therefore concentrated on providing a competitive set of 'core' benefits to supplement cash remuneration. The wilder extremes of tax-efficient 'beyond the fringe' benefits only exist in areas where extremely high pay is given in response to severe market pressure and for directors/owners of private companies where shareholder pressure is not an issue.

A balanced approach

Benefit entitlements are an area which employees watch closely and where perceived injustice can rapidly cause problems. They are also a major component of employee costs, particularly at management level where keeping up with 'best practice' can add 40 per cent or more to basic salary costs for a fairly average group of executives. The costs can rise sharply above that level where special pension provisions have to be made for older directors, who are earning over the pensions 'cap', and who have been newly recruited with little by way of preserved pension entitlements and expectations of retiring on two-thirds salary in line with Inland Revenue limits. Luxury cars are also a major cost item and other benefit costs can sometimes rise rapidly and unpredictably.

In this chapter we look first at all the major benefits currently provided by UK employers to give an overview of the options available. We then discuss:

- intangible benefits as an important part of the total benefits package
- the development of employee benefit strategies
- how to recognize the need to review benefits
- the steps to take when modifying the benefits package
- the important subject of communications.

Principal types of benefits

Benefits can be divided into the following categories:

1. *Pension schemes*: these are generally regarded as the most important employee benefit. They are sometimes referred to as deferred pay because they are financed during the working lifetime to provide a guaranteed income for employees or their dependants on retirement or death. Pension schemes are so important that they are dealt with separately in Chapter 17.
2. *Personal security*: these are benefits which enhance the individual's personal security with regard to illness, health, accident or redundancy.
3. *Financial assistance*: loans, house purchase assistance, relocation assistance, discounts, etc.
4. *Personal needs*: entitlements which recognize the interface between work and domestic needs or responsibilities, eg holidays and other forms of leave, child care, career breaks, retirement, counselling, financial counselling, personal counselling in time of crisis, fitness and recreational facilities.
5. *Company cars and petrol.*

6. *Other benefits* which improve the standard of living of employees such as subsidized meals, clothing allowances, refund of telephone costs and credit card facilities.
7. *Intangible benefits*: characteristics of the organization which make it an attractive and worthwhile place in which to work.

Personal security

Death-in-service benefits

Provided either as part of the pension scheme or as a separate life assurance cover, this benefit provides for a multiple of salary to be paid to an employee's dependants should he or she die before retirement. The range of multiples of salary payable, generally ranges from one to four times (currently the limit set by the Inland Revenue). Entitlements may be dependent on employee status or they may be the same for all employees in organizations with harmonized or single status benefit provisions. This is not a particularly expensive benefit to provide and is usually appreciated by employees because it saves on the personal life insurance cover needed to provide for their liabilities if they die prematurely. Death-in-service benefits are also discussed on pages 327–8.

Personal accident cover

This insurance cover provides for compensation should an employee be involved in an accident causing serious injury or death. It is a very common benefit, particularly where there is a great deal of travel involved or where the work can be hazardous for environmental and sometimes political reasons.

Permanent health insurance

Also called long-term disability cover, this form of insurance provides for continued income once the provisions of the company sick pay scheme are exhausted. It is therefore used to provide security of income for those struck down with chronic or terminal illnesses, normally payable after the first six months of sick leave and continuing until death or retirement, when the employee's pension becomes payable. Cover can be provided either through a separate insurance or through the ill-health early retirement provisions in the pension scheme. The income provided under permanent health insurance schemes typically ranges from between one-half to two-thirds of salary at the time illness occurred, usually with some provision for escalating payments in relation to rises in the cost of living. This benefit is not particularly expensive to provide as a percentage of payroll for a group of employees. It is certainly much cheaper than any cover available to individuals. The cost will vary in relation to the age profile of employees and any special health risks involved in employment. It is a much appreciated benefit – the dependants of an employee with terminal cancer or multiple sclerosis can be saved from financial hardship by the scheme's payments. This is an expected benefit for employees at all levels among major employers.

Business travel insurance

Arguably a benefit, business travel insurance is normally provided as a matter of course for all employees who have to travel extensively on company business. The insurance cover may be more generous than that obtainable by individuals and it will be offered at advantageous rates.

Given the generosity of some provisions it is not surprising that benefits experts occasionally amuse themselves by working out how much an employee would be worth dead if he or she died in service (4 times salary), in a plane crash (personal accident cover pays out in full), while travelling abroad on company business (business travel insurance pays out too), with an entitlement to dependants' pensions (typically due for the spouse and children under the age of 18).

Medical insurance

There are two basic forms of medical insurance available in the UK:

1. Schemes which cover the costs of private hospital treatment at rates which vary with the location and status of hospital selected by the employer (BUPA, PPP, WPA, etc).
2. Schemes which pay out cash to those being treated under the National Health Service, eg Hospital Savings Association (HSA).

The former type of scheme may also pay out if the employee chooses to be treated under the National Health Service. Cover for private medical insurance may be taken out by employers either:

(a) on a group discount basis, so that employees can obtain cover more cheaply for themselves and their families than they could as individuals; or
(b) at no cost to employees. In this case free cover may only be extended to employees with the possibility of covering families under group discount arrangements – or it may cover spouse and often dependent children too.

Apart from the obvious comforts of private health care, the real benefit to employers of medical insurance is the freedom it provides for employees to be treated at times that suit their work commitments. For as long as the National Health Service has to run long waiting lists for non-emergency surgery, then medical insurance is a very necessary benefit. It can prevent months of performance below par. Private medical cover also has connotations of status which can increase premium costs. If employees go for minor surgery in unforeseen numbers, partly at least to say they have received private treatment, such costs can escalate rapidly. Some organizations have had to resort to requiring employees to pay, for instance, the first £50 of any treatment costs to keep their schemes within reasonable limits. Medical insurance is an increasingly competitive market. Apart from the three main organizations providing private medical cover mentioned earlier, there is a growing number of other insurers competing for business. It is always worth negotiating with insurance companies and provident associations to see if they can come up with a more appealing quote – or getting brokers to do this for you.

Health screening

Looking after employee health by providing screening can mean anything from providing for mass X-Rays to screen for chest ailments, to cervical smears for female employees to the full panoply of total health checks. Full screening is often provided for executives, especially for those over 40 or subject to particular stresses and hazards. At its most sophisticated, screening will look not just at an employees' current state of health but analyze their lifestyle and diet to provide advice on the prevention of future problems and the management of stress. Such screening may be far more appreciated than more expensive benefits, particularly if it picks up a health problem early and facilitates immediate treatment before the condition has got out of hand.

Extra-statutory sick pay

Although all employees are covered by statutory sick pay provisions, most major employers supplement these provisions by continuing sick pay for longer than the statutory period. Typically they provide for a given period at full pay and then a further period at half pay until the scheme's provisions are exhausted, sometimes after six months or more. Sick pay entitlements are generally service related. Entitlements may vary with status or be harmonized depending on the employment philosophy prevailing in particular sectors. Generous sick pay provisions are usually much appreciated, but absenteeism often needs to be strictly monitored and controlled to prevent abuse of the system.

Extra-statutory redundancy pay

Although the statutory redundancy payments available in the UK provide some cushion for longer-serving employees losing their jobs, they are not very helpful to shorter service and indeed higher paid employees made redundant through no fault of their own. Trade union agreements therefore frequently cover both redundancy policy and extra-statutory redundancy entitlements to provide additional job security or at least compensation for those covered by them. Many organizations too, faced with a redundancy arising from restructuring or a change of business direction, are more generous with redundancy provisions. This normally takes one or more of the following forms:

- extra notice compensation
- additional service-related payments – these vary considerably, two weeks per year of service being fairly common and one month per year of service not being uncommon and many ignore the statutory weekly pay limit
- *ex-gratia* payments given as compensation for loss of office (golden handshakes)

Policy on redundancy is obviously influenced by what the organization can afford, but account should be taken of the fact that the relative generosity of treatment may well affect the morale of those whose jobs are safe. Redundancy exercises are very unsettling for everyone concerned. They need very careful planning and handling to ensure that the minimum disruption and hardship are caused.

Information on the severance package

When employees are told that they are to be made redundant, they should also be given precise details of the severance package. Preparing this is a major task for company pay specialists – one which often has to be performed in secret and at great speed. The information to be given to newly redundant employees typically comprises the following:

- actual date of redundancy
- notice payments and additional notice payments due
- statutory and extra-statutory service-related redundancy payments
- any *ex-gratia* payments included in the package
- accrued pension rights and any augmented rights given on

redundancy (eg early retirement provisions where it is technically possibly to turn redundancy into compulsory or voluntary early retirement)

- the position on other benefits eg continued medical insurance or retention of the company car for a limited period to provide protection and continued mobility while a new job is found
- when and how payments of all kinds are to be made
- provisions to deal with special cases of hardship
- sources of information and advice both within the organization and outside

The humanity and consideration for individuals shown when the package is explained can do much to ease their shock and sense of loss on being made redundant. This is always a situation that needs to be dealt with on a one-to-one basis and for which training in counselling skills is helpful.

It is probably worth emphasizing – even in a chapter such as this – that redundancies should never be announced on Fridays – an early or mid-week breaking of the news provides time for advice to be given and for personal adjustment to the trauma before employees have to face the weekend, and often their social life, without any form of support.

Outplacement advice (career counselling)

One of the benefits which an increasing number of employers are offering to redundant employees is professional help in sorting out what it is they really want to do next and in learning how to apply effectively for the jobs they want. This service can be called outplacement, career counselling or one of a variety of other names dreamed up by the consultants who provide it. It can be given on a one-to-one basis for managerial staff leaving in mid/late career or as a series of lectures and advisory sessions for more junior employees. Good outplacement consultants or career counsellors have a high success rate in helping people replan their lives, build on their strengths and present themselves effectively to potential employers. The provision of career counselling does of course have wider spin-off benefits and a positive effect on the morale of those still in post in the organization who see their ex-colleague learning to survive the trauma of redundancy.

As with any consultancy work, it is always wise to see several outplacement consultants or career counsellors, review their track record and see who provides the most appropriate service for the employees in question.

Financial assistance

Company loans

Loan schemes either provide for modest sums to be lent interest-free or for more substantial sums to be loaned at favourable interest rates. Small sums tend only to be loaned on a compassionate basis where there is personal hardship. Larger loans tend to be for defined purposes such as home improvements or car purchase, but may come without any strings attached at all. Repayments are normally made by regular deductions from salary on a basis specified or agreed between employer and employee. The benefit is more common in the finance sector. The taxable threshold for loan benefits should be monitored (see Chapter 18).

Season ticket loans

The high cost of commuting into London and other major conurbations has led many employers to offer interest-free loans for annual season tickets. Such loans normally fall below the taxable threshold for loan benefits (see Chapter 18) and are repaid in instalments over the year.

Mortgage assistance

Subsidized mortgages are a very substantial benefit, especially for those who have to buy property in high-cost housing areas. The benefit is mainly confined to the finance sector and is usually provided by subsidizing interest payments (down to between three and five per cent in mid-1990) on mortgages up to a given price threshold – often a multiple of salary. Where given, this benefit tends to be provided for all employees subject to set age and service requirements. Service requirements may, however, have to be dispensed with if they cause recruitment difficulties for staff categories already likely to have subsidized mortgages with other employers. The amounts available for subsidy normally rise either with seniority or salary level.

Housing assistance can also be given in the form of bridging loans and guaranteed selling prices (usually based on averaging of current valuations), especially for employees who move at company request and who cannot sell one house before they have to move into the house they buy near their new place of work.

Relocation packages

Companies recruiting managers and specialists from other parts of the country, or requiring employees to move, normally expect to pay the costs of removal. They also expect to compensate to some extent for the personal upheaval involved as well as paying for legal and agents fees and the costs of moving their possessions, buying new carpets and curtains and even school uniforms. The Inland Revenue keeps a strict eye on payments, but there is an extra-statutory concession covering the proportion of salary that can be paid tax-free. Companies can, where they wish to be generous, use this to the full or exceed it on a taxable basis if they believe this is necessary to induce an employee to make a move essential to business needs to an area not of their choice. Packages can either be drawn up individually or be controlled by set guidelines. Several specialist consultants offer assistance with the property side of relocation and this is a growing area of business.

Company discounts

Where a company has products or services which can be offered to employees at a favourable discount, this is normally much appreciated. Such schemes can run from free sweets or a fixed weekly allowance to employees in sweet factories, to low-cost second and third cars for people working in car manufacturing. Some organizations, unable to give discounts on their own products, negotiate discounts for their employees from suppliers. British trade unions are also active in the area of negotiating discounts as a means of attracting and retaining membership.

Fees to professional bodies

Fees for recognized professional bodies such as the Institute of Chartered Accountants or the Institute of Personnel Management may be refunded.

Personal needs

Holidays

Annual leave entitlements are a major benefit. Very few UK companies give less than four weeks to employees at any level and basic holiday entitlements are often five weeks. The maximum seems to have stopped at six weeks for most people. This is granted either to senior executives (who in practice may rarely have time to take full benefit of the provision) or on a service-related basis to more junior staff. Long entitlements may also be given in recognition of working unsociable hours or agreeing to flexible working practices. Some organizations specify minimum as well as maximum holidays, requiring employees to take one break of two weeks from their entitlement to ensure that they get away from work for at least one reasonably lengthy period a year. Many employers also need to specify when holidays can be taken, either to ensure that everybody is not off work at the same time when continuous working has to be maintained, or to ensure that everybody is off during the annual shutdown.

Compassionate leave

Granted when close relatives are ill, or die, or to deal with other unforeseen events, compassionate leave is normally the subject of formal policy in larger employers. It is usually paid leave for a limited period and unpaid for longer periods. This provision gives the opportunity for the organization to show concern for the individual and recognition of the importance of family responsibilities at times of personal hardship. Sensitivity in dealing with requests for compassionate leave, or offering it when it is clearly necessary can do much for employee morale – not just for the employee concerned, but for the immediate work group who see that a colleague has been well treated at a time of personal crisis.

Maternity leave and maternity pay

A growing number of women choose to or have to return to work after their babies are born. This reflects changing demographic patterns: the requirement for both partners to work to make ends meet where housing costs are high, the growing number of single-parent families, and the fact that professional women are starting families later with no intention of breaking their career. The nuclear family with a wife at home is a reality for only a small proportion of the population and, for better or worse, a diminishing one.

UK employment law provides for six months' maternity leave after the birth of a child with a right to return to work at the end of this period. Some companies however, often as a result of union negotiations, provide for longer maternity leave with a right to return to the old job. They may also provide additional maternity pay on top of statutory provision. Where employers find that they employ large numbers of women and are dependent on their skills, generous maternity provisions can help with long-term recruitment and retention. It can also be a very useful and cost-effective policy in areas of professional skill shortage, enabling employers to attract qualified women, provided this is achieved without infringing the sex discrimination legislation.

The management of maternity leave and pay requires care. It is not helped currently because women have to make firm statements about their intention to return to work after childbirth, whether or not they know what they want to do and in order to protect themselves in the event of stillbirth. Many of the potential difficulties can be avoided by ensuring that employees have a clear idea of the legislation and that their employer respects this and will make sensible and reasonable provisions for them. Poor treatment of a woman taking maternity leave will affect morale for all her immediate colleagues.

Paternity leave

Outside those who make provisions as the result of union negotiations, few UK employers yet make formal provisions for paternity leave. Where they do, it is for a few days either while the partner is in hospital or when she returns home. Otherwise, compassionate leave may be granted or the employee is expected to use part of his annual leave entitlement. Other European countries tend to be more generous, recognizing perhaps that most families stop at two children and the amount of leave involved for most men in a lifetime is less than many need to take as sick leave in a year. In deciding policy in this area employers need to take account not just of the cost, but of the benefit obtained from recognizing and encouraging involvement in family responsibilities.

Career breaks

A growing number of UK employers are providing for employees (both men *and* women) to take up to five years off to rear children. People taking breaks are usually brought in regularly to keep up to date with developments both in their skills area and the organization in general and are entitled to return full or part-time to work with no loss of job status.

Sabbaticals

Although sabbaticals are a comparatively rare benefit in the UK, they can be a useful retention factor for professionals able to use the time to travel and update their knowledge. They may also be granted to long-serving employees either as straight leave or as time to get involved in something of value to the community. There is no set pattern to the length of leave given – it varies from a few weeks up to a year.

Other leave

Policies also need to be developed by most organizations to cover leave for territorial army training, jury service, civic duties and other special requirements.

Child care

In order to attract or retain employees with young dependent children, employers can offer financial or practical child care provisions. For example, companies such as the Midland Bank are providing workplace nurseries or crèches. Although expensive to provide, such arrangements work well where travel with a child to the workplace is relatively easy. They can pose problems where parents reject the idea of commuting with a toddler in the rush hour. Cash payments or child care vouchers are also now being offered by a growing number of organizations to offset employee costs for childminders, nannies, or after-school babysitters.

Practical or financial help in finding, recruiting or retaining child care providers may be welcomed. For instance, arranging a 'nanny-share' for two or three employees; retainer payments for child-minders for part-time workers.

Other types of provision, such as flexible hours, or help with transport can ease practical problems for employee and employer, and be perceived as a benefit.

Pre-retirement counselling

Many larger employers now provide a series of lectures and an information pack for employees nearing retirement. The areas typically covered are:

- personal financial planning
- managing increased leisure time
- health in retirement
- local sources of information and advice.

Personal financial counselling

Top executives and other higher rate tax payers are not always as effective as they might be in organizing their own personal financial planning. Even finance directors able to work wonders with corporate financial policy may have little time or inclination to deal properly with family financial matters. To help with this problem and provide the necessary specialist advice, many major employers offer senior executives the chance to go to independent advisors for personal financial counselling. This should be provided by advisors who are not going to benefit from the sale of particular financial products, ie those who typically return commissions to either the company or the individual executive where commission-earning products are bought on recommendation. The advice given usually covers areas such as:

- making a will
- inheritance and other planning
- required insurance cover
- provisions for dependents
- savings and investment strategy
- finance and property
- planning for school fees
- trusts and covenants
- tax planning.

Advice is generally provided on a one-to-one basis once the executive has produced an inventory of his or her personal financial situation under guidance. The position is usually reviewed regularly to take account of changed personal circumstances.

Companies may also offer this service to widows and widowers of employees to help them plan how best to make use of death-in-service benefits and take stock of the financial situation in which they have been left. Given that many widows of an older generation may have little idea about financial management, this can be a valuable and much-needed benefit.

Personal counselling

Traditionally provided as part of company 'welfare' services, a new generation of personal counselling services is growing up among major employers. Their purpose is to help employees deal with the traumas of bereavement, divorce, alcoholism and the spectre of AIDS. Larger employers typically provide specially trained 'in-house' counsellors on a confidential basis. Others provide a referral service to counsellors in the community, eg to Relate, Alcoholics Anonymous, etc.

Sports and social facilities

Most employers recognize that work is also a social institution. They therefore try to provide at least some leisure activities so that colleagues can meet together outside working hours. Depending on the size, location and culture of the organization, provisions vary considerably. It may be entirely appropriate to negotiate favourable membership terms at nearby health and sports clubs. Whatever the cicumstances, providing a social focus can have beneficial effects on the organization's culture (eg assisting team building) and should therefore be regularly reviewed as part of the remuneration package. It can certainly be a retention factor where staff are difficult to find and keep.

Company cars

Virtually no other country in the world provides company cars to the same extent as the UK. Foreign parent companies setting up in the UK often experience difficulty in persuading head office that such generous provisions are necessary to compete in the salary market. Employees seldom move from a job where they have a car to a non-car job, even if it carries a much higher basic salary. This is because in the private sector, and now in parts of the public sector too, cars are a mark of managerial status. Company cars are normally taxed, insured and maintained at company expense. They are, therefore, a much larger benefit than even the 1990 tax scale charges suggest and create a major differential and, some would say, distortion at the point in a salary structure where they are given on the basis of status alone.

The cash value to an employee of a company car can be as much as £5,000 to £7,000 a year (or more) depending on the model. The gap in a reward structure between the 'haves' and 'have nots' in company car terms is therefore considerable and can and does frequently cause heartache.

Company car policies are often a benefit 'trouble spot' and can take an inordinate amount of top executive time to get right. Car fleet management is not an area for amateurs. Most large organizations have a fleet manager in charge of the acquisition and maintenance of the company car fleet, leaving the details of allocation policy and the way in which cars fit into remuneration policy as the main problems of the compensation and benefits specialists. Here a number of problems arise. People who are not entitled to them often try to get cars on the basis of business need, or to get their jobs regraded to a level where car provision is automatic. When they eventually get cars there may still be problems about the model, the permitted extras or the replacement cycle. In devising the remuneration policy element of company car policies, the following areas have to be dealt with in relation to what the company can afford in the face of competitive practice:

1. *Allocation policy*: this deals with who is to get cars on the basis of status, and what the annual mileage threshold is, before cars are given in response to business need (somewhere

between 5,000 and 10,000 miles is common – dependent on the type of journeys made).

2. *Car model entitlements*: when deciding car model entitlements the choice is between setting them rigidly in relation to a small number of models at each status level or, as is now more common, in relation to a bench-mark price or lease cost, allowing varying degrees of freedom of choice. Few companies allow open sports cars, while others restrict the choice to models manufactured in EC or Scandinavian countries or even to British manufacturers' models (although the latter policy becomes confused when cars manufactured in Europe are sold by British-based firms). The market trend is to allow as wide a choice as possible within a given cost framework.

   Organizations may also choose to allow some flexibility either on the additional extras that may be added to the car at employees' expense or, indeed, over whether they can make a contribution out of salary to either the lease cost or the purchase price of a more expensive car if they want one. In either of these cases, strict limits must be set because there is a strong tendency to stretch allowances to their limits and indeed beyond! A typical example of the problem is the organization which leases cars and sets an absolute price limit of, say, £300 a month, and finds that a remarkably high proportion of employees will passionately want metallic paint on this model, which takes the leasing cost to £324. If they are then told that the limit is £300, they may complain bitterly that the company can surely afford an extra £24 a month.

   An increasingly common response is to let employees pay the extra – typically with a cost ceiling that might be 20 per cent above the monthly lease cost or purchase price. Some organizations set no ceilings on additions, typically those with a high proportion of young professionals who can then at least try having a Porsche for three years before moving on to a less personally costly family Volvo. If ceilings are imposed it is critical to stick to them *without exception.*

   Most car fleet managers know that if they allow themselves to be swayed by these specious arguments, the level will creep up incrementally and the allocation policy will be in tatters. It can however be very hard to hold the line in times of severe market pressure. Chief executives can, and sometimes do, intervene to ensure a favoured candidate gets the car he or she wants. As we have already said, car policy demands far more boardroom time than it should. Getting top executive commitment to the imposition of firm limits each time they are reviewed can help contain abuse of policy by directors with 'special cases'.

3. *Replacement cycles*: cars are commonly replaced every two to four years, or 50,000 to 60,000 miles, but this varies with the use and durability of the cars involved. Three years is the most common replacement period. Salesforce cars suffer more wear and tear and therefore tend to be replaced more frequently than top executive cars, especially where annual mileages for the latter are relatively low.
4. *Eligibility to drive*: the policy on who may drive the car, eg employee/spouse/family/named drivers, is usually determined by the provisions agreed under the insurance cover negotiated. Flexibility in this area is often appreciated – especially in dual career families where the nanny or au pair needs to be insured to drive the car to get children to school and ferry them around.
5. *Permitted fuel* ('Green' issues): the majority of UK employers now specify that all new company cars should run on unleaded petrol – for both environmental and (as the UK Government intended when it reduced the tax) cost reasons. The use of all-diesel fleets is also growing – again encouraged by the Government via the diesel price differential. Buying cars with catalytic converters is also a major contribution to pollution abatement.
6. *Fleet management*: the management of the car fleet involves not only selecting, purchasing and disposing of cars, but also encouraging drivers to treat their cars properly so that their resale value holds up when they fall due for replacement.

Company car policies are normally set out in a manual for drivers which is regularly updated.

Company cars – the future

The Government is progressively increasing the income tax liability for the benefit of a company car, both to implement its policy of encouraging clean cash pay and, more recently, in response to a strengthening 'Green' lobby to restrict the number of cars on the road – cars being a major source of 'greenhouse gases', notably carbon dioxide, in the atmosphere. The motor manufacturers' lobby does its best to restrain the Government because British firms are very dependent on the car fleet market and have to some degree tailored their model ranges to meet company status hierarchies. (Why, it may be asked, can foreign firms like Saab or Volkswagen be successful without this lifeline?) But this very tangible benefit is disliked intensely by the Treasury and there is every sign that it will continue to be attacked through the tax system. It can be argued that this is a good thing. Company cars are an all too visible status symbol and in these days of single status organizations (following the example of many US and Japanese-owned companies), should something as divisive as this be allowed to continue? Company car policies can effectively demotivate as well as motivate. They cause a lot of pain as well as pleasure and perhaps the best, long-term, solution if the tax advantage disappears, is for people to be rewarded financially according to their contribution. This would give them the final choice of whether they want to come to work in a Porsche, a more environmentally acceptable Ford Fiesta or on a bicycle.

Private petrol

Free petrol for private mileage remains a predominantly top and senior management benefit. It is taxable and care should be taken where annual mileage is low that the tax charge does not exceed the cost of petrol for the occasional driver. Employers will also have to decide whether to give private petrol provision for holidays and overseas trips. A return journey to Athens can add significantly to an individual's annual employment cost! Not surprisingly, therefore, most employers restrict the benefit to UK travel.

Car allowances

Where cars are not provided but are used regularly for business purposes, many employers pay car allowances. These should be designed to make a sensible contribution to the cost of depreciation, maintenance and other running costs. A car used on business will inevitably need replacement earlier than one used more occasionally. Organizations such as the Automobile Association provide guidelines on running costs as a basis for settling allowances. In 1990 the tax treatment of car allowances changed (see Chapter 18).

Mileage allowances

The cost of fuel used on business journeys is normally reimbursed. For company cars this will be on a mileage rate which reflects the actual cost of petrol or diesel. For employees' own cars, there will be an addition to compensate for wear and tear. These rates vary both in relation to the price of fuel and market practice. They may also vary in relation to the length of journey made. The full allowance may be payable for short journeys, but a lower allowance can apply for much longer journeys. Again, the Automobile Association figures are often used in setting the level of allowances.

Other benefits

Other benefits include:

- subsidized meals in staff restaurants
- luncheon vouchers – especially where employers are sited in large towns/cities
- clothing allowances/cleaning tokens for employees who have to wear company uniforms
- the refund of telephone rentals and the whole or part of the cost of calls – for those required to work at home or from home on occasions
- educational allowances for expatriates – to ensure continuity of education for their children
- credit card facilities for petrol or other purchases – especially for those who do a lot of travelling
- mobile telephone/fax machines – typically job need related but perceived as a reward too
- funding of non-job related evening classes/training to encourage employees to broaden their interests and skills – an area where 'leading edge' employers such as Ford and Mars have taken major initiatives.

Intangible benefits

It should already be clear from much of this book that the authors do not believe that people work for money alone. There are in fact many determinants of the decision to work for, and stay with, a particular employer. Throwing money at recruitment and retention problems may be the worst possible strategy because this only deals with one aspect of what may be a complex problem. It is also, of course, self-limiting, because there has to be an ultimate ceiling on employment costs. The role of money as a motivator was discussed in Chapter 2. What we want to emphasize here is the simple fact that employees weigh up a number of tangible and intangible factors when looking at what employers have on offer. The list below sets out in more detail the main items involved. Most of them are strongly related to the need for personal recognition and the desire to go on learning and developing as a career goes through different stages. Recognition of the overlap between private and working life is also important. Most people prefer to work for an employer who is caring and supportive as well as challenging and successful.

The principal items are:

- status – recognition of seniority and professional excellence
- power – the opportunity to influence the course of the business and take responsibility for a growing number of functions and people
- recognition for achievement – a culture in which managers praise and reinforce individual success

- training opportunities – the chance to acquire a wider range of skills in preparation for promotion and to function more effectively and confidently
- career progression – the prospect of promotion, preferably in relation to a properly designed succession plan to ensure that the right experience is acquired at the right time to enable new responsibilities to be taken on when the individual has been properly prepared for them
- good working conditions – pleasant, spacious and well-designed offices and other work environments which facilitate effective working both for individuals and teams
- a well-managed organization – an appropriate organization structure infused with a sense of purpose and commitment. The reputation for running a 'rough shop' spreads quickly and prevents successful recruitment of all but those who believe they can change it – until they give up!
- recognition of the need to balance work and family responsibilities – employees knowing that they are treated as responsible individuals whose family commitments are important to them. This means not developing a culture where becoming a workaholic and risking family breakdown is a key means to promotion. It also means taking a reasonable view on attendance, for instance, at school functions and other family occasions. Organizations seeking to recruit women returners are finding that they have to pay greater heed to the family responsibilities of their men to enable women to feel free to take up employment with adequate partner support. One is mindful of Rosabeth Moss Kanter's paradox – 'succeed, succeed, succeed and raise terrific children' (*When Giants learn to Dance*, p. 21)
- flexibility – a willingness to tailor conditions to the particular needs of individuals. Companies can rapidly develop this when they have to attract staff in great demand, but there may also be benefits to be gained, in terms of commitment and stability, from using the principle in other areas.

Developing employee benefit strategies – key factors

The key factors to be taken into account in developing employee benefit strategies are that they should:

- be an integral part of the total reward management strategy of the organization, which in turn should specifically support the achievement of its business objectives
- add value to basic remuneration and performance-related pay policies by extending the purely financial provisions of these

policies into areas where the company will benefit from providing additional rewards and which will support the achievement of employees' specific needs

- be in line with and supportive of the culture of the organization and its value system
- demonstrate to employees that they are members of a caring and enabling organization which is concerned in highly practical terms with meeting their needs for security, support and other forms of help so that they are able really to give their best
- meet the needs of the organization to increase the commitment of its members, to develop their identification with its objectives and to increase unity of purpose
- meet the real needs of individual employees rather than those needs which management believes they should have
- help the organization to recruit and retain high-quality and well-motivated staff by being competitive in the market-place
- ensure that benefits are cost effective in the sense that the increase they produce in commitment and improvement in recruitment and retention rates justify their cost
- take account of relative tax efficiencies in structuring the package
- establish an appropriate degree of flexibility in operating the benefit package
- provide a measure of individual choice to employees
- aim to avoid an over-divisive approach which places employees into clearly defined 'have' and 'have not' categories
- bear in mind the importance of the non-tangible benefits as well as those which provide extra remuneration or financial assistance
- be creative – not simply offering what competitors offer but devising new approaches to structuring the package and to providing individual benefits which are tailored to the strategic needs of the organization (like giving secretaries having to cope in poor, if temporary, office conditions, fresh flowers on their desk every week in recognition of their commitment and tolerance of the environment)

Recognizing the need to review benefits

The impact and effectiveness of the benefits package should be kept under constant review to identify its impact and effectiveness. The symptoms that might indicate the need for attention include:

- problems in managing the expectations of prospective employees on their benefits package (the 'every other employer I'm talking to provides mobile 'phones' syndrome)

- problems in retaining staff because of dissatisfaction with the package (as established at leaving interviews)
- discontent expressed by management on the extent to which the benefits package provides value for money
- general information on trends in the provision of benefits which indicates that the level of benefits provided by the company is out of line with good practice elsewhere
- discontent expressed by staff on the scale of benefits provided by the company or the basis upon which they are allocated
- pressure from staff to be allowed more choice in the benefits they get
- changes in fiscal law which reduce the tax efficiency of individual benefits
- problems in administering benefit policies, for example company cars.

Modifying the benefits package

The steps required to modify or re-design the benefits package are as follows:

1. Analyze trends in the market-place using survey and other data for the provision of benefits, and assess what is regarded as the best practice in each area.
2. Analyze trends in the recruitment and retention of staff to assess, in the light of the market survey, any areas where it is believed that improvements in the benefits package and/or the way it is applied might improve the ability of the organization to attract and retain staff.
3. Assess in discussions with management what it wants the employee benefits, strategies and policies of the organization to achieve and the extent to which the present arrangements satisfy these objectives.
4. Consult employees on their needs (consider using an attitude survey for this purpose).
5. Obtain the views of relevant trade unions or staff associations.
6. Assess the tax implications of current and projected government policies.
7. In the light of these processes of analysis and consultation:
   (a) conduct an overall review of employee benefits strategies under the headings listed above
   (b) review each of the main policy areas as set out in the key dimensions part of this section
   (c) decide, on the basis of these reviews, any changes required to strategies and policies and the steps required to get these changes formulated, agreed and introduced.

8. In the light of revised strategies and policies and by reference to the analytical and consultative steps taken earlier (stages 1 to 5):
   (a) subject each benefit to careful scrutiny to determine any changes required to content or application
   (b) examine the costs of each benefit and assess whether it is providing value for money (this involves comparing the cost of providing and administering the benefit with an assessment of the extent to which it is meeting the needs of the company and its employees – clearly low cost to employer/high value employee items will be the most attractive)
   (c) decide if any additional items should be included in the package and assess their likely contributions to meeting organizational and individual needs and their overall cost effectiveness
   (d) decide if any items should be eliminated on cost effectiveness grounds – but beware of taking away traditional benefits if the timing is poor and the change is the wrong symbolic act
   (e) plan the steps required to make the changes, include the design of the benefit, consultation with staff and methods of communicating information on the changes to all those affected (including tax implications).
9. Introduce the changes, ensuring that the supporting administrative systems are properly installed and that the communication programme takes place as planned.

Communicating the benefits package

Employee benefits can easily be taken for granted by staff, and it is therefore important to tell them about what they are getting and its value. This can be done in company newsletters or, better still, by means of employee benefits statements which set out in full the scale and cost of the benefits for each individual employee.

Trends in employee benefits policy

To summarize, the main trends in benefits policy are:

- less attention being paid to tax avoidance
- greater simplification of benefit packages
- more attention to individual needs
- greater emphasis on individual choice
- a move towards clean cash rather than benefits in kind

- greater concentration on assessing the cost/effectiveness of the total benefits package and planning a strategy for benefits which is integrated with an overall reward management policy, which is in turn linked to the business strategy of the organization
- more attention paid to communicating the benefits policy.

Chapter 17

Pensions

Approved pension schemes

Pensions are generally regarded as the most important employee benefit. They are often defined as deferred pay because they are financed from contributions which build up rights to a guaranteed income for employees or their dependants on retirement or death. Some people, however, would rather classify pensions as benefits provided by the employer. This may seem like a distinction without a difference, but those who prefer the term benefits are saying, in effect, that while the organization believes in pensions and sees them as a legitimate part of employment costs, it does not regard them as negotiable alongside other financial elements of the pay packet, which counting them as deferred pay would imply. Many employers firmly refuse to include pensions in the pay deal and thus reserve their right to decide on the scale and scope of this benefit alongside others which are non-negotiable, such as restaurants and sporting facilities. This view, however, should not absolve them from the obligation to communicate full details of pension arrangements to employees (including the implications of the choice between the company scheme and a private pension). Neither should it prevent employers consulting with their staff on the scheme's arrangements and including employee representatives on the management committee of a pension trust. Companies should almost always aim to provide the best pension arrangements they can afford because:

1. There is a moral obligation to provide a reasonable level of security for employees, especially those with long service.
2. A good pension scheme demonstrates that the company has the long-term interests of employees at heart.
3. A good scheme helps attract and retain high-quality staff.

The area of pension scheme administration is increasingly dominated by highly skilled in-company specialists and external suppliers of software or administration services. Nevertheless, it is essential for the general salary administrator to understand the major policy considerations in order to contribute effectively to pension policy development. The check-list at the end of this section lists the main questions that should be asked when assessing current or proposed pension scheme practice.

Apart from their internal complexity, pension schemes are subject to a number of legal and fiscal regulations, and in recent years the volume of legislation on pensions has increased dramatically. The process of balancing the requirements of the legislation against the optimum benefits levels and funding arrangements almost always requires expert independent advice from leading actuaries or benefits consultants before final details of a new or revised scheme can be decided.

The most significant change in recent times was perhaps the requirement that from April 1988 membership of a company pension scheme can no longer be compulsory. Employees can opt out of the company scheme and are then free to choose whether or not to make their own personal pension arrangements or rely solely on the State pension scheme. The employer is less able to adopt a paternalistic approach in deciding what is 'best' for his employees, and new attitudes may range from 'this is the company pension scheme, take it or leave it' to a concerted effort to provide good benefits and to sell the advantages of the company scheme over the personal pension or 'State pension only' routes.

Inland Revenue approval

All company pension arrangements other than those of a purely voluntary nature require the approval of the Inland Revenue, if the director or employee concerned is not to be liable to income tax on the cost of providing the pension benefit. Inland Revenue approval also confers significant tax advantages on the scheme. The 1989 Finance Act introduced the facility for companies to provide benefits under unapproved pension schemes in addition to those under approved schemes. These unapproved schemes are discussed later in this chapter.

The current code of approval was introduced in the 1970 Finance Act, which has been incorporated into the Income and Corporation Taxes Act 1988, and became mandatory on 6 April 1980. This Act sets out the conditions under which the Inland Revenue will automatically approve a pension scheme for advantageous tax status. In addition it confers discretionary powers on the Inland Revenue to approve schemes which do not fully conform to stated conditions. Most schemes are approved under this discretionary power because the stated conditions are too restrictive.

The Inland Revenue issues guidance as to how it will exercise its discretionary powers in a booklet entitled *Occupational Pension*

Schemes: Notes on approval under Chapter I Part XIV Income and Corporation Taxes Act 1988, commonly known as the 'Practice Notes' or 'IR12'. The main conditions of Inland Revenue approval are in the form of restrictions on the maximum benefits that can be provided. The main maxima are summarized below.

1. *Normal retirement pension*: one-sixtieth of final remuneration at normal retirement date for each year of service up to 40. The 1989 Finance Act introduced an 'earnings cap' for new schemes established on or after 14 March 1989 or new entrants to existing schemes on or after 1 June 1989. This cap restricted the amount of final remuneration used in the calculation of maximum benefits to £60,000 in the year ending 5 April 1990. The Act provides for the cap to be increased each year in line with the increase in the Retail Prices Index (suitably rounded). A higher pension fraction under an 'uplifted scale' may be permitted for late entrants to the scheme, who are unable to complete a full 40 years. This uplifted scale rises to two-thirds of final remuneration after only 10 years for members who joined their scheme prior to 17 March 1987, or after 20 years for those who joined on or after that date.
2. *Lump sum option on retirement*: three-eightieths of final remuneration at normal retirement date for each year of service up to 40. As for the pension, a higher fraction under an uplifted scale may be permitted for late entrants to the scheme, who are unable to complete a full 40 years. This scale produces the maximum 120/80ths, or 1.5 times final remuneration after only 20 years, but those who joined their scheme on or after 17 March 1987 are permitted uplifted cash only if their pension benefits are uplifted, and are also subject to a limit of £100,000 on final remuneration in the calculation of the tax-free cash. For new schemes established on or after 14 March 1989 or new entrants to existing schemes on or after 1 June 1989 the earnings cap introduced by the 1989 Finance Act also applies to final remuneration in the calculation of the tax-free cash.
3. *Spouse's benefits on death in service*: two-thirds of the member's pension achievable at normal retirement date (based on current earnings), plus a cash sum equal to four times current earnings plus a refund of all the members' own contributions with interest.
4. *Spouse's pension on death after retirement*: two-thirds of member's pension.
5. *Inflationary provisions*: benefits may be escalated in line with the increase in the Retail Prices Index.

State pensions and contracting out

State earnings related pension scheme (SERPS)

The Social Security Pensions Act 1975 (the 1975 Act) changed the whole face of UK pensions practice and introduced the new State Earnings Related Pension Scheme (SERPS) on top of the State Basic Pension. SERPS started on 6 April 1978 and originally provided a pension of 1.25 per cent of a person's average annual 'revalued band earnings' for each year completed after April 1978, up to a maximum percentage of 25 per cent by 1998.

Revalued band earnings are earnings between a lower and upper earnings limit, which are increased in line with earnings inflation for the period up to retirement. The lower earnings limit is approximately equal to a quarter of national average earnings and the upper earnings limit is about one and three-quarters times national average earnings.

Subsequently, the Government considered that the cost of SERPS would be too high in the next century, and has introduced changes in the Social Security Act 1986 which became effective from 6 April 1988. The changes should not affect the SERPS pension of anyone reaching state pension age before the end of this century. The SERPS pension for anyone retiring after that will be gradually reduced to an ultimate level of 20 per cent, rather than 25 per cent, of average revalued band earnings. Furthermore, this average will be based on all earnings rather than the best 20 years as originally provided.

Contracting out

The 1975 Act empowered good occupational pension schemes to contract out of SERPS. This meant that the occupational pension scheme undertook to provide benefits at least equal to a guaranteed minimum pension (GMP) in place of the SERPS pension, in return for a reduction in employer and employee National Insurance contributions. A person's GMP is calculated in a similar way to the SERPS pension.

Until April 1988, only final salary schemes which guarantee a minimum level of earnings-related pension could contract out of SERPS. The Social Security Act 1986, however, allowed schemes to contract out of SERPS from April 1988 without having to guarantee any level of minimum benefits. Such schemes are Contracted Out Money Purchase schemes, or COMP schemes, and will provide benefits equal to whatever the contributions accumulated for a member will buy at the time of retirement.

Main features of company pension schemes

The main sources of more detailed information on UK pensions practice are the regular surveys conducted by the National Association of Pension Funds (NAPF) and the government actuary. In addition, there are a number of loose leaf works on pensions and several specialist pensions periodicals. Most leading firms of pension consultants and actuaries produce their own newsletters and other information aids for employers. Guidance on the statutory requirements is published by the Superannuation Funds Office and the Occupational Pensions Board.

The short sections below are not exhaustive and merely summarize the main aspects of current pensions provisions.

Eligibility

Membership of any company pension scheme must be on a voluntary basis. Before 6 April 1988 companies could, and usually did, make joining the company pension scheme a condition of employment.

Eligibility conditions for membership of a pension scheme often express a minimum age and/or length of service before an employee can join, although there is usually a power to waive these conditions in any particular case.

The 1975 Act introduced equal access requirements. These meant that admission to membership of an occupational pension scheme should be on terms which are the same in respect of age and length of service for both men and women.

Pensionable age

The Sex Discrimination Act 1986, which applies to new employees joining a company after 7 November 1987, prohibits employers from forcing women to retire at a different age from men in similar circumstances. This Act does not require pension schemes to adopt a common normal *pensionable* age.

However, various EC directives and judgments handed down by the European Court of Justice have systematically removed elements of sex discrimination from company pension schemes. In particular, the judgment by the European Court in the case of Barber vs Guardian Royal Exchange, which was handed down on 17 May 1990, ruled that pension benefits count as pay under Article 119 of the Treaty of Rome, which requires equal pay for work of equal value. The Court also determined that contracted-out company pension schemes could not impose age conditions which differ according to sex, even if the difference between the pensionable ages for men and women is based on that provided for by the national statutory scheme. Thus this single judgment has the effect of requiring all pension schemes in future to adopt common pensionable ages for men and women and common eligibility conditions for benefits. Unfortunately the wording of the judgment has left in doubt the extent of its applicability to benefits earned before 17 May 1990. It may take some considerable time for clarification of this to be obtained, bearing in mind that more than nine years elapsed between the event which triggered Mr Barber's original claim and the judgment being handed down.

A number of schemes have already adopted a common normal pensionable age, or alternatively, have introduced a system of flexible retirement, whereby members can retire at any time between 60 and 65 without any early retirement deduction from their pension. The 1989 NAPF Survey found that 44 per cent of schemes had equalized pensionable age, with approximately equal numbers choosing age 60 and 65 and very few choosing an intermediate age.

Retirement formulae and pension on retirement

Final salary

The principal method for determining the benefit formula of retirement income is final salary. Pension is calculated as a fraction of either the salary at retirement or an average of salary over the closing years of service multiplied by the length of pensionable service. The most common fraction is sixtieths, giving the full pension allowed by the Inland Revenue after 40 years' service of 40/60ths or two-thirds of final salary. The maximum scheme pension will be subject to the Inland Revenue maximum referred to earlier.

Money purchase

The main alternative to a final salary pension scheme is a money purchase scheme. Under a money purchase approach, the company fixes the contribution it wants to pay in respect of each member. This may be a sterling amount eg £2,000 per annum, or a percentage of the member's salary, eg 10 per cent. The pension payable to a member on retirement is then whatever annual payment can be purchased with the money accumulated in the fund for him.

The company may pay the same rate of contribution for all members, or it may vary its contribution according to status, age, length of service, and the level of the employee's contribution. Alternatively, the company can adjust the contribution paid each year in respect of a member, to home in on a target level of benefit, perhaps determined by reference to a final salary formula.

Hybrid schemes
In order to meet the pension aspirations of different types of employee, some schemes have adopted benefit structures which combine both final salary and money purchase principles. This may take the form of a money purchase 'underpin' to a final salary benefit, whereby a member gets a pension based on a money purchase formula if this gives a higher pension than the final salary formula. Other forms of hybrid might be a final salary benefit based on a fairly low fraction with a money purchase benefit on top, or a money purchase formula below a certain age with a final salary formula above that age.

Other formulae
Other possible pension formulae are:

1. *Average salary*: fixed amounts of pension are given for each year spent in a salary bracket and these are added up and paid at retirement.
2. *Flat rate*: a given rate paid for each year of service.

These methods are rarely used nowadays.

Lump sum on retirement

The Inland Revenue allows up to 3/80ths of final salary for each year of service up to a maximum of 40 years to be paid as a lump sum on retirement. This gives a maximum lump sum of 120/80ths or 1.5 times final salary. Under a final salary scheme, the lump sum is usually obtained by the member exchanging, or commuting, part of his pension entitlement for the lump sum, although some schemes provide a (smaller) pension *plus* a lump sum. With a money purchase scheme, the lump sum will usually be paid from the fund available at retirement, before applying the balance of the fund to buy pension benefits. A lump sum provision of some kind is almost universal in modern schemes.

The 'uplifted scales' and Inland Revenue limits referred to earlier will apply to employees who complete less than 40 years and to those who joined their company pension scheme on or after 17 March 1987.

No tax is payable on the lump sum whereas the pension is subject to income tax. This usually means that a member is better off taking the lump sum and most members do so, whether for this reason, or because the capital is required for immediate material needs such as the purchase of a retirement home, or repayment of a mortgage.

Late retirement

Money purchase pension schemes automatically provide for an enhanced pension for members who continue to work after normal retirement date, through the continued growth of the money purchase fund. The rules of final salary pension schemes will also usually provide for an enhanced pension on late retirement. If contributions continue to the final salary scheme during the period after normal pensionable age, the employee will normally earn additional benefits on the scheme's normal scale, based on the extra years of service completed.

For somebody who has already completed 40 years by their normal retirement date and earned the maximum pension of 40/60ths of final salary, the Inland Revenue permit a further 1/60th of final salary for each year of additional service up to a maximum total pension of 45/60ths. The normal maximum lump sum option of 120/80ths of final salary is similarly increased by an additional 3/80ths for each year, up to an overall maximum of 135/80ths.

If contributions cease at normal retirement age, it is usual for an actuarially increased pension to be paid when retirement takes place, although employees whose benefits are subject to the earnings cap introduced by the 1989 Finance Act may be ineligible for such increase because there is no corresponding limit in the Inland Revenue maximum benefits.

Post-retirement pension increases

Increases to cushion pensioners against at least some of the inroads of inflation are now considered an essential part of most company pension schemes.

Under a contracted out final salary scheme, the part of a member's pension forming the guaranteed minimum pension (GMP) is already inflation proofed by the state, although the company scheme must pay the first 3 per cent per annum of that inflation proofing. Similar increases will be payable to pensioners of contracted out money purchase schemes.

In addition to these statutory increases, most employers will provide for annual escalation by a fixed, funded percentage, commonly three to five per cent of the member's pension, to which the scheme is committed in the trust deed and rules. The 1989 NAPF Survey found that 62 per cent of schemes guaranteed some level of increases. Alternatively, *ad hoc* or discretionary pension increases may be granted. Some employers give both types of increase. Pension schemes in the public sector go further on pension increases by formally linking the whole of the employees' pensions to the Retail Price Index.

In the mid 1980s, low rates of inflation, together with good investment returns on pension fund investments, has meant many good pension schemes in the private sector giving discretionary pension increases as good as, or better than, RPI increases, although these have, in part, represented a catching up from previous years. The 1990 Social Security Act has introduced a provision whereby, from an appointed day, all final salary pension schemes will be required to provide annual increases to pensions earned after that day in line with the RPI up to a maximum of 5 per cent per annum. In addition, any surplus revealed by an actuarial valuation of the scheme after that day will have to be used to provide this level of pension increase on pensions already earned before any part of it can be returned to the company, either in cash or by means of a contribution holiday.

The extent to which schemes can continue to afford pension increases which compare well with inflation will depend largely on the government's success in keeping inflation under control. The successful performance of pension fund investments, and the willingness of companies to fund for future increases are equally important factors.

Death in service benefits

Most employees are concerned about the effect their untimely death would have on the financial security of their dependants. It is therefore usual for this problem to be catered for by the pension scheme in one or, usually, a combination of the following ways:

1. By providing a lump sum, usually calculated as a multiple of salary at the time of death.
2. By providing a spouse's pension, normally a proportion of pension due at normal retirement date.
3. By providing a child's pension in order to assist with family costs until the children have reached, say, 18.

Lump sum payments typically vary between one and four times annual salary; a good staff entitlement would currently be three or four times salary. This payment needs to be a significant amount if it is to fulfil its purpose of meeting short-term financial commitments and provide a financial cushion for dependants during the immediate period after bereavement. Most employers provide this cover for all staff regardless of service and make special provisions to allow at least some degree of cover prior to entry to the pension scheme. The earnings cap introduced by the 1989 Finance Act also affects the maximum level of lump sum death benefits for those employees who are subject to it.

Spouses' pensions are commonly one-half of the pension due on the employee's retirement based on his salary at death, although some more generous schemes provide the maximum permitted of up to two-thirds of the prospective pension (4/9ths of pay at the date of death).

Child pensions are also increasingly common but normally cease when the children reach 18 or finish full-time education.

Death in retirement benefits

As with death in service benefits, the principal objective is to ensure that the surviving spouse retains an acceptable level of income until her/his death. For this reason, the most common entitlement is a spouse's pension of one-half of the member's pension. The maximum permitted pension is two-thirds of the member's maximum pension entitlement before death, ignoring any pension reduction as a result of taking a lump sum at retirement.

Early retirement

Most final salary schemes allow employees to retire before normal pensionable age (but after age 50), and receive an immediate early retirement pension, but at a reduced rate. This is the most realistic approach in terms of costs to the company where early retirement is voluntary. Retirement through ill-health, which may be at any age, is usually given more sympathetic treatment under long-term disability provisions, which either allow for payment of the full pension earned up to the date of early retirement or even give credit for the years between the actual and normal retiring age.

Leaving service

For many employees, career progression depends on the ability to gain experience and promotion with several employers. Fewer and fewer staff stay with one employer for life. But older employees who might otherwise move, and benefit in career terms by doing so, often tend to stay on in companies they have outgrown or jobs where they are not particularly happy, because they feel themselves locked in by the pension rights they cannot afford to lose. Unless they gain substantial pay increases, or are very senior and able to negotiate 'top hat' arrangements, most employees lose out on the final value of their pension by changing jobs.

The loss arises from the way pensions are calculated in final salary schemes. The pension at retirement is a fraction, typically 1/60th, of final salary at retirement for each year of service. On leaving service, however, the pension is based on salary at the date of leaving.

Statutory and discretionary increases on the leaving service pension now go some way in making up the difference, but are unlikely to match the rate of increase in salary.

By contrast, a money purchase scheme will not normally distinguish between a leaver and a stayer. On leaving a money purchase scheme, a member's entitlement is usually the full amount accumulated for him in his individual account to the date of leaving. Thus members do not suffer the reduction in benefits that takes place on leaving service under a final salary scheme.

This does not always mean that leaving service benefits are better under a money purchase scheme. This will depend on such factors as the rate of contribution paid under the money purchase scheme, the success of the scheme's investment performance for the relevant period, the scale of benefits under an alternative final salary scheme, the level of pension increases under the final salary scheme, and the age of the member at the date of leaving.

'Top hat' arrangements

The tax efficiency of approved pension arrangements encourages many employers to provide benefits for senior executives and directors of the company up to the maximum levels permitted by the Inland Revenue. This can be done by exercising powers under the company pension scheme to augment individual members' benefits, or by effecting additional individual pension policies for the members concerned. Some companies operate a separate pension scheme for senior executives and directors.

The 1973 Finance Act removed the restriction on controlling directors joining occupational pension schemes, and this eventually led to the establishment of separate schemes, typically for just one or two controlling directors, and operated on a self-administered basis. This gave the directors the opportunity to decide on the investment of their pension contributions themselves rather than pay them to an insurance company. These schemes, known as 'small self-administered pension schemes', are subject to special additional conditions imposed by the Superannuation Funds Office to prevent abuse of the tax privileges.

Financing of approved pension schemes

Employee contributions

The 1989 NAPF Survey found that 78 per cent of schemes required contributions from members and 22 per cent were non-contributory. The arguments usually given in favour of contributory schemes are that sharing the cost between employer and employee often enables better benefits to be purchased and that employees appreciate benefits more – and see the schemes as their own – when they have had to pay for them. This can create an area of joint interest and co-operation which may help to improve the industrial relations climate. Employees in contributory schemes are also able to obtain tax relief on contributions – as well as refunds if they leave – after a short period of membership.

Non-contributory schemes generally allow the employer greater flexibility, while providing an attractive benefit at no obvious cost to the employee. The administrative costs are less and the total costs may not necessarily be more than those of contributory schemes, because the type of pension scheme can be taken into account in salary-market comparisons which affect the level at which salary scales are set.

Additional voluntary contributions

All schemes must provide a facility for members to pay contributions on a voluntary basis. Such Additional Voluntary Contributions, or AVCs, may be invested in the main scheme, or through a separate contract with a building society or insurance company. AVCs may operate on a cash accumulation principle, whereby the AVCs earn interest, or on a with profits basis whereby they earn bonuses, or they may be unit linked. In a final salary scheme they may be used to buy additional years of service.

The Finance (No 2) Act 1987 removed the requirement that, once started, AVCs could only be stopped after 5 years or in cases of financial hardship, and thus allowed for AVCs to be paid on a one-off basis. However, the same Act also required that AVC arrangements commencing after 8 April 1987 must eventually be taken in pension rather than lump sum form on retirement.

Since November 1987, members have been able to take out a free-standing AVC contract with an insurance company (or other free-standing AVC provider) of their own choice instead of the company's AVC arrangements.

Employer's contributions

Under a final salary scheme, the employer is usually responsible for paying the 'balance of the cost of the benefits'. This will usually result in the employer paying more, often considerably more, than the employees, perhaps between one and three times the employees' contribution rate.

The employer's rate of contribution to a final salary scheme will vary from time to time. If pension costs escalate, eg through high-pay inflation, the employer may need to increase his contribution or pay special additional contributions. Conversely, if the experience goes well, eg investments perform better than expected, the employer may be able to reduce or temporarily suspend, his contributions.

With a money purchase scheme, the employer simply decides what contribution he wishes to pay. Hence the term 'defined contribution' for a money purchase scheme, and 'defined benefit' for a final salary scheme.

Pension scheme surpluses

At periodic intervals, usually every three years, although sometimes more frequently, a final salary scheme will be valued by an actuary. One of the purposes of the valuation is to compare the value of the investments in the fund against the estimated value of pensions earned up to the date of the valuation. If the investments are worth more than the pensions the difference is described as surplus.

The Finance Act 1986 attempted to limit the extent to which surpluses could build up in tax exempt funds. Excessive surpluses must now be reduced by a combination of benefit improvements and contribution reductions or holidays, or repaid to the employer less a 40 per cent tax charge. If no such action is taken to eliminate an excessive surplus, part of the investment income and capital gains of the fund will lose their tax exemption.

Investment medium

A pension scheme will invest the current contributions received from the employer and employees to build up funds from which to provide the benefits when they fall due in the future. The trustees of the scheme, using the services of professional investment managers such as stockbrokers and merchant banks, can invest in their own portfolio of stocks and shares. These schemes are usually referred to as directly invested or self-administered pension schemes. For smaller and medium-sized pension schemes, investment in managed funds operated by insurance companies and other fund managers offers the opportunity to participate in investment experience directly without the costs of individual portfolio management.

Alternatively, the pension contributions can be paid as premiums under an insurance contract. The insurance company will then invest the premiums in stocks and shares, and channel the investment earnings to the pension scheme in the form of interest or bonuses on the insurance contract. The insurance company will generally hold back part of the investment earnings to smooth out market value fluctuations.

The choice of funding arrangements is a complex process and it is usually necessary to obtain independent advice on the approach to be adopted.

Communication

The Social Security Act 1985 provided for greater disclosure of information about company pension schemes to their members. This includes access to scheme trust deeds and rules, annual benefit statements, and annual reports containing a copy of the scheme's audited accounts, actuarial statement and other general information about the scheme.

Apart from the statutory requirement to give information to members, the prohibition of compulsory membership of company pension schemes from April 1988 – and the introduction of personal pensions from July 1988 has led many employers to make greater efforts to 'sell' their schemes to employees.

The advice which pension scheme managers and administrators give to employees can, in some cases, be subject to the Financial Services Act 1986. The Act covers advising on investments and arranging deals in investments, and only persons authorized under the Act may engage in such investment business. Advising employees about joining the company scheme is not investment advice, but advice on the relative merits of particular insurance policies might be.

Unapproved schemes

In addition to introducing the earnings cap for approved schemes the 1989 Finance Act made changes to the tax laws governing unapproved pension arrangements so as to make it possible for companies to provide additional benefits through unapproved schemes for employees who are subject to the earnings cap. Two types of unapproved scheme are possible, funded or unfunded.

A funded unapproved scheme operates in the same way as an approved scheme except that:

- the employer's contributions paid are taxable on the employee as earned income
- the employee's contributions, if any, are paid from taxed income
- the fund is taxed at the basic rates of income tax and capital gains tax on its income and capital gains respectively
- retirement benefits can be taken entirely in the form of a tax-free lump sum (although any benefits paid as pension are taxed as earned income).

Under an unfunded unapproved scheme the employer makes no contributions, but undertakes to provide benefits at retirement. All benefits received are taxable on the employee.

At present very few companies have established unapproved pension schemes. However, the number is likely to grow as more employees become subject to the earnings cap.

Pensions check-lists

A. Information about the present arrangements

Information about the present arrangements can be obtained from the following documents:

- Trust Deed and Rules, plus subsequent deeds of amendment, variation, etc.
- Insurance policies if the scheme is fully or partly insured.
- Member's booklet and any announcements issued to members.
- Annual reports to members, incorporating trustees' report, audited accounts and actuarial statement. An individual statement of benefits will usually be issued to each member with the report.
- Actuarial reports (usually every three years) on the financial position of the scheme.

From these documents, it should be possible to discover basic information about the scheme as follows:

Administration

- Who are the scheme's trustees?
- Who is responsible for the scheme's administration?
- What external advisers does the scheme have?

Inland Revenue approval

Has the Superannuation Funds Office of the Inland Revenue confirmed that the scheme is fully approved under Chapter I, Part XIV of the Income and Corporation Taxes Act 1988, or does the scheme only have interim approval?

State pensions

Is the scheme contracted out of the State Earnings Related Pension Scheme (SERPS)?

Eligibility

- What categories of employee are eligible to join the scheme?
- What are the minimum and maximum entry ages, if any?

- Is there a minimum service requirement?

Pensionable age
What are the normal pensionable ages for men and women?

Benefits on retirement

- Is the scheme final salary or money purchase, or some other basis?
- If final salary, what is the rate of pension for each year of service? What definition of earnings is used to calculate the pension?
- If money purchase, how is the pension determined?
- Is there an option to take a lump sum at retirement, or does the scheme provide a lump sum as well as pension?
- Can employees who work beyond normal pensionable age remain in the scheme? How are their benefits affected?
- What provisions are there for early retirement? How are early retirement benefits calculated? Do these distinguish between early retirement on ill health grounds, redundancy, and voluntary early retirement?
- Is there any provision to increase pensions in payment? Are increases guaranteed or discretionary? What increases have been awarded in recent years?

Benefits on death

- What lump sums and/or spouse's pensions are payable on death in service or after retirement?
- Are children's benefits payable on death? Are these increased if there is no surviving spouse?
- Are death in service benefits limited to pension scheme members?

Benefits on leaving service

- What benefits are payable on leaving service? Does the scheme treat leavers with less than a minimum number of years' service differently from longer servers?
- What increases does the scheme give to any deferred pensions left in the scheme by early leavers?
- What interest does the scheme pay on refunds of members' contributions?

Financing and investment

- Are members required to contribute, and at what rates?
- What are the facilities for paying Additional Voluntary Contributions (AVCs)?

- What is the company's rate of contribution, currently and historically? How is the company's contribution determined?
- How are the contributions invested; in a self-administered fund, managed fund, or other insurance contract? Who are the investment managers?
- Is the investment return linked directly to the performance of investment markets, indirectly linked, or related to interest rates?
- What have the investment rates of return been historically, or rates of bonus, if applicable?

B. Analysis of present arrangements

State Pensions
Has the right contracting out decision been taken? Should the company operate both contracted out and contracted in arrangements?

Eligibility
- Are the conditions for joining the scheme unnecessarily restrictive? Should coverage be extended?
- Should members who opt out of the company scheme in favour of personal pensions be re-admitted on request? More than once?

Pensionable age
- Is the company's policy on pensionable age equally fair to men and women?
- Should a policy of flexible pensionable ages be adopted, whereby retirement is permitted within a range of ages without reducing a member's pension?

Benefits on retirement
- How does the benefit formula compare with other schemes? Does it result in worthwhile pensions?
- Is the definition of final salary appropriate? Can it be simplified or improved on?
- Does the scheme permit lump sum commutation up to the maximum permitted by the Inland Revenue? Are the rates for commuting pension for cash fair?
- Are the benefits for working beyond pensionable age reasonable?
- Are pensions on early retirement reasonable? Are they consistent with the company's personnel policies (see also Pensionable age)?
- How have past pension increases compared with inflation over the same period? Are pensions reviewed frequently enough?

Benefits on death

- Are the benefits on death adequate for the needs of dependants left behind?
- Are widowers' pensions provided in respect of female members on the same terms as widows' pensions?
- Should death in service benefits be provided for all employees regardless of scheme membership?

Benefits on leaving service

- To what extent are early leavers from the scheme penalized, compared with the benefits they would have received for their past service if they had stayed in the scheme?
- If final salary, does the scheme offer a money purchase underpin, or some other method of limiting the early leaver's loss?
- On leaving service, what assistance does the scheme offer in helping members choose between a deferred pension, transfer value to another scheme, or buy-out policy?

Financing and investment

- If contributory, does the scheme provide good value to members in respect of their own contributions?
- Are the AVC arrangements competitive?
- Is the company getting good value for its contributions?
- If final salary, how well funded are the benefits? Are the benefits in respect of past service, after allowing for projected salaries, fully covered by the current assets?
- What allowance is built into the funding rate for discretionary pension increases?
- Under what circumstances can the scheme be wound up? What are members' entitlements in this event?
- How well have the investments been managed? Is the performance independently monitored and reported on?

Communications and administration

- Does the scheme produce attractive and intelligible literature about the scheme? Do they get individual statements of benefits which illustrate their entitlements clearly?
- Do members have sufficient access to scheme managers to obtain advice?
- Do the administration systems allow membership data to be readily accessed and processed? Are benefits calculated promptly and accurately?

C. Introducing or amending a pension scheme

The steps a company will need to take when introducing or amending a pension scheme are as follows:

1. Analyze present arrangements.
2. Consult member representatives for members' views on present arrangements.
3. Make a preliminary assessment of the need to change present arrangements and select advisers to help in developing new or revised scheme.
4. In conjunction with advisers, identify and evaluate the alternatives for each aspect of the pension scheme design from the point of view of:
   - market practice of similar companies
   - employee appreciation
   - costs
   - administration
5. Make decisions on type of scheme, ie insured or self-administered, final salary or money purchase, contracted out, etc.
6. Decide on benefit and contribution levels. Consider special provisions for certain individuals or categories of staff.
7. If a scheme is new, appoint scheme trustees and an administrator, and engage services of any external advisers as required, eg consultants, actuaries, investment managers, insurers, etc. If the scheme is in place, consider any changes to present advisers. Scheme advisers would be responsible for the remaining tasks, or would assist with them.
8. Notify members of new or revised pension provisions. If appropriate, advance notice of intentions may be given to allow for employee representations. Presentations and discussions may be held to explain pension provisions, and allow for queries.
9. Notify relevant authorities in prescribed forms.
10. Establish new or revised administration procedures.

Chapter 18

Tax Considerations

Why tax efficiency matters

There are many messages that can be given by an employer to an employee in the design and implementation of sophisticated remuneration packages, especially for senior management and other highly paid employees. To the extent that taxation reduces the amount of salary, bonus or benefit given by an employer to an employee, it reduces the strength of the message that the latter receives. It follows therefore that a tax-efficient package can benefit both employer and employee. From the employer's perspective it can reduce costs, from the employee's perspective it can enhance the benefits of working for that employer. Unfortunately the government has a monopoly on devising tax-free remuneration products. However those that do exist should be used to the full provided that they support the corporate objectives of the employer.

Tax efficiency

A tax-efficient benefit is one for which the tax payable on the cost of providing the benefit is less than the tax that would be payable by the employer and employee on the equivalent cash sum. In the past, tax efficiency was one of the main reasons for the proliferation of benefits, but it has become progressively less important as governments have tightened up the fiscal rules relating to employee benefits. Pension schemes, however, are still highly tax efficient, as are company cars although, in the latter case, this is being steadily eroded by government legislation.

Although the pursuit of tax efficiency is not of such paramount importance as formerly, it is still necessary to understand the principles and practice of tax law on benefits, and the law as it stands in 1990 (post-Finance Act 1990) is summarized later in this chapter. But because fiscal regulations are constantly changing, it is essential to update these after every Budget or other piece of fiscal legislation or court decision. It is also necessary to remember that tax legislation, like any form of legislation, can be interpreted in many different ways. It is therefore always advisable to obtain advice from a tax specialist and/or the Inland Revenue before introducing or changing a benefit. It is also advisable to review benefits after each Budget to assess the implications of any changes.

The tax considerations affecting benefits are the most important ones from the point of view of reward management policies and practices. But they need to be considered within the context of the general provisions of tax law, which are summarized below.

The basics of tax law

For most employers, the tax considerations affecting their employees' rewards are contained in that body of law and practice known to taxation practitioners as Schedule E. Income tax was introduced in the UK as a temporary measure to finance the war against Napoleon, and to this day it remains a 'temporary' tax that must be re-enacted each year or lapse. The schedular system of taxation in the UK has its roots in the earliest days of income tax, when the notion was introduced that, before you could compute the income of a taxpayer, it was first necessary to allocate each specific source of income received to a particular schedule. Specific rules were drawn up to deal with the income of each schedule. For example, rents from land were assessed under Schedule A; income from woodlands were assessed under Schedule B; income from Government Securities under Schedule C and so on. This schedular anachronism was reintroduced in 1842 and it and its anomalies have been with us ever since. Its practical effects are to complicate simple matters and to puzzle taxpayers as to why a simple tax computation can lead to three different demands for tax all payable on three different dates! However, what is important for employers to know is that the schedules are mutually exclusive and employees who are taxable under Schedule E will not have their employment income taxed under any other schedule.

Schedule E

Schedule E is found in the Taxes Acts, but in a sense it transcends those Acts and carries with it its very own charging paragraphs:

> Paragraph 1 of Schedule E provides that tax under the schedule shall be charged in respect of any office or employment on the emoluments therefrom, and provides that tax shall not be chargeable in respect of emoluments of an office or employment under any other paragraph of Schedule E. It is divided into three cases: Case I where the employee is resident – and ordinarily resident –

in the UK, Case II where the employee is not ordinarily resident in the UK, and Case III where the employee is resident in the UK.

Paragraph 2 taxes under Schedule E certain annuities and pensions paid by the crown.

Paragraph 3 taxes pensions paid in the UK.

Paragraph 4 charges pensions paid by government departments to public servants who have been employed abroad; and last of all.

Paragraph 5 states that the preceding provisions of the Schedule are without prejudice to any other provision in the Tax Acts, directing tax to be charged under the Schedule, and tax so directed to be charged shall be charged accordingly.

Defining emoluments

It follows, therefore, that any *emoluments* will be taxed under Paragraph 1 and that *emoluments* may not be taxed under any other paragraph. Paragraph 5 by contrast provides that, notwithstanding Paragraph 1, if any section in any Tax Act states that tax shall be charged under Schedule E, Paragraph 5 enables such a charge to be made. The obvious conclusion which is to be drawn is that, while Paragraph 1 taxes emoluments, Paragraph 5 brings within the charge to income tax under Schedule E items which are not emoluments.

Two categories of income therefore fall within the potential scope of Schedule E – emoluments and other items which are not emoluments, but which are specifically legislated to be taxed under Schedule E.

The scope of Paragraph 1, commonly known as the general rules of Schedule E, is extremely broad. The definition given by the Taxes Acts is that the expression emoluments shall include all 'salaries, fees, wages, perquisites and profits whatsoever'. One advantage of having an antiquated tax system is that we have the benefit of many years of litigation between the crown and taxpayers and by the time we come to consider the precise meaning of words such as 'perquisites and profits whatsoever', we have the benefit of generations of judicial thought giving us their learned opinions. The 1990 edition of *Tolleys Tax Cases* reported 115 cases dealing with the simple matter of interpreting whether or not certain benefits or payment constituted 'perquisites and profits whatsoever'. Generally it is fair to say that a consensus of tax advisers would be that any payment of money by an employer to an employee on account of services rendered, or to be rendered, be they in the past, present or future, will constitute emoluments.

If assets are provided to employees rather than cash payments made to them, then the value which, in the first instance, would be assessable on the employee is the value of the cash into which they could convert that asset. However, special rules have been introduced for the taxation of directors and other employees earning more than £8,500 a year, and the basis of the taxation liability was shifted to the cost to the employer rather than the second-hand value of any asset. The level of remuneration at which an employee is caught by these benefit rules has not been lifted since 1979 and anyone earning the now modest sum of £8,500 per annum, including all benefits and expenses, will be treated as a director for these purposes. This is called the P11D limit from the designation of the return that has to be submitted to the Inland Revenue, listing the benefits and expenses received by an employee. The erosion of this P11D limit is a deliberate Government policy.

The scope of Paragraph 5 of Schedule E, which charges to income tax items which are not emoluments, encompasses many types of transaction that would not fall within the general rules of Schedule E. For example, restrictive covenants, golden handshakes, share transactions, vouchers, expenses and benefits of directors and higher paid employees, and living accommodation all have their own legislation specifically creating a tax charge under Schedule E.

The PAYE obligations

The Inland Revenue rely on the employer to provide them with details of transactions between the employer and employee. In the first instance, the PAYE system requires the deduction by the employer of tax at source from emoluments paid to the employee and the accounting for that tax direct to the Inland Revenue. For items where a PAYE deduction cannot be made, there are a number of reporting obligations and deadlines which place onerous responsibilities on the employer. For example, all expenses and benefits for higher paid employees have to be reported to the Inland Revenue (on form P11D) by 5 May each year in respect of the tax year ended on 5 April, unless specific dispensation for certain types of expenses has been granted by the Inland Revenue. Similarly, when an employer grants share options to an employee, a return showing full details must be made to the Inland Revenue within 30 days of the end of the tax year.

A table of income tax rates for 1990/91 is set out below.

Table 18.1 *Income Tax Rates 1990/91*

Rate	Slice	Tax Payable
	£	£
25%	20,700	5,175
40%	*any further income*	

The table shows how the rate of tax increases from the basic rate of 25 per cent to the higher rate band of 40 per cent as taxable income grows from £20,700 (all of which will be taxed at 25 per cent), after which each pound will be taxed at 40 per cent. It should be noted that taxable income is the income of the individual after deduction of all reliefs and other tax-deductible expenses or payments. From the employer's perspective, the reliefs and taxable benefits will usually be reflected in the PAYE notice of coding given by the Inland Revenue to the employer and approximately the correct rate of tax will be withheld from the individual's earnings by operation of the PAYE system.

The PAYE system may not, however, fully match up with the tax liabilities of the individual employees and a tax assessment may be issued by the Inspector of Taxes to charge any shortfall. There has been a major change on the basis of assessment to Schedule E. Prior to Finance Act 1989 the taxable amount was based on amounts *earned* by the employee in a tax year irrespective of whether payment was made of the emoluments. Post Finance Act 1989 the taxable amount is now based on sums *received* in a tax year rather than the amount earned.

For the majority of employees on a monthly salary this change will be of little practical effect, but for directors and those paid bonuses there will be some changes. This is a very important change for deferred bonus plans and it makes their introduction and implementation easier from a tax perspective, since only when the incentives are paid are they taxable. The main problem area is the definition of when amounts are deemed to be received and when PAYE must be accounted for.

For non-directors this is defined as when payment is made or when the employee becomes entitled to payment, whichever date falls earlier. Thus, if payment of, for example, a bonus is deferred, PAYE should still be accounted for on the date when the employee becomes entitled to payment. For directors, however, the position is more complex in that payment is regarded as being made on the earliest of:

(a) when payment is actually made;
(b) when the director is entitled to be paid;
(c) when earnings of the director are credited in the company's accounts or records (even if they cannot immediately be drawn);
(d) if the amount of the director's earnings for a particular period is determined before the end of that period, when the period ends; and
(e) if the amount is determined after the period ends, when the earnings are determined.

The Revenue's guidance note is somewhat confusing in relation to (c) above as it states that an entry for remuneration in accounts being proposed for the company's AGM would not normally constitute the crediting of remuneration to a director, although if the directors are also the controlling shareholders this may not necessarily be the case. It also suggests that a general accounting provision for remuneration not relating to any specific directors will not fall within (c).

An amount will be treated as credited in the company's accounts, even if there is a legal block which prevents the director drawing on the sums, or even if the credit is to an account not specifically in that director's name. However, if the director only becomes entitled to an amount when certain conditions are met, the amount is not 'paid' until the conditions are satisfied.

Taxation of benefits

A benefit in kind is defined as accommodation (other than living accommodation), entertainment, domestic or other services, and other benefits and facilities of whatever nature. This definition is provided by section 154, Taxes Act 1988 and is intended to cover all benefits where no other specific section sets out a charging mechanism such as is stated for company cars, free petrol and cheap-rate loans. The law relating to the taxation of benefits is summarized below.

Benefits for directors and employees paid over £8,500 a year

Special rules have been introduced for the taxation of directors and employees paid over £8,500 a year which provide for the basis of the tax liability to be shifted to the cost to the employer rather than the second-hand value of the asset.

This level is called the P11D limit from the designation of the return that has to be submitted to the Inland Revenue listing the benefits and expenses by an employee. The threshold of £8,500 includes the value of benefits and expenses. The low level of this threshold, which has been maintained deliberately over a number of years, means that the great majority of full-time staff in organizations are above the limit.

Non-taxable benefits

The following benefits are at present (1990) not taxed:

- *Approved Pension Scheme*: in Inland Revenue approved pension schemes no tax charge arises on employees in respect of the contributions made to the pension scheme by the employer; the contributions made by the employees to pension schemes are deductible from earnings for tax purposes; the income accruing to the pension fund does so on a tax-free basis and tax-free lump sums can be given to employees when they retire. To be Inland Revenue approved, the scheme must, amongst other things, limit the pension to two-thirds of final remuneration. There is, however, a pensionable earnings limit on new tax-approved schemes of £60,000, which means that the maximum pension which will attract tax relief is £40,000 ($\frac{2}{3}$ final salary). These limits were introduced in Finance Act 1989 and will increase each year in accordance with the increase in the retail prices index rounded up to the next full percentage point of £60,000 so that no increase will ever be less than £600. In 1990/1 the limit was £64,800
- *accommodation*: where this is used solely in performing the duties of the appointment. Apart from exemptions for the Prime Minister and Chancellor of the Exchequer, this is unlikely to affect any employer
- *meals*: as long as they are served to employees generally
- *car-parking space*: if this is at or near to the place of work
- *subscriptions*: to approved professional institutions or learned societies

Benefits for which special taxation rules apply

- *company cars*: where a car is made available to a director or an employee paid over £8,500 a year or to his or her family for private use, the employee will be liable to income tax on the cash equivalent, otherwise known as the scale benefit or scale rate. Tax is paid at the highest rate of the employee. For example, the scales applicable in 1990/91 provided for a car of 1401–2000cc, under four years old and costing up to £19,250, to have a scale rate of £2,200. If the employee's business mileage for the tax year was between 2,500 and 18,000 miles and if his or her marginal tax rate was 25 per cent, the tax cost to the employee would be £550.

  The cash equivalent is increased by half if business travel is less than 2,500 miles in the tax year and is reduced by half if business travel in the year exceeds 18,000 miles

- *petrol*: petrol or other car fuels provided by the company are chargeable to income tax on the basis of the cash equivalent of the benefit in accordance with a car fuel benefit scale or cash equivalent. For example, the scale applicable to higher paid employees in 1990/91 for a car between 1401–2000cc was £600. Thus employees on a marginal tax rate of 25 per cent would pay £150 tax. There will therefore be a benefit as long as they consume more than about 80 gallons a year on private motoring.

  The cash equivalent for car fuel is reduced proportionately if the motor car is not available to the employee for the complete tax year (in the same way that the cash equivalent for the motor car is reduced). Similarly, if the motor car is used predominantly for business purposes then the cash equivalent for car fuel is reduced by half. However, there is no provision for increasing the cash equivalent for car fuel by half if the motor car is not used substantially or is a second or subsequent motor car.

  If the employee is required to make good the entire expense incurred in providing fuel for his/her private use and he/she does so, or if car fuel is provided only for business travel, then the cash equivalent is reduced to nil. Journeys between the employee's home and normal place of work are regarded as private motoring. If the employee makes good only part of the expenses incurred in providing fuel for his/her private use, the cash equivalent will not be reduced by the amount contributed and the full amount of the cash equivalent will remain taxable. This can be contrasted with payments for the private use of a company car where even a part payment will serve to reduce the cash equivalent.

  The cash equivalent for car fuel is only chargeable in respect of motor cars provided by the employer where there is a private use by the employee. It does not apply to fuel provided for an employee's privately-owned motor car where there are different tax considerations.

  Changes have been introduced in the Finance Act 1990 to amend the tax rules for employees who use their own car for business purposes. Such employees can claim a deduction for the business proportion of the running costs, eg insurance, road tax, petrol etc and, in certain limited circumstances, can also claim capital allowances and a deduction for loan interest paid. Mileage allowances paid are taxable if they exceed costs for which relief is due. The Finance Act 1990 has extended the circumstances in which capital allowances and loan interest deductions may be claimed; these are now available (on a pro-rata basis for business use) to any employee who uses his or her car for work. Previously, these were only available if the car was 'necessarily provided' for use in the employment.

Major changes have also been made in the voluntary fixed profit car scheme (FPCS) which many employers operate rather than calculating tax relief based on actual costs. This scheme previously prescribed tax-free mileage rates as follows:

Car engine size:

Up to 1,000 cc	24.5p
1,001–1,500 cc	30p
1,501 cc upwards	34p

Mileage rates paid above these limits were taxable.

It is now considered that these rates are too high and the scheme could give more relief than the costs incurred, particularly if business mileage is high. Accordingly they have been amended as follows:

Car engine size	*Up to 4,000 miles*	*Over 4,000 miles*
Up to 1,000 cc	24.5p	9.5p
1,001–1,500 cc	30p	11.5p
1,501–2,000 cc	34p	13.5p
2,001 cc upwards	43p	16.5p

It is considered that the addition of the new engine size band and the differing rates for mileage under and over 4,000 will mean that the tax-free rate is more closely matched to actual business costs for the typical employee. In particular those driving more than 4,000 business miles per annum will not be able to benefit from excessive tax-free reimbursements.

Transitional arrangements ensure that any increases in tax liability will be phased in gradually. Taxable mileage allowances in 1990/91 will be limited to the amount taxable in 1989/90, and increases in each subsequent year will be limited to £1,000, assuming business mileage does not increase.

It is worth pointing out that the FPCS is a voluntary scheme, and any employee is free to 'opt out' of the scheme and have his liability calculated by reference to actual costs incurred. This will require detailed records of business and private mileage and costs incurred to be kept, but it may mean a lower tax liability in some cases

- *relocation allowances*: these can be tax free within limits allowed by the Inland Revenue. Disturbance allowances, however, are taxable
- *ex-gratia payments given as compensation for loss of office* (golden handshakes): these are taxable if they amount to more than £30,000

- *uniforms provided by the employer* (within strictly defined limits) are tax free
- *luncheon vouchers*: up to the value of 15p a day are tax free
- *loans*: the benefit from interest-free or low-interest loans is not taxable if the cash equivalent – the difference between the interest charged to the employee, if any, is less than £200. If the cash equivalent is more than £200, then the whole benefit is taxable (including the first £200)
- *workshop nurseries*: are not counted as benefits in kind as long as they are registered nurseries and playgroups for children under five and are provided by the employer at a workplace or elsewhere, or are similar facilities provided for the care of older children after school hours or during holiday periods. Note, however, that a subsidy provided by an employer for a private nursery is treated as a benefit in kind.

Share schemes for directors and employees

A company normally introduces an employee share scheme for the following reasons:

- to provide an incentive for certain key members of the management team by rewarding them according to the performance of the company
- to encourage employees generally to identify with the success or failure of their company by giving them a financial interest in its results.

A simple share scheme might involve giving shares to employees or allowing them to subscribe the shares at less than their market value. However, many employees will not wish both their savings and their jobs to be dependent on the continuing success of the company and therefore may quickly dispose of their shares. If this happens the scheme will achieve its objective only to a limited extent.

More commonly, an employee share scheme is designed to give the individual an equity interest which does not involve any immediate capital outlay and which cannot immediately be sold or realized. One way of achieving this is to grant the employee an option to buy shares at or below their current value, the option to be exerciseable only after a period of years. In the past, partly-paid share schemes, where the major part of the issue price is left outstanding, have also been used.

It should be remembered that the incentive effect of employee share schemes may be limited in larger enterprises, since the return which they provide is linked to the performance of the company as a whole measured in terms of the share price and not to the performance of the particular division or section in which the individual is employed. Such schemes will not necessarily lead to employees retaining a long-term equity interest in the company since, if the scheme is to provide any incentive, there must be a date when the participant is freely entitled to dispose of his or her shares and to realize his or her profit in cash.

The basic tax legislation does not permit artificial manipulation to provide remuneration in a disguised form through increase in share values.

Since 1978 however, three types of approved schemes have been introduced which, if certain conditions are met, avoid the tax penalties imposed by the basic legislation and may provide additional tax benefits:

1. Approved profit sharing schemes introduced in the Finance Act 1978.
2. Approved savings-related share option schemes introduced in the Finance Act 1980.
3. Approved share option schemes introduced in the Finance Act 1984.

Although the rules applying to each of the three schemes are similar in many areas, the schemes are very different in concept.

The main contrasting features are as follows:

- shares or options – under an approved profit sharing scheme participants are given shares in the company, whereas under the other two schemes they are given options to subscribe for shares
- eligibility for participation – an approved share option scheme may be applied to selected personnel only, the other two approved schemes must allow all full-time directors and employees to participate on similar terms
- limits on benefits – the maximum which can be provided to an individual under an approved savings-related share option scheme or under an approved profit sharing scheme is much lower than the limit under an approved share option scheme
- cost of shares – shares are provided to participants at no cost under an approved profit sharing scheme, at up to a maximum discount of 20 per cent under an approved savings-related share option scheme, and at no discount under an approved share option scheme
- tax benefits – an approved profit sharing scheme can provide a tax-free benefit since the initial value of the shares which the participant is given is free of all taxes if the shares are held for at least five years. The other two schemes do not provide tax-free benefits but ensure that the benefits obtained are subject to capital gains tax rather than to income tax. Now that the rates of

income tax and capital gains tax are equal, this advantage is diminished
- tax deduction – in the case of an approved profit sharing scheme the company may obtain a tax deduction for the cost of providing the shares to the participants, but a deduction is not available for new shares issued when options are exercised under the other two approved schemes.

Taxable benefits

The following cash benefits or benefits in kind are taxable (1990/91) for employees above the earnings limit, apart from certain exceptions noted below:

- payments for expenses which have not been wholly, exclusively and necessarily incurred in the performance of the relevant duties of the employee
- entertaining non-employees of the company
- the cost of medical insurance subscriptions
- the cost of luncheon vouchers above 15p a day.
  (N.B. this ruling applies to staff earning *below* the earnings limit of £8,500 – it is an archaic practice which persists from the time when 3 shillings bought a reasonable three-course meal!)
- the cost of accommodation if not used solely in performing the duties of the appointment
- the cash equivalent of loans or mortgage subsidies (the difference between the interest paid by the employee and the official rate)
- payment of telephone rental charges and private telephone calls (also applies to *all* employees)

It is necessary to re-emphasize, however, that the application of the basic principles of benefit taxation is by no means clear-cut, and it is always advisable to get a ruling from the Inland Revenue on any benefit, for example relocation allowances, where there may be some doubts about tax liabilities. It is particularly important to ensure that employees are warned of potential tax liabilities and the fact that they will be reported on their P11D *before* a benefit is offered to them so that they do not receive any unpleasant surprises when they receive their tax assessment.

Tax and the self-employed

The income tax position for individuals will depend significantly on whether they are liable to income tax as employees under the rules of Schedule E or as self-employed traders under the rules of

Schedule D. The tax legislation determining the basis of taxing income either under Schedule D or E has not changed substantially since 1842. Although it is very difficult to state with any certainty whether a particular activity will constitute a trade or an employment because of the great number of conflicting legal decisions there are on the subject, generally speaking companies are aware of whether they are making payments to employees or to independent traders. However, it is not always a clear-cut matter and there is the possibility that, if taken to the Commissioners of Inland Revenue or to the courts, the tax status could be altered with consequent taxation implications. The Inland Revenue has published a leaflet (called IR56 – obtainable from local tax offices) which attempts to help individuals decide if they are employees or self-employed traders.

Using outside advisers

The changing nature of taxation makes it vital to keep up to date with developments in law and Inland Revenue practice. Most personnel departments use a number of publications and from time to time consult outside experts in taxation. These experts will be either tax specialists within the finance function or their external advisers. Or the remuneration function may need to seek independent advice.

One of the difficulties often found after such an encounter is that the tax advice, although sound, is not capable of implementation. Because taxation experts tend to have a narrow perspective, it is essential that the personnel department briefs the expert well and explains the business objectives and context that have created the need to seek advice. It will also need to give an indication of the solutions that will and will not be acceptable, stressing that 'artificial constructions' which run counter to the general direction of salary policy are unlikely to be worth considering.

Chapter 19

Total Remuneration – Putting the Package Together

Application of the total remuneration or 'remuneration package' concept involves treating all aspects of pay and benefits policy as a whole. It gives valuable discipline and perspective to the overall process of salary and benefits planning and creates a framework within which the different elements of remuneration can be adjusted according to the needs of the organization and the individual. The cost to the company and the value to the individual of each element is assessed with the aim of achieving an appropriate balance between the various components of remuneration for each employee grade or category. The concept applies to all levels of staff, but it is usually of more importance at senior levels because competitive practice and tax considerations have led to the development of a much wider range of benefits in addition to salary for senior executives.

It is generally agreed that senior executives should be paid salaries and be provided with benefits which give enough 'headroom' for the establishment of a series of properly graduated differentials between each level of responsibility below them. At the top level as indeed elsewhere in most organizations motivation is not just a matter of money: success, power and influence have substantial incentive value (see Chapter 1). Nevertheless, companies are often judged by their competitors on the salaries paid to directors, whose level of annual remuneration has to be stated by law in the annual report. Despite this, top executive remuneration is not generally as high in cash terms in the UK as it is in the USA and some of Europe although with the internationalization of company operations and executive recruitment this picture is beginning to change. In many cases, however, the benefit provisions are greater, reflecting the tax and other pressures of the last three decades. The distribution of directors' and senior management salaries within this general pattern still varies enormously and is often more unpredictable than one might expect in terms of company size and type (see Chapter 4).

As we have said many times in this book, the approach adopted to remuneration is a matter of individual organization philosophy about the acceptability for each employee level or category of different forms of reward. Practice varies enormously by industrial sector: the pressures imposed by a heavily unionized manufacturing base are very different from those current in the financial sector or from a newly constituted Government Agency.

Assessing and managing the total remuneration package

In assessing the best mix of possible components of remuneration at each level, both from its own and from the employees' point of view, the organization should have a clear idea of the climate and attitudes and culture it wants to achieve and how these meet business needs as well as individual aspirations. Apart from the statutory contributions to state insurance and pension schemes the main elements of total remuneration are:

1. Basic salary, pensions, sick pay, holidays, all-employee profit shares or SAYE share options and other entitlements normally provided for all staff.
2. Benefits or additional remuneration that is available only to staff in limited employee categories: eg incentives and bonuses, executive share options, company cars.
3. Benefits available to all or some staff categories which are only used according to individual need: housing and removal assistance, medical insurance, permanent disability cover, etc.

These will need to be considered in terms of policy on differentials and comparisons with other competing organizations.

All the major salary survey producers give at least an outline of current practice and trends. Consultants with major databases such as Hay and TPFeC provide much more detailed analyses of total remuneration packages. As the quality of benefits data improves, especially in club surveys, reasonably reliable information on the components of total remuneration for each job should be available to assist decision making.

It is still, however, not easy to assess the total value of all benefits in addition to pay and to evaluate the pattern of total remuneration against cost parameters for each employee category, because items such as sick pay are always variable and the age and requirements of employees in competing organizations will often be different and so give misleading comparisons. It may be helpful, therefore, just to list the items involved by employee category (see Table 19.1) and check the balance to see if any policy adjustments seem necessary. At the same time the fundamental reason for providing each item and its cost to the organization should be analyzed.

In reviewing policy in this way the following questions which lead on from those in Chapter 16 covering benefits strategy (see p 314) should be asked:

1. Are basic salary levels set at an acceptable and competitive place in relation to the market?
2. Are merit payments, incentives, or bonuses and other performance rewards achieving the results intended?
3. Are basic benefit entitlements of a satisfactory standard?
4. Are status-related differences in benefit entitlements set at the right level? If problems exist what solutions are possible?
   (a) Extension of the benefit to more employee categories if not ruled out by cost considerations?
   (b) Revision of the rules to restrict future entitlement to business need only, phased in at some appropriate time – such as a general salary review – and bought out on an acceptable basis?
5. Are the current entitlements which are based on status differences acceptable in terms of any incentive value that may be gained?
6. What improvements would increase the effectiveness and competitiveness of the package within the organization's remuneration budget limits?
7. Does the remuneration budget need to be amended or enlarged to take account of measures that may produce long-term benefits in terms of attracting and retaining employees?
8. Is the communication of remuneration entitlements effective and up-to-date? Is it putting the right message across?

This kind of review really needs to be conducted annually as part of overall compensation policy planning. Proposals for change will need to be considered in the following terms.

1. For which employee categories is the new measure most appropriate?
2. What are the short- and long-term costs?
3. What are the likely effects in terms of employee attitudes? Is the proposed change high in perceived value and low in cost to provide – or the reverse?
4. Is government intervention likely to affect the value or tax effectiveness of new benefits or approaches to salary policy?
5. If this happens could they be bought out without undue resistance?
6. What are the administrative implications of any of the above? Will additional time and/or manpower be involved within the salary function or elsewhere?

Table 19.1 *An example of total remuneration for a medium-sized employer*

	Employee category	Directors	Senior and middle management	Junior management and clerical staff	Manual employees
	Salary levels	Ungraded	Grades 1–4	Grades 5–9	Grades 7–12 Union-negotiated in relation to skill
	Range (£)	65,000–120,000	25,000–65,000	8,500–25,000	9,000–18,000
Benefits/Entitlements	Pension	Contributory, contracted out of state scheme and 'top hat' pension and provisions for new entrants over the pensions cap	Contributory, contracted out of state scheme	Contributory, contracted out of state scheme	Contributory, contracted in to state scheme
	Life assurance	Annual salary × 4	Annual salary × 4	Annual salary × 3	Annual salary × 1
	Sick pay	Full pay for 6 months, then permanent disability insurance benefits at ⅔ salary	Full pay for 13 weeks and half pay for 13 weeks then permanent disability insurance	Full pay for 13 weeks and half pay for 13 weeks then permanent disability insurance	Statutory sick pay entitlements
	Medical insurance	Free for directors, spouses and children	Free for managers and spouses	Group scheme discount	Savings scheme to provide income when in hospital
	Annual holiday	25 days	25 days	23 days	23 days

Benefits/Entitlements	Incentive	Target-related–based on profit before tax	Performance-related merit bonus	Merit payment system	Team-based performance rewards
	Profit Share		1987 Finance Act Profit Related Pay Scheme	1987 Finance Act Profit Related Pay Scheme	1987 Finance Act Profit Related Pay Scheme
	Loan facilities (interest-free)	Season tickets in excess of £250 pa	Season tickets in excess of £250 pa	Season tickets in excess of £250 pa	Season tickets in excess of £250 pa
	Company car	Value £25,000,	Value £20,000 senior management and £12,000 for middle management with some flexibility to 'top up' from salary	Salesforce–plus others on a 'job need' basis–value £11,500	On a job need basis only *eg.* service engineers
	Private petrol	Free			
	Payment of fees to professional associations	Paid in full	Paid in full–for 2 bodies	Paid in full–for 2 bodies	–
	Discount facilities	15% on company products	15% on company products	15% on company products	15% on company products
	Subsidized meals	In management dining room	In staff/works restaurants	In staff/works restaurants	In staff/works restaurants
	Early/late retirement option	Available	Available	Available	Available
	Sports and social facilities	Open to all	Open to all	Open to all	Open to all

*This does not in any way present an ideal distribution of pay and benefits, but it does illustrate a framework for assessing acceptability and the necessity for change.

7. Is the company verging on the creation of a 'welfare state' within its own walls, so cushioning employees excessively against the realities of the world outside?
8. Would it be more effective to pay higher salaries, provide a limited range of benefits and concentrate on providing a challenging and stimulating work environment in which employees stay and commit themselves to the company's success?
9. How can communication be improved?

Choice – the 'cafeteria' remuneration concept

One way of giving employees a measure of choice on their benefits is to introduce a 'cafeteria' or flexible remuneration system. This allows employees to exercise choice over a range of benefit options within the constraint of total remuneration. Employees, particularly executives with a wider range of benefits, can alter the balance between the range of benefits by cutting back the level of benefits that have less value to them and using the surplus this generates for redistribution to other benefits. For example, an allowance of £500 a month for the contract hire of a car could be reduced to £300 a month, freeing £200 to be allocated to other benefits or, possibly, to be paid as additional salary. The approach is widely used in the USA and now in Australia where the tax regimes encourage the use of this approach, and the range of benefits available – particularly in health care is wider. In the USA, such systems are used as much to control benefit costs (by having a restricted benefits core and allowing employees to buy 'add-ons') as to meet the requirement for greater choice.

A cafeteria system can enable companies to:

- discover which benefits are popular and which are not, leading to more effective concentration of resources on those benefits welcomed by employees
- develop mechanisms to manage benefit costs more effectively
- inform employees about the real costs of benefits
- make use of a single strategic concept to meet diverse employee needs.

A typical way of managing flexibility in a cafeteria system is to establish a core package of benefits topped up by a percentage of gross pay available for additional components. But a cafeteria system can be an elaborate affair because of the need to produce comparative valuations of different parts of the package and construct methods of transferring the cash released by foregoing the whole or part of a benefit to another benefit or aspect of remuneration. This is far more difficult to do than it sounds and specialists disagree over approaches to benefits valuation.

Some companies are trying to move away from a complex benefit package to a 'clean cash' system, which provides basic core benefits such as pensions, sick pay and holidays but translates all other items into cash. This may conflict with a policy of maximizing tax efficiency, especially in the case of company cars, but it does give freedom of choice and also reduces administrative costs in the longer term.

The downside of the cafeteria approach

On paper the policy has many attractions for the freedom of choice and improved level of satisfaction with employment conditions it offers. In practice, however, UK experience of the cafeteria approach has been beset with problems, administrative and otherwise, and full applications are therefore still very rare. It is not just a question of devising the alternatives, costing them and working out the possible combinations of options available. There is concern that in the absence of specific legislation to allow flexible benefits, giving choices could adversely affect the tax position of those content with current benefits. Changes in an employee's domestic arrangements can also have a dramatic effect on remuneration options. A manager may have a mid-life crisis and divorce his wife, for instance, and want to exchange a family sized car and high dependants' benefits for a sports saloon and higher cash earnings to pay for exotic holidays. With a UK divorce rate of 1 in 3 this poses very real problems. Such an occurrence is not only inconvenient and costly for the employer; it can also involve making moral judgements on the employee's private life which are best avoided.

The cafeteria approach is relatively rare and occurs principally as the negotiation of individual packages on recruitment or flexibility between individual benefit entitlements. But the idea of 'menu-driven' remuneration lives on especially for highly paid employees (such as those in the City) with widely varying ideas of how they want their package structured.

Experience indicates that cafeteria arrangements are likely to be most successful when devised by experienced specialist management or employee benefits consultants, and when personal financial counselling is an integral part of the package. There will always need to be a basic level of pay and benefits and the practical reality is that the options available are normally limited in the UK to additional pension provisions, extra life or other insurance cover, variations in the value and model of car supplied, the availability of loans, share

Items typically covered in an employee benefits statement

- The assumptions and basis on which the statement has been drawn up to provide background on reward policies;
  - individual employment status
  - type of pension arrangements including spouse's/children's pensions
- Employees personal details – taken from payroll records;
- Current remuneration and benefits – typically;
  - basic salary
  - allowances (eg London allowance)
  - profit sharing/share scheme entitlements
  - annual leave entitlements
  - discount entitlements
  - sick pay entitlements
  - permanent disability cover/ill health early retirement
  - personal accident insurance
  - private medical insurance cover
  - dependent's benefits actually payable for death before or after retirement (including current statutory entitlements)
  - personal retirement benefits actually payable including additional voluntary contribution possibilities/scheme details
  - the basis for reviewing/increasing pensions in payment
  - provisions for early retirement
  - pension entitlements if the employee leaves
  - a total valuation for current benefits

Such statements can also usefully give summary advice on personal financial planning, eg making a will and reviewing personal assets and liabilities. They may also contain brief details of the pension fund trustees' report to show its financial status.

purchase or profit sharing, additional leave entitlements and a small collection of more fringe items.

Without specific enabling legislation it remains unlikely that 'cafeteria' schemes will become widespread although at top executive level and where executive search consultants are involved and individual service contracts are negotiated, there is usually some flexibility over the balance of pay and benefits finally agreed. What certainly *is* happening is that flexibilities in individual benefit provinces continue to grow.

Communicating total remuneration (see Chapter 25)

Informing employees about pay and benefits policy in a clear, appealing and carefully presented manner can have a tangible effect on the level of their satisfaction with employment conditions. Appreciation of the value and cost of the elements involved is instructive and ensures that employees are fully aware of what their total remuneration package includes. An approach to this which is increasingly used by major employers is the annual benefits statement. The list on page 358 shows what a statement of this kind typically contains, to illustrate how these statements can improve employees' understanding of the policies that affect them. These statements can be produced on an in-house basis provided the payroll and all the necessary associated data are available (preferably computerized). They are usually printed out annually and sent to employees' home addresses as a document to be kept for reference.

Part 6

Special Aspects of Reward Management

Chapter 20

Boardroom Pay

Setting the style of remuneration policy

The principles affecting boardroom pay are generally the same as those described elsewhere in this book for all employees. What is often different is the public visibility of pay decisions and the fact that salary policy for directors can be a determinant of corporate culture. Statements in many company annual reports confirm this, especially when an organization decides to change, and usually sharpen, rewards at the top. The press has always reacted badly to major pay hikes – playing on the politics of envy and the so-called 'bosses' bonanza' syndrome. More recently, major institutional shareholders have taken considerable interest in the link between executive rewards and corporate success. In 1990 the advertizing agency Saatchi and Saatchi, for example, cut board-level remuneration to reflect falling profitability.

In the USA the profit/payout link is coming under increasing scrutiny. Minority shareholders are now sueing US corporations for excessive executive remuneration, where they believe this prejudices their long-term interests. A particular target is incentive plans, which pay out regardless of profitability as part of the institutionalization of executive capital accrual. Regular articles in *Fortune* and *Business Week* in the US bear witness to growing impatience with unjustifiably high levels of reward.

The way in which boards of directors are paid, or choose to pay themselves, tends to affect the pay philosophy of the organization as a whole. Boards who have adopted and believe in the value of incentives for instance, will push the concept of performance-related pay down through the whole organization. Those who choose to reinforce other values such as loyalty and commitment may place more emphasis on these – but they may, of course, offer performance rewards too.

Critical to the success of the remuneration policies for more junior staff is the level at which boardroom pay is set in relation to the competition. Boards, especially in family companies where remuneration does not come from basic salary alone, do not always appreciate that the level of their basic pay sets the ceiling below which all other salaries generally have to fit. Failing to recognize this can create 'headroom' problems which have an impact on both recruitment and retention. Also potentially damaging are salary levels which employees perceive as excessive in relation to their own rewards. High boardroom pay can and often should be an outward sign of corporate achievement. But the taste can go sour if employees perceive that their pay is 'just a cost to be controlled' and that there is no potential share for them in the organization's success. It is no coincidence that many companies that have gone for generous bonus or incentive schemes or executive share options have also opted to introduce performance-related pay further down, often in addition to some form of all-employee profit sharing or share scheme. Such actions have not just tempered possible accusations of executive greed but have given everyone a potential share in success. They have also of course, in public companies, reassured shareholders that good and competitive remuneration practice has been introduced at all levels. It is, after all, in the interests of shareholders that an effective board be properly remunerated and so be free to get on with the work of running the business.

Non-executive remuneration committees

In larger public companies and indeed in a growing number of organizations as a whole, directors' remuneration is determined by a non-executive committee of the board. This committee is comprised typically of directors of other organizations and sometimes 'public figures' in the industry sector, and acts on the behalf of shareholders to ensure that:

- basic salaries are maintained at a level which allows the organization to compete effectively for good calibre executives.
- annual pay increases are awarded both in relation to performance and to an assessment of market movement based on data from one or more reputable sources
- the basis, targets and payments of executive incentive schemes serve the needs of the business and are satisfactory to shareholders in both the short and the longer term
- the balance of pay and benefits is maintained on a sensible, competitive and defensible basis
- contractual obligations to individual directors are honoured and the contracts themselves are reviewed from time to time to ensure they remain up to date and defensible
- the relationship between boardroom remuneration and policy for employees below this level remains consistent and sensible
- proper and professional advice is sought when policy changes are envisaged either from the organization's own remuneration

specialists or, where appropriate, from reputable outside advisers on remuneration, tax and especially on the complexities of the new executive pensions environment.

Composition

As we said earlier, board remuneration committees are normally composed of a group of non-executive directors plus the company chairman or chief executive. The personnel director may well sit in the committee or act as official adviser (often briefed by the company's remuneration specialists). The use of non-executive directors can act as a valuable source of independent experience in reviewing policy as well as a useful brake on enthusiasm for major change until it has been properly considered. Sometimes it may also have to provide a check on excessive boardroom greed – a desire to come top of the salary market can still be a problem at the more aggressive end of some sectors, and this is not always wise for the company. Directors who sit as non-executives on a number of company boards often get a very good idea about which approaches to, say, incentives will or will not work in a particular environment – and why.

Method of operation

Board remuneration committees normally review and authorize pay recommendations put by the Chief Executive for subsequent Board approval. This provides the basis for the annual pay review. Such reports will also include revisions to incentive targets, policy on share options and payment structures, reviews of differentials between different directors and, where necessary, changes to pension provisions, car entitlements and other benefits. It cannot be emphasized too strongly that all policy reviews and pay recommendations made by non-executive remuneration committees should be based on well researched fact, as well as the anecdotal experience of the members, however valuable that may be.

Paying non-executive directors

There are two fundamental considerations to be taken into account when setting fees for non-executive directors:

(a) providing reasonable recompense for the time and commitment they contribute to board meetings;
(b) not paying them so much or tying them down with perquisites of various kinds so that they are afraid to be independent and

speak their mind when their judgement and experience tells them that the executive directors are wrong about something.

'Reasonable recompense' depends on the following factors:

1. How many board meetings per year the non-executive director is required to attend.
2. Whether he or she also sits on a board committee such as the audit committee or the remuneration committee which involve extra duties and an additional time commitment.
3. How eminent the director is. If he or she is a well-known figure, much sought after for their particular wisdom and expertise, then the fees will have to be greater than they might be for someone with less 'star quality'.
4. Company size – research from sources such as Hay and Monks/Charterhouse shows a fairly clear relationship betwen the size of non-executive directors' fees and the size of the organization in terms of annual sales turnover. This is of course also related to the relative eminence of the directors in question – major employers seek non-executives from other major employers or the City who expect, and get, a higher consideration for their services than those from smaller or less prominent organizations.
5. Position – Non-executive chair people are normally paid substantially more than ordinary non-executive directors. This differential partly reflects the additional time input involved and partly the additional responsibility and public exposure that goes with this role. It is also a reality that some non-executive chair people are appointed at milestones in an organization's history when there can be a high risk of failure as well as success. 'High risk' factors usually raise the rewards on offer because a public reputation is at stake.

Maintaining objectivity and independence by not paying too much remains critical to the effectiveness of non-executive directors. If they become dependent on their fees from a company on whose board they sit, they will not perform the independent role required of them by shareholders. For this reason the provision of company cars, pensions etc is generally to be avoided. Most non-executives will in any case already have adequate benefit provisions from their full-time employment and will expect nothing but fees in the form of cash. They should therefore feel free to ask the difficult and searching questions that need to be asked when companies experience problems, when directors make mistakes or when enthusiasm for change needs dispassionate review before the go ahead is given. If non-executives really feel that the organization is taking a wrong turn, they should be in a position to resign, often very publicly, to make their point. Dependence on fees could prevent this.

Fees for non-executive directors should be reviewed regularly in the same way as directors' remuneration as a whole. An annual review is sensible, although in times of low inflation an adjustment is not always carried out. Trends in this area should be monitored from reputable sources to ensure that practice is kept competitive.

The balance between basic salary and incentives for full-time directors

Basic salary differentials

Differentials in basic salary exist in the UK between directors in different functions and between the board as a whole and the chief executive. Differences between directors by function are normally market related – based on survey and other evidence of competitive remuneration practice.

To set the basic salary differential between the managing director or chief executive and other directors, survey evidence should also be sought. In the early 1990s, evidence from a number of sources suggests that board salaries are on average, some 70–80 per cent of chief executive's pay. The earnings differential with sales directors may sometimes be lower, or even the reverse (ie higher than the chief executive), where special commission arrangements exist. It may also be narrower for other directors in response to market forces or where recent recruitment has dictated a higher basic salary that has not, as it often does, yet triggered a general review of boardroom pay.

As we have already shown in Chapter 11, the majority of major UK employers operate executive incentive schemes and the payments involved continue to grow as a proportion of basic salary. In more aggressive and performance orientated organizations, incentive payments which exceed 100 per cent of basic salary are being made, sometimes with no 'cap' when profits rise unexpectedly. In good times such payments are, as we have already said, an outward visible sign of company and indeed executive success – the 'applause' given to those who perform well.

The credibility of this approach however, probably depends in the long-term on whether the beneficiaries are prepared to take the decline in payments inevitable under the currency rules of their schemes when profits fall, or when the country faces an economic recession from which even they cannot escape. Warnings about this have come over the last couple of years from all the major remuneration consultants active in helping companies install sharper rewards for performance.

Such considerations inevitably affect the decision on where to set basic, pensionable salary and what to provide as performance reward. If basic salaries are set competitively, there will be less temptation to 'fudge' the incentive payments in lean years because executives have become more dependent than they should on 'risk' payments. Provision of the benefit of independent personal financial counselling, to help directors plan their incentive payments sensibly in 'good' years, is worth considering (see Chapter 17). People who are creative with the company's money may not always be as shrewd with their own. Professional and confidential assistance from a reputable, independent, outside adviser (check the provisions of the Financial Services Act to see what this now means) should help executives plan their investments and personal financial strategy. It may also help prevent them from giving in to the temptation of overstretching themselves on the back of high incentive payments with an unwise, 'rosy' view of the future.

Before a board decides to implement change in its current salary and incentive arrangements, it needs to consider how this will affect salary policy for staff lower down. A particular concern should be the differential within the level of management just below. The basic salary differential should provide for sensible progression and a reasonable jump on promotion to the legal responsibilities of a full-time directorship.

Ensuring long-term commitment

The use of fixed-term service agreements is often perceived as a benefit as well as a legally required written contract of employment. Such agreements are thought of as status symbols – signs of company commitment to its top executives which also, of course, set out the way in which directors are to be paid and the benefit entitlements they are to get. They are therefore very important in terms of the messages they provide on how remuneration can be expected to reward success.

Deferred incentives and share options are the two main ways in which remuneration policy can provide messages on the need for loyalty and commitment to the organization.

Deferred incentives are based on the setting of longer-term targets – say those which may take two or three years, sometimes more, to achieve and which are rewarded accordingly. This approach is gaining favour in the UK and is already widespread in the US. The principles covering incentive scheme design set out in Chapter 10 apply. The tax implications of the timing of payments should also be explored (see Chapter 18 on tax considerations). The lowering of top rates of tax to 40 per cent introduced and maintained since the 1988 Budget should help to make deferred incentives more appealing.

Following the 1984 Finance Act, there was an explosion of executive share option schemes in public companies and in private firms able to take advantage of the legislation. These were introduced to cover boards of directors and take maximum advantage of the Act's provisions. Few schemes have been introduced on a performance-related basis, although this pattern may now begin to change (see Chapter 14). What the introduction of this benefit has achieved is a level of commitment among directors to stay in an organization until options can be exercised on a tax effective basis and, more importantly, a very real personal sense of identity with corporate success (although prospective employers can, and do, buy them out). The introduction of these schemes has had a noticeable effect on directors' awareness of what affects their company's share price and which of its activities make City analysts report optimistically on their expectations. This does not, of course, as 'Black Monday' at the end of 1987 and its aftermath showed, prevent share prices falling rapidly, almost regardless of profitability, when a bear market supersedes a raging bull one. But although a bear market can dash the hopes of executives expecting to make a killing when they exercise their options (in practice they just do not exercise while the options are 'under water' – preferring to wait for an upturn in the market) they are good times to give out share options. The gains will be greater if they come to be exercised at a time when the market has risen again. Chapter 14 on share ownership schemes covers the detail of share options and Chapter 15 covers all-employee share schemes and profit sharing.

Individual remuneration packages

Over the last decade or so, a lot has been written about the concept of 'cafeteria' or 'menu-based' remuneration packages. Most of the work, and the practice, has occurred in the US and other countries where the tax regime is helpful to this approach. The idea essentially is that highly paid executives should be offered the chance to select how they wish to be paid in terms of cash and benefits and so have their remuneration tailored to their personal ambitions and lifestyle. In practice, in the UK, formal schemes of this kind are a rarity. Our tax regime renders the exchange of benefits for cash unfavourable (tax experts will refer to the case of Heaton v Bell) and the main options come in the form of being able to supplement pension provisions or contribute out of taxed income to a more expensive car (p. 357).

The story does not end there. Many remuneration packages are individually negotiated and tailored at the time of recruitment to a board level appointment. As companies find that they cannot always promote to board level from within, they face increasingly tough negotiations on remuneration packages from those they seek to recruit from outside. There are a number of reasons for this:

1. Directors, perhaps comfortably in post somewhere else and approached by executive search consultants, often feel they are in a good position to negotiate major improvements for themselves as an 'incentive' to move (they might be being enticed into a volatile and precarious environment where job security cannot be guaranteed, or one which is much more publicly exposed).
2. People are more aware than ever of market rates for top executives and see a move as an opportunity to 'catch up' to a more realistic level. People at board level probably expect something of the order of a 20 per cent improvement in earnings to make it worth their while. This makes recruiting top calibre directors from outside very expensive, unless they are working in a sector or organization where they are currently underpriced (a trick the City learned to good effect for people with transferable skills in less well paid sectors in the rapid expansion surrounding the 'Big Bang' in 1986). Internal relativities may then be upset and cause 'knock-on' costs as other directors' pay is increased to match the new market rate.
3. Directors may employ their own specialist remuneration and sometimes pension advisers to make sure they get a good deal.
4. Being an effective director generally goes with having an ambitious and assertive personality – it is unreal to expect such people not to be shrewd negotiators and to look after their own interests. They may perceive, quite rightly, that they are being brought in to wake up a 'sleepy' organization and see a shake-up on the pay front (which usually means moving to the more competitive end of market practice), as part of a necessary process of change.
5. More rarely, they may be simply greedy, with unrealistic ideas about the remuneration they can command. These ideas are usually based on fragmentary market data, either from contacts who may have exaggerated the package, or from the newspapers. And an exaggerated view of their worth may be reinforced by the special kind of inexperience that goes with being a high flyer who has risen too far too fast. Such individuals need tactful handling, since their potential contribution may far outweigh the drawbacks of apparent greed, and they may have powerful 'champions' already on the board.

Whatever the circumstances, personnel directors, company secretaries and indeed chief executives increasingly find themselves unable to offer just a 'standard' remuneration package to new boardroom recruits. Faced with demands from an executive they may have spent a long time trying to entice they will need to have:

(a) a willingness to tailor the remuneration package to fit individual requirements;
(b) a clear idea on which items of pay they are prepared to negotiate on;
(c) the ability to cost out alternatives quickly;
(d) a maximum total earnings cost they are prepared to go to to get the executive they are after – this can mean 'anything it takes';
(e) a prepared case to defend a package which other directors or even shareholders may perceive as an unacceptable anomaly.

Chapter 21

International Remuneration

The continuing development of Third World countries and improved global communications have made it essential for UK companies to compete with an international market in order to survive. UK staff in many organizations will, therefore, find themselves sent abroad to further the development of their employer's overseas interests.

Terms and conditions of employment

The terms and conditions of employment while abroad typically depend upon the nature of the work as in the following two examples:

1. *Feasibility studies*: Where an employee or team of employees visit a territory to assess the potential market for their company's goods or services. These visits rarely last longer than a month and the method of payment is usually no more sophisticated than a reimbursement of expenses.
2. *Contract work*: Construction or civil engineering companies typically recruit contract staff for specific projects. Food and accommodation is often provided on site, in which case there might be no local currency payment. A lump sum for the contract, agreed in advance, is then paid in the UK.

Alternatively, or additionally, terms and conditions of employment may be determined by the type of assignment as in the following three examples:

1. *Short-term assignments*: The definition of a short-term assignment varies from company to company but often refers to a period which does not exceed six months. Some companies choose to make the break point at three months; others at twelve.

   Managers from company headquarters frequently spend periods of approximately six months in the offices of an overseas subsidiary when it is newly acquired or established and, in this capacity, are typical short-term assignees. If the assignment does not exceed three months or so, these employees are usually retained on their UK salary and given a 'daily rate' ('per diem' allowance) in local currency calculated to incorporate the likely costs of hotels, meals, taxis and sundry items such as laundry. Once an assignment exceeds three months' duration, some companies, such as those in the construction or contract software industries, would seek to reduce any per diem rate, possibly by calculating a package which acknowledged the employee as almost of expatriate status. Short-term assignees often benefit from regular trips home.

2. *Expatriate status*: Indigenization is cheap and has distinct local political advantages by comparison with expatriation, but many multinational companies adhere to a policy of mixing the local workforce with at least some management from UK headquarters. These managers are still employees of the parent company and may be kept on the UK payroll although it is increasingly common for expatriates to be transferred to the local payroll in 'developed' countries.

   In order to be operationally effective and win the co-operation of local trading partners, the expatriate is deemed to require at least two years in any territory. The typical length of a 'tour' is three years and the method of payment must, therefore, be more sophisticated than any of the three methods mentioned above. The bulk of the section 'Salary and Allowances' in this chapter deals with alternative methods of expatriate compensation.
3. *Secondment*: Secondment is frequently confused with expatriation and some companies do not distinguish between the two. However, it is generally accepted that the difference is contractual; for the duration of an assignment, a secondee is employed by the subsidiary company rather than the parent company and the source of remuneration is local.

Level of pay

How much expatriates are paid depends upon their job and status, personal commitments, the territory to which they are assigned and other variables.

An expression commonly found in the policy documents of multinational companies runs approximately thus: 'the aim of the expatriate remuneration policy is to ensure that individuals are "neither better nor worse off" as a result of their overseas tour of duty'. This is quite an understatement of the reality and many individuals actively campaign for expatriation in the hope of a substantial improvement in their bank balances.

Annual gross salary	£ 48,309
Recruitment costs	£ 14,493
Briefing	£ 2,244
Medical screening	£ 513
Medical and Repatriation	
Insurance (BUPA)	£ 1,126
Removal costs	£ 4,270
Furniture storage	£ 500
Air fares	£ 9,528
Boarding schools (UK)	£ 8,249
Local school	£ 3,891
Outfit allowance	£ 610
Accommodation	
Agent's fee	£ 2,920
Rent	£ 38,910
Club	
Entrance fee	£ 1,945
Annual subscription	£ 513
Utilities	£ 1,743
Company car	£ 3,669
Total cost	£143,433

A further consideration is the employer's contribution towards national insurance for the first year of assignment.

In the example where free accommodation is given, the contributions would be:
620773 × 0.1045 = HK$ 64,870 = UK£ 5,048

Where an accommodation allowance is given the contribution would be:
1198053 × 0.1045 = HK$ 125,196 = UK£ 9,743

Figure 21.1 *The effective cost of a failed one-year assignment to Hong Kong*

Source: Information provided by Employment Conditions Abroad limited, a leading European information and advisory service specializing in expatriate salaries and benefits worldwide, and terms and conditions of employment.

Note: The assumptions about the employee's circumstances are given in Figure 21.2 on p. 380.

Such discretion in the wording of policy documents does, however, safeguard the employer against massive expenditure in times of straitened circumstances. The cost of sending an employee abroad far exceeds the salary outlay. In addition, the company must consider the air fares to and from the destination which are not insignificant when individuals are accompanied by their families and may return once or twice a year for leave, or need to go to a holiday resort for rest and recuperation. Accommodation costs, relocation expenses, language training and UK boarding school fees are further financial burdens to be carried by the employer.

As Figure 21.1 (which illustrates the horrendous cost of a failed assignment) shows, many of these costs are incurred at the outset of the tour and will not be refunded if the incumbent proves unsatisfactory and returns home. On the contrary, the company will be forced to duplicate costs if the market is valuable and an immediate replacement must be sent.

The financial embarrassment of a failed expatriate assignment has led some of the major multinationals to concentrate carefully upon their expatriate selection techniques. A variety of questionnaires and psychometric tests are in use but most employers still base their decisions on interviews. Likewise, research into the stress caused by international relocation has strengthened the case for comprehensive briefing sessions prior to departure. Language tuition and independent financial counselling are often arranged for expatriates at this stage and are recognized as diminishing anxiety quite considerably.

Companies should remember that this anxiety and sense of displacement recurs when the individuals are repatriated. The problems of re-entry have been researched in some detail in recent years and good employers now recognize that the assignment does not end with the expatriate's return to the home country. Employees should be made aware that practical assistance and counselling are available to them, should they require them.

Salary and allowances

Methods of payment vary not only between companies but also between locations. There are three principal methods:

- budget system
- market rate
- balance sheet

Budget system

This payment method aims to assess the costs incurred by the expatriate, both in the home country and in the host country. These costs are then combined and expressed in a single currency – usually that of the host country – and grossed up for tax.

The major drawback of this system is that, in areas with high inflation or volatile exchange rates such as Central America, it requires constant adjustment and is therefore time-consuming and costly to administer.

UK-based companies are really the only organizations which operate the budget system, and those that do tend to be the larger, more paternalistic ones which cling to well-established but somewhat obsolete administrative procedures through laziness or sentimentality.

Market rate

Market pressure in certain industries or functions is familiar to recruitment and personnel professionals in the UK. International markets are no different. Certain territories – notably the USA and Switzerland – have a higher standard of living which is more than compensated for by high pay expectations, in relation to those of other Western countries.

In territories such as these, it is rare that a salary which would begin to compete with those offered locally could be justified by a cost-of-living survey or inducement payment. The ignominy of UK managers, sent abroad on perfectly adequate budget or balance sheet packages, who find that their subordinates are earning considerably more than they themselves, would prove insupportable. Consequently, the local market standards are absorbed by foreign companies in high paying countries.

Balance sheet

The balance sheet method is often referred to as the 'build-up' method and is the commonest form of expatriate remuneration package. It is preferred to the budget system for two main reasons: first, it is less cumbersome in administrative terms and is open to greater flexibility, second, it avoids the rather unrealistic expedient of combining the home country and host country commitments. Figure 21.2 shows a worked example of this method for an assignment in Hong Kong.

Its advantage over the market rate is that it is usually less expensive (although the costing-in of certain variables can make it competitive with the market rate if this is politically desirable). It is favoured by personnel departments since its 'build-up' structure is easy to communicate, both in justifying the cost to the company directors and in explaining the 'bottom line' to the outgoing expatriate.

The three components of the balance sheet system – notional home salary, spendable income, and allowances – are described below.

Notional home salary

The notional home salary is a more appropriate term for this component than the alternative 'home-base salary'. The expression 'home-base' implies an element of reality whereas this component is, in almost all organizations, hypothetical.

Its purpose is to serve as the foundation upon which the other components are built. It is used as the basis for pension contributions and is expressed in terms of the salary which the expatriate will receive upon return. It should be updated annually in line with salary increases for home-based 'peer' group staff.

Spendable income
The expression 'spendable income' is so phrased as to distinguish it from deductible income and is sometimes known as 'net disposable income'. It refers to the portion of income which remains after tax, social security, pension and, sometimes, housing and personal savings obligations have been met. It is used as a measure of expenditure levels and is a vital yardstick when ensuring that the expatriate will be 'no worse off' abroad than at home.

Certain companies deduct housing costs from the gross income, taking the view that individuals are committed to the payment of mortgages and rental in the same way as they are to tax, social security and pension conributions. However, housing has proven such an emotive issue over the years that many companies have removed it from the balance sheet altogether and treat it separately.

Allowances
Companies calculate a number of allowances in arriving at the total expatriate remuneration package. These are designed to compensate for disruption and to make the assignment attractive to the employee. Most are applied to the notional home salary but one of them, the cost of living allowance, is based on spendable income.

Cost of living allowance: The cost of living allowance is reached by applying an index to the home country spendable income. The index measures the relative cost, in the host country, of purchasing conventional 'shopping basket' items such as food and clothing.

In an effort to ensure that the expatriate maintains his or her home standard of living, indices inevitably include the pricing of items peculiar to the home country. It follows that many components of the shopping basket will be imported and it is, consequently, rare to find a cost of living index which is lower than that of the home country.

Cost of living information can be obtained from various sources such as: Employment Conditions Abroad Limited and ORC (UK) Limited (see Bibliography).

Like all indices, these should be treated with caution. Some cover diplomatic rather than commercial centres and are, therefore, based on a diplomatic lifestyle which may be very different from that adopted by an expatriate employed by an industrial concern.

Overseas premium: The 'overseas' or 'foreign service' premium is not paid by all companies since many feel that, by awarding a hardship allowance, they are providing sufficient incentive for an employee to move abroad.

Those companies which do award an overseas premium might do so in the form of a flat sum but it is more usual to find a percentage of notional home salary such as 10 per cent or 15 per cent.

The premium is designed to recognize and compensate for disruption. Being away from home, family and friends is seen as a hardship which does not vary with location and this premium is therefore available to all expatriate staff.

Hardship allowance: This allowance constitutes a financial recognition of potential discomfort and difficulty in the host country. Some of the factors to be taken into account are:

- an excessively hot or cold climate
- health hazards
- poor communications
- isolation
- language difficulties
- daily possibility of burglary, kidnap, mugging etc.
- scarcities of food
- poor amenities
- political risk
- *force majeure*, floods, typhoons, earthquakes etc.

As distinct from the overseas premium, the hardship allowance is variable and, for countries such as North America, Australia and parts of Western Europe, a zero percentage is common (although companies which build an overseas premium into their hardship allowance may have a minimum allowance of 10 per cent). Hardship allowances are usually expressed as a percentage of notional home salary. The maximum, for locations of extreme difficulty, rarely exceeds 30 per cent.

Other allowances: There are a variety of other allowances which are peculiar to locations, companies or individual circumstances. Some will be used instead of one of those listed above and some in addition. Some examples are as follows:

- Separation allowance – if personal circumstances or unpleasant conditions in the host country prevent expatriates from taking their family abroad, a separation allowance may be paid. Alternatively, additional trips home may be permitted.
- Kit allowance – a one-off payment for clothing and accessories which expatriates need to buy on account of the particular territory to which they are assigned. Tropical countries requiring light clothing are the obvious examples where kit allowances might be payable.
- Added responsibility allowance (position allowance) – occasionally applicable when the overseas job carries greater

responsibility than the notional job in the home country. It is a difficult allowance to manage and, in practice, many expatriations are seen as promotions so the notional home salary is increased accordingly. The added responsibility allowance, therefore, is seldom found.

– Tax equilization allowances are often paid but company policies towards tax on expatriate emoluments are highly variable and are the subject of a separate section later in the chapter.

– Certain locations with punitive tax rates make fiscal concessions for allowances and it is common, in these countries, to find the multinational companies have developed a large portfolio of allowances – for items as far-fetched as soft furnishings – which they do not award elsewhere in the world.

Make-up of the 'balance sheet'

The 'balance sheet' is, therefore, built up in two parts: the 'local' or 'host country' component and the 'home' or 'base country' component.

The local component is calculated by applying the cost of living index to the net (home country) spendable income and converting the result at an appropriate exchange rate.

The home component consists of any other allowances added to that portion of the notional home salary which remains after deductions for home country tax, social security, pension contributions and other expenses. Where spendable income is distinct from commitments such as housing costs and savings, this, too, will be deducted. The remainder tends to represent 25–30 per cent of the notional home salary and is converted at the same exchange rate used for the local component and the two, combined, form the total net pay which is then grossed up for host country tax and social security.

The calculations in Figure 21.2 on page 380 reflect the costs to the company of expatriating a senior executive (notional UK salary £ 40,000) to Hong Kong. For the purpose of this exercise it has been assumed that the expatriate is married with two children, one of whom will remain in a boarding school in the UK, with the other at school in Hong Kong.

The first calculation represents the ongoing costs of a successful assignment using a build-up approach to determine the assignment salary.

Senior executive. Married with two children. Non-contributory pension fund.

Index for Hong Kong	UK	= 100
	Hong Kong	= 116

Exchange Rate UK£ 1 = HK$ 12.85

UK salary	£ 40,000
Net	£ 26,529
Income	£ 16,588
Housing and savings	£ 9,941

Local spending component = UK Spendable Income × Index/100 × exchange rate

= 16,588 × 1.16 × 12.85
= HK$ 247,261

Home component	: Housing and savings	£ 9,941
	: Expatriate incentive (i)	£ 6,000
	: Location allowance (ii)	£ 4,000
	: Class I contributions (iii) or first year	£ 1,155
	Total	£ 21,096
		= HK$271,084

Notes (i) Given as an incentive to be expatriated – 15% of UK notional salary.

(ii) Specific to location of assignment ranging from 0% to 30% of UK notional salary – 10% for Hong Kong.

(iii) Assume contracted in to UK social security. After the first year class I contributions will cease and class III contributions will be paid.

Total Hong Kong dollar requirement = HK$ 518,345 net

This figure assumes that the expatriate receives free accommodation.
Therefore the following options exist:

(a) provide free accommodation and gross the salary up to give the expatriate sufficient to cover the extra tax liability;

(b) give an accommodation allowance in addition to the guaranteed net salary and gross this up for Hong Kong tax.

N.B. At this level of salary Hong Kong tax is equivalent to 15% of gross salary.

Assume cost of accommodation = HK$ 500,000 (3 bedroom flat)

(a) free accommodation – taxable value 10% of gross salary

Gross	= HK$ 620,773
Taxable gross	= HK$ 682,850
Tax	= HK$ 102,428
Net	= HK$ 518,345

(b) Accommodation allowance of HK$ 500,000 (full rental cost)

Net	= HK$ 518,345
+ Acco. Allowance	= HK$ 500,000
Total net	= HK$ 1,018,345
Gross	= HK$ 1,198,053

Figure 21.2 *Example of a build-up' calculation for an assignment to Hong Kong*

Source: Employment Conditions Abroad Limited.

One can see from this that the extra cost of providing an accommodation allowance rather than free accommodation in this example is:

HK$ 1,198,053 – HK$ 518,345 – HK$ 500,000 = HK$ 179,708
= £ 13,985

Additional ongoing costs to company (other than salary)

Company car	HK$	47,150	
Utilities	HK$	22,400	
Local Education (one child)	HK$	50,000	
Home Education (one child)	HK$	106,000	
Club	HK$	6,600	(annual subscription)
Medical Insurance	HK$	14,469	
Furniture Storage	HK$	6,425	
Air fares	HK$	122,435	(12 × economy returns)
Accommodation	HK$	500,000	
Total	HK$	875,479	
Total ongoing cost =	HK$	1,496,252	

N.B. Those costs which have been incurred in £ have been converted to HK$ at a rate of UK£ = HK$ 12.85

Source: Employment Conditions Abroad Limited.

Method of payment

When the total earnings have been calculated and expressed in local currency, the company will opt for one of several methods of payment. Many elect to split the salary between home country and host country, particularly in countries such as Greece, Kenya or Indonesia where the home country currency is more stable than that of the host country or where the local remittance facilities are limited. The expatriate thus has the opportunity of building up some capital and is assured of a lump sum in the home country for the servicing of continuing domestic commitments such as mortgage and insurance payments.

A split salary also has political advantages in countries where the market rate is low and where marked contrasts in income and expenditure patterns would be demotivating for the local workforce. If the pay and corresponding lifestyle of the expatriate can be seen as broadly similar to those of the local business community, blind eyes may well be turned to sizeable 'offshore' payments in hard currency.

Most multinationals quote and pay a gross salary but a few guarantee net emoluments to their expatriates. Paying net throughout the world is extremely costly but it does mean that the employer rather than the employee benefits from any exchange rate fluctuations in favour of sterling.

Benefits

Housing

Housing allowances, where paid, are sometimes built into the balance sheet method of remuneration but it is more common for them to be treated as separate items. It is commoner still for accommodation to be provided free of charge although many companies place a ceiling on the annual rental costs that they are prepared to accept. Such ceilings, where enforced, tend to increase in proportion to the seniority of the expatriate. Where employers meet the total rental cost, no matter how high, it is often the case that entertainment is an essential part of the incumbent's expatriate job.

Some of the longer-established multinational companies still own houses around the world. They acquired properties in the early days of business expatriation and have never got around to disposing of them. Thus, a small family, posted to Central America, may find itself forced to live in an immense colonial-style mansion, with three or four servants per person. Relics of the past like this are, however, the exception rather than the rule.

Until recently, employer involvement in home country housing commitments was minimal. Expatriates whose companies paid for pre-departure financial counselling benefited from expert independent advice as to the disposal or otherwise of their home country residence, but few employers went so far as to offer the services of professional relocation companies to their employees.

This lack of involvement seems to be on the decline and there is evidence of a trend among certain companies to assist with home housing. The choices between selling (and risking re-entry during a property boom), letting (and risking bad tenants) and leaving the property empty (and risking squatters) are no longer regarded as decisions that can and must only be made by the home owners and their families.

Utilities

The cost of utilities can be exorbitant in certain overseas locations – particularly in hot climates where the electricity bill is distorted by the constant use of air-conditioning.

Most companies accept that it is their responsibility to make bottled gas, water, electricity and telephones available to their employees abroad but some exact a contribution from the expatriate

– usually no more than 20 per cent – to discourage them from wasting power or making too many extravagant international telephone calls. Other companies put a ceiling on the total cost of reimbursing rental and utility costs.

Car

Cars are a common perquisite for expatriate staff of all grades. In many countries, for status or security reasons, a chauffeur/guard is provided by the company in addition to the car. In certain European locations, however, the company car is not as tax-efficient a benefit as it is in the UK and it is not, therefore, local custom to provide any but the most senior employees with a car – or those whose job demands it, such as salesmen. Sensible multinational companies fall in line with market practice in such territories. Likewise, although an expatriate may be entitled to a car in, for instance, Hong Kong or Tokyo, they may elect to waive the benefits on the grounds that driving in such over-populated cities is more difficult and more frustrating than using the public transport system.

Servants

Although the employment of servants may sound like a relic of a bygone century, there are still many countries in the world where it represents affluence, power and status. In such locations, expatriates – and the companies which they represent – are expected by the local populace to conform to best market practice and it is probably not unreasonable to infer that the esteem in which they are held will increase in proportion to the number of servants they employ. They will also, in many cases, be providing much-needed employment and so be contributing to the wealth of the community.

In addition, there are locations, notably African and Central American, where security poses a real threat to anyone whose affluence is notable. In such places, merely being foreign might be enough to trigger thoughts of theft, kidnap or brutality in the minds of the local criminal fraternity. It therefore goes without saying that security guards are an essential part of these remuneration packages.

Club subscriptions

Wherever appropriate, club membership fees and subscriptions are usually paid for by an expatriate's employer. The social environment is seen as an important part of the 'settling-in' process as well as a useful source of business contacts.

Sports clubs are the commonest form of benefit and, in some

areas, it may be necessary to provide access to more than one club – for instance where a golf club does not have separate facilities for squash and swimming. This benefit is not to be underestimated since, in many expatriate communities, the waiting list for club membership is long and the cost of joining correspondingly high.

Education expenses

Most companies will pay for the children of expatriates to be educated in the host country. The cost is rarely as high as subsidizing home country (boarding) school fees. In many overseas territories, there may be a limited choice of foreign language schools. Where the method of instruction is, for instance, American, it may be appropriate for the children of English expatriates to attend only for primary education, owing to UK university entrance requirements.

Many companies will take the view that it is unreasonable to expect students following one syllabus, such as GCSE, to be interrupted by a transfer to the American curriculum and will assist with UK school fees. The level of assistance varies but is commonly a percentage (such as 75 per cent) of basic boarding and tuition expenses up to a set annual maximum. It is most uncommon for companies to finance 'extras' such as fencing, tap dancing or scuba diving!

Some companies place a financial ceiling on their school fee assistance, others: age or grade minima and maxima. A few make provisions for kindergarten in the host country. In general, it is fair to say that global policies are a thing of the past. Cost conscious multinationals are now careful not to pay for UK boarding school fees unnecessarily but aim to take a flexible country-by-country approach, simultaneously assessing the individual requirements of each expatriate family.

Holiday

Annual leave

Holiday entitlement is usually in line with or slightly above home country practice, 25 or 30 working days being the norm. Comparatively ungenerous host country practice – such as the standard fortnight in the USA – tends to be over-ridden. Particularly high hardship regions may encourage companies to allow for holidays in excess of 30 working days.

Public holidays

Host country practice is usually followed with respect to public holidays although, in non-Christian countries, certain UK public holidays such as Christmas Day and Easter Day may be allowed in addition to the local festivals.

Home leave

If a norm had to be quoted, it would probably be a fair generalization to suggest that companies will pay for expatriates and their families to fly back to their home country once per year. However, the variations on this practice are too numerous to mention and are increasing all the time as the issue of home leave becomes more emotive and a matter of as much heated negotiation as the annual pay review.

Location affects the frequency of home leave; areas of extreme hardship often merit a second home trip while areas of low hardship, separated from the home country by a prohibitive air fare, such as Australia, might not even qualify for an annual return trip. Indeed, it is quite common for one home trip per tour (usually three years) to be provided from the Antipodes.

Marital status, however, has the most profound effect upon the regularity of home trips. Employees on married accompanied status, particularly those with children, will, as a rule, be provided with the minimum (ie, one return trip per annum). Not surprisingly, bachelor status or married unaccompanied personnel fare rather better. Where companies distinguish between these two latter categories, the bachelor status staff tend to be provided with one extra trip per year on the grounds that it is cheaper for the employer to pay for two single fares than one family trip. In a company where this distinction is understood by the staff, it acts as an incentive for single-status employees to volunteer themselves for expatriate posts. Married unaccompanied personnel, by contrast, would be likely to benefit from three return trips per annum in an effort, on the part of the employer, to minimize their separation from their families.

Rest and recuperation

'R&R' is usually a feature of a remuneration package for an expatriate in a high hardship territory. The intention of the employer is to fly the expatriate (plus family if appropriate) to the nearest 'civilized' location where decent meals, temperate climate and good communications may be enjoyed. R&R visits rarely exceed one week and are often no more than long weekends. The advantages to the employer are twofold: the trip is relatively cheap and the employee returns to work refreshed with minimum disruption to the work schedule.

Pensions

Care should be taken to ensure that the expatriate's final pension is never adversely affected as a result of an overseas assignment. The method for maintaining home country contributions may be complex and specialist advice should be sought from a firm that specializes in this field, such as:

International Pension Plan
Unilife Assurance Group SA
5 Boulevard Joseph II
1840 Luxembourg City
Grand Duchy of Luxembourg

David Callund Esq
Hall-Godwins (Overseas) Consulting Company
Briarcliff House, Kingsmead
Farnborough
Hampshire GU14 7TE
Telephone: 0252 521701
Telex: 858241

Clarkson Puckle Overseas Limited
Ibex House
Minories
London EC3
Telephone: 071–709 0744

Health insurance

It is essential that all overseas personnel are adequately covered for private treatment by health insurance; few countries have National Health Services as sophisticated or generous as that of the UK. The cost of private medical care in the USA, for instance, is exorbitant and the national provisions are almost non-existent. The major UK schemes such as BUPA and PPP have international plans for which the premium rates will vary, depending on the country assignment and the cost of medical treatment there.

Third country nationals

The term TCN (third country national) is literal; it describes an employee, whose home country is not that of his employer, who is expatriated to a third country. They are popular animals for political and economic reasons; they appease international antagonism towards massive corporations with reputations for imposing home country culture upon an array of host countries and they render more credible the corporate claims of 'globalization'. Simultaneously, they are often cheap to employ: Filipinos, Pakistanis and Bangladeshis have proven much more willing to work on construction sites and oil rigs in the Middle East than, for instance, Americans who demand extensive financial incentives to compensate for working in regions which take a dim view of alcohol and women.

The catch phrase which is often used of TCNs is 'getting the balance right', and this can be a problem. As with any expatriate, a decision must be made as to which remuneration method to use but, once an option has been elected, there remain further decisions to be taken. For example, in the case of the balance sheet method, the moment a third country is introduced (the home country of the employee), the question arises as to which home country – that of the employer or the employee – should be used as the base country.

If the employer's home country is used as the base country, some TCNs will be worse off than if their own home country were used as the base (for instance Swiss nationals employed by a UK company) while others will be so ridiculously well-off (for instance a Portuguese national employed by an American company) as to be discontented and demotivated when repatriated to their home country.

If the employee's home country is used as the base country, and the number of TCNs employed is high, the administrative burden of calculating balance sheets from a variety of bases to a variety of hosts would be immense. Nor does this method eliminate internal inequities; it is quite possible for a company to be employing an expatriate (say, British) and a TCN (say, American) in one host country. They might be on the same grade but, owing to the contrast in their home country base, will be earning substantially different host country packages. The problem will be compounded if the host country is lower paying than either home country and their immediate superior, a local national, is earning less than either of them.

That said, the balance sheet system, using the TCN home country as base, is one of the more likely methods to succeed, if handled sensibly and sensitively. TCNs from high-paying home countries are ideal candidates for split salaries and are usually acceptable to local management if the latter are fully briefed as to the potential difficulties. It helps, of course, if the assignment is limited to two or three years. In a similar way, TCNs from low-paying home countries will be more likely to accept internal inequities if the reasons are discussed with them at the outset. Any wounded pride at being worse off, relatively, than other expatriates – and, in high-paying host countries, their local national peers – is usually counter-balanced by their being better off than their contemporaries at home. The budget system is expensive and unwieldy to administer when only two countries have to be considered. The problems multiply when third countries are introduced. It is used increasingly rarely for expatriates and almost never for TCNs.

The market rate is expensive for the employer but quite effective for TCNs when used for high-paying countries; most TCNs will be better off than at home and equity with local managers will render the assignment politically smooth. TCNs sent to low-paying countries may not maintain their home country level of income if they are from a high-paying country and offshore payments will, therefore, have to be introduced into the package. This offshore payment rarely does more than compensate for deficits in the host country market rate and the system, therefore, lacks any element of incentive.

Unfortunately, there is no perfect TCN strategy but there are companies which have applied the balance sheet or market rate successfully – and will continue to do so since the number of TCNs employed around the world is increasing all the time.

Taxation

In most cases, a UK expatriate working abroad for more than 365 days is not liable for UK tax unless his salary is paid in the UK. Local taxation rates, in host countries, however, are enormously variable. True to the policy of 'keeping the expatriate whole' (ie ensuring that they are 'no worse off' in the host country), companies may elect to safeguard them from fiscal penalization by one of the following two methods.

Tax protection

When an expatriate is paid a gross salary and working in a location where the tax rates are low, the employer need make no adjustment, but when the host country tax rates are higher than in the employee's home country, the difference is reimbursed, usually in the home country.

Tax equalization

The system of tax equalization is more equitable than that of tax protection and is therefore favoured by multinationals with large numbers of overseas employees. An expatriate who has benefited from a tax 'windfall' through the protection system, having, for instance, worked in a zero tax country such as Saudi Arabia, may, justifiably, be reluctant to be transferred to a country with rates similar to the UK where 'windfalls' and reimbursements will be equally negligible.

The tax equalization system offers a fairer global policy in that it reimburses tax excesses to those in high tax areas but makes a deduction from the total remuneration of those in low or zero-rated countries. Thus, all staff are maintained on a tax standard which reflects that of the home country.

Net payments

The payment of a net salary not only ensures expatriates throughout the world of fiscal equity but removes the onus of tax administration from the employee in countries which have no equivalent of the PAYE system. However, as mentioned above, it is extremely expensive to operate a net payment system and few companies do so. Several systems have been developed to assist companies with grossing up. Two examples are:

ECA Tax Program
Employment Conditions Abroad Limited
Anchor House
15 Britten Street
London SW3
Telephone: 071–351 7151

Sedgwick Financial Services
The International Employer Ltd
Winterton House
Nixey Close
Slough
Berkshire 0753 516151

Chapter 22

Mergers and Acquisitions

The implications of a merger or acquisition on pay and conditions of employment do not seem to be considered seriously in most take-over battles. Employees are too often pawns in a game of chess played by remote grand masters. However, acquisitions or mergers do not always live up to expectations and one of the principal reasons for failure is the demotivation of managers and staff. This is inevitable if insufficient attention is paid to their needs and fears.

The degree to which staff are affected by a merger or acquisition does, of course, vary. At one extreme the holding company adopts a completely 'hands off' approach, leaving the acquired company to run its own business, in its own way, and with its own terms and conditions of employment, as long as it delivers the goods. At the other extreme, the acquisition is merged entirely into the parent company and all terms and conditions of employment are 'harmonized'. The employees affected, however, might have different views about the extent to which the process is harmonious.

Between these two extremes there is a measure of choice. In some cases it is only the pension scheme that is merged. In others, it is the pension scheme and all the other benefits that are harmonized, leaving separate pay structures. In making decisions about what should be done and how, the points on the following check-list should be considered jointly and in advance by the parties concerned.

Merger and acquisition check-list

Salary structure

1. To what extent, if at all, should a common salary structure be introduced?
   To answer this question information will be needed, first on the economics and strategy of each business unit to see how far they conform. Then, if the business case emerges, details will be needed on:

(a) existing salary structures
(b) organization structures, with salaries and grades for each job
(c) the distribution of salaries within each grade
(d) the method of job evaluation used
(e) policies and procedures for grading or re-grading jobs and for fixing salaries on appointment or promotion
(f) any terms and conditions negotiated with trade unions or staff associations
(g) the similarities and differences between the work carried out in each company and, therefore, the type of people employed.

2. What are the advantages and disadvantages of merging salary structures?
The advantages seem obvious. A common basis is established throughout the group which facilitates movement and a consistent approach to salary administration. The disadvantage is the disturbance and potential cost of merging, bearing in mind the re-gradings and salary increases that might be necessary as well as the expense of job evaluation. Why go to all this trouble if the operations in the respective companies are dissimilar and they are located in entirely different parts of the country? It could even be damaging.
3. If salary structures have to be merged, how should this be done?
The choice is between:
(a) a full job evaluation exercise which will be disturbing, time consuming and expensive but may now have to be looked at in the light of recent equal value cases; or
(b) the arbitrary slotting of jobs into the new structure using existing job descriptions (if any). This could result in gross inequities unless very full job descriptions are available or there is already a good fit between the two salary structures; or
(c) a compromise between (a) and (b), slotting in jobs without a full evaluation if the fit is obvious, but evaluating doubtful or marginal cases.
Note that if pay is negotiated with a trade union or staff association they would have to be involved and they will obviously fight against any detrimental changes.
4. When the merger takes place, should action be limited to the creation of a common grade structure, defining benefit levels but allowing different salary scales to reflect regional or separately negotiated variations in rates?
It is possible to have common grade structures with

different salary levels as long as the differences can be justified by reference to market rates.

5. What should be done about staff whose grade or salary range is changed as a result of merging pay structures?

   To re-grade people and adjust their salaries to higher levels could be prohibitively expensive. To reduce salaries could be impossible, especially if there are trade unions in existence who carry any weight at all. It might then be necessary to 'red circle' staff affected by grade changes, that is, give them 'personal to job holder' gradings and salary brackets which they retain as long as they are in the same job.

General salary reviews

6. Should general salary reviews be centralized and take place simultaneously in all locations?

   The answer is clearly yes if a common salary structure exists or pay is negotiated centrally. If structures or pay levels vary or if site negotiations continue, then it may be best to maintain local arrangements.

Merit reviews

7. Should performance appraisal systems and merit review procedures be standardized?

   It is tempting to say that they should, in the interests of consistency and control and to facilitate career and salary planning for the new group as a whole. But there are strong arguments for maintaining the local scheme if it is operating effectively. Managers who are familiar with one system might resent change. They could be forced to accept it but reluctant appraisers are bad appraisers.

Salary administration procedures

8. Should standardized procedures operate throughout the new group?

   A bureaucratic centralized approach is inevitable in some organizations, but if local arrangements work well why change them for change's sake?

Bonus schemes

9. Should different arrangements for bonuses be allowed to continue?

   The answer to this question again depends on how close the links between establishments are. There is much to be said for retaining effective local bonus schemes which have an immediate link to performance as long as they do not conflict too much with group policies.

Profit sharing schemes

10. What should be done about profit sharing, assuming a scheme exists in one or other or both of the companies?

    Clearly, if there has been a complete takeover and the merged company loses its status as a separate profit centre or can no longer issue shares under arrangements such as ADST (Approved Deferred Share Trust), then the scheme in the company which has been taken over must be discontinued and employees moved into the takeover company's scheme, if one exists. If there is no scheme in that company, consideration would have to be given to some form of compensation, which could be as high as three times the average of the last three years' payments.

Pension schemes

11. Should the employees of the acquired firm be transferred into the acquirer's pension fund?

    This is quite common and, obviously, there is no problem for staff if benefits are better. However, the back-funding of previous pension arrangements in order to pay for improvements can be very expensive, and it may be necessary to maintain separate schemes.

    When the pension scheme in the acquiring company is inferior, it may be possible for members to choose under which scheme they will retire in the unlikely event that both schemes can continue. This could be divisive when staff in the takeover company see that employees in the taken-over company are better off than themselves. However, many employees may leave the taken-over company before retirement and there will only be a handful of genuine anomalies reaching retiring age.

    The Government regulations on personal pensions and the development of portable pensions (see Chapter 17) would also have to be taken into account. Employees in the acquired firm should be told about their rights and given advice on what is best for them to do in their own interests.

Other benefits

12. To what extent should employee benefits be harmonized, for example:
    (a) company cars
    (b) free petrol for company cars
    (c) life insurance
    (d) sick pay
    (e) private medical insurance

(f) mortgage subsidy
(g) season ticket and other staff loans
(h) lunch arrangements, including luncheon vouchers
(i) educational subsidies
(j) discount facilities?

The degree to which benefits should be harmonized is, like other areas of reward management, a policy question the answer to which depends first on the philosophy of the controlling company (the extent to which it believes in centralization and absolute consistency in the treatment of employees) and secondly, on the circumstances in each company (the degree to which their operations and their geographical locations are linked or adjacent). Considerable variations in benefits between employees in different parts of a group are undesirable, especially if there is any interaction or inter-change between establishments. But a brutal approach to harmonization which significantly reduces the total remuneration of the affected employees will damage morale – will the takeover company want its acquisition to be operated by demotivated people?

Trade unions or staff associations

13. If a trade union or staff association has negotiating rights, how should they be involved?

It is desirable in these circumstances to enter into discussions as soon as possible. The two companies should already have considered the approach they want to adopt and this will provide a basis for consultation and, where negotiated terms and conditions are affected, negotiation.

Communication strategy

Apart from any discussions with bodies representing staff, it is essential to have a communication strategy which ensures that staff in *both* companies know what is going to happen and how it is going to affect them.

This strategy must be prepared in advance and this implies that the question in the check-list will have been considered before the merger is announced.

Chapter 23

Reward Policies for New and 'Start-up' Organizations

Key characteristics and influences

Designing reward systems for new organizations is often fraught with difficulty. Most new organizations start with a small group of top executives who introduce their own previous experience and prejudices with the system before anyone like an HR professional gets to look at it. The thinking of the 'start-up' cadre of top executives will typically be based on:

- reward systems from previous employers (bringing the staff handbook/salary policy with you)
- throwing out the bits of these that they found demotivating
- 'cherry picking' from reward policies they have known or liked the sound of from other employers
- selection of benefits (notably pensions) provided on a basis that suits a small high-powered cadre but can't be extended to a more balanced group of employees in a maturing organization
- failure to understand the underlying pluralism of employment – that inevitably not all employees will be fired with the same enthusiasm as top management – they are in it for different reasons, like having a job just round the corner from home, rather than wanting to make their first £1 million by 30.

Where to start

The objectives of a reward system designed to meet the needs of a business start-up are to:

- attract and keep people anxious to make the organization grow and flourish
- reward the risk of coming into a new venture with high rewards if the risk pays off – for those who have real control over development. It is more difficult and probably unrealistic to reward support and mere junior staff on a high risk basis
- provide a sensible basic salary that is reasonably competitive with the market for most staff and highly competitive if rare

skills have to be brought in. This is one time to pay at the *top* of the market
- lock people in to give the business a chance – typically with generous share options for senior executives and an all-employee SAYE share scheme or profit sharing for everyone else
- minimize overheads by keeping benefits to a decent basic core until there is some 'fat' in the system or where competitive pressure indicates additions to the various benefits
- pay out bonus or provide more cash rewards (have a party!) when key milestones in the business plan are successfully achieved
- recognize that in the early days office accommodation may be at best basic and demonstrate willingness to improve conditions as soon as practicable (fresh flowers in an aged but clean reception area – or even in the staff lavatories – can have a significant effect on the way the company is perceived).

Preparing for growth

Whatever the basic components of the reward system in a 'start-up' they should be developed with an eye to appropriateness in a larger organization. Particular attention will be needed in these areas:

- *pensions*: schemes for small partnerships/groups of professionals or the self employed will *not* easily adapt to cover 140 to 200 employees after three years. Professional advice will be needed to achieve this
- *pay relativities*: starting on a 'spot salary' basis is logical, but internal relativities should always be defensible as the organization grows
- *share options/share schemes*: should be capable of extension – again an area for good professional advice
- *performance rewards*: need to relate to the milestones in the business plan and be based on achievement of agreed objectives/performance standards. Chief executive-driven discretionary bonuses are typically suspect unless the boss really is in the 'tough but fair' (or preferably just the fair) category.

The involvement of investors/auditors/other advisers

If the business is promising and set to grow then sooner rather than later investment will be sought from providers of venture capital. Such organizations typically take a very robust view of reward systems, requiring introduction of share options and highly geared incentives to ensure that the top management group they have entrusted with their money really are fully committed to the business. Fixed term contracts will be required and the high risk/ high reward approach mentioned earlier will be what counts.

If the company decides to take itself to the market, typically the unlisted securities market (USM) in the first instance, it will have to ensure that its financial house is in order. Auditors, lawyers and others providing advice at this stage will again go over the elements of executive reward policy and the structure of payroll costs with a fine tooth comb. This is the time when beyond the fringe benefits (company yachts etc) come under scrutiny to potential institutional shareholders.

Such advisers may, or may not always, be mindful of the rationale for pay systems and the messages the individual elements can give. Sad to say, while some are very helpful and constructive others may have a perspective that is sometimes narrow and confined to their specialism and its accompanying prejudices – be it over-zealous cost control or a desire to pin down every last detail in fine print. This can come as a shock to a free-wheeling entrepreneurial organization. Faced with criticism about 'unorthodox' approaches to pay from such sources the important questions to ask are:

- is what we are doing illegal in any way (in terms of employment law)?
- are there tax implications we don't know about?
- is it uncompetitive for any reason?
- what messages will the symbolic act of taking it away give?
- are you mistaking 'unorthodox' on our part for real creativity in finding rewards that match our developing culture?
- what culture *should* we be aiming for as a larger/listed organization?
- where can we get advice about putting our house in order if necessary?

Reinforcing the culture of success

Much of the success of a growing organization depends on close and effective team-work. Reward systems need to support this. This means that as organizations grow they have much to gain from implementing:

- performance rewards which reflect team as well as individual achievement
- consistent and as far as possible harmonized benefits
- the beginnings of a formal approach to setting internal relativities so that a defensible 'pecking order' emerges
- management of the reward system by an individual who is a wise custodian of both policy and implementation until the organization

is large enough to have a personnel/HR/remuneration professional to do the job.

This last point is, in fact, critical. Experience shows that most of the mistakes made by new business in the reward area are because the wrong person had accountability for it. If they perceive reward management as merely an administrative system, fail to take a broad view of its purpose or (at worst) incompetently develop policies that divide and cause dissent then the business is at risk. Good and promising businesses have foundered on disagreements over pay. Sensible pay policies are the oil in the works of any organization. In a small, growing organization oil can turn to grit very fast indeed.

Part 7
Managing the Reward System

Chapter 24

Reward Management Procedures

Salary administration procedures are needed to control salary costs and ensure the consistent application of salary policies. They should be based on an overall system of salary control, as discussed in the first section of this chapter. This should lead to specific procedures, as considered later in the chapter, for:

- controlling salary budgets
- monitoring the salary system
- conducting general salary reviews
- conducting individual salary reviews
- grading jobs and fixing salaries on appointment or promotion
- using computerized salary administration systems.

Salary control systems

The salary control systems should be based on:

- a clearly defined and understood salary structure
- defined methods of salary progression
- budgets of salary costs
- methods of monitoring salary costs and the implementation of salary policies
- clearly defined salary review guidelines
- well defined procedures for grading jobs and fixing salaries
- clear statements of the degree of authority managers have at each level to decide salaries and increments.

A senior member of management should be given the responsibility for developing and maintaining the salary control system, monitoring its implementation and taking or recommending corrective action when necessary.

Salary budgets

The annual salary budget is a product of the numbers of staff to be employed and the rates at which they will be paid during the budget year. It is therefore based on manpower plans, present salary levels and forecasts of additional costs arising from general or individual salary reviews. Actual costs should be monitored against budget using a return such as that illustrated in Figure 24.1.

Category of staff	Budget for year		Budget for period		Period actual		Year to date	
	No	Cost	No	Cost	No	Cost	No	Cost
Grades 3–2 Grades 7–4 Grades 12–8								
Total								

Figure 24.1 *Salary cost return*

There are two other useful techniques for monitoring salary costs and providing additional information on the stability and effectiveness of the salary system. These are *measuring attrition* and *compa-ratios.*

Measuring attrition

Attrition takes place when entrants join on lower salaries than those leaving so that salary costs over a period are likely to go down, given a normal flow of starters and leavers and subject to the effect of general and individual salary increases. In theory, at least, attrition helps to finance merit increases. It has been claimed that fixed incremental systems can be entirely self-financing. But the conditions under which this can be attained are so exceptional that a completely self-financing system rarely, if ever, occurs. But some amount of attrition to merit increase costs is normal and should be measured in order to assess actual costs and to forecast future expenditure.

Attrition can be calculated, crudely, by the following formula: *Total percentage increase to payroll arising from general promotional and merit increases minus total percentage increase in average salaries.* An example of this formula in operation is given in Table 24.1. This is simplified to show only three groups of staff, but it could be done for each grade, especially if a computer program, which would be necessary in larger organizations, is used.

Compa-ratio

A compa-ratio (short for comparative ratio) provides a measurement of how far average salaries in a range differ from the target salary,

Table 24.1 *Calculation of attrition*

	Group A	Group B	Group C	Total
1. Average salary at beginning of year (£)	8000	10,000	12,000	9200
2. Average salary at year end (£)	8560	10,900	13,320	9975
3. Increase in average salary (%)	7	9	11	8.4
4. General increase (%)	5	5	5	5
5. Merit increase (%)	5	5	5	5
6. Promotional increase (%)	0	1	2	0.6
7. Total increase [4+5+6] (%)	10	11	12	10.6
8. Total attrition [7−3] (%)	3	2	1	2.2
9. Residual cost of merit increase (%)	2	3	4	2.8

defined as the salary which should be earned by a fully competent individual in a job. A line drawn through the target salaries for each range in a salary structure is the salary policy line for an organization and it is this line which is related to market rates. If, typically, the target is the midpoint of the salary range for a grade, the compa-ratio can be calculated as follows:

$$\frac{\text{average of all salaries in grade} \times 100}{\text{midpoint of range}}$$

If the distribution of salaries is on target (ie the average salary is equal to the midpoint) the compa-ratio will be 100. If the ratio is above 100 this would suggest either that staff are overpaid or that there are a large number of long-service employees or 'fast track' paid at the top of the range. Conversely, if the ratio is below 100, the causes would probably be that salaries are too low or that a large number of entrants on lower salaries have affected the relationships. The identification of the reasons for a high or low compa-ratio can suggest policy adjustments to correct the imbalance, although there can be many situations where a ratio of over or under 100 is perfectly justified.

Information on compa-ratios and changes in average salaries can be recorded on a form such as that illustrated in Figure 24.2 and used for annual comparisons and to provide guidance on the likely effects of attrition.

		Number in grade		Average salary		Compa-ratio	
Grade	Salary range	Last year	This year	Last year	This year	Last year	This year

Fig. 24.2 *Compa-ratio summary*

Monitoring the salary system

The salary system needs to be monitored to check that:

1. Salary levels are keeping pace with changes in market rates so that salary policies on external relativities are being maintained.
2. The salary structure is not being eroded by grade drift (unjustifiable upgradings) or because salaries for new starters or promoted staff are fixed at too high a level.
3. Appropriate differentials are being maintained internally.
4. Salary progression policies are being implemented properly.

Much useful information can be obtained by measuring attrition and by the use of compa-ratios. In addition it is necessary (a) to conduct regular exercises to check on external and internal relativities, and (b) to carry out regular checks to ensure that salary policies and procedures are being implemented.

Monitoring external relativities

Market rate surveys should be conducted or analyzed regularly and comparisons made with salaries paid within the company to assess whether salaries are generally keeping pace with the market or whether any particular groups of staff are out of line. The best way to summarize and compare the data is to chart, (as shown in Figure 24.3).

1. The salary practice line (the average of actual salaries paid in each grade).
2. The salary policy line (the line joining together the target salaries for each grade – usually the midpoint salary).
3. The median and/or upper quartile market rate trend lines.

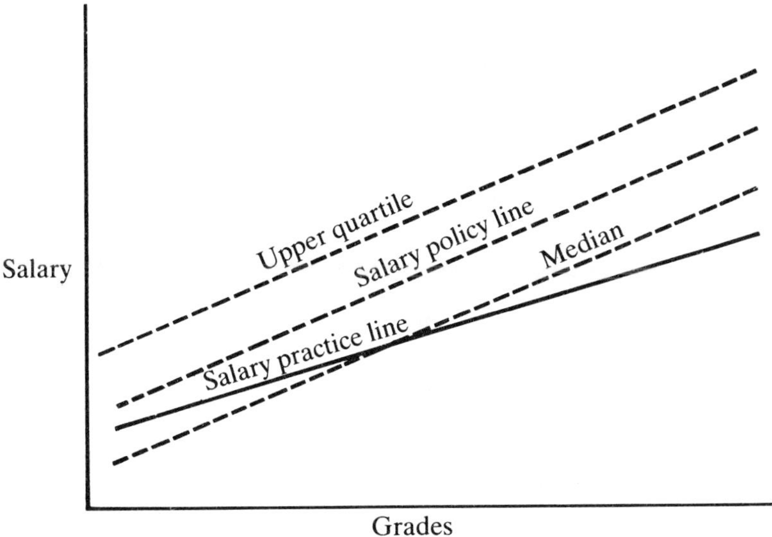

Fig. 24.3 *Analysis of salary structure policy and practice in relation to market rates*

Monitoring internal relativities

Internal relativities should be monitored by carrying out periodical studies of the differentials that exist vertically within departments or between categories of staff. For example, if there is an established hierarchy in departments of, say, departmental managers, section heads, senior and junior clerks, the average salaries at each level should be analyzed periodically to reveal any changes in differentials between levels. There is nothing sacrosanct about the pattern of differentials. Structural adjustments within the company and alterations in market rates can justify changes. But it is desirable to know what is happening so that action can be taken, if required and if feasible, to restore the proper relationships.

It may also be interesting to analyze key ratios, for example, between the salary of the chief executive and the average earnings without overtime of semi-skilled employees. If, for example, this ratio has changed from 7:1 to 5:1 the implications will need to be studied, not only for the chief executive but also for intermediate jobs in the hierarchy.

General salary reviews

General salary reviews take place when an across-the-board increase is given to all staff in response to increases in the cost of living or in market rates, or as a result of pay settlements with trade unions or staff associations.

It is necessary to make a decision on whether to have separate general and individual reviews or whether to combine them, unless policy is dictated by a union agreement or a fixed date for making incremental payments. Practices vary. If pay settlements are negotiated with trade unions it is usual to conduct merit reviews at a different time. Some companies separate them in any case because they believe they can exercise better control over merit payments, or because they think the staff will be more highly motivated if they receive distinct merit payments at a different time. Experience shows, however, that equally good, if not better, overall control can be achieved over costs if the general and individual reviews take place at the same time. And staff can still be motivated if they know how much of their increase is attributable to merit and how much is common to all employees. More companies are now, however, taking the view that increases should be related entirely to the combined impact of individual performance and any changes in the market rate applicable to the individual's job. This approach is, of course, not favoured by trade unions.

Companies also sometimes combine general and individual salary reviews in order to reduce costs by cutting down on merit increases when a large market-driven general increase has to be given. This may be unavoidable, but it ought to be a conscious decision arising from the need to restrict increases to payroll costs.

Following a general percentage increase to salaries the salary structure should be revised by making proportionate adjustments to the midpoints of each salary range. If the policy on range widths is retained, this results in similar increases to the minima and maxima of the ranges. In hard times, however, companies that do not negotiate or publish salary structures have been known to reduce range widths following a general review. Some have even tried to negotiate a reduction, but it is not easy to get anyone to accept a change which restricts the salary progression available to staff. Companies who do not negotiate pay settlements may reserve the right to withhold general increases or give smaller increases to staff who are overpaid or who are not performing effectively.

Individual salary reviews

Individual salary or merit reviews are usually held annually although companies occasionally allow half-yearly reviews for junior staff or high flyers who are thought to need encouragement. Some companies pay merit increments on birthdays or the anniversary of staff joining the firm. This, they say, allows more individual attention to be given to staff and removes the emotion associated with a review affecting all staff at once. But phasing reviews in this way makes it difficult to control costs and is an administrative headache without effective computerised systems.

A fixed incremental system is an automatic process and therefore cannot be classified as an individual salary review. If minor variations to a fixed system are allowed, such as double increments, special performance bonuses or withheld increments, special guidelines should be issued to managers indicating the circumstances in which these variations are allowed. These guidelines can be related to the performance review, indicating, for example, that only outstanding staff should receive anything extra and only unsatisfactory staff should be left out. It is usual to restrict the proportion of staff who can receive a double increment or a bonus to, say, 10 per cent.

Variable progression systems, as defined in Chapter 11, need to be controlled even more carefully by means of budgets, guidelines and control procedures. These matters are discussed below.

Individual review budget

The individual review budget should be expressed in terms of the percentage increase to the payroll that can be allowed for merit payments. The factors that should be taken into account when deciding on the budget figures are:

1. The need to adjust average salaries either because compa-ratio analysis reveals that averages are falling below target levels or because market rate analysis shows that the salary practice curve is out of line with the salary policy curve, ie the market rate policy of the company is not being achieved.
2. The amount the company thinks it can afford to pay on the basis of budgeted revenue, payroll costs and profits and an analysis of the effects of salary attrition on costs.
3. The company's policies on salary progression. These will cover the rates of progression and the amounts which it is customary to pay for different levels of performance in addition to market adjustments. Over the last 10 years or so, merit budgets have stayed at around two and a half to three per cent in addition to cost of living increases. The actual range of merit pay typically goes from 0–10 per cent (or more), ie 0–20 per cent in 'all merit' systems. If the company cannot afford to give, say, an average of three to five per cent for the majority of its staff it would be preferable to restrict increases to those whose performance is above average rather than to spread derisory payments around the rest of the staff.

The agreed individual review budget is normally expressed as a percentage of payroll costs and this is the limit given to each departmental manager for increasing his or her own payroll.

Individual salary review guidelines

Guidelines are necessary to tell managers how they should distribute their budget for merit payments among their staff. The aim of the guidelines should, as far as possible, be to minimize inconsistencies in the treatment of staff in different parts of the company. Such consistency can, of course, be achieved by taking away authority from managers and imposing rigid control from the top. But deciding on the rewards for his or her staff is an important part of a manager's job: removing this responsibility would rightly cause resentment. However, if managers are to be given some discretion, they should be given guidance on how to exercise it, and it is still necessary to use control procedures to check that the policy on guidelines has been implemented.

Guidelines can be given in various forms, depending on the extent to which consistency of treatment throughout the organization is required, bearing in mind that complete uniformity is an impossible and undesirable ideal. Only fixed incremental systems deliver total uniformity. Once the principle of giving rewards according to performance is agreed, it has to be accepted that the amount of the reward will depend on human judgement. That judgement can be subjected to guidance and control, but if some freedom is given to exercise it, as it must be, a measure of inconsistency will creep in. The advantages of allowing managers to use their judgement far outweigh the disadvantages, as long as managers are working within budgets and according to the guidelines.

The main types of guidelines are described below. In each case, final control would be exercised by imposing an overall budget limit on the increase to the departmental payroll arising from merit awards.

1. *Average and min/max guidelines*: these indicate the average merit award – say five per cent, with restrictions on the minimum and maximum increments that can be given, if any award is to be made (for example, three per cent minimum and 10 per cent maximum). This is the simplest form of guideline and can be used in the absence of an elaborate performance appraisal system.
2. *Performance/reward guidelines*: these link the overall performance assessment with the merit award (see Table 24.2).

Table 24.2 *Awarding salary increases according to merit*

Assessment	*Increase (%)*
A (outstanding)	10
B (highly effective)	7–8
C (effective)	5
D (barely effective)	3 or nil
E (ineffective)	nil

If the salary progression system used by the company includes limits within salary ranges according to the level of performance, as described in Chapter 11, these limits would also be issued to managers. This form of guideline depends on the existence of a formal appraisal system and is slightly more directive than the average, minimum/maximum approach. But it can help managers to achieve a more consistent relationship between their own assessment and the reward. What this guideline does not achieve, however, is any measure of control over the distribution of awards between the different performance levels.

3. *Forced choice distribution guidelines*: these, as the name implies, indicate the way in which the different levels of assessment and hence the awards should be distributed among the staff by defining the percentage of staff who should be assessed at each level (see Table 24.3).

Table 24.3 *Assessing staff within forced choice guidelines*

Assessment	Distribution amongst staff (%)	Award (%)
A (outstanding)	5	10
B (highly effective)	15	7–8
C (effective)	60	5
D (barely effective)	15	3
E (ineffective)	5	nil

This distribution would produce an average award of about five per cent and could be adjusted if higher or lower averages were required. It takes a fairly tough line on the proportion of staff who are rated as barely effective or ineffective, and some companies increase the proportion at higher levels on the assumption, which may or may not be correct, that they only employ high quality staff. Salary range limits, if they exist, would also be applied. This method provides the most rigid guidelines and is therefore the easiest to control, where the objective is to achieve the greatest degree of uniformity.

Managers may resent the way in which it restricts their degree of choice, and the assumption that the distribution of talent is evenly spread throughout the organization is questionable. It is also difficult to apply in small departments.

4. *A performance matrix*: as described in Chapter 10, this can be used to define exactly what increase individuals should have in various segments of the salary scale according to performance. To exercise control over the costs of the increase it is usual to analyze the distribution of performance ratings first (preferably with the help of a computer) and then adjust the figures in the matrix to ensure that the total percentage increase to the payroll is in line with the budget.
5. *Ranking*: as described in Chapter 10, this is a form of forced distribution. Managers are asked to rank comparable groups of staff in order of merit and the rank order is divided into groups.

   The percentage increase is governed by the group which individuals are in. Thus someone in the top 10 per cent might get a 10 per cent merit increase while someone in the next 20 per cent might receive an 8 per cent increase, and so on.
6. *Salary modelling*: the use of software packages for modelling salary systems has enabled some large organizations such as building societies and insurance companies with formal salary systems to relate salary increases very precisely to performance ratings (often expressed as percentages). The merit increase may be entirely determined by a formula which allocates money according to merit points, each grade having different rates. For example, in a range of £12,000 to £15,000 with a scale of 200 points, anyone awarded 50 points or more would receive a merit payment at the rate of £6 per point. Thus, someone with 60 points would get an increase of 3 per cent of the bottom of the scale, ie £360. Someone with 100 points would get 5 per cent, ie £600, and so on. The value of the points would be determined by the model on the basis of what the company was prepared to pay and the distribution of points ratings. This distribution could be forced along the lines described above.

The choice between methods depends on the degree to which the organization believes that the benefits of uniformity and consistency are more important than the benefits of giving a reasonable degree of choice to managers. It is a matter of opinion. In the authors' view, forced choice systems can go too far if they are operated rigidly. They are best treated as broad guidelines which can be varied at management's discretion as long as (a) the overall budget is not exceeded, (b) the upper limit is not exceeded, and (c) the distribution

SALARY REVIEW FORM									Sheet:
Department:			Proposed by:			Date:			Date:
Name	Job title	Present salary (£)	Last increase			Assessment (Note 1)	Proposed increase (£)	Proposed salary (£)	Comments (Note 2)
			Amount (£)	Date	Reason				

Note 1: Assessment – A = outstanding, B = very effective, C = satisfactory, D = barely satisfactory, E = unsatisfactory
Note 2: Comment on any special reasons for proposed increase or for amending the proposal

Figure 24.4 *Departmental salary review form*

of awards looks sensible overall, ie it is not skewed unreasonably in either direction.

Control of individual salary reviews

Individual salary reviews should be controlled by:

1. Defining who has the authority to propose and authorize awards.
2. Allocating responsibility to a manager to co-ordinate the review.
3. Agreeing and issuing budget limits and guidelines.
4. Generating control information which will ensure that the review is co-ordinated, that awards are made in accordance with the guidelines and that the increase to payroll costs does not exceed the budget.

The basic control information should consist of a departmental salary review form (see Figure 24.4) and a company salary review summary form (see Figure 24.5).

Merit only reviews

Organizations are increasingly adopting the practice of a merit only review which does not contain any general element, although the size of the merit increases will be related to market rate increases for staff in comparable jobs. This enables the company to adopt a flexible approach which discriminates much more effectively between different levels of performance. Significantly large increases can be given to the top performers while poor performers may get nothing or an amount which is less than inflation (a decrease in real terms). At mid-1990 competitive rates top (A rated) individuals would be given increases of between 17 and 20 per cent, the next group of B rated staff could get 13 to 16 per cent, C rated staff could receive 9 to 12 per cent, while the poor performers would get 0 to 9 per cent.

Procedures for grading jobs and fixing salaries

Grading jobs

To avoid grade drift (ie unjustified upgradings simply to achieve higher salaries) it is necessary to:

1. Ensure that jobs cannot be graded or regraded until they have been evaluated by the appropriate job evaluation officer or committee using the company's standard job evaluation procedure.

Department	Number employed	Payroll (£)	Number receiving increase	Proposed payroll (£)	Increase to payroll (£)

Figure 24.5 *Company salary review form*

2. Resist demands from managers for jobs to be regraded simply because of market rate pressures, difficulties in recruitment or retention, or threats to leave. Methods of dealing with these problems are discussed in Chapter 27.
3. Instruct the manager responsible for salary administration to monitor pressures on the pay structure arising from market rate changes so that problems can be anticipated.

Fixing salaries on appointment

Guidelines on who has the authority to grade new jobs should be issued to managers. Gradings should be approved by whoever is responsible for salary administration. Starting salaries should normally be close to the minimum of the salary range for the job. There should be some scope for fixing starting salaries above the minimum when it can be shown that this is the only way to attract suitable staff. Limits of authority should be set: for approval at one level to starting salaries up to 25 per cent above the range minimum, and, perhaps, for approval at a higher level for starting salaries up to the range midpoint. These should be exceptional cases. To provide room for salary progression, staff should not start above the midpoint. If this is the only way to recruit people it would show that there was something fundamentally wrong with salary levels in relation to market rates or to grading policies. These problems would then have to be tackled separately.

Fixing salaries on promotion

Promotions should be dealt with as they arise. The increase should be meaningful, say 10 per cent or more, and should normally take the promoted employee to no more than half-way up his or her new salary range. Promotions above that level should be exceptional and subject to special authorization.

New trends in computerized salary management

The changing environment

The 1980s marked a significant change in the role of human resource professionals in the salary management process – from reactive administrators at the beginning of the decade to proactive decision makers at the end.

This change was helped and, to some degree, stimulated by the rapid developments in information technology that enabled the HR function to break free from the mainframe computer environment which had previously been dominant and so use the output of the technology more creatively. In most organizations the main source of pay data was the payroll system which was maintained either on an in-house mainframe computer or managed externally via a specialist bureau. As these systems were divorced from peronnel and designed to meet the requirements of the finance function, they were of limited use to the reward specialist other than as a source of raw data.

With the emergence of the personal computer (PC) came the development of a range of software from databases to spreadsheets that gave managers the freedom to record and analyze data in a way that had previously been impossible. Suddenly, those responsible for reward management had the opportunity to take a much more systematic approach to the salary planning process, and it became possible to test out a range of alternative proposals in short timescales. As the development of end-user computing grew there became a greater need to integrate systems. Manually maintaining different systems which hold common data is an inefficient use of resources and inevitably leads to anomalies.

To overcome this problem the computer industry has developed industry standard file formats such as ASCII and DIF that allow data to be transferred between systems. Most software is now designed with interfacing facilities which means systems can 'talk' to each other and are no longer isolated. Thus payroll, the personnel record system and other reward management software can receive and transmit common items of data.

With the potential for information to move freely between different systems some form of verification and validation process is essential where key programs are being affected. For example, audit trails need to be incorporated into software that updates the payroll system.

Data itself is becoming more accessible. The development of multiuser software and the introduction of LANs (Local Area Networks) mean that it is now possible for several users to 'log onto' the same software simultaneously. The performance problems associated with the early networks has diminished with the introduction of 386 and now 486 technology.

Most PCs are used as stand alone systems. However, it is still possible for two computers to communicate with each other without the need to download files onto diskette. Over larger distances data can be transmitted over the telephone via a modem. Over short distances software, such as Laplink, allow information to be sent via a cable attached to one of the printer ports.

It is not just data that is becoming more portable, computers themselves are becoming smaller and more powerful. Only a few years ago, the term portable computer referred to a luggable beast weighing 30lbs and capable of running only off the mains. Nowadays it is possible to purchase laptop computers weighing only a few pounds that operate on batteries and yet have more storage capacity and greater processing power. As this book was being finalized the 40Mb, 4lb laptop became a reality.

As the power of computers increases, it is not only the software that is becoming more sophisticated. HR professionals themselves need to adapt this changing environment and develop more efficient management practices. Only a few years ago, it would have been difficult to imagine that a compensation manager could plan the salary review for each operating division on site, with line managers, using a portable computer. Now they can 'own' the decisions as they are being made!

The computerized options

Within the increasingly complex pay environment, some sort of computer-based system is now considered essential in all but the smallest operation – and often there too! There are a number of different options available to choose from. Deciding which is the best for a particular organization depends on a number of factors, namely:

- the availability of resources – both human and financial;
- the number of employees involved;
- the complexity of the pay structure;
- the stability of the pay structure.

Defining system requirements

Any solution should allow the remuneration specialist to analyze the following:

- *Internal equity* – between individuals and across divisions/ functions, (see Figure 24.6) illustrates how salary practice can be analysed using a scattergram. Using a system such as Hay's HayXpert, it is possible to highlight individuals on the scattergram by positioning the cursor on a selected data point. This will instantly provide details of the person and their salary details
- *External comparisons* – by tracking current practice against survey and other market data
- *Overall policy development* – testing out new pay initiatives against the employee population they are to cover to determine what the outcomes will be and decide which is the most acceptable. Figure 24.7 analyses the impact on individuals of applying a new pay policy to the existing practice.

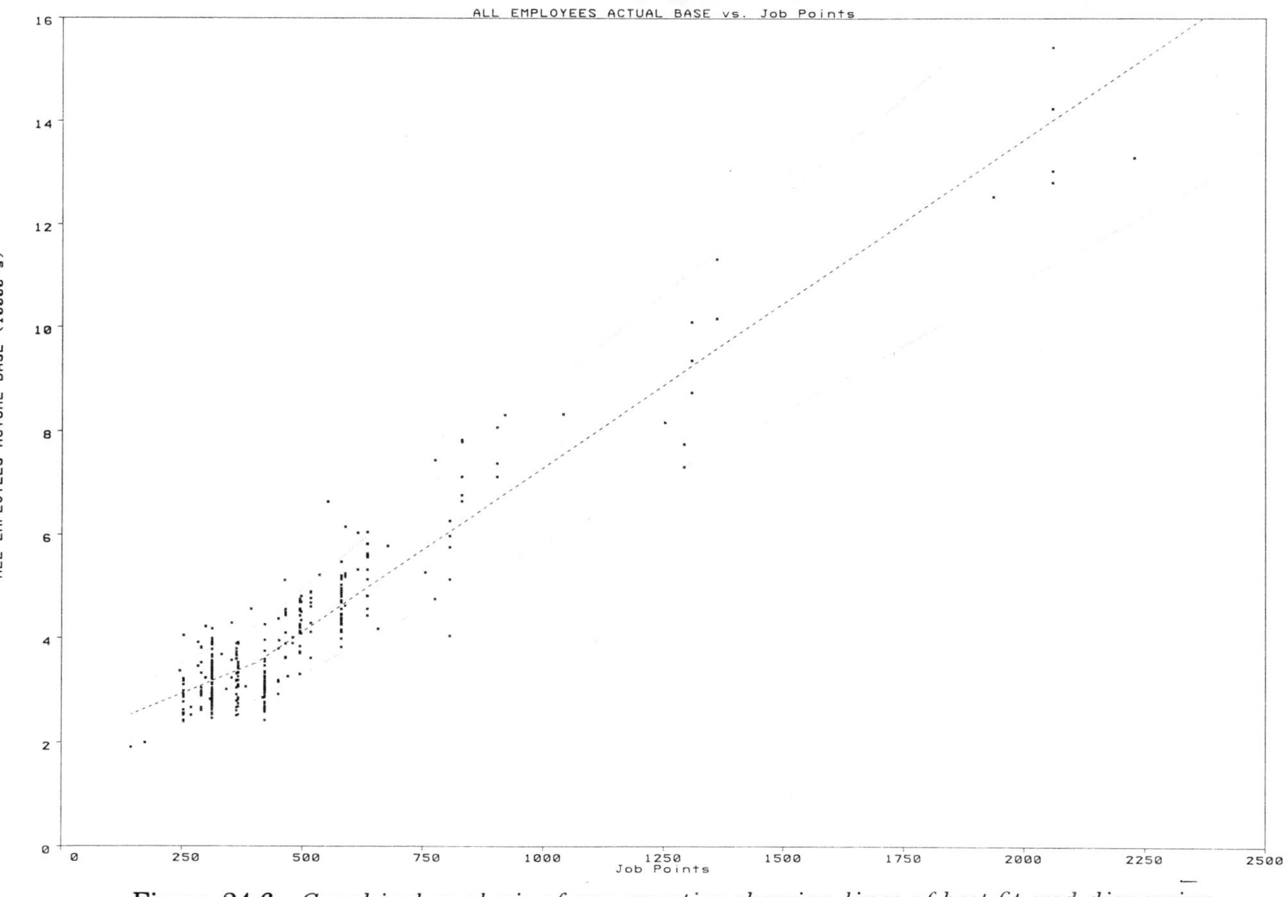

Figure 24.6 *Graphical analysis of pay practice showing lines of best fit and dispersion*

Name Job no	Init Title Job Title	PSF	Job units	Current salary	Compa ratio	80% Min	100% Midpt	120% Max
Adams 11001	AS Managing Director	1.00	2448	77186	90%	68467	85584	102701
Carrington 13001	I Operations Director	1.00	1628	41966	72%	46819	58524	70229
Williamson 12001	CJ Sales/Mkting: Director	1.00	1628	51708	88%	46819	58524	70229
Thomson 13078	W Factory Manager Nwch:	1.00	1192	33723	76%	35309	44136	52963
Johnson 15001	JG Personnel Director	1.00	1182	42759	98%	35045	43806	52567
Comben 12002	MJ Marketing Mgr: – UK	1.00	1096	38069	93%	32774	40968	49162
Cooper 13003	J Factory Manager – SOTON:	1.00	1040	30725	79%	31296	39120	46944
Smith 12003	TJ Sales Manager – UK	1.00	1040	37619	96%	31296	39120	46944

Figure 24.7 *Tabular analysis showing current pay practice against proposed policy*

- *Individual pay increase models*
  Once pay policies are agreed reward specialists need to be able to allocate pay awards for instance on the basis of factors such as market movements, performance, position in range, time in job and other influences on particular jobs. The system should have the facility to develop models that allow optimization of the distribution of funds based on the criteria used in that organization.

When the pay increase guidelines have been finalized the results need to be communicated to managers for approval or fine-tuning. This requires the preparation of reports showing all the relevant facts about their subordinates and the funds available. A typical example is illustrated in Figure 24.8. When all the increases have been approved and signed off, employees need to be notified of their new salaries. This is usually communicated via a standard letter which can be produced on a proprietary wordprocessing package, using a mail merge facility to incorporate data from the database. Such letters are now commonly personalized to recognize particular achievements and performance ratings. Figure 24.9 is an example of a letter template, which contains a number of variables. The resulting output appears as per Figure 24.10 when the variables are inserted from the merge file.

In addition to the specific functional requirements outlined briefly above, an effective computer-based solution needs to be able to have some general features. These include:

- Data transfer facilities

The facility to receive from, and send data to, other systems should be seen as an essential feature of any salary management system.

At the beginning of the planning process the compensation specialist needs access to the most up-to-date information. A lot of this data, such as salaries, divisional, functional information etc., is already held on the payroll or the main personnel record system. Why reinput the data manually when it can be transferred electronically?

During the review process itself the data may need to be exported into a business graphics or spreadsheet package in order to enhance the presentation of reports and produce some *ad hoc* analyses.

Once the review process is complete relevant data needs to be output into a wordprocessing package to produce the salary notification letter, and updated salaries sent back to the payroll or personnel record system.

There are now industry standard file formats such as ASCII and DIF that enable data to be transferred between different computer systems.

Cooper Products Ltd
Preliminary Salary Increase Report

Job No	Job Title	Surname	Inits	Job Units	Perf Rating
13006	Purchasing Manager	Stevens	DT	805	3
13008	Distribution Manager	Wilson	K	732	3
12010	Account Manager – Export	Weekes	SA	682	2
12017	Sales Manager	Jones	AC	516	3
12021	Brand Manager A	Abthorp	AB	479	3
13030	Factory Services Engineer	Barker	J	466	1
13031	Works Services Manager	Patel	T	451	3
13057	Quality Controller	Adamson	E	344	2
13059	Production Supervisor	Bartley	A	344	3
13058	Q.C. Controller	Barry	KJ	344	3
13060	Process Technician	Barnes	JG	342	4
15008	Factory Personnel Manager	Watson	G	342	3
13064	Warehouse Manager – Soton	Bannister	SE	312	3
13070	Work Study Officer – Soton	Evans	PJ	291	3

- Flexible reporting facilities

The salary review process in every organization is different and each has its own reporting requirements. It is unlikely that these requirements will remain the same year after year. Changes in the pay structure, for example, will result in changes to the reporting requirements for both the compensation specialist and individual managers. If the system is unable to respond to these changes and also any *ad hoc* queries that may be requested from time to time, it will rapidly become redundant.

The solutions

The customized database

In the past personnel have commissioned customized programs in order to incorporate all aspects of the salary management process into a single system. Although the advent of 4GLs (Fourth Generation programming languages), such as DBase, Paradox and Clipper, have made systems programming quicker this can still be an expensive option both in terms of time and money. Besides the obvious programming time involved, the end-user must devote a considerable amount of time to system specification and design, testing and implementation. The customized approach tends to be valid for a set, established management process, but this can become a straitjacket, restricting salary planning options. Building flexibility into the system design requires a much greater degree of skill and invariably increases both the cost and lead-time to implementation.

Inc (£)	Proposed Salary	PIR	Inc (%)	Min	Proposed Midpt	Max	Current Salary	Curr Pos in Range
2735	30087	103 %	10	23401	29251	35101	27352	102 %
2878	26858	92 %	12	23401	29251	35101	23980	90 %
3381	24514	84 %	16	23401	29251	35101	21133	79 %
735	25240	113 %	3	17837	22296	26755	24505	120 %
1686	20421	104 %	9	15680	19600	23520	18735	104 %
2518	20503	105 %	14	15680	19600	23520	17985	100 %
1896	19132	98 %	11	15680	19600	23520	17236	96 %
1709	15948	104 %	12	12298	15373	18448	14239	101 %
1484	14973	97 %	11	12298	15373	18448	13489	96 %
1386	15250	99 %	10	12298	15373	18448	13864	98 %
600	15588	101 %	4	12298	15373	18448	14988	106 %
1335	16173	105 %	9	12298	15373	18448	14838	105 %
1484	14973	97 %	11	12298	15373	18448	13489	96 %
859	15173	111 %	6	10983	13729	16475	14314	113 %

Figure 24.8 *Salary increase report used as a basis for testing out options and costs*

Spreadsheets

Spreadsheets, such as Lotus 1–2–3, Quattro and Excel, are now widely used. These provide the user with a worksheet area, divided into cells, into which can be inserted, text, numbers or formulae. This allows the user to carry out complex 'what if' analyses, giving the flexibility to make individual or group adjustments and accommodation policy changes or the demands of individual managers. Each set of analyses can be saved as a separate file for future recall when final agreement or approval is received.

Spreadsheets can be printed out in report format or as any one of a number of different types of graph – XY, histograms, pie-charts etc. Figures 24.11–24.13 illustrate some typical examples. For enhanced presentation it is possible to use specialist business graphics packages such as Harvard Graphics and Freelance.

On the whole, spreadsheets are a very powerful medium for carrying out pay analyses. However, they do have their limitations. Complex pay structures and/or medium-sized databases can become quite cumbersome to deal with and require a significant degree of skill on the part of the operator. Also, most spreadsheets will only function within the available memory on your computer. This means that on the average pc you are likely to run out of processing space when dealing with medium/large populations.

Proprietary software

Micro-based packages, such as Hay's HayXpert, have been designed specifically to help managers cope with the more sophisticated and flexible remuneration policies that are now emerging.

```
PERSONAL


<DATE>


<TITLE> <INITS> <SURNAME>
<DEPT>


Dear <KNOWN_AS>


I am writing to confirm that with effect from March 1st 1991
your base salary will be increased to £<SALARY>. The
attached sheet also details your revised pension and bonus
arrangements.

During the last financial year Cooper Products continued to
experience steady growth in profits and market share despite
increased levels of competition, particularly in the Far
East sector. The year end figures showed both revenue and
profits significantly ahead of budget with performance in
the final quarter exceptionally strong.

This places us in an excellent position for the coming year
and I would like to take this opportunity to thank you for
all your efforts in the last twelve months and look forward
to your continued support during 1991/1992


Yours sincerely



A B Jones
Managing Director
```

Figure 24.9 *Template for salary notification letter*

Most proprietary software of this nature is designed as a standard software shell within which there are a number of functions that allow users to customize the system according to their own requirements.

Before making any commitment, it is important to carry out a detailed evaluation of any package that might look useful to determine whether or not the system is going to meet your requirements both now and in the foreseeable future. Each organization is different but these are the basic points to consider when making your assessment.

1. Does the software do what you want it to do? This might sound obvious, but you need to consider whether the system is

Ms R. Lawson
Marketing Dept.

Dear Rosemary

I am writing to confirm that with effect from March 1st 1991 your base salary will be increased to £25000. The attached sheet also details your revised pension and bonus arrangements.

During the last financial year Cooper Products continued to experience steady growth in profits and market share despite increased levels of competition, particularly in the Far East sector. The year end figures showed both revenue and profits significantly ahead of budget with performance in the final quarter exceptionally strong.

This places us in an excellent position for the coming year and I would like to take this opportunity to thank you for all your efforts in the last twelve months and look forward to your continued support during 1991/1992

Yours sincerely

A B Jones
Managing Director

Figure 24.10 *Salary notification letter as printed after the merge routine*

capable of providing the sort of outputs that will answer most of the foreseeable questions that either you, managers or employees are likely to ask. It is extremely difficult to find any software that will meet all your requirements – so draw up a list of priorities.

2. Can the standard software shell be tailored to meet the requirements of your organization?
3. Can it accommodate the complexities of your pay structure and adapt to any possible future changes? Consider, for example, how easily the system would be able to handle a change in the

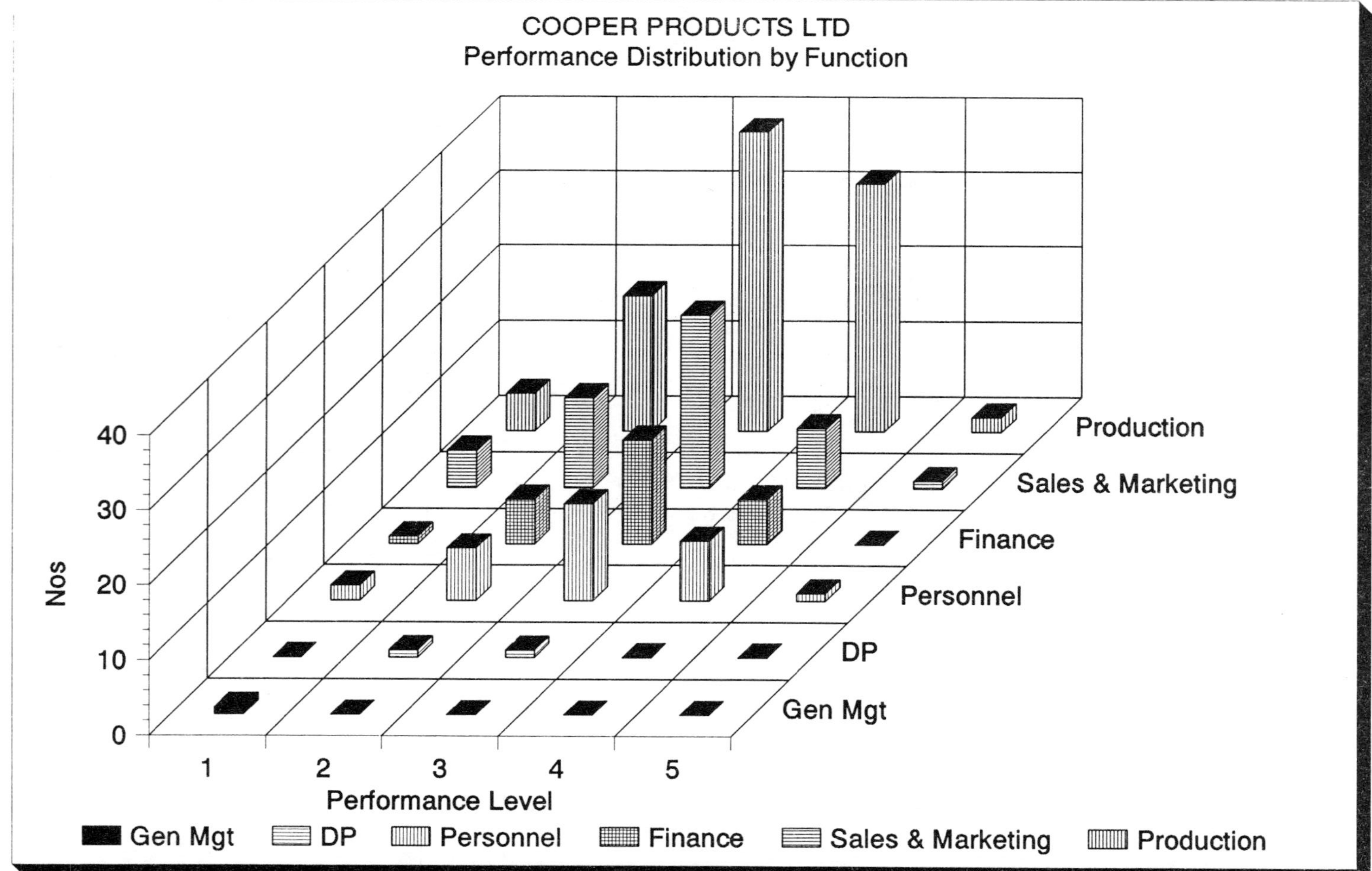

Figure 24.11 *Graphical illustration of performance level by function produced from a spreadsheet*

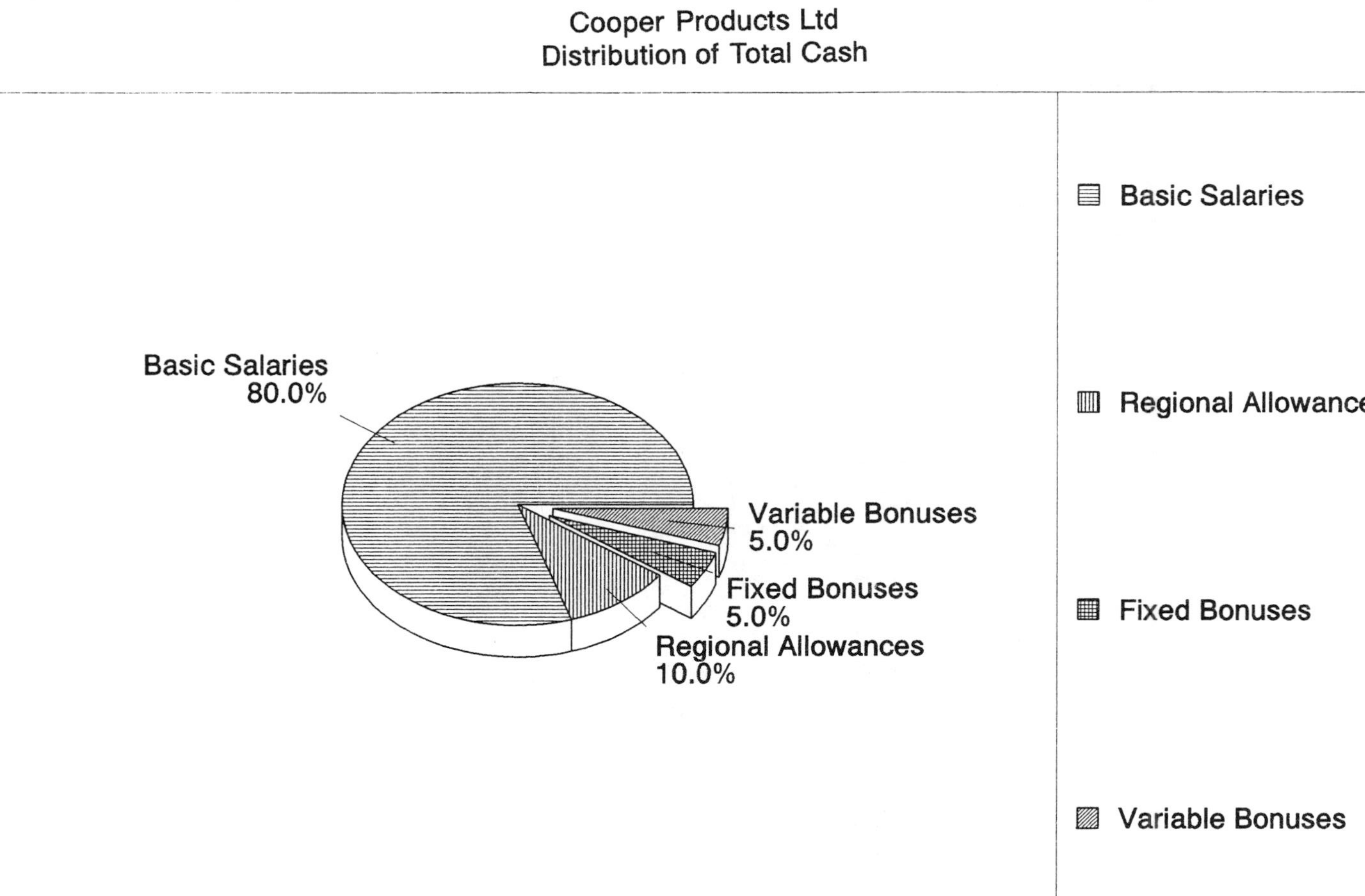

Figure 24.12 *Pie-chart showing distribution of total cash*

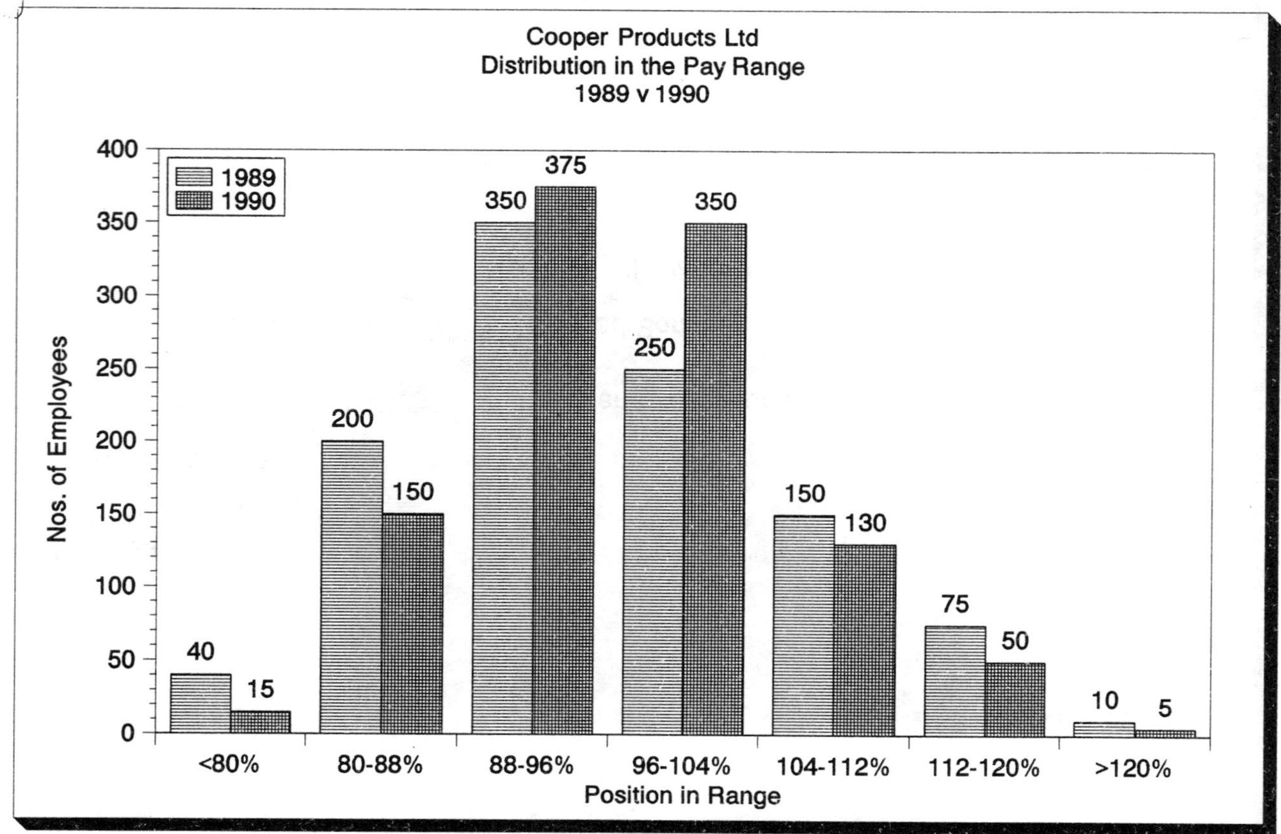

Figure 24.13 *Bar chart showing change in distribution through the range from 1989–90*

grade structure, or a move from a single pay policy to multiple policies based on functional lines.

4. How will the system perform in your environment? Will it provide acceptable response times on existing and anticipated future volumes of data? Demonstrations on small databases provide impressive response times but enquire about the sort of performance you can expect with your hardware configuration and database size.
5. How does the system fit in with your overall strategy? You should think about how the system is going to communicate with your existing software and other systems in the pipeline.
6. What support and training does the supplier offer? Do they understand your business and the issues you are trying to address?
7. What developments are planned and does the company have a record of delivery?
8. What other resources will you have to budget for? Additional financial resources may be required to fund extra training, the upgrade of existing computer equipment etc. Don't forget about manpower resources. The successful implementation of any new computer system requires a significant time commitment from end-users.
9. Ask for references and speak to existing users. They are a valuable source of independent advice and can help to highlight potential problems in advance.

A flexible database – some considerations

The database design is an important feature of any system as this ultimately determines the flexibility of the software and the degree to which it can be adapted to your own organization's requirements.

A proprietary system should have a user-defined database ie the field labels should not be pre-determined. The reason for this is that organizations vary in their structure and employee groupings. Most have a number of types of employee groups each with it's own characteristics. An organization must therefore be able to look at its employee groups on a global basis using those elements that are common between them. The user should specify which employee groups need to be set up in the system, the individual elements of each group and their relationships.

For example, within HayXpert, users are able to organize the database into employee groups, referred to as compensation mixes. Typically these groupings are based on the various discrete pay populations within the organization. For example, a manufacturing company may have the following employee groups:

- Executives
- Management
- Technical/Professional specialists
- Supervisory
- Clerical
- Manual

Each of these groups has some element of their overall remuneration that is unique and needs to be identified separately. The executives have incentives and share options, management may have a different bonus structure, the manual level is paid on an hourly rate.

Once the different compensation mixes have been defined, the individual pay elements associated with each group must be specified. From these individual elements compensation mix aggregates can be defined. For example, the management compensation mix may contain the following discrete elements:

- Basic Salary
- Fixed Bonus
- Variable Bonus
- Paid Benefits (cash equivalent)

The type of compensation mix aggregates that could be derived from these might be Total Cash (Basic Salary + Fixed Bonus + Variable Bonus) or Total Remuneration (Basic Salary + Fixed Bonus + Variable Bonus + Value of Benefits). Having defined all the groups the final task is to identify those global aggregates that relate all defined compensation mixes to one another on a common basis for organization-wide analysis. For example, one global aggregate may be annual base salary. To continue with our earlier example, the global aggregate may look like this:

Global Aggregate – Annual Base Salary

Compensation Mix	*Comp. Mix Aggregate*	*Individual Elements*
Executives	Annual Base	Basic + Fixed Bonus
Management	Annual Base	Basic + Fixed Bonus
Tech/Prof Spec.	Annual Base	Basic + Fixed Bonus + Market Premia
Supervisors	Annual Base	Monthly ×12 + Fixed Bonus
Clerical	Annual Base	Monthly ×12
Manual	Weekly Wages × 52	Hourly Rate × 38 + Bonus

This now gives us a common basis for comparing the different compensation mixes as well as a means of evaluating the organization as a whole, or in part, to the external market.

In addition to different compensation mixes, every organization has different ways of categorizing employees into certain populations by function, division, cost centre etc. An important feature of the user-definable database is the ability to create your own code groups and definitions.

For example, you could create two code groups location and function with the following values:

Location	*Function*
A London HQ	1 Finance
B Southampton	2 Marketing
C Norwich	3 R & D

By assigning the appropriate codes to each employee you are now able to analyze populations defined by any combination of function and/or location in addition to a selected compensation mix.

With this degree of flexibility built into the database it is possible to analyze internal equity, make external comparisons, develop new policies, and allocate individual increases for any population of employees.

Conclusions

Deciding on the best approach is very much a matter of individual choice for each organization. Invariably one has to reach some sort of compromise with any solution that is implemented but the following guidelines might be useful. For a small/medium-sized population of jobs with uncomplicated salary structures, satisfactory results can be obtained by setting up a simple database linked into a spreadsheet. This can be achieved relatively quickly and at a low cost. If you already have a suitable database, such as a personnel record system, storing the information you need to analyze, ensure that it can output data into the spreadsheet software used in your organization. For medium/large populations with more complex pay structures it is best to consider one of the commercially available alternatives, such as HayXpert. This is more cost-effective than in-house development and considerably more efficient.

Salary planning

In any salary system where progression rates vary according to performance there will be anomalies. These can arise when performance suddenly improves or gets worse and staff are either under-

or over-paid because it is not possible, using the normal guidelines, to place them on the right curve immediately. In this situation these people would have to be treated individually and their salary increases adjusted to accelerate or decelerate their progression through the range so bringing them back in line.

It is in these circumstances that managing the reward system requires judgement and a sensitive approach. Inevitably, this book has largely been about systems and procedures. But ultimately we are dealing with people who want and deserve to be treated as individuals, and this applies equally to those who manage as to those who are being managed. Mechanistic systems of salary administration may make life easier for the personnel department but that is not the object of the exercise. No members of an organization can be really happy, well motivated and committed if they feel they are part of a machine which pays no attention to their individual needs.

Salary planning and administration must adopt the stance of thinking first of what is right for individuals in terms of their aptitudes, abilities, skills, performance and needs. Of course, this approach must always be tempered with the knowledge that the organization also has needs which demand satisfaction. But an integrated approach to reward management can optimize the needs of the organization and those of the individuals, and these should be seen as complementary, not opposed.

Salary planning therefore has to treat people as individuals who are pursuing a career. This means looking at how that career is developing and ensuring that the incentives and rewards for increasing competences and improving performance go hand in hand with progress within and through the organization.

Chapter 25

Communicating the Benefits

Why communicate?

One of the prime objectives of the reward system should be to motivate people and so ensure their commitment. Hence the theme of paying for performance which has run throughout this book. But how can the system motivate if left to its own devices – if people are unsure why the system was developed, suspect that it is unfair, or are unsure about how their pay will be linked to performance, or what their future rewards are going to be as they take on greater responsibility? And how can the company get any mileage out of its logical, equitable, competitive and even creative reward system, its high level of rewards or its generous employee benefits package if it does not tell its employees all about them?

Payment systems can sometimes demotivate even more effectively than they motivate, as Herzberg established by his classic research on *The Motivation to Work*. This is because they often seem to be unfair. Pay is perceived as being either inequitable or not commensurate with performance. Elliott Jacques called this the felt-fair principle. He suggested on the basis of extensive research that people feel their pay ought to be fair in relation to their personal contribution, to what other people are being paid within the organization and to what is being paid by other organizations for similar jobs. If management wants to motivate its employees, these expectations must be satisfied. It is worth remembering that the most respected theory of motivation – the expectancy theory – states that it is what people *expect* to get, if it is worth having, which will motivate them most effectively, rather than what they have already got.

So it is important to motivate people by telling them that what they have got is worth having – if that is the case – and even more important to tell them what they can expect. This starts with the recruitment process and ends with the way in which retirement or indeed severance is handled. If they have been rewarded for doing well that has to be communicated to them. If they are going to get higher rewards for doing even better in the future, that must also be communicated, but more forcibly.

What to communicate

The following is what you should communicate to staff in general and to individual employees:

Staff in general

1. *The company salary policy*: This will set out the principles followed in setting pay and benefit levels.
2. *The pay and benefits structure*: This will define the salary brackets for each grade and the benefits available, including details of the pension scheme.
3. *Methods of grading and re-grading jobs*: Where job evaluation exists, details will be given of the job evaluation scheme, including how evaluations are carried out and the right to appeal against gradings.
4. *Salary progression*: The method by which salaries are progressed within grades or within a salary curve system.
5. *Incentive/bonus schemes*: Details of any incentive, bonus, profit sharing or share purchase schemes including how bonuses or profit shares are calculated and distributed and the procedures for purchasing shares.
6. *Reward systems and organizational change*: How remuneration policy will be affected by mergers/takeovers, change in corporate direction and indeed the bad news of liquidation and closure.

Individual employees

1. *Job grade*: What their grade is and how it has been determined.
2. *Salary progression*: The limit to which their salary can go in their present grade and the rate at which they can progress through the grade, depending on performance.
3. *Potential*: Their potential for higher salaries following promotion, subject to meeting defined performance criteria and the availability of suitable positions. In other words, this information, plus that contained under the heading of salary progression, should create expectations of what staff can get and define the action or behaviour they have to do to get there.
4. *Performance appraisal*: How performance and potential are assessed, including details of the criteria used, the method of assessment and the right of the employee to know what his or her assessment is and why it has taken that form.
5. *Salary levels*: The reasons for the level of reward they are getting or the salary increase at the last review and what the employee must do to get more.

6. *Benefit statement*: The value of the benefits the individual employee receives so that he or she appreciates the level of his or her total remuneration.

How to communicate – general information

The best way to communicate general information about salaries and benefits is to include the details in a staff handbook which is issued to all employees on joining the company and is updated regularly. This can be supplemented by brochures specially written for employees describing, for instance, the pension scheme and other profit sharing or share ownership schemes. In these publications discrete emphasis should be placed on the scale of benefits that employees enjoy and the scope provided for rewarding improved performance and loyalty to the company. Many large companies such as IBM mount continuing internal PR campaigns to explain the system and its benefits.

The written statement should be supplemented by initial briefings during the induction period. Whenever major changes are made, the information should be disseminated widely in the company magazines, or notice boards, through joint consultative committees and by means of team briefing (face-to-face briefings made by managers or supervisors to their staff).

How to communicate – individual information

Individual members of staff will, of course, receive letters of appointment which should tell them their grade and refer them to a staff handbook which gives details of the grading and performance schemes. Whenever they are upgraded or promoted they should receive another letter congratulating them on the event and providing encouragement for the future. Considerable attention should be given to the wording of these letters to ensure that they come over as warm and sincere rather than cold and bureaucratic or, worse, patronizing. They should *always* be handed over personally by the manager to ensure that the opportunity to get needed messages across is available.

Face-to-face

The best way to communicate personal information is face-to-face. Employees should be seen regularly by their immediate superior for discussions about their performance. Personal explanations should be given to them of the reasons for the employee's rate of salary progression or most recent increase. These meetings should discuss what actions the employee has to take to progress faster or to get more next time.

Potential for promotion and salary progression in the longer term should also be discussed at these meetings. Ideally, employees should be given the opportunity to talk to their immediate supervisor's manager in order to get a broader view. People with strong potential should also meet a career planning advisor who can act as a mentor in discussing future career steps, the further training or experience they need and, without painting too glowing a picture, the glittering prizes that await them if they do really well.

Implementing communications

Considerable care will be needed in preparing handbooks, brochures and letters. They need to be clear and informative and, while they should emphasize the scale of benefits employees receive, they should not over-do it. Experts' help in preparing and presenting this information can be useful.

Individual managers and supervisors should be trained both in how to appraise their staff and in how to convey information about assessments and rewards in a way which will motivate them. Their performance in doing this should be monitored.

Auditing communications on reward systems

Whoever is responsible for the reward system, and the messages which communications about them should convey should regularly audit their quality, consistency and effectiveness. The key items that usually need looking at and the main questions to ask are:

- job advertisements/recruitment literature – do descriptions of the remuneration package do justice to what is on offer and what the organization is seeking to pay for?
- offer letters/contracts – is as much attention paid to highlighting the attractiveness of all elements of the package as stating the bald elements of entitlements?
- staff handbooks – is layout clear and unambiguous and is the style one that will have immediacy and meaning to the groups of employees covered? Is the information sensibly grouped?
  (*Do not* use complicated language if most of the readers left school at 16, respond better to visual presentations and have reading habits that centre on the *Sun* and *Hello*. Remember that it *is* possible to describe share options without using arcane legal terminology and that if the way in which incentive measures are described is impenetrable this will hardly focus motivation.)

- salary increase letters – do they properly thank people for their efforts and contribution? Is delivery made an occasion of?
- policy changes – are these communicated to convey the logic and the benefits.
- severance (retirement/redundancy) – is the approach perceived as caring and concerned? If not, what is the likely effect on remaining employees?
- company videos communicating change – do these come across as sincere and provide helpful information or do they look hastily assembled and have too high a 'cringe factor' to be useful?

Major changes to reward systems

Most employers now recognize, or have learned the hard way, that major changes to reward policy not only take time to implement but that implementation has to be a carefully planned campaign. Communication is the key. The quality of communications will largely determine the acceptability of the proposed changes.

In the IDS/IPM publication *The Merit Factor – Rewarding Individual Performance* 12 rules for Internal Communications were reproduced. As background to any communication plans we believe they have continuing value and list them below:

1. There is no such thing as a stone cold certainty in business decisions and it is important everyone in a business realizes this.
2. If a Board cannot or will not clearly spell out its business strategy, employees are entitled to assume it does not have one.
3. Assume that in an information vacuum, people will believe the worst.
4. Never take it for granted that people know what you are talking about.
5. Always take it for granted that people doing a job know more about it than you do.
6. Telling people something once is not much better than not telling them at all.
7. Never assume that people will tell you anything that reflects unfavourably upon themselves.
8. Remember that employees read newspapers, magazines and books, listen to the radio and watch television.
9. Do not be afraid to admit you were wrong; it gives people confidence that you know what you are doing.
10. Asking for help, taking advice, consulting and listening to others are signs of great strength.

11. Communicating good news is easy but even this is not often done by management; bad news is all too often left to rumours and the grapevine.
12. Changing attitudes in order to change behaviour takes years – changing behaviour changes attitudes in weeks.

Bearing these in mind (and some of the cynical, if realistic, perceptions they contain) the following means of communications media can be used to draw from, together with some of their more appropriate uses:

- poster campaigns – for creating expectations for say, a new pay or performance management system
- staff newsletters – for explaining new policies or providing updates on how a new policy (job evaluation for instance), is being implemented
- personal letters – to explain the personal impact of policy developments
- brochures – where a major policy has to be explained, eg a PRP system or a new pension scheme
- individual meetings – where a personal, confidential or difficult message has to be got across and maximum impact is needed
- videos – where large number of staff in distributed sites have to be reached – good if a charismatic Chief Executive can convey his or her commitment to policy changes or development
- team briefings – to inform groups of employees, consult with them and ensure they properly understand change (eg to an incentive scheme).

Whatever the chosen media, the presentation should be as professional as possible. Ill-conceived, hasty and scruffy presentations will always give employees the impression that the organization does not really care about them and that it is doing as little as it can get away with. This is not the area for penny-pinching – the price in terms of justifiable resistance and cynicism is too high.

Chapter 26

Developing the System – The Use of Management Consultants

Why use consultants?

There are four possible reasons for using management consultants:

1. They bring expertise in solving problems based on their understanding of relevant techniques and their experience in analyzing similar situations.
2. They can open closed doors, releasing ideas already developed within the organization which have been stifled by the universal habit of resisting change. The saying: 'A prophet is not without honour save in his own country and in his own house' (Matthew 57) is as true today as it was in New Testament times. Consultants can play the role of catalysts or change agents.
3. Consultants can act in an independent and disinterested way, unaffected by local politics and pressure groups.
4. Consultants have the time to concentrate on the problem they have been set. They can act as an extra pair of hands, leaving management more time to get on with the day-to-day task of running the business.

How can they help?

In reward management, the areas in which management consultants can help are:

- advizing on remuneration strategy eg following a merger or change in corporate direction
- developing and introducing tailor-made job evaluation schemes
- introducing and maintaining their own brand of job evaluation
- designing and reviewing pay structures
- conducting salary surveys
- advizing on salary levels for individual jobs; for example, non-

executive directors seeking information on the right remuneration for a managing director
- designing bonus schemes
- developing profit sharing plans, including share ownership schemes
- advizing on pension schemes
- developing total remuneration packages covering the whole range of benefits
- advizing on the personal tax implications of remuneration policies.

How to choose a consultant

The golden rule in selecting consultants is to be absolutely clear in advance about what you want them to do. Objectives and terms of reference need to be defined as a basis for briefing any firms pitching for the assignment and, later, for monitoring progress.

Having defined objectives, the next step is to identify possible consultancies. The comparative advantages of large or small firms need to be considered. A large firm will have ample resources and back-up facilities. It will be able to tap a reservoir of experience and expertise. A smaller firm may be able to provide exactly the type of advice you need because it specialises in a particular area. It may also provide you with more individual attention.

Unless you are absolutely certain from personal knowledge that one firm is exactly right for you, it is always advizable to approach three or four different consultancies and get them to pitch for the job. Select firms on the basis of recommendations you can trust, or on the advice of organizations such as, in the UK, the Institute of Management Consultants and the Management Consultancy Information Service (see Bibliography).

Give the consultants your terms of reference and any further information they need to prepare a proposal. You can get some measure of their ability by the speed and accuracy with which they size up your situation and the quality of the questions they ask.

Always ask them to submit a written proposal which should set out:

(a) the terms of reference
(b) their understanding of your situation and requirements
(c) how they would carry out the assignment
(d) what they would achieve
(e) how the assignment would be staffed
(f) the proposed programme of work
(g) the cost of their fees quoted as daily or hourly rates and as a

total based on their estimate of the length of the assignment. Make sure that this specifically includes or excludes fee increases in the pipeline and ask for an estimate of expenses.

In coming to your decision on which firm to select, the following points should be taken into account:

1. The reputation of the firm.
2. The initial impression they made.
3. The quality of their proposal with particular reference to:
   – the relevance of their proposed solutions;
   – the practicality of their proposals from the view of implementation;
   – the realism of the programme.
4. The cost of the proposals.

When you have made your choice, confirm it in writing by reference to the proposal, subject to any modifications that have been agreed. If you want to be certain about the costs of the assignment and if you believe that the length of time estimated for completing it is reasonable, it may be worth agreeing a fixed price.

Using consultants

A responsible firm of management consultants will stick to its brief, but it is natural for people with enquiring minds – and if consultants don't have those, they are in the wrong business – to identify new problems and to offer solutions to them. Even the most professional firms are not averse to drumming up more work. It is up to you to make sure that no extra time is spent on the assignment unless you agree that it is worthwhile and unless the costs are also agreed.

You have every right to expect consultants to complete their programme within their own estimate of time and costs. They could take longer if they come up against unforeseen snags and this is a joint problem if the delay has adverse effects on your business. But unless you have misled the consultants in your brief, it is their responsibility to overcome the problems and to carry the burden of any extra costs they may have incurred.

Ensure that liaison arrangements with consultants are agreed. There should be regular progress or 'milestone' meetings when you can check how the assignment is going and deal with any problems as they arise. You should expect the consultants to discuss their preliminary findings with you and to present their interim conclusions and initial recommendations. It is in everyone's interest that alternative proposals should be evaluated jointly and that the feasibility of the implementation programme should be reviewed.

The final report should include a convincing analysis of the situation and any problems that have been identified. Recommendations should be derived logically from this analysis and they should include an assessment of costs and benefits and a plan for implementation which sets out precisely who does what and when.

Chapter 27

Reward Management – Myths and Issues

Our aim in this book has been to present reward management in its fullest sense as a key element in achieving sustainable competitive advantage and organizational effectiveness. We have constantly stressed the need for reward strategy to be business driven, flexible, innovative and, importantly, closely and clearly linked to the core values and beliefs of the organization. We have also emphasized that reward policies and practices can and should drive and support desired behaviour.

The pursuit of excellence in reward management is, however, a tough route to follow. There are a number of myths which have to be exploded, and there are five major strategic issues to which there are no easy answers. We explore these myths and issues in this chapter.

Myths of reward management

The main myths of reward management, whose origin, like all myths, is buried in the mists of antiquity, are:

There is one right way to run a reward management system

This myth is perpetuated by those who want a quick fix in a complex world.

They believe that performance related pay will magically transform everyone overnight into the sort of hard-working, dedicated, productive, well-motivated, performance orientated individuals the organization wants, forgetting that these individuals might have other views (more of this later).

They think that by simply telling everyone to agree objectives and review results in relation to those objectives it will automatically happen, with the help of elaborate procedures. But it doesn't. Managers, understandably, find it difficult to set clear and measurable objectives and even more difficult to counsel their staff on how to do better next time.

They consider that a new magic formula in the shape of a different pay structure, a cafeteria remuneration plan or a performance management system will operate effectively of its own volition because it has been well conceived and carefully implemented. But it won't unless, first, top management are behind it all the time, second, those running the system are prepared to put a lot of hard work into guiding and helping the managers who are using it and, third, a continuing communications campaign is mounted which informs all concerned why the change is happening, what they have to do to help implement it and how they will benefit from its successful implementation.

Performance related pay always improves performance

It won't. Margaret Ellis of Sainsburys recently did six months' full-time research at Oxford University on the relationship between pay and performance. She identified only one piece of reliable research, which was conducted by Pearce, Stevenson and Derry in 1983. This studied the impact of what they called 'performance-contingent compensation' in the Social Security Administration. Rigorous analysis provided no evidence that it had any significant effect on performance.

Recent research on motivation has, in fact, suggested that tangible rewards can actually lower the level of performance, particularly in jobs requiring creativity. Study after study has shown that intrinsic interest in a task – the sense that something is worth doing for its own sake – typically declines when someone is given only external reasons for doing it. Deci, for example, has argued on the basis of his extensive research in this subject that contingent pay plans should be avoided because they reduce intrinsic motivation, lead individuals to develop strategies that will enable them to get rewards with least effort, and can easily break down if, for example, no one is looking.

Getting people to chase money can produce nothing except people chasing money. Waving twenty pound notes in front of employees can lead them to think of themselves as doing work *only* for the reward. And performance tends to suffer as a result. Digital, for example, do not pay their sales representatives commission because the number one goal of the company is continuing customer satisfaction and loyalty, not sales earnings in a given period. This avoids overselling and nurtures long-term relationships with customers.

Badly conceived performance related pay schemes – and there are a lot of them about – can encourage people to focus narrowly on a task, to do it quickly and to take few risks. This is short-termism, a major contributor to poor performance and hardly the behaviour we want in the innovative, flexible and responsive organizations of the 1990s.

It should not, of course, be inferred from these arguments that people ought not to be paid more when they do good work. Neither do we mean that all payment for performance schemes should be scrapped. What they do suggest is that higher quality work, particularly in jobs requiring creative thinking, is more likely to occur when a person focuses on the challenge of the task itself, rather than on some external motivator, thus developing a sense of self-determination, as opposed to feeling controlled by means of praise and reward. This means that incentives announced in advance may be less effective in encouraging sustained high performance than are unexpected bonuses that recognize an outstanding job after the fact.

Performance related pay systems can convey the right messages about what the organization considers to be important, not only in terms of performance, profit and productivity but also with regard to the 'softer' but equally important values of quality, customer service, innovation and team-working. But you should always bear in mind the enormous difference between saying: 'I'm giving you this reward because I recognize the value of your work' and 'You're getting this reward because you have lived up to my standards'.

Pay systems must be driven by market rates

Market rates are important and it is certainly necessary to find out what they are and to relate pay structures and salary progression to them. But you can go too far and allow your pay system to be dominated by short-term and insignificant market trends. You are then in danger of fragmenting your pay policies. A job family structure as described in Chapter 7 is a good way of flexing rewards for different market groups but it must be based on a coherent approach to how performance is rewarded in the various job families, and the rationale for differentiation must be sound. The difficulty faced by all people managing reward systems is the myth that there *is* a market rate. As we pointed out in Chapter 4, there is no such thing. There are market rate trends and one can infer from a variety of sources that there is a range of market rates, but to design a structure on the concept of a single market rate would result in it being built on a foundation of sand.

Issues

The main issues facing those concerned with the development and implementation of reward strategies and policies are how to achieve:

- creativity
- flexibility

- a good fit between corporate strategy and reward strategy
- a good fit between corporate culture and reward policies
- the right balance between extrinsic and intrinsic rewards.

Creativity

As Alistair Wright of Digital said at the Compensation Forum 1990 conference: 'Companies spend millions on innovation researching new products. When they feel that they should innovate in the area of pay practice, organizations still ask "has anyone else got one of these?"'

Of course, innovation has to take account of new developments elsewhere and how well they function. But creativity begins at home: what works well somewhere else will not necessarily work with you.

To be creative about reward management you need to concentrate on what your organization is, on where it is going and on what needs to be done to get there. Creativity is rooted in the present but is focused on the future. You need to:

- look at the situation differently, exploring all possible angles, identifying alternative approaches on the basis that 'there must be a better way'
- list as many approaches as possible without seeking the 'one best way' (there is no such thing)
- arrange discontinuity by thinking about other and apparently irrelevant ways of doing things, deliberately exposing yourself to new influences (cross-fertilization of ideas) and switching yourself from problem to problem
- question everything – the pay structure, the performance appraisal system, bonus and incentive schemes, the employee benefit package and the ways in which salaries are reviewed
- set objectives – more or less flexibility, looser or tighter control, greater or lesser emphasis on individual as distinct from team rewards, more attention to intrinsic motivators and less dependence on financial incentives, increased or decreased opportunities to choose benefits
- relate these objectives to what is desirable and what is achievable in the light of your analysis of the present and future needs of the organization and its members and the attitudes of management, employees and trade unions.

We must also remember that performance and human resource requirements change over time and within the same organization. Yesterday's innovations can quickly become today's problems. Flavours of the month sometimes have a short shelf life. It is therefore essential to build flexibility and a drive for creativity into the system. This means continually monitoring current arrangements so that plans can be made for their development or replacement.

Flexibility

Greater flexibility has become almost a parrot cry when discussing organizational structures and systems. But this belief in freedom to act, which is coupled with an emphasis on decentralization, has to be reconciled with the need to avoid anarchy and to provide some form of structure within which people can operate. Most of us are lost without structure; to paraphrase T S Eliot: mankind cannot bear too much flexibility – dissonance sets in.

While conventional wisdom has stated that decentralization and the creation of virtually independent strategic business units are good things, there is a backlash against this nostrum for organizational effectiveness. This backlash emphasizes synergy by suggesting that the whole is greater than the parts and that it is necessary at corporate level to make the best use of human resources across divisional boundaries and ensure that reward management strategies assist in this process.

Methods of increasing flexibility in the operation of reward management systems were discussed in Chapter 2. These, however, need to be tempered with a reasonable degree of structure in most organizations.

Achieving a fit between corporate and reward strategy

Achieving a fit between corporate and reward strategy is a matter of identifying the key areas of corporate strategy and then deciding how reward strategies can support them. The corporate strategic areas are likely to include:

- market and product development
- technical innovation
- acquisitions and mergers
- organization restructuring
- reliable delivery to customers
- quality
- cost reduction.

These have to be analyzed against a background of an understanding of external competitive, social, economic and political trends and the internal strengths and weaknesses of the organization in the areas of human resource management and development. Factors such as the demand for new skills, skill shortages (the influence of demographic trends), market rate pressures, international influences, new methods of working and the culture and values of the organization (see below) will have to be taken into account.

Achieving a fit between corporate culture and reward policies

As we have emphasized repeatedly in this book, culture management and reward management interact. Reward management policies must take account of the organization's climate, management style, values and beliefs. But they can also help to shape these and assist in the process of cultural change.

To achieve a fit between the two it is necessary first to analyse the culture of the organization under these headings:

- *norms*: unwritten rules of behaviour such as:
  - the work ethic
  - status
  - ambition
  - formality/informality
  - openness
  - trust
- *values*: what is regarded as important, expressed as beliefs on what is best or good for the organization and what ought to happen. These are expressed under such headings as:
  - balance between needs of the organization and its members
  - care and consideration for people
  - care for customers and clients
  - competitiveness
  - cost control
  - enterprise
  - equity in the treatment of staff
  - excellence
  - flexibility
  - growth
  - innovation
  - market/customer orientation
  - need for order, systems and control
  - performance orientation
  - provision of opportunity for employees
  - quality
  - social responsibility
- *organization climate*: its working atmosphere, which can be described in one or more of the following ways:
  - action orientated
  - bureaucratic

- emphasis on individualism
- emphasis on team work
- hierarchical
- informal
- open
- people orientated
- proactive
- reactive
- relaxed
- stressful
- task orientated
- *management style*: the extent to which managers are:
  - autocratic
  - task-centred or people-centred
  - distant or approachable
  - hard or soft on people.

This culture will, of course, be strongly influenced by the type of organization – its size, technology, market position, traditions, achievements, performance and the extent to which it is:

- entrepreneurial and risk taking
- marketing led
- service led
- product led
- research led.

All these factors need to be analyzed so that a complete picture can be gained of the organization. This will indicate how reward management policies and systems can help to reinforce the functional aspects of the culture and to change the dysfunctional parts.

Balancing extrinsic and intrinsic rewards

In this book we have consistently warned against an over-dependence on a crude system of extrinsic rewards. We fully recognize that relating pay to performance is an appropriate and necessary way of providing incentives and rewards. But dependence on this approach at the expense of the intrinsic reward system can be detrimental to the overall impact of reward management strategies.

The balance can be achieved by emphasizing that performance management is a total approach to the motivation and development of staff. Managers can use the financial reward system to recognize good performance in the past and to encourage it to continue in the future. But performance management is as much about helping people to grow and to achieve self-determination, as it is about providing direct incentives. This message should be clearly conveyed from the top and reinforced by means of communication and training programmes.

Chapter 28

Trends in Reward Management

Influencing factors

Reward management strategies, policies and processes in the 1990s will be influenced by the following factors:

Environmental change

- a move from the entrepreneurial 1980s to the post-entrepreneurial 1990s with less emphasis on gain and greed and more on values such as concern for people, quality, customers and the environment
- an increasing trend for people to want to be treated as individuals coupled, perhaps paradoxically, with more emphasis on team-work, co-operation and synergy.
- even higher consumer expectations and demands for quality and service
- continued emphasis on business growth
- more mergers and acquisitions
- increased internationalization (more competition from European – especially German – firms and the Japanese)
- shorter product-life cycles, hence more emphasis on individual firms retaining their leading edge position by innovation to remain competitive in increasingly segmented markets
- new technology playing a much greater part in the information flow aspects of management as well as in manufacturing, distribution and other operations.

Social and attitudinal change

- increased emphasis on the importance of managing corporate cultures to meet the challenge of change
- a risk of 'change fatigue' as people have to cope with the problem of too much turbulence
- an increasingly multi-cultural approach to managing organizations which have to adapt quickly to different cultures when operating globally

- continuous renewal within organizations as they learn to adapt to the changing environment
- more sharing of learning in organizations in order to innovate, compete, and manage change – as Revans has said: 'Doubt from below speeds wisdom from above'
- multi-skilling within flatter and more flexible organizations
- shortage of some key skills because of new demands and demographic pressures.

Organizational change

Organizations will become more:

- responsive, reacting quickly to changes in the market place and the needs of their customers and clients
- pro-active, businesses having to make markets as well as adapt to them, and public sector and voluntary organizations having to anticipate the needs of their clients
- flexible, able to adjust structures, technologies, product ranges, marketing strategies and facilities to respond quickly to change and, more importantly, to anticipate it
- information-based, ie knowledge-orientated and composed largely of specialists who direct and discipline their own performance through organized feedback from colleagues, customers, clients and the divisions or strategic business units into which the organization is divided in accordance with the markets or clients it serves
- compact, with flatter organization structures as superfluous layers of management are stripped out
- project team based as groups of managers and individuals work together at all levels in the organization to deal with strategic and tactical issues
- networked or distributed as activities and functions are carried out in separate but linked units
- decentralized as strategic business units or divisions are placed firmly in their market or service niches in order to respond quickly to opportunities and threats
- managed to achieve well-defined goals, with individuals and teams being allowed more freedom to operate and organize their activities (self-determination) as long as they deliver expected results.

Trends in strategies, policies and systems

The directions in which reward management strategies will develop will, of course, vary considerably from organization to organization.

Bureaucratic or mechanistic type organizations which continue to exist in a fairly steady state may buck the trends elsewhere by retaining bureaucratic and mechanistic reward management systems.

Most organizations will, however, be more exposed to the environmental, social and organizational trends listed above. It is against this background that they will be likely to develop their reward management policies and systems in the following ways, if they have not already done so:

1. More attention paid to releasing the potential of *all* employees (not just the favoured few) by empowering and enabling them to perform more effectively in fluid situations.
2. Skills, not job based, pay structures which are related to well-defined competences rather than to rigid job grade hierarchies (pay curves rather than graded structures).
3. Integrated performance management systems which, while based on reviewing results in comparison with agreed objectives, also provide a foundation for personal and career development.
4 The assessment of performance not only in relation to the achievement of quantifiable objectives but also by reference to the extent which behaviour supports company values in such areas as innovation, team-work and staff development.
5. A focus on self-determination and self-development.
6. Less emphasis on performance related pay systems as universal panaceas – those which are retained will be thought through much more carefully to ensure that they motivate rather than demotivate.
7. More careful monitoring of market trends and the consequential adjustment of pay levels and progression rates.
8. Where properly based schemes for rewarding merit have been established, annual increases which are entirely merit based and do not separately identify a cost of living element (although they will take account of the increases in the market values of the individuals concerned).
9. More individual bonuses related to achievements and provided as alternatives to permanent increases in base rates.
10. More emphasis on choice of benefits, although not necessarily through fully developed 'cafeteria' systems.

These are the approaches that will be most appropriate in the flexible, responsive, people and performance orientated organizations of the 1990s.

Appendices

Appendix A

Statistical Terms Used in Pay Surveys and Analysis

Pay data

Most commonly used statistical methods and computer packages assume that the data under analysis is normally distributed. In such a distribution the individual items are more likely to be close to the average than far from it but are evenly distributed above and below the average. There are very few instances of data being exactly 'normal' but many are close enough to make no real difference. An example would be the heights of children at a given age; most would cluster round the average with a few extremes. Figure A.1 illustrates a normal distribution.

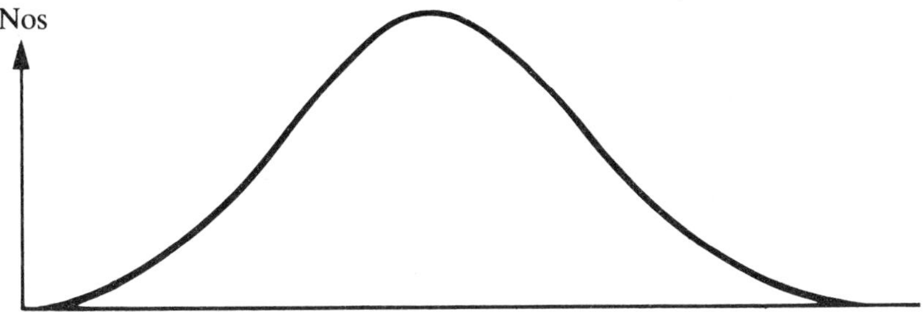

Figure A.1 *Normal distribution*

Pay data, however, tends not to be symetrically distributed; typically there is a greater spread above the average than below it. Overall this reflects the fact that there are more people in lower paid jobs and the differences in pay between lower paid jobs is less. Pay data therefore tends to have a skewed distribution similar to that illustrated in Figure A.2. The distribution which pay typically has is known as 'lognormal'. Technically this means that the logarithm of pay is normally distributed – in simple terms it reflects the fact that an additional £1,000 has a much greater impact on a salary of £10,000 than on a salary of £50,000.

Because pay is not normally distributed, most statistical methods should only be used with care.

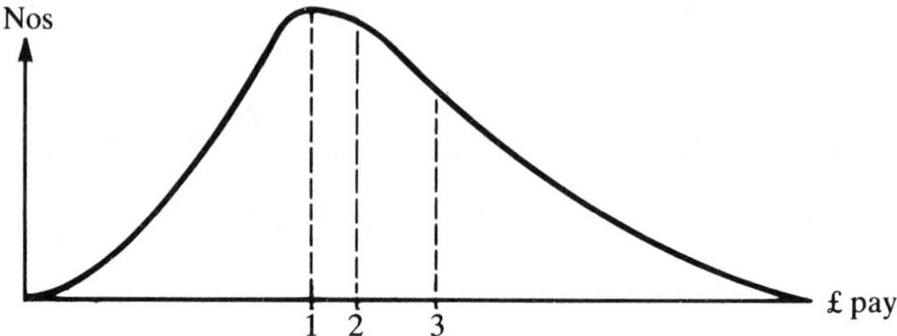

Figure A.2 *Lognormal distribution (eg pay)*

Salary surveys

Salary and benefits surveys collect together a mass of useful, and not so useful, information. Rather than just presenting listings of the data collected, most surveys present summaries or analyzes of the data. This section provides explanations of the more usual terms used in salary surveys.

Measures of central tendency

There are three statistics that are commonly used to describe the middle or centre of a set of data, the average or mean, the median, and the mode.

Average or mean

The arithmetic average, or mean, is calculated by adding all the reported salaries together and dividing by the number reported. In salary survey data the mean can be unduly influenced by one or two extremely high (or low) values. Some surveys, therefore, also quote averages with the two highest and lowest values omitted which reduces the likelihood of the answer being distorted. If the data is lognormally distributed as in Figure A.2 the mean will be at position 3; the higher values at the top pull the mean up more than the low values pull it down.

Median

The median is the middle ranking salary, ie that which 50 per cent of the reported salaries are equal to or above and 50 per cent equal to or below. This measure is less influenced by outlying values than the average or mean and is therefore used widely in salary surveys as a measure of central tendency. In Figure A.2 it would be at position 2; this divides the area under the curve into two equal parts.

Mode

The mode is that value which appears most frequently in a given set of data. This is not always a central value and indeed in some sets of data there can be more than one modal value. Where data is clustered around a centre it can be useful to show which value(s) occur most frequently.

As salaries can vary by small amounts, they are usually grouped into ranges before a mode is derived and the range with the most reported salaries is known as the modal range. However, this is only useful if the ranges are of consistent widths. In Figure A.2 the mode is at position 1, the point where the curve is at its highest.

The mode is more commonly used in describing benefit provisions where there are often only a limited number of possible alternatives.

Relationship of mean, median and mode

As already mentioned, pay is usually lognormally distributed as in Figure A.2. If this is so then the mean will be higher than the median and the median higher than the mode. In a normal distribution as in Figure A.1 the mean, median and mode all coincide at position 1.

Measures of spread

Most surveys give some indication of the relative spread of the data as well as statistics describing its centre. The relative spread shows whether the reported salaries are close together or whether there is great variability.

Range

The range is the total spread from the highest value to the lowest value and is shown in most surveys by actually quoting the highest and lowest values. Although this is a very simple measure it can be misleading if the extremes are unrepresentative of the data as a whole.

Standard deviation

The standard deviation is of great importance in many branches of statistics, especially those linked to experiments, but has little relevance in the field of reward management. It requires a relatively complex calculation, and the main reason for its use in salary surveys is that it is available on statistical packages. Technically it is the square root of the average of the sum of the squares of the difference from the mean for each observation. If the data is normally distributed then roughly 95 per cent of all the data lie within two standard deviations each side of the mean. However, as already mentioned, pay data tends not to be normally distributed, so this approximation does not always hold good.

Quartiles

There is great confusion as to whether a quartile is a point or a range. Quartiles, in the original statistical definition, were the three points which divided the data into four equal parts; the upper quartile, the median and the lower quartile. However, in recent years it has been used increasingly to mean a range – one of the four equal parts. Indeed the confusion has spread so far that recent editions of the Oxford dictionary give both definitions.

Where salary surveys refer to upper and lower quartiles they are using the original technical sense of a point. The upper quartile is that value which 25 per cent of values exceed and 75 per cent are less than. The lower quartile is that value which 75 per cent of values exceed and 25 per cent are below. As with medians and other quantiles discussed below, the quartiles can be (and often are) equal to one or more of the values.

The quartiles, unlike the standard deviation or the range, are little influenced by one or two outlying values.

Inter-quartile range

This is a measure of spread between the upper and lower quartiles. It is therefore the range which covers the middle 50 per cent of values; 25 per cent of values lie below and 25 per cent above the inter-quartile range.

Deciles, percentiles and other quantiles

Other quantiles are similar to quartiles. For example the ninth decile is that value where 10 per cent of values exceed and 90 per cent are less than; the 99th percentile is that value which one per cent exceed and 99 per cent are below. These other quantiles are sometimes used in salary surveys but are more frequently used by companies to set their salary policy.

Calculation of medians, quartiles and other quantiles

When calculating quartiles and other measures the critical point is whether the sample is sufficient to support the results. In broad terms it is usually accepted that for a measure to have any validity there should be at least three observations in each part in which the sample of data is divided, and preferably more. For example medians should not be defined on less than six observations and even this can be misleading if the data included in the sample is in any way unrepresentative.

There are various formulae for calculating quantiles. The following are the most commonly used. If there are N observations and the observations are ranked in descending order:

median $\frac{N + 1}{2}$ observations from the top

(If there are 20 values this gives 10.5 – ie the average of the 10th and 11th observations)

upper quartile $\frac{N + 3}{4}$ observations from the top

(If there are 20 values this gives 5.75 – ie a weighted average of the 5th and 6th observations calculated by taking 3 times the 6th values and 1 times the 5th and dividing by 4)

lower quartile $\frac{3N + 1}{4}$ value from the top

ninth decile $\frac{N + 9}{10}$ value from the top

first decile $\frac{9N + 1}{10}$ value from the top

Pay analyses

There are three other common statistical techniques used in analyzing pay data.

Correlation

Correlation measures how closely two variables are related, for example salary and company size. Correlation coefficients vary from +1 to −1 and typically assume a straight line relationship. A value close to +1 indicates that a high value in one variable will be reflected by a high value in the other. A value close to −1 indicates that a high value in one variable will be reflected in a low value in the other, and near 0 indicates that there is no correlation and so a high value in one variable can reflect any value in the other.

For example, in low level jobs there is little correlation between pay and company size and therefore the correlation would be close to 0. For senior jobs such as managing directors there is a much stronger link and the correlation would be, say, +0.5 or +0.8. Interpreting a correlation coefficient is difficult as it depends to a certain extent on the size of the sample and the type of relationship between the variables.

Regression

Data with two variables such as pay and job size can be plotted as a scattergram (see Figure A.3). If the data is highly correlated then the data can be approximated by a (usually straight) line; this is known as a regression line. This is calculated by a complex formula, but one of the underlying assumptions is that the data is evenly distributed about the regression line. In most cases the dispersion in pay increases as the level of pay increases and so the underlying assumption is not valid. However, regression lines can be useful, especially over small variations in pay levels.

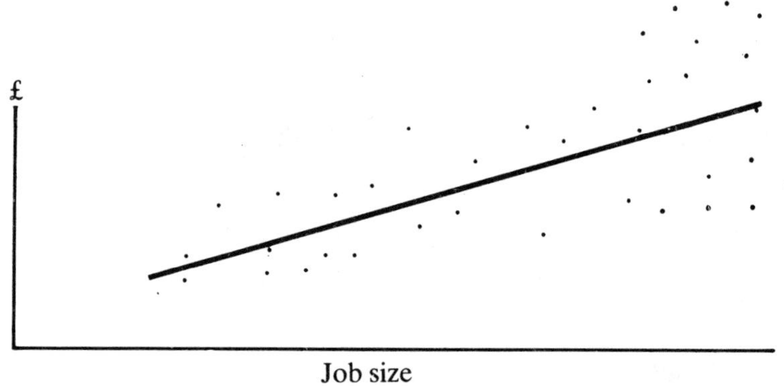

Figure A.3 *Relationship between salary and job size*

Multiple regression

This is similar to the linear regression outlined above but instead of relying on one explanatory variable it depends on two or more. For example salary could be linked with age, experience and job size. It can be a helpful technique but the statistical assumptions underlying it assume that the explanatory variables are not correlated with each other. However, this is not always true (eg age and experience tend to go together) and therefore this method should only be used with great care.

Appendix B

Job Ranking Scheme Using Paired Comparisons

Basic features of the scheme

The scheme uses the paired comparison technique to compare one whole job with another so that the jobs under review are ranked in order of importance. The jobs are then divided into grades by taking into account the following factors:

1. The number of grades required to accommodate the range of jobs under review. This will be influenced by:
   (a) the market rates for the highest and lowest jobs
   (b) the width of the pay brackets – this could be 50 per cent of the minimum rate for the grade on management jobs
   (c) the degree to which pay packets overlap.
2. The natural ladder of promotion or hierarchy of skills in the organization.
3. Natural groupings of jobs because of common features such as similar duties, skills or training requirements.
4. The market rates for the jobs.

Jobs may be ranked vertically for the organization as a whole or, initially, on a functional basis. In the latter case the separate functional rankings are amalgamated into an overall ranking.

Procedure

The procedure consists of the following steps:

1. Select bench-mark jobs.
2. Analyze the bench-mark jobs and produce outline job descriptions; this would normally be carried out by the evaluator, but in a large study which has to be completed quickly, draft descriptions might have to be prepared by functional or departmental heads for editing by the evaluator. In these circumstances, it is necessary to brief the executives concerned on methods of preparing job descriptions (the notes for guidance set out in Appendix L can be used for this).

3. Rank the jobs by paired comparison. Depending on the complexity and size of the organization, the speed with which the exercise has to be completed and the degree to which managers and staff are to be involved, this can be carried out by:
   (a) the evaluator alone, possibly with the assistance of one or two other managers
   (b) a working party of functional or departmental heads agreeing an overall ranking
   (c) a working party of functional or departmental heads initially ranking jobs in their own functions and then agreeing an overall ranking (this is a useful approach in a complex or large organization)
   (d) an evaluation committee consisting of managers and employee representatives.

   Typical notes for guidance issued to a working party of managers initially ranking jobs in their own functions are set out below. The instructions on completing the paired comparisons ranking form provide an appropriate basis for carrying out ranking independently or for briefing other types of working parties or committees as described above. An example of a completed paired comparison ranking form is shown in Table B.1.
4. Determine grades and salary levels in accordance with the factors listed at the beginning of this appendix.

Instructions for completing the paired comparison ranking form

Purpose

The purpose of this procedure is to establish the order of importance within the company of the jobs selected for evaluation. This will provide the basis for grading the jobs and deciding on the appropriate differentials between them.

General method

The heads of each function in the company are being asked to compare each job individually with every other job. A list of the jobs is attached together with a brief description of each job (not included here).

The comparisons should be based on the information supplied in the job description and the department head's knowledge of the job. The assessment of the relative importance of jobs should be based on an appraisal of the following factors:

1. The scope and impact of the job in terms of the size of resources controlled (money and/or people); impact on end results; amount of discretion allowed; level and range of personal contacts made.
2. The complexity of the job in terms of the number and variety of tasks to be carried out, the range of skills to be used and the range and difficulty of the problems to be solved.
3. The level of knowledge and skills required to carry out the job in terms of business, technical or professional knowledge, managerial and supervisory skills, communicating skills or manual skills and dexterity.

It is important to note that it is the content of the jobs and the level of knowledge and skill required that is being evaluated and not the competence of the job holders.

Procedure for completing the paired comparison ranking form

The procedure for carrying out comparisons is to:

1. Enter the name of your function and department and your own job title and name on the attached job ranking form. This includes a list of the titles of the jobs to be evaluated (a completed form is shown in Table B.1).
2. Compare each job listed on the vertical column of the form and indexed with capital letters (A,B,C, etc) with each job listed across the page and indexed with lower case letters (a,b,c, etc). Score each comparison (eg Job A with Job b) in the section of the form above and to the right of the diagonal line as follows:
   (a) start with Job A, compare it with Job b and if you consider that:
- Job A is more important than Job b, enter 2 in square Ab
- Job A is less important than Job b, enter 0 in square Ab
- the jobs are of equal importance, enter 1 in square AB.
   (b) continue comparing Job A with the other jobs listed across the page (c,d,e etc) in the same way
   (c) repeat the procedure with Jobs B,C,D, etc.
3. Complete the section of the form below and to the left of the diagonal line by reference to the scores for the equivalent box above and to the right of the diagonal line (eg compare Ad with Da). The scores in the two sections of the form for each pair of jobs are images of one another, for example:
   (a) if 2 is recorded in square Ad, 0 should be recorded in square Da

COMPANY XYZ Ltd		DEPARTMENT Production
EVALUATOR	NAME J.Smith	
	JOB TITLE Production Director	

Job Letter	JOB TITLES	a	b	c	d	e	f	g	h	i	j	k	l	m	n	o	p	q	r	s	t	TOTAL SCORE	OVERALL RANKING
		Packer	Plant Operator	Chargehand	Foreman	Superintendent	Production Manager	Maintenance Craftsman	Plant Engineer	Lab. Assistant	Lab. Technician	Clerical Assistant	Senior Clerk										
A	Packer		0	0	0	0	0	0	0	0	0	0	0									0	12
B	Plant Operator	2		0	0	0	0	0	0	0	0	2	0									4	10
C	Chargehand	2	2		0	0	0	2	0	2	0	2	1									11	6=
D	Foreman	2	2	2		0	0	2	0	2	1	2	2									15	4=
E	Superintendent	2	2	2	2		0	2	1	2	2	2	2									19	2=
F	Production Manager	2	2	2	2	2		2	2	2	2	2	2									22	1
G	Maintenance Craftsman	2	2	0	0	0	0		0	1	0	2	0									7	8=
H	Plant Engineer	2	2	2	2	1	0	2		2	2	2	2									19	2=
I	Lab. Assistant	2	2	0	0	0	0	1	0		0	2	0									7	8=
J	Lab. Technician	2	2	2	1	0	0	2	0	2		2	2									15	4=
K	Clerical Assistant	2	0	0	0	0	0	0	0	0	0		0									2	11
L	Senior Clerk	2	2	1	0	0	0	2	0	2	0	2										11	6=
M																							
N																							
O																							
P																							
Q																							
R																							
S																							
T																							

Figure B.1 *Paired comparison ranking form*

   (b) If 0 is recorded in square Ae, 2 should be recorded in square Ea
   (c) if 1 is recorded in square Af, 1 should be recorded in square Fa
4. When both halves of the form have been completed, add up the total points scored for each Job A,B,C, etc and enter in the right-hand column headed total points.
5. Rank as 1 the job with the highest score and enter in column headed overall ranking. Rank the remaining jobs in sequence depending on their points score.

Appendix C

Job Classification Scheme: Clerical Staff

Grade 1
Work where no specific clerical knowledge or skills are required such as maintaining simple records or basic clerical systems, sorting, messenger work or operating the simpler kinds of office machines. Full proficiency can be attained in a few days and the job is carried out under strict supervision with completely detailed instructions covering every aspect of the work. The job is highly repetitive – the same task or group of tasks has to be performed continuously.

Grade 2
Work where knowledge is required of basic clerical procedures, such as maintaining records, carrying out routine calculations (including decimals), fairly complex filing and dealing with routine inquiries by means of mainly standardized replies. Or the work may include straightforward copy-typing or operating a fairly complex office machine. A reasonable degree of proficiency can be attained after a concentrated training period of a few weeks. The work is closely supervised and thoroughly checked and most of the tasks simply require the straightforward application of easily understood rules. The job is fairly repetitive and the limited variety of tasks are carried out to a strict daily routine.

Grade 3
Work where knowledge is required of more advanced clerical procedures, such as basic bookkeeping, the maintenance of fairly complex records, writing routine letters, more advanced calculations or preparing statistical statements. Or the work may involve shorthand writing, a high degree of typing skill to transcribe machine dictation and lay out complex reports and schedules, or the operation of a complex office machine. The job might also involve the supervision of a small (less than 10) group of grade 1 or grade 2 staff. To attain a reasonable degree of proficiency a training period of some months is required. The work is generally standardized and fairly close supervision is exercised, although there is some scope for interpreting the rules to decide on the best method of completing

a task. A variety of clerical or secretarial skills has to be used.

Grade 4
Practical knowledge is required of accountancy or another area of professional or technical work where direct assistance is provided to professionally or technically qualified staff and a full understanding of the special terms and procedures is required. Broad knowledge of company policies and procedures is necessary. The work may require the ability to deal with correspondence on a variety of subjects, although replies can usually be based on well established precedents. The work could also include preparing straightforward reports based on the analysis of standard returns and data, or acting as a personal assistant to a senior executive. The job might involve supervising a large group (over 10) of grade 1 and 2 staff or a small group (less than 10) of grade 2 and 3 staff. Some years' experience is usually required to attain a reasonable degree of proficiency. The work is carried out under general guidance and supervision. Programmes and procedures are laid down, but it is often necessary to use judgement in deciding how to complete the programmes or in selecting the most appropriate rule or precedent to deal with a problem. A considerable range of clerical or secretarial skills has to be used to perform a wide variety of tasks.

Grade 5
Knowledge may be required of accountancy or another area of professional work where the work is carried out in conjuction with professionally qualified staff. A thorough knowledge of company policies and procedures is necessary. The work may include correspondence on non-routine matters, or the ability to analyze data which is often varied in nature, or the preparation of detailed reports. The job might also involve the supervision of a large group (over 10) of grade 2 and 3 staff or the control of grade 4 or grade 3 supervisory staff. Several years' experience is usually required to attain a reasonable degree of proficiency. Much of the work is carried out without reference to management and some judgement has frequently to be exercised in dealing with problems which are coverd by broad rules or procedures. A wide variety of tasks has to be performed involving the use of many different skills in frequently changing circumstances.

Appendix D

Grade Definitions: Managerial Staff

Grade 1
Senior supervisors in charge of a large group or section in which the work is mainly routine; or assistant to grade 2 specialists.

Grade 2
Senior supervisors in charge of a large group or section where some of the work is non-routine; or specialists giving advice or services or carrying out research work when a professional qualification or its equivalent is required.

Grade 3
Managers of medium-sized departments consisting of several sections where the work is mainly routine; or senior specialists leading a section or team of grade 2 or grade 1 specialists.

Grade 4
Managers of large departments consisting of several large groups or sections where the work is mainly routine; or managers of medium-sized departments where a considerable amount of non-routine work is required; or managers of small specialized departments entirely engaged on high level professional, technical or scientific work.

Grade 5
Managers of very large departments consisting of a number of large units each carrying out similar but mainly routine work and headed by grade 4 managers; or managers of large departments where the work is mainly non-routine, or heads of specialized functions providing advice or services for a division.

Grade 6
Managers controlling a number of different functions headed by grade 5 managers; or heads of major functions providing services throughout the division and contributing to the formulation of divisional policies and plans.

Grade 7
Divisional directors accountable for the results achieved by major activities or functions of the division and for the formulation and implementation of divisional policies and plans for their area of responsibility; or heads of group functions providing advice and services throughout the group and advising on group policies and plans.

Grade 8
Chief executives of medium-sized divisions; or group directors responsible for co-ordinating functional services throughout the organization or for formulating group policies in relation to a major service function.

Grade 9
Chief executives of major divisions accountable for the results achieved by their division; or senior group directors in charge of major functions and responsible for formulating group policies and plans in key operating and financial areas.

Grade 10
Group chief executive.

Appendix E

Points Rating Job Evaluation Scheme: Factor and Level Definitions

Factor 1 – knowledge and skills

Factor definition

The knowledge and skills gained through education, training and experience required to achieve the overall purpose of the job by attaining the outputs and standards specified for each key result area.

Level definitions

1. Ability to carry out certain tasks which can be acquired after a brief period of practical experience and/or training lasting up to one month.
2. More practical experience lasting between 1 and 6 months is needed to obtain the knowledge and skills required. Alternatively, proficiency can be attained after a concentrated training period of 1 to 3 months.
3. The knowledge and skills required to perform the job satisfactorily can only be acquired by intensive education and/or training lasting 6 to 12 months, or by up to 2 years of practical and relevant experience.
4. A high level of knowledge and skill is required in an area of professional, technical or administrative work. This can be attained either by professional or vocational training lasting 1 to 2 years or through practical and relevant experience over a period of 3 to 5 years.
5. Advanced knowledge and skills are required. These are normally attained by following an education and training course lasting over 2 years leading to a professional qualification, plus at least 2 years' practical experience. Alternatively, the standard required can be reached by at least 5 years' relevant

experience during which the advanced knowledge and skills demanded by the job have been used or practised at an appropriate level.

6. The job demands the use of a wide variety of advanced knowledge and skills which have been gained at level 5 for at least 5 years.

Factor 2 – responsibility

Factor definition

The responsibilities of a job are the particular obligations that have to be assumed by job holders who are called to account for what they do. The level of responsibility in a job is measured by reference to:

- the impact of of the job on the end-results of the organization
- the consequences of errors
- the size of the resources controlled.

Level definitions

1. Although job holders are expected to contribute at their level to the effectiveness of their department or section, they have little or no impact on the end-results of the organization. The consequence of errors is evident within hours and job holders exercise no control over resources except the equipment, tools or material they use in carrying out their job.
2. The impact on the end-results of the organization is very small and will be limited to the unit or section within which job holders work. Errors can be detected readily, coming to light within a day or two at most. Job holders may exercise limited control over physical resources related to their own job or their section.
3. The impact on the end-results within the job-holders' unit can be fairly high but is not significant in a wider context. Errors are not immediately detectable and might not come to light for a number of days, having meanwhile created noticeable operational problems within the section or department. Job holders may supervise one or two people carrying out entirely routine work and/or exercise control over resources within a small section.
4. Job holders can make considerable impact on the department or unit within which they work and this could affect the end-results of the organization as a whole, although not to a very significant extent. Errors of judgement may not become evident for some time (weeks, even months) and could seriously damage the effectiveness of the department.

5. Job holders are entirely accountable for the results obtained by their department or unit within a major function of the organization. The impact on the end-results of the function and therefore the total operation is high. Errors of judgement may not be detected for a considerable time, and they can seriously affect departmental and organizational effectiveness.
6. Job holders are entirely accountable for the results obtained by a major function. Their impact on the results of the organization is considerable and the effect of the errors of judgement (which may be extremely difficult to detect) can be devastating.

Factor 3 – decisions

Factor definition

This factor assesses the degree to which the job involves choice of action. It therefore covers the extent to which the work is prescribed or routine and the degree of supervision received. The amount of guidance and detailed instruction provided and the availability of standard procedures, manuals and clearly defined precedents are also taken into consideration.

Level definitions

1. The job is routine and is carried out under direct supervision with detailed instructions covering every aspect of the work. Thinking is entirely patterned.
2. The work is fairly routine and is carried out under quite close supervision. Most of the tasks simply require the straightforward application of easily understood rules, although there is a need from time to time to interpret the rules or procedures to decide on the best method of completing a defined task. Thinking is on the whole patterned.
3. The work is carried out under general guidance and supervision. Programmes and procedures are laid down, but it is often necessary to use judgement in deciding what action to take in particular circumstances. Non-routine problems, however, are referred to the job holders' managers or supervisors.
4. Freedom of action is within wide but clearly defined limits. Judgement has to be exercised in making decisions and this involves the ability to analyze and interpret data where the solutions are not immediately obvious. Guidance is, however, readily available when required from the job holders' managers or supervisors and there are a number of defined decision

points which must be referred upwards. Thinking requires some creativity in developing new ideas or concepts.

5. Freedom of action is considerable within broad policy guidelines except for a few major decision points which have to be referred upwards. Little guidance is available except in the form of definitions of overall objectives, targets and standards. Original thinking and creativity are required in making decisions and preparing plans.
6. Works under general policy guidelines only. Considerable judgement and initiative is required in making decisions without any guidance from above. Constantly required to exercise creativity and ingenuity in dealing with new and challenging situations.

Factor 4 – complexity

Factor definition

This factor covers the variety of tasks that have to be carried out, the range of skills required and the degree to which the work is subject to sudden changes.

Level definitions

1. Highly repetitive work where the same tasks or group of tasks have to be performed continuously.
2. Repetitive work where a limited variety of skills have to be used.
3. Work which involves some diversity of activities within a unit. However, the basic tasks and role do not change significantly.
4. Work which involves a diverse range of tasks and decisions within a major function. The decisions to be made change fairly often but seldom to a significant extent.
5. Work which involves a wide range of tasks and diverse decisions spread over more than one major function. Job holders frequently have to face change, which is often of some significance to the organization.
6. Work which involves a wide range of tasks and diverse decisions spread over all major functions. The management of significant change is a constant feature of the job.

Factor 5 – contacts

Factor definition

This factor covers the extent to which the work includes making personal contacts inside and outside the organization. The contacts may involve fact-finding, dealing with queries, interviewing, providing information, influencing others or negotiating. The level and importance of contacts should also be considered.

Level definitions

1. Contacts of little importance.
2. Contacts of a routine nature within the organization, not at a level above that of the job holder, which are only concerned with furnishing or providing information. Or routine contacts with people outside the organization where no more than normal courtesy and tact are required.
3. Contacts with members of other departments, sometimes above the level of the job holder, where information is requested or provided or where routine queries are dealt with; or contacts outside the organization dealing with routine queries or exchanges of information. These contacts, however, may require the exercise of special tact and diplomacy.
4. Periodical contacts with more senior members of organization outside the job holders' department where some non-routine queries are dealt with and some persuasive ability may be required. Or external contacts, where non-routine matters are handled occasionally or minor grievances settled and where a fair degree of tact or diplomacy is needed to deal with the person concerned.

Factor	Level					
	1	2	3	4	5	6
1 Knowledge and skills	50	100	150	200	250	300
2 Responsibility	50	100	150	200	250	300
3 Decisions	40	80	120	160	200	240
4 Complexity	30	60	90	120	150	180
5 Contacts	30	60	90	120	150	180

Figure E.1 *Score matrix*

5. Frequent internal or external contacts at high levels in which advice may be given or negotiations carried out within the competence of the job holder, or non-routine queries are answered. Considerable persuasive ability or tact may be required to handle the contacts.
6. The job constantly involves internal and external contacts at the highest level which will require very considerable communicating, persuading and negotiating skills.

Appendix F

Job Evaluation: Management Consultants' Schemes

This appendix gives brief details of the following most commonly used management consultants' job evaluation schemes:

- Hay Guide Chart – Profile
- PE International – Pay Points and Direct Consensus Method
- PA Personnel Services – PAGE Method
- Price Waterhouse – The Profile Method
- Saville-Holdsworth – the SHL Method
- The Wyatt Company – The EPFC and MULTICOMP systems
- Ernst and Young International (Employment Relations Associates) – The Decision Band Method

The Hay guide chart-profile method of job evaluation

History and development

The Hay Guide Chart-Profile Method of Job Evaluation is the most widely used single job evaluation method in the world, being used by over 7000 profit and non-profit organizations in some 40 countries. While it is perhaps best known for its application to management, professional and technical jobs, it is also extensively used for clerical and manual jobs, and when a single top-to-bottom evaluation method is required as the basis for integrated pay and grading structures.

It was initially conceived in the early 1950s, having its roots in factor comparison methods in which Edward N Hay was a pioneer, and has evolved by practical application into its present form.

Its widespread use, and the consistency of the job size numbering scale used, enables it to provide the basis for valid pay comparisons between organizations, nationally and internationally. Comprehensive pay and benefits surveys, using job-size-based comparisons are conducted by the Hay Group in over 35 countries.

The method can be applied by a wide variety of processes, both manual and computer assisted (see Appendix H), tailored to the particular requirements of the user organization.

Basis of the method

The method is based upon the following principles and observations.

- While there are many factors which could be considered in developing a job evaluation scheme, these can be grouped into three broad factors: the knowledge and skills required to do the job; the kind of thinking needed to solve the problems commonly faced; and the responsibilities assigned to the job.
- This provides the basis of the three main factors of the Guide Chart-Profile Method – Know-how, Problem Solving, and Accountability – which are common to all jobs, and which are subdivided into several elements.
- For any given job, there will be a relationship between the three factors. Thus the output or end results expected from the job (the Accountability), will demand a certain level of input (Know-how), and processing of this Know-how (Problem Solving) to enable delivery of the output.

  This can be represented by the simple model:

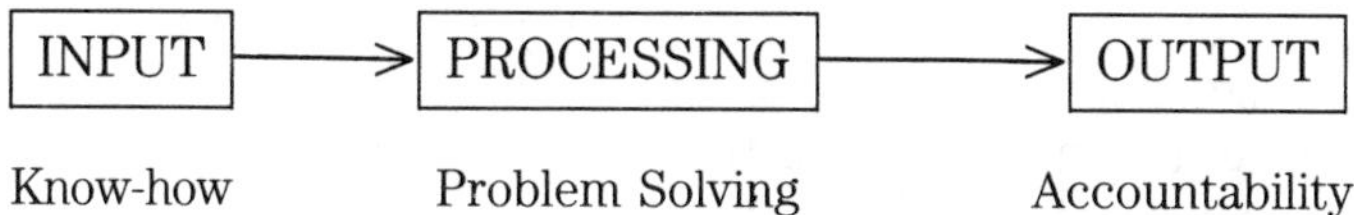

Know-how Problem Solving Accountability

- Thus jobs can be characterized not only by the size or level of each factor, but also by the balance between the factors – the Profile – which reflects the 'shape' of the job. Thus for example a research job is likely to be heavily loaded towards Know-how and Problem Solving, whereas for a sales representative or production manager, the balance will be shifted towards Accountability. In addition to evaluating each factor, evaluators also assess the profile of the job, which provides an important check on consistency of treatment.
- The ability of evaluators to discern a difference between two jobs depends not only on the absolute difference, but on how big this difference is in relation to the size of the jobs themselves. Thus the numbering patterns used in the Guide Charts are based upon a geometric scale, each number being a constant percentage greater than the previous one. This percentage has been empirically determined at 15 per cent, as best representing the ability of experienced evaluators to discern a difference in any factor between two jobs. This 'step difference' concept provides the basic building block for the scales and for comparisons between jobs, with one step representing a 'just discernible difference'.

- Jobs should not be evaluated in isolation, but viewed in their organizational context, so that working relationships both vertically and horizontally throughout the organization are taken into account.
- In order that the focus is on jobs, not the performance of jobholders, 'standard acceptable performance' is assumed. Similarly, jobs are evaluated independent of any market-driven pay conditions which may pertain, recognizing that these require addressing explicitly as pay issues, not job-size considerations.

Components of the method

The method has three main factors and eight dimensions as follows:

Know-how
The sum of every kind of knowledge, skill and experience, however acquired, needed for acceptable job performance. Its three dimensions are requirements for:

1. Practical procedures, specialized techniques and knowledge within occupational fields, commercial functions, and professional or scientific disciplines.
2. Integrating and harmonizing the diverse elements involved in managerial situations. This involves, in some combination, skills in planning, organizing, executing, controlling and evaluating and may be exercised consultatively as well as executively.
3. Active, practising person-to-person skills in work with other people, within or outside the organization.

Problem Solving
The original, self-starting use of know-how required by the job to identify, define, and resolve problems. 'You think with what you know'. This is true of even the most creative work. The raw material of any thinking is knowledge of facts, principles, and means. For that reason, Problem Solving is treated as a percentage of know-how.

Problem Solving has two dimensions:

- the environment in which thinking takes place
- the challenge presented by the thinking to be done.

Accountability
The answerability for action and for the consequences thereof. It is the measured effect of the job on end results of the organization. It has three dimensions in the following order of importance:

HAY GUIDE CHART FOR EVALUATING KNOW-HOW

•• PLANNING, ORGANISING, CONTROLLING – BREADTH OF MANAGEMENT KNOW-

••• HUMAN RELATIONS SKILLS

1. **BASIC**: Ordinary courtesy and effectiveness in dealing with others is required
2. **IMPORTANT**: Understanding, influencing, and communicating with people are important but not overriding considerations
3. **CRITICAL**: Skills in influencing, developing and/or motivating people are critical to the achievement of job objectives

• DEPTH AND RANGE OF TECHNICAL KNOW-HOW	O. TASK: Performance of a task (or tasks) highly specific as to objective and content and not involving the supervision of others			I. ACTIVITY: Performance or supervision of work which is specific as to objective and content with appropriate awareness of related activities			II. HOMOGENEOUS: Internal integration of operations which are relatively homogeneous in nature and objective, and which involve external co-ordination with associated functions			III. HETEROGENEOUS: Operational or conceptual integration of functions which are diverse in nature and in objective in an important management area or central co-ordination of a strategic function	
••• HUMAN RELATIONS SKILLS	1.	2.	3.	1.	2.	3.	1.	2.	3.	1.	2.
PRACTICAL PROCEDURES — **A PRIMARY**: Jobs requiring Secondary education only plus some work indoctrination	38	43	50	50	57	66	66	76	87	87	100
	43	50	57	57	66	76	76	87	100	100	115
	50	57	66	66	76	87	87	100	115	115	132
B ELEMENTARY VOCATIONAL: Jobs requiring familiarisation in uninvolved, standardised work routines and/or use of simple equipment and machines	50	57	66	66	76	87	87	100	115	115	132
	57	66	76	76	87	100	100	115	132	132	152
	66	76	87	87	100	115	115	132	152	152	175
C VOCATIONAL: Jobs requiring procedural or systematic proficiency, which may involve facility in the use of specialised equipment	66	76	87	87	100	115	115	132	152	152	175
	76	87	100	100	115	132	132	152	175	175	200
	87	100	115	115	132	152	152	175	200	200	230
SPECIALISED TECHNIQUES — **D ADVANCED VOCATIONAL**: Jobs requiring some specialised (generally non theoretical) skills gained by 'on the job' experience or through part professional qualification	87	100	115	115	132	152	152	175	200	200	230
	100	115	132	132	152	175	175	200	230	230	264
	115	132	152	152	175	200	200	230	264	264	304
E BASIC PROFESSIONAL: Jobs requiring sufficiency in a technical, scientific or specialised field based on an understanding of concepts and principles normally associated with a professional or academic qualification or gained through a detailed grasp of involved practices and procedures	115	132	152	152	175	200	200	230	264	264	304
	132	152	175	175	200	230	230	264	304	304	350
	152	175	200	200	230	264	264	304	350	350	400
…NAL DISCIPLINES — **F SEASONED PROFESSIONAL**: Jobs requiring proficiency in a technical, scientific or specialised field gained through broad and deep experience built on concepts and principles, or through wide exposure to complex practices and precedents	152	175	200	200	230	264	264	304	350	350	400
	175	200	230	230	264	304	304	350	400	400	460
	200	230	264	264	304	350	350	400	460	460	528
G PROFESSIONAL MASTERY: Jobs requiring determinative mastery of concepts, principles and	200	230	264	264	304	350	350	400	460	460	528

Figure F.1 *Know-how*

1. Freedom to act: the extent of personal, procedural, or systematic guidance or control of actions in relation to the primary emphasis of the job.
2. Job impact on end results: the extent to which the job can directly affect actions necessary to produce results within its primary emphasis.
3. Magnitude: the portion of the total organization encompassed by the primary emphasis of the job. Where possible, magnitude is expressed in annual financial figures representing the area of primary emphasis of the job.

Beyond these three factors of job content, additional scales can be used to assess factors relating to the context in which the job operates; for example unpleasant working environment, hazards, physical demands, sensory attention, etc. When such factors are important for the jobs under consideration, scales are generated to enable their assessment within the context of the organization.

The Guide Charts

A Guide Chart for each factor (see Figures F.1, F.2 and F.3) contains semantic scales which reflect degrees of presence of each dimension. Each scale, except for Problem Solving, is expandable to reflect the size and complexity of the organization to which it is applied. The language of the scales, carefully evolved over many years and applied to literally millions of jobs of every kind, has remained fairly constant in recent years but is modified, as appropriate, to reflect the unique nature, character, and structure of any given organization. The numbering pattern in each chart is based upon the 15 per cent difference concept noted above.

To illustrate the use of the charts, consider the Know-how chart (F1). If for example a job is considered to fall squarely into E Technical Know-how, II Breadth of Management and 3 Human Relations skills, then the chart indicates a Know-how value of 304 units. The 264 and 350 values are to allow for fine tuning or shading, when one of the elements is considered light or heavy compared with the basic definition, or with comparator jobs.

The same total of Know-how score of 304 units can of course be arrived at in a variety of ways. For example F+I2 304 indicates a job which is significantly more technical, but less demanding in terms of management and human relations skills – but on balance requiring the same total volume of knowledge and skills. In addition to their primary purpose of arriving at a job size, this illustrates the way that the Guide Charts are frequently used to provide a language in which jobs can be described and characterized in a consistent way.

HAY GUIDE CHART FOR EVALUATING ACCOUNTABILITY

●●● MAGNITUDE	(0) MINIMAL				(1) VERY SMALL				(2) SMALL				(3) MEDIUM			
Figures for use in 1989/90	Under £28,000				£28,000 – £280,000				£280,000 – £2.8M				£2.8M – £28M			
Adjusted figures for 19 (Magnitude figures for use in the following year are published each September)																
●● IMPACT	R.	C.	S.	P.	R.	C.	S.	P.	R.	C.	S.	P.	R.	C.	S.	P.
A PRESCRIBED: These jobs are subject to — Direct and detailed instructions — Close supervision	8	10	14	19	10	14	19	25	14	19	25	33	19	25	33	43
	9	12	16	22	12	16	22	29	16	22	29	38	22	29	38	50
	10	14	19	25	14	19	25	33	19	25	33	43	25	33	43	57
B CONTROLLED: These jobs are subject to – Instructions and established work routines – Close supervision	12	16	22	29	16	22	29	38	22	29	38	50	29	38	50	[illegible]
	14	19	25	33	19	25	33	43	25	33	43	57	33	43	57	[illegible]
	16	22	29	38	22	29	38	50	29	38	50	66	38	50	66	[illegible]
C STANDARDISED These jobs are subject, wholly or in part to – Standardised practices and procedures – General work instructions – Supervision of progress and results	19	25	33	43	25	33	43	57	33	43	57	76	43	57	76	[illegible]
	22	29	38	50	29	38	50	66	38	50	66	87	50	66	87	[illegible]
	25	33	43	57	33	43	57	76	43	57	76	100	57	76	100	[illegible]
D REGULATED: These jobs are subject, wholly or in part to – Practices and procedures which have clear precedents or are covered by closely defined policies – Managerial control – Review of results	29	38	50	66	38	50	66	87	50	66	87	115	66	87	115	[illegible]
	33	43	57	76	43	57	76	100	57	76	100	132	76	100	132	175
	38	50	66	87	50	66	87	115	66	87	115	152	87	115	152	200
E DIRECTED: These jobs are subject to – Broad practice and procedures covered by functional precedents and policies – Achievement of a circumscribed operational activity – Managerial direction	43	57	76	100	57	76	100	132	76	100	132	175	100	132	175	230
	50	66	87	115	66	87	115	152	87	115	152	200	115	152	200	264
	57	76	100	132	76	100	132	175	100	132	175	230	132	175	230	304
F GENERALLY DIRECTED: These jobs by their nature or size are subject to – Functional policy objectives – General direction	66	87	115	152	87	115	152	200	115	152	200	264	152	200	264	350
	76	100	132	175	100	132	175	230	132	175	230	304	175	230	304	400
	87	115	152	200	115	152	200	264	152	200	264	350	200	264	350	460
G GUIDED: These jobs are subject only to guidance and broad direction on orientation of policy	100	132	175	230	132	175	230	304	175	230	304	400	230	304	400	528
	115	152	200	264	152	200	264	350	200	264	350	460	264	350	460	608
	132	175	230	304	175	230	304	400	[illegible]	[illegible]	[illegible]	[illegible]	304	400	528	700
			[illegible]	350	200	264	[illegible]								[illegible]	800

● FREEDOM TO ACT

Figure F.2 *Problem solving*

HAY GUIDE CHART FOR EVALUATING PROBLEM SOLVING

● THINKING ENVIRONMENT – FREEDOM TO THINK	●● THINKING CHALLENGE: 1. REPETITIVE Identical situations requiring solution by simple choice of things learned	2. PATTERNED Similar situations requiring solution by discriminating choice of things learned	3. VARIABLE Differing situations requiring the identification and selection of solutions through the application of acquired knowledge	4. ADAPTIVE Situations requiring ar cal interpretative a constructive thinking significant degree of e ative judgement
A STRICT ROUTINE: Thinking within detailed rules instructions and/or rigid supervision	10% / 12%	14% / 16%	19% / 22%	25% / 29%
B ROUTINE: Thinking within standard instructions and/or continuous close supervision	12% / 14%	16% / 19%	22% / 25%	29% / 33%
C SEMI-ROUTINE: Thinking within well defined procedures and precedents somewhat diversified and/or supervised	14% / 16%	19% / 22%	25% / 29%	33% / 38%
D STANDARDISED: Thinking within substantially diversified, established company procedures and standards, and general supervision	16% / 19%	22% / 25%	29% / 33%	38% / 43%
E CLEARLY DEFINED: Thinking within clearly defined company policies principles and specific objectives, under readily available direction	19% / 22%	25% / 29%	33% / 38%	43% / 50%
F BROADLY DEFINED: Thinking within broad policies and objectives, under general direction	22% / 25%	29% / 33%	38% / 43%	50% / 57%
G GENERALLY DEFINED: Thinking within general policies, principles and goals under guidance	25% / 29%	33% / 38%	43% / 50%	57% / [illegible]
H ABSTRACTLY DEFINED: Thinking within busi-	29%	38%	50%	66%

Figure F.3 *Accountability*

Use of the other two Guide Charts is similar, though in the case of Problem Solving, the chart yields a percentage value which is applied to the Know-how score to give Problem Solving units. Total job size is the sum of the three factor scores.

Consistency checks

- Profile: this is used as a powerful check for internal consistency within an evaluation. If for example the evaluation shows an Accountability score three 15 per cent steps higher than the Problem Solving score, it would be recorded as A3 (sometimes 'plus 3' or 'up 3').
- Evaluators make a separate judgement on the profile expected for the job. Thus, typically, jobs in line functions would be expected to have strongly Accountability (A) oriented profiles, jobs in basic research would have strong Problem Solving orientation (P), while jobs in many staff functions like personnel, finance, etc. are likely to have the two more in balance. If the profile which emerges from the evaluation does not agree with the evaluators' view of the appropriate profile, it indicates an inconsistency of treatment between the factors, and causes the evaluators to reconsider the evaluation.
- Rank Order: Testing of rank order to identify anomalies is an important part of the process. It can be done at the level of total job size; by factor (eg total Know-how); or by individual dimension (eg Freedom to Act).

Application of the Guide Chart profile method

The basic measuring instrument of the Guide Charts can be applied through a wide variety of processes, both manual and computer assisted. The choice of a particular application process depends principally upon the purpose for which the job evaluation is being undertaken, the size and diversity of the job population under consideration, and the time and resource constraints which exist. Thus traditional processes based upon multi-functional evaluation committees can provide great sensitivity to a wide diversity of jobs, and can generate valuable output in terms of organizational analysis and clarification, though they are demanding in terms of time and resources. Computer assisted processes reduce the time and resource demands, particularly for large populations, but may reduce the opportunity for organizational debate and analysis. Hay consultants advise client organizations on the most appropriate process to meet particular needs and circumstances. The range of processes is illustrated in the following examples:

Committee-based process
In this, the most commonly applied traditional process, evaluation judgements are made by a committee (or committees), trained in the use of the Guide Charts, and using job information in the form of job descriptions.

The process usually starts with the selection of a benchmark of jobs, to reflect the range of job types and levels in the population, and to enable basic evaluation standards and interpretations to be set.

Job descriptions for the benchmark jobs may be prepared by trained analysts, by jobholders or their managers – depending on circumstances. In most cases, approval of the final document by both jobholder and manager is adopted, whoever has prepared the description. A variety of job description formats may be used, but an important feature of Hay job descriptions is an emphasis on the results expected from a job – the Principal Accountabilities – which assists clarity and conciseness, and can provide links into related processes such as organizational analysis and performance management.

The benchmark committee is selected, usually including members from a range of functions, not purely HR specialists, so as to provide a range of inputs and perspectives, and foster ownership of the results. Depending on the organization's needs, the committee may be a management group, or may include peer group members and/or Trade Union representatives.

The committee is trained and guided by a Hay consultant, and evaluates the Benchmark sample to provide clear reference points, and standards and principles to assist evaluation of non-benchmark jobs.

An important component of this process is the establishment of evaluation interpretations which reflect the organization's values and emphases, within the Guide Chart framework.

For a small population or in a highly centralized organization, the same committee may proceed to evaluate the remaining jobs. Otherwise, additional committees are selected and trained, (for example Divisional committees in a diversified business), and processes established to ensure application of common standards.

Computer-based administrative support is available to assist this process, in the form of the HayQED component of the HayXpert suite of software. This enables recording and storage of job evaluation data, evaluation rationales, and if required, job descriptions, for rapid sorting and access when comparisons or rank order checks are being made.

Comparisons and classification methods
The Guide Chart-profile method can also be used to underpin a variety of comparison or classification approaches, particularly for large and relatively homogeneous populations.

These processes normally start with committee evaluation of a benchmark sample, using the Guide Charts in the conventional way.

Based on the results of this sampling and standard setting, a classification of 'slotting' framework can be established, to facilitate evaluation of remaining jobs by direct comparison. This can be presented in written 'workbook' form, or as a computer-based framework in HayXpert software.

Such methods can achieve very rapid evaluation of large populations and provide for significant devolution of responsibility for evaluation, with relatively low training requirements.

Computer assisted evaluation processes
In these processes, the use of job descriptions and committees for the bulk of the job population is replaced by structured questionnaires, processed by computer to generate evaluations directly, using an algorithm which has been established from full evaluation of a benchmark sample.

Where a single approach is required to cover all (or most) of the jobs in an organization, a single, comprehensive questionnaire is constructed. A benchmark sample of jobs is evaluated conventionally, using the Guide Charts, to provide the basic standards to underpin the process. The same jobs are also rated on the questionnaire and an algorithm built to replicate Hay job unit results from the questionnaire responses and programmed into HayXpert software. For non-benchmark jobs, questionnaires are completed and processed through the computer (batch or interactive) to yield comparative evaluations. Quality checks are built in, both to the software and processes, to ensure consistency.

An alternative approach, for a more tightly defined job group is the Job Family Questionnaire. This provides a shorter, more focused questionnaire which is typically developed in conjunction with members of the family in question to reflect quite explicity the key differentiating factors which affect job size in that family, expressed in their language. It is often used when relationships between job evaluation, career development and competency analysis are important. The process for its implementation is similar to that described for the 'Universal' questionnaire.

Mixed processes
Since all these application processes are underpinned by the same Guide Chart principles and numbering scales, they yield compatible results, and so different processes can be applied to different job groups without loss of compatibility.

Advantages and disadvantages

Advantages

- It is a very thorough and sensitive form of factor comparison method, using a structured language and job size units to express relationships between jobs.
- It is applicable to any type or level of job, and can be used throughout an organization.
- It is extensively tried and tested over many years, worldwide, and supported by an international consulting network.
- Cross-organizational comparisons are easily made and extensive external remuneration comparisons are available internationally.
- As a process guided and controlled by principles rather than rigid rules, it is sensitive to organizational values and emphases, and able to deal with new and evolving organizational arrangements.
- It can be applied by a wide variety of processes, both traditional and computer assisted, geared to the requirements of the user organization. Different processes can be mixed within an organization for various job groups, but still provide compatible results.

Disadvantages

- It is based on a view of organisations which reflects Western industrialized hierarchies, decision-making processes and values, so organizations and job categories not conforming to this pattern may find the evaluation results less acceptable.
- It is open to the same form of abuse as any other job evaluation scheme

Commentary

Hay's success in the UK and international job evaluation market is undeniable as is its influence on both national and international remuneration practice. The basic method has changed little over the years but it is normally sufficiently sensitive to reflect different cultural values and the process by which it is applied can be geared closely to the organization's needs. Those evaluating in, say, an oriental environment must be ready to reflect different values and accept evaluations which may be unfamiliar to Western experience. To recognize such differences Hay advise that the evaluation of jobs, with perhaps the exception of the top international jobs, should be undertaken locally with local nationals on the committee.

PE International Pay Points

History and development

PE International Pay Points was developed in 1979. It can be applied to determine market-related salaries for senior executives and middle management jobs and as an analytical method of job evaluation extending down to clerical level. The system has the advantage of an automatic link to PE International extensive salary database derived from their regular surveys of executive salaries and fringe benefits.

The evaluation process

Simple job descriptions are prepared and points are awarded under five factors in the traditional points rating manner. The factors cover:

- knowledge and experience
- complexity and creativity
- judgements and decisions
- influence on results
- contacts.

Depending on the number of jobs to be considered the system may be applied to a sample of jobs first which can then be used as benchmarks or reference jobs for evaluating others. Jobs can be left individually scored or put into a grading structure with each grade having a specific range of points. Job scores are converted into market-related salaries by the application of two multipliers derived from PE International's own extensive database. The first multiplier called 'Company Factor' takes account of the size and characteristics of the particular company or operating unit in which the job is situated. The second multiplier called 'Salary Factor' simply converts points scored into an assessed market salary for the job which then becomes the mid-point of a salary range. There is provision in the system for taking account of industry and regional salary differentials and of specific Job Premiums where a market scarcity applies. Salary ranges can also be pitched at market median, upper quartile or other intermediate values depending on a particular company's salary policy.

Salary data

PE International's Annual Survey of Executive Salaries and Fringe Benefits has been established for over 25 years and for some time now has had the largest sample of companies of any UK management survey. The company sample in the survey changes from year to year. In fact on average around 60 per cent of companies take part in consecutive years. This has the advantage of a regular input of data from fresh sources contrasted with many club surveys where information tends to be compared among the same group of companies each year.

The PE International sample probably includes a larger number of medium-sized companies than any other survey, and is particularly useful for providing salary data related to medium-sized manufacturing companies and subsidiaries of large corporations. Before the development of the pay points system, job evaluation clients of PE International, who also participate in the salary survey had no direct mechanism for linking their grading structure with the market, other than by matching jobs according to title, function and general responsibility level.

Advantages and disadvantages

Advantages

- quick and simple to install and maintain
- can be used simply for establishing market rates as well as for job evaluation
- provides an automatic link to a well established and extensive salary database. (PE International provide an annual updating service for users of the system.)

Disadvantages

- the 'company' and 'salary' factors need updating annually to reflect market movements in salaries and any significant changes which may have occurred in company size
- job evaluation scores are translated into the values annually thrown up by the survey. The inevitable fluctuation in the composition of the varying sample and the rate of response might result in internal relativities being distorted, year on year, if the system were rigidly adopted.

PE International Direct Consensus Method (DCM)

History and development

DCM was first developed by PE International some 25 years ago, and uses job ranking by paired comparisons. Jobs are compared within a number of different factors to develop a factor plan. The system is highly flexible and is suitable for both large and small organizations. It can cover senior management, as well as clerical and manual jobs.

DCM can be applied with full employee participation, or purely as a management exercise.

The evaluation process

For job populations above 70–80, a series of jobs, typically 40–60, would be selected for ranking as benchmarks. In the case of a participative exercise, employees whose jobs will be covered by the evaluation are first of all briefed on the project, and a judging panel of 6–16 panelists is chosen to represent a cross section of the organization by level, function and sex. The panel then decides the factors which will be used in the evaluation.

There is complete flexibility as to the factors chosen. The main criteria are that they need to suit the jobs which are being evaluated. Thus, it may be expedient to use different factors for managerial, clerical and manual jobs, although otherwise the approach is the same. Care must be taken to ensure that the selected factors are free from sexual bias. If job descriptions do not already exist, these must be prepared with due prominence being given to each of the selected factors. Jobs are then arranged in pairs on a ranking form with each job paired with every other job against each of the chosen factors.

Although job descriptions are available, the judges are required to familiarize themselves with the jobs to be ranked. They then record their decisions on the ranking forms provided, by marking the 'winning job' in each pair of jobs against each factor. After individual factor assessments hve been completed, each pair of jobs is separately compared on a 'total factor' basis.

Analyzing the results and providing weightings

The judging panel's decisions are processed by computer, which prints out the rank orders of jobs as decided by the panel, both for each factor and also on a 'total factor' basis. The programme also produces decision matrices, which highlight judgements contrary to the general consensus so that these can be examined and resolved. The implied factor weights are then calculated by computer, based on the judges' decisions in ranking jobs against individual factors and on a total factor basis. In this way, a factor plan is prepared which is unique to the organization and the evaluated jobs. The ranking is divided into a number of grades and the remaining jobs, ie those not ranked, are then fitted into grades by the application of the factor plan.

Advantages and disadvantages

Advantages

- the system is simple to understand and apply
- it is quick and relatively inexpensive to implement and maintain
- it can be used to cover all jobs, management, clerical and manual and it enables factors to be chosen which best suit the jobs to be evaluated
- it is easy to involve employees and their representatives in the evaluation process; alternatively the system can be applied purely as a management desk exercise.

  The outcome of the evaluation is generally highly acceptable; when participative it represents a consensus of a group of employees and the factor plan developed is unique to the organization and the jobs covered by the evaluation.

Disadvantages

- no automatic link with salary data
- not easy to explain to employees why their jobs have been evaluated in the way they were.

Commentary

The Direct Consensus Paired Comparison method has been widely used over a number of years in a variety of industries. The 1979 BIM survey of job evaluation found this method in use in 12 per cent of their sample, being adopted at all levels of seniority, but slightly more popular at clerical and junior to middle management levels. The method has also been used in the public sector.

The PE International Pay Points system is currently used by over 200 companies across a wide spectrum of industry and commerce including the public sector. The majority of applications have been at middle and senior management levels covering executive, technical and administrative posts although the system can also be applied to clerical jobs.

PA Personnel Services: 'PAGE' (developed from the factor/paired comparisons method).

History and development

The factor-based approach to job evaluation developed by the PA Consulting Group gives greater prominence to internal relativities than external comparisons. PA emphasize that their experience has shown people at work place a relatively higher importance on pay comparisons with colleagues than with those doing similar work in other organizations. Each scheme is therefore developed to meet the client's own needs, particularly in the section of factors. The approach utilizes the advantages of the traditional paired comparison method in developing the system parameters by using cross ranking, allowing a line of best fit between results obtained from the paired comparison and the factor plan. All jobs are finally ranked by their weighted factor scores alone.

Particular care is taken throughout the process, both at the stage of factor choice and definition and during evaluation meetings, to avoid any bias and this applies particularly to sex bias, in line with the spirit of the Equal Pay (Amendement) Regulations.

Recent developments involve the use of psychometric concepts in factor selection and the use of electronic voting. A microcomputer (PC) is used to process results and develop the final system based on the factor weighting which are most appropriate for the client concerned. Software and data discs are left with the client for future updating and addition of new jobs.

Scheme development

There are three broad stages involved in developing a scheme for a client:

- factor selection and definition
- evaluation of benchmark jobs
- analysis and review of results and development and testing of the final structure.

The end of the development phase results in a unique, validated scheme for each client.

Basis of the scheme

Factors are selected and defined uniquely for each client and, typically, between six and ten factors are chosen. A set of core factors may be suggested including, for example, 'knowledge', 'experience' and 'decision-making'; or management factors such as 'contribution to business performance' or 'impact on profitability'. But it is up to the client organization to select which factors it considers important. Each factor will normally be divided into five or six levels or degrees, each with a narrative description using client terminology.

The evaluation process

The client is encouraged to set up a steering group to oversee the process. That group will select 30 to 40 benchmark jobs which are representative of both senior and junior levels in the organization and of all functions. The steering group will appoint a panel including a wide cross section of people in the company, to evaluate the jobs.

Company job descriptions are completed, either by the job holder or by an analyst, depending on time and cost constraints. As well as a traditional job description, a factor-based questionnaire is also completed. These are reviewed for consistency prior to the panel meeting.

At the evaluation meeting, each job is considered in turn, separately from the other jobs. The chairman of the panel introduces the job and ensures there is sufficient discussion to enable each panel member to examine the scope and responsibilities of the job. Factors are considered one at a time and the appropriate degree finally selected by a majority vote. The panel votes using specially designed equipment to enable simultaneous, confidential voting. Each panel member has an input device to a central console and can change his or her vote at any time if convinced to do so by the arguments put forward. The chairman's console shows the state of voting and discussion is stopped when a solid consensus emerges. At least a two-thirds majority is required and discussion continues until there is this level of consensus.

Each panel member then separately completes the paired comparison exercise. This involves comparing each job with each other job on paired comparison sheets. This process of course involves subjective judgement, but panel members will have gained an up-to-date knowledge of the scope of these jobs during their discussion in the factor analysis process. Again stress is placed on the need to avoid sex discrimination, and to think to the future rather than to justify the status quo.

Analysis, development and validation of the scheme

All results are processed by computer, using PA's own software. First, the paired comparison results are checked for consistency between judges and the average rank order then compared with the factor analysis scores. Weightings are produced which give the closest fit between the paired comparison results and the factor analysis.

These results are then carefully reviewed with the client to ensure that the scheme which has been developed is the optimum scheme for that client. Thus the parameters of the system are tested and refined before proceeding to the application stage.

Application and use of the scheme
The remaining jobs are evaluated using the factors; weightings are developed in the previous phase. (The benchmark jobs, having been evaluated during the development phase, do not need re-evaluation.)
Participation and disclosure: There is potential for this system to be highly participative at every stage. A manual is produced for use by the job evaluation panel at its meetings, containing all the information necessary to conduct future evaluations and to deal with new jobs as they are created. The information disclosed to employees will typically include a summary of the purpose, processes and results of the scheme but will usually exclude factor weightings.

When the results are announced, employees are normally allowed to appeal against the grading, following a procedure recommended by the consultant. Once these appeals have been considered and settled, the scheme is in full operation. New and changed jobs are evaluated as necessary.
Maintenance: To ensure the scheme keeps up to date and is responsive to changes in the clients' situation, various levels of maintenance are recommended, and detailed in the manual. In the short-term, annual job content reviews are recommended, in the longer term (three to five years), factor and weighting audits.

Salary data

Clearly the flexibility allowed in designing and implementing the PA method means that no automatic basis for salary comparisons across organizations exists. However, in addition to all the published survey data they hold, PA also undertake a number of special 'club' type surveys on request, as well as being able to draw on salary information available via PA's extensive recruitment and executive search activities.

Advantages and disadvantages

Advantages

- flexible and participative
- relatively cheap to install
- although no automatic linking mechanism is available, there is access to a wealth of pay data through PA's pay research and recruitment activities.

Disadvantages

- direct comparisons across companies are not possible because of the individual tailoring of factor plans
- paired comparisons are used in the calculation of factor weightings. These can be perceived as subjective and may need to be updated every few years.

Commentary

The system has been used across a wide range of organizations and industries including the public and financial sectors, covering all types of jobs from top management to shop-floor, including some organizations covering this whole range in one, harmonized scheme.

The PA system has the advantages of flexibility and participation. It can be applied with relative ease using microcomputers for ongoing administration. It is a relatively cheap system to install and once running would probably need a minimum of consultant involvement. But like most job evaluation schemes, a major audit would probably be necessary within five years of installation.

The major disadvantage of the system relates to the subjectivity inevitable in the use of paired comparisons. They are only used once, when the system is being set up, but this is in the crucial step of establishing factor weightings for the company. PA stress that all jobs are finally ranked by their weighted factor scores.

Comparisons across organizations can be difficult because PA prefer companies to use those factors which are most appropriate. Recognizing this problem, PA have developed a technique which allows each company or division within a group to develop its own system (using its own factor weightings or even its own factors), while a keying process using the standard set of factors enables the group head office to compare jobs across subsidiary units.

The methods used for the choice and definition of factors means that an organization's job evaluation system can be tied in with other personnel areas such as recruitment specification, performance appraisal, organization planning, promotion criteria etc.

Price Waterhouse: The Profile Method

The Profile Method was developed in the 1960s by Urwick Orr and Partners who are now part of the Price Waterhouse consultancy group and who were among the pioneers of job evaluation itself, in the mid 1960s. The method is designed to help organizations develop schemes to meet their own needs quickly and easily. In recent years it has been used increasingly to cover all jobs ranging from board level to the shop-floor.

Main components of the scheme

The system uses a set of factors termed 'characteristics' which are selected according to the client's own needs. Similarly, weightings are specific to each client company. Urwick stress the difficulty in consistently evaluating jobs when the rating scale comprises too many points or levels. Their analytical profile method therefore uses only four to eight levels within each characteristic or sub-characteristic. Each of the benchmark jobs is 'profiled' by scoring within each characteristic and sub-characteristic. As experience is gained, guidelines are drawn up for ensuring consistency. Typically, the characteristics cover responsibility, knowledge, social skills, mental skills, physical skills and working conditions.

Benchmark jobs are selected by the steering committee, and job descriptions completed. (Emphasis is placed on training a team of analysts to minimize dependency on external consultants.)

The benchmark jobs are compared first analytically characteristic by characteristic to produce 'profiles of the jobs' with the aid of a sorting computer program. They are then placed in a simple felt-fair rank order. These two comparisons are matched statistically to produce a set of weightings that enable the profiles to be converted into numerical evaluations. The weighting computation is carried out using a specially developed computer program designed to place greatest weighting upon those characteristics that are most highly correlated with the felt-fair rank order. The analysis enables weightings to be calculated so as to bring the ranking of benchmark jobs into the felt-fair order.

The remaining jobs are then also profiled and scored using the weighted factors, so providing detailed evaluations of all jobs. Alternatively, as in the case of British Steel middle managers, the profile patterns obtained from the benchmark exercise are used to develop the grading structure. Then the other jobs can be slotted into grades by simply comparing with the grades of benchmarks.

Throughout each assignment consultants encourage full participation and discussion. They say that the atmosphere in which the evaluations are conducted is important and that involvement in the development of the scheme ensures greater acceptability. It also prolongs the life of the scheme by achieving higher consistency in assessment.

Salary data

No off-the-peg salary surveys are provided, although a club survey facility is available. Comparisons will be made on clients' behalf with companies in the same line of business and only jobs with similar profiles will be compared.

Coverage

The Profile Method has been used to devise over 300 schemes across a wide range of industries, principally in the manufacturing sector. The 1979 BIM survey on job evaluation found that the scheme was equally popular at manual as well as clerical and junior managerial level. In recent years the proportion of schemes covering top management has been increasing.

Advantages and disadvantages

Advantages

- can involve a high degree of participation
- consistent across job function and at various locations (in cases where the same set of characteristics is used)
- a single scheme can cover almost any range of jobs (where the same set of characteristics is used for all groups)
- the scoring system is easy to use
- less grading drift likely
- as with other factor points schemes, new and changed jobs can be readily accommodated.

Disadvantages

- no automatic pay database is provided
- weightings depend on felt-fair ranking which could be subject to change over time as new jobs are introduced and others disappear.

Commentary

The tailoring of characteristics to suit the job range and the scoring or rating system used are key features of the Profile Method. When only a few levels are available to score any one characteristic (or sub-characteristic) a high level of consistency can be attained. The scheme can be easily applied across a number of job functions and at various locations for which a single factor plan appears suitable.

The resulting grading structure is likely to suffer less drift than with the standard points rating system, because fewer choices are available when scoring jobs.

Maintenance of the scheme involves reviews to ensure consistency of interpretation of the levels as well as keeping job descriptions up to date. Computer assisted processes are now well developed.

Saville and Holdsworth – The SHL approach to job evaluation

History and development

An integral feature of the SHL approach to job evaluation is the linkage with the Work Profiling System of job analysis, which provides a comprehensive range of human resource management applications.

The WPS is a standardized job analysis questionnaire which is normally completed by the job holder and is then read by an optical scanner. The computer produces both a detailed Technical Report and a short Summary Report on the job. It is possible for a number of job holders in the same job to complete the questionnaire and produce a combined report showing the mean and standard deviation for up to 99 job holders.

The WPS has been developed over four years and was sponsored by 21 major UK organizations, such as Barclaycard, BP, British Coal, British Telecom, Courage Ltd, Halifax Building Society, ICL, Milk Marketing Board, Plessey, Tesco, and Whitbread.

More than 1,000 jobs were submitted to quantitative scaled questionnaires (Critical Component Questionnaires) as well as qualitative research via Repertory Grid, Critical Incidents and Paired Comparisons techniques. This led to three structured trial questionnaires with over 800 questions between them and the generation of a Human Attribute model covering over 200 attributes.

Main components of the scheme

The use of the WPS allows information to be collected about a job in a structured way using either paper and pencil or computer administration. The expert aspect of the WPS computer system is in the:

- 800 plus equations used to predict human attributes from job task and context information
- linking assessment methods to the Human Attribute model
- matching procedure for individuals to jobs
- standardized guidance in setting interview questions and personality link caveats.

For job evaluation purposes organizations have the choice of selecting relevant factors from the 28 sections in Part II of the WPS questionnaire or if necessary the 32 sections in Part I of the WPS. Thus each organization may develop a unique job evaluation system from the same menu of variables.

The scheme is introduced by means of the following eight steps:

Step one: steering committee appointed
The steering committee, comprising management and staff representatives, has three main tasks:

- agreeing the principles of the job evaluation scheme
- helping in the smooth introduction of the scheme
- monitoring the long-term performance.

Ideally, the steering committee should collectively have knowledge of all the jobs covered by the scheme. This helps in the various decisions that need to be made and provides confidence to staff that the scheme will be administered fairly.

It is important that all members of the steering committee have a basic understanding of the job evaluation process and the Work Profiling System. The first meeting will be largely devoted to these two objectives.

It is desirable for the appeals procedure to be defined at an early stage. This is likely to take the form of a sub-committee of the steering committee. Time periods should be set for the receipt of appeals following the announcement of the results of job evaluation.

A sample of benchmark jobs need to be selected which reflect a clearly perceived hierarchy within the current pay structure. Benchmark jobs are chosen to represent the full range of job values and are jobs about which there is substantial agreement on current relative value. Being selected as a benchmark does not mean that a job will necessarily remain on the same grade once the exercise has been completed. Those jobs selected as benchmarks would then be analyzed using the Work Profiling System.

Step two: job analyst training
Validating the Work Profiling System questionnaires will be a key element in the job evaluation process. Job analysts will require comprehensive knowledge of the WPS and specific training in the validation interview. This will help to develop the skill and expertise of the organization's own job analyst team.

Step three: selection of evaluation dimensions
From approximately 30 main sectors in Part I of the WPS and the 32 sectors in Part II the steering committee selects those dimensions which reflect the needs of the organization. At this stage it is possible to attach additional items that may not appear in the WPS, and yet be of importance to the organization and relevant to the jobs under review. Having identified the key dimensions for the scheme it is then required to allocate weightings to them for inclusion in the WPS analysis. SHL provides guidance on the various ways of doing this.

Step four: evaluation of benchmark jobs by steering committee
Using job objectives and key job tasks produced via the WPS, the steering committee evaluates the benchmark jobs on a 'felt-fair' basis, and creates a metric derived from the rank order of jobs. Paired comparison technique can be used for this procedure, although other methods are available.

Step five: evaluation of bench-mark jobs by WPS
The bench-mark jobs are put through the WPS and evaluation scores generated as weighted aggregates. These are then validated by correlating against the felt-fair metric. If the degree of correlation is inadequate, a review of differences is undertaken. This could result in a revision of weights and re-validation.

Step six: preparation of explanatory documentation
To keep staff informed of the scheme, a general explanatory document and technical manual will need to be prepared. These documents may well be supported by other activities – for example, staff meetings to introduce the evaluation method.

Critical monitoring of the job analysis process will be required on an ongoing basis, including the validation interviews.

Step seven: data preparation
Once all the jobs have been analysed using the WPS it will be necessary to collate the scattergram of scores and present this to the steering committee to aid their decision on relating points to salary grades.

Step eight: review of appeals
Due to the thoroughness of the WPS as a means of analyzing jobs it is unlikely that many appeals will arise on the grounds of an inadequate job description. However, some appeals may occur where job holders feel there is inequity in the grading of their own job compared to that of another staff member perceived to be performing similar duties.

Advantages and disadvantages

Advantages

- the time of the job evaluation committee is used much more effectively in the initial benchmarking of jobs and final agreement on grades
- little time is required to evaluate jobs other than the benchmark ones
- consultancy time is kept to a minimum

- computer administration saves much time and effort on producing job descriptions
- fairness and objectivity with the use of standardized job descriptions
- employee participation is encouraged by job holders completing the WPS and in effect writing their own job description (subject to the validation interview conducted by the job analyst and agreed by the management)
- the job descriptions can be used for multifarious human resource applications.

Disadvantages
The fact that the scheme relies largely upon the inputs of staff rather than consultants does require a considerable degree of commitment from top management and the staff involved. This is as it should be, but everyone must be prepared to make the efffort.

Wyatt – The Employee Points Factor Comparison Method (EPFC)

History and development

This new variation on points rating was developed in 1978–79 by Wyatt Harris Graham (now the Wyatt Company UK Ltd). It is the product of a search for a method which is quantifiable, which avoids the problem encountered in some factor schemes of scoring jobs twice on the same factor, and yet which arrives at an integrated evaluation of jobs at all levels. Since such a scheme would provide an acceptable framework for the collection of comparative pay information, Wyatt devised the EPFC as a necessary preliminary to the establishment of their Remuneration Data Service (RDS). At that stage the scheme was not primarily intended for use by companies as a method of in-house job evaluation. Company 'in-house' adoption of the scheme came at the request of individual participants and is not a condition of membership of the RDS. The EPFC approach is essentially a factor-based points rating scheme which superficially, because of the use of detailed scoring charts, resembles elements of the Guide Chart-Profile Method.

Current components of the scheme

The EPFC method starts from a different point from most conventional job evaluation. It is based on the premise that since jobs cannot be carried out without people, why not measure them by reference to human characteristics, ie the demands the job makes on the people doing them? Employees have two attributes to offer in fulfilling the requirements of any job: knowledge and personal skills. Wyatt therefore base their scheme on a detailed analysis of these two dimensions as follows:

Knowledge
The axes on the chart for measuring knowledge are education and experience. The education breakdown measures the job holders' required store of knowledge that can only be gained by formal education or training. The experience analysis measures the knowledge and skills which cannot be gained by formal education or training but which are essential for satisfactory job performance. A section illustrating the knowledge chart is shown below. The full chart contains eight degrees of education and seven degrees of experience.

Skills
The axes for the chart measuring skills are mental aptitude, human relations skills and physical skills. The mental 'aptitude' elements

EDUCATION	I. Experience is limited to basic exposure to the routines of life. Little or no previous business or commercial experience required.			II. Jobs requiring work related experience to gain limited but specialised knowledge of machinery, processes, procedures and work routines.			III. Jobs requiring experience of a range of business procedures, specialised experience of complex industrial machinery or processes, or technical sufficiency in a specialised subject.		
A. Jobs requiring minimum formal education or general work training.	23 27 32	27 32 38	32 38 44	32 38 44	38 44 52	44 52 61	44 52 61	52 61 72	61 72 85
B. Jobs requiring either general schooling in a range of subjects, probably to 'O' level GCE standard, or specific training in one specialist subject or skill.	32 38 44	38 44 52	44 52 61	44 52 61	52 61 72	61 72 85	61 72 85	72 85 100	85 100 115
C. Jobs requiring a craft apprenticeship, City and Guilds, qualification or ONC.	44 52 61	52 61 72	61 72 85	61 72 85	72 85 100	85 100 115	85 100 115	100 115 132	115 132 152
D. Jobs which require either: general schooling in a wide range of subjects, probably to 'A' level GCE standard, or specialist training eg City and Guilds technical qualifications or HNC.	61 72 85	72 85 100	85 100 115	85 100 115	100 115 132	115 132 152	115 132 152	132 152 175	152 175 201

Figure F.4 *Section of a knowledge chart*

define the range of mental skills required and start from simple observance of limited rules governing basic tasks through various levels of analysis, decision-making and original thought. The human relations breakdowns define the levels of social skill required for effective job performance. Physical skills are scored against three levels from no special skills to highly developed skills. A section of the skills chart is illustrated below. The full chart contains six degrees for human relations and seven degrees for mental aptitude. This chart is more complex than the knowledge chart because it has to represent three factors rather than just two.

MENTAL APTITUDE	PHYSICAL SKILLS	I. No more than ordinary courtesy required.	II. Jobs requiring the serving of others, perhaps in answering queries from the public, explaining instructions, supervising a team on routine work or in circumstances requiring tact and diplomacy.	III. Understanding and serving people is important for supervising a small team on technical work or a larger team on routine work, explaining complex technical material or organising others outside the establishment.
A. Simple repetitive duties requiring no special mental skills. Job limits are defined by regulations and procedures and continuously available direction.	1 2 3	61 72 85 85 100 115 115 132 152	85 100 115 115 132 152 152 175 201	115 132 152 152 175 201 201 231 266
B. Routine duties requiring mental or visual concentration, attention to detail or simple analysis. Judgements are uninvolved and based upon standard instructions and procedures with readily available direction.	1 2 3	85 100 115 115 132 152 152 175 201	115 132 152 152 175 201 201 231 266	152 175 201 291 231 266 266 306 352
C. Jobs requiring mental alertness and concentration for controlling machinery or making judgements within well defined procedures and precedents, and with readily available advice.	1 2 3	115 132 152 152 175 201 201 231 266	152 175 201 201 231 266 266 306 352	201 231 266 266 306 352 352 405 465

Figure F.5 *Human relation skills chart*

For the purposes of comparison with the RDS the scheme divides into level or grades from 1, eg cleaner/janitor, to 24, eg international chief executive. Company structures vary from this pattern but are carefully cross checked by Wyatt for the purposes of salary comparisons on the data bank.

The evaluation process

Wyatt recommends that evaluations are based wherever possible on up-to-date job descriptions, although it is recognized that the design of these will in each case need to be consistent with the needs, goals and culture of the organization. Jobs should be evaluated where practicable by panels of four to six members (although larger groups may be necessary where wider representation is required) including representatives of different areas of the organization. All evaluation decisions should be recorded formally with a written justification of the score allotted to each job. Within this framework it is understood and accepted that no two organizations will want their job evaluation systems to be implemented in the same way, and Wyatt's approach is appropriately flexible. Wyatt prefer to use the method most suitable to an organization's culture. However, they insist that good records are the key to a fully supported job evaluation programme and full notes of both job details and the evaluations are kept as part of the programme.

Although there are as yet no instances of this scheme being used either on a union negotiated and/or participative basis Wyatt say there is no reason why the scheme could not be so operated in the future.

Salary data

Detailed six-monthly comparisons are provided for RDS participants. All participants also have access to the database at any time. Wyatt also produce regular surveys of specialist functions eg, pensions investment managers, office automation, engineering and sales personnel.

Advantages and disadvantages

Advantages

- the scheme is relatively easy to explain and use once the basic philosophy is accepted
- the use of standard charts greatly assists grading consistency

- it copes well with manual and technical jobs as well as the general range of clerical and administrative functions
- it avoids over-emphasis of the financial dimensions of any job
- it avoids double counting of evaluation factors
- it can be used internationally provided the education definitions are amended to fit local qualifications
- because 'in-house' EPFC gradings are allowed to differ or diverge from those given for the purposes of RDS participation, accurate job-for-job external pay comparisons are not affected by any bias or inconsistency in interested evaluations.

Disadvantages

- adoption of the scheme requires rejecting the traditionally used factors of responsibility/accountability
- because of this the differences in scoring of very top and lower level jobs may not appear large enough from those lower down to reflect real differences in job scope. This 'squeezing' can affect the scheme's credibility.

Commentary

Although Wyatt's consultants advise and assist companies with the implementation of in-house EPFC schemes, their principal task is the use of the scheme for pay comparisons. They do not therefore expect to have long-term involvement in scheme operation, maintenance, and audit unless this is specifically requested by clients.

Effective use of the scheme depends on accepting that the analysis of knowledge and skills successfully measures job scope and that the degrees given indicate satisfactorily the levels of responsibility and accountability involved. This is a concept which, Wyatt say, is fairly easy to explain to personnel professionals but more difficult for general management to accept. They also point out that although the 'squeeze' on scores for top level jobs does present problems, in their experience it still provides grade differences which reflect the true requirements of the jobs concerned except in the largest international companies.

The EPFC system has now been used for a number of years for matching jobs into the RDS survey database, over 300 organizations use it for this purpose. It is currently used by a small but growing number of companies as an internal evaluation system and levels of acceptance, particularly from employeees and their representatives, have been high. Wyatt has recently established a full-time job evaluation team in their London office to support EPFC as well as Multicomp and other job evaluation products.

Wyatt–MULTICOMP

Basis of the system

MULTICOMP was developed in the United States and is available in the UK from the Wyatt Company. It is described by them as a computerized, multiple-regression-based job evaluation system.

Components of the system

MULTICOMP uses a questionnaire, specially tailored to the needs of the organization, which is filled out by incumbents or their supervisors to create a comprehensive company database which measures how each job reflects the key factors which are specific to the organization.

Benchmark positions are selected and, using multiple regression analysis, MULTICOMP then evaluates questionnaire responses to develop a statistical model for each benchmark position. Mathematical relationships are then established between benchmark data and grades which enable benchmark jobs to be slotted into a grade structure.

Using what Wyatt calls the 'Electronic Devil's Advocate' feature the reasonableness of employee questionnaire responses are monitored by the computer against the benchmark jobs. Every answer is verified and invalid responses are flagged for further investigation. If the response in a questionnaire is verified as falling within acceptable limits, MULTICOMP calculates the grade appropriate to the job responsibilities.

Advantages and disadvantages

Advantages

- both qualitative and quantitative job information is tracked
- since all employees answer the same questions, the resulting database compares all jobs against the same dimensions
- because of the nature of the database, statistical analyses can be conducted to isolate the impact of specific variables on grades
- the approach is designed to adapt to rapid change and can be easily modified to account for new policy decisions, revised organizational values and continually changing job descriptions
- management and staff time is saved in producing job descriptions and sitting on job evaluation committees. Questionnaires are filled in, often by groups of employees at the same time under the guidance of consultants or analysts. The job evaluation committee is largely replaced by the computer.

Disadvantages

- MULTICOMP is a system with many attractive features but it is relatively new to the UK, although it is now being tested thoroughly in the UK environment.

Commentary

MULTICOMP's adaptability to a wide range of industries and operating environments gives management freedom to explore all the options with the help of the low cost, high speed and complete flexibility provided by today's technology. The questionnaire approach provides real opportunities for employees to get involved. The use of this and schemes like it in the United States is growing and the approach appears valid across both the private and public sectors.

Ernst and Young – Employment Relations: the decision band method (DBM)

History and development

DBM was devised by Dr T T Paterson who applied it in Africa and Europe. It has been applied extensively in the USA and Canada by Arthur Young Management Consultants. In 1981, Arthur Young acquired the world rights to implement DBM, DBM is available in the UK through Employment Relations Associates Ltd – part of Arthur (now Ernst and Young) Young (UK). DBM is a registered trademark.

DBM is derived from Dr Paterson's work on organizational theory and practice. As such it is an aid to organizational analysis as well as a job evaluation and pay determination method.

In common with many other job evaluation methods, DBM requires three stages: analysis of jobs, grading of jobs and pricing of jobs. DBM is a relatively simple method to implement.

Components of the scheme

A common characteristic of all jobs is that they are required to make and/or advise those making decisions. As such decision-making/advising can be used as a means of comparing jobs in an organization. The nature of the decision ranges from the most far-reaching decisions on policies to simpler decisions such as how fast to clean an area or key in data. Dr Paterson observed that there are six levels (termed bands) of decision-making/advice present within organizations. The bands for an end-means continuum, ie the higher band, sets the end for the next band etc. These six bands form the basic framework of the grading approach and incorporate various aspects of decision-making which are treated as separate factors in some other methods. Other factors such as skill are also considered as explained below.

The six bands are summarized below.

Band F – corporate policy-making decisions
Decisions that determine the scope, the direction, the overall goals of the total enterprise, subject to few constraints other than those imposed by law and/or economic conditions. These decisions take into consideration the functions of the enterprise. Such decisions also set the goals of the major functions and set the limits of the funds available to each and to the extent of their intended programmes. Band F decisions are of the kind made at Board or chief executive level.

Band E – programming decisions
Decisions on the means of achieving the goals (ends) established by Band E decisions – specifying goals for the constituent functions of these major functions, and allocating resources (facilities, people, money, materials) among these constituent functions in order to achieve the goals).

Band D – interpretive decisions
Decisions on the means of achieving the goals (ends) established by Band E decisions specifying what is to be done in lower bands, and deploying the allocated resources. If circumstances change, involving uncertainty of information or outcome, a Band D decision is required to establish what is to be done in similar circumstances in the future.

Band C – process decisions
Decisions on the means (selection of a process) of achieving the goals (ends) established by Band D decisions, subject to the limits imposed by the available technology and resources, and the constraints set at Band D. The selection of the process is a decision that must precede the carrying out of the operations that constitute the process. That is, the process decision specifies what is to be done at Band B.

Band B – operational decisions
Decisions on the carrying out of the operations of a process specified by a Band C decision. There is, within the limits set by the specific process, a choice as to how the operations are carried out, but not as to what operations constitute the process.

Band A – defined decisions
Decisions on the manner and speed of performing the elements of an operation. There is, within the limits set by the prescribed operation, a choice as to how the elements are performed, but not as to what elements constitute the operation.

The grading method

When each job has been analyzed, the jobs are then banded, graded and sub-graded, if appropriate. The need and the extent of sub-grading depends upon the nature and requirements of the organization. The three steps as shown in Figure F.6 are:

1. Banding: Each job is placed in an appropriate band.
2. Grading: Each band has an upper and lower division (termed grades). If a job has a co-ordinating responsibility for other jobs in the same band as itself, it is placed in the upper division, if not it is placed in the lower division.
3. Sub-grading: Degrees of job difficulty can be distinguished within the grades by comparing jobs on aspects such as diversity and complexity of tasks, need for special alertness, precision, technical or professional skills.

The grading steps are illustrated in Figure F.6. It does not mean that posts must appear in all the bands and grades. This will depend on the organization, eg Band E tasks are often undertaken by Band F postholders in small/medium-size organizations. In practice, it is often found that a maximum of three sub-grades are required for the lower grades of each band and two sub-grades for the higher grade.

The grading of jobs is usually undertaken by a group of managers and employees.

Pricing of jobs

DBM provides a method of comparing jobs throughout an organization and of providing an equitable pay structure. When it comes to determining the pay of a particular job, aspects such as market rates, abnormal working conditions are considered. These are not included at the grading stage because this would distort valid comparisons between jobs. Determination of pay for bands etc, is usually undertaken by an assessment group within the organizations, using the DBM pay curves for the organization as a guide to current and future action, treatment of anomalies etc.

Regular pay surveys are not provided by Arthur Young as many organizations have their own methods for collecting such information.

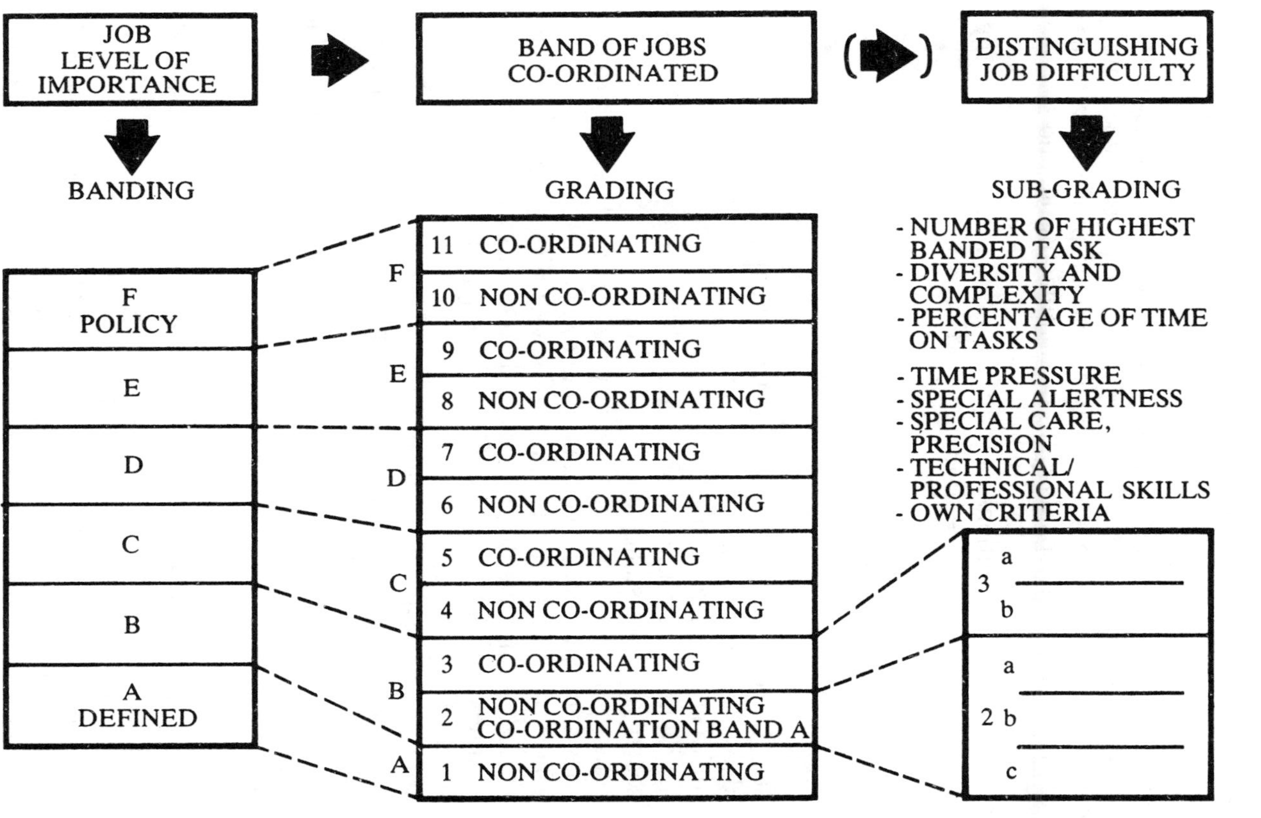

Figure F.6 *Decision banding method*

Special surveys will be undertaken or information provided from their resource centre on pay rates etc.

Coverage

Although use of the scheme is in its infancy in the UK its use is widespread elsewhere. In the US and Canada it has been successfully applied in local government, financial institutions, professional firms, research institutes, hospitals and in manufacturing and service industries. UK use may grow from the present handful, particularly among smaller organizations new to job evaluation who find the underlying concepts simple to understand.

Advantages and disadvantages

Advantages

- easy to understand and communicate even to those new to the idea of job evaluation
- relatively quick and easy to implement
- maintainable by the organization without dependence upon consultancy assistance
- benchmark jobs are unnecessary as each job is compared consistently against a common framework
- evaluation is concentrated on the analysis of work itself and may be less subjective than measuring responsibility, knowledge qualifications levels of contact and effort related to person specifications
- appropriate at all employment levels
- the scheme appears to cope better with evaluation of technical specialists than many factor-based points schemes
- ease of salary comparison between organizations using DBM who wish to pool data.

Disadvantages

- as yet no established track record of success in the UK – too new
- the primary criteria for grading is the decision-making/advisory content of each job. Other aspects of jobs are considered under sub-grading. The name and initial emphasis on decision-making means that explanations are needed for managers and employees to understand how other aspects are considered by this method.

Commentary

The number of Ernst and Young consultants trained in the philosophy and implementation techniques of DBM is growing. Use of the scheme is tied in with the consultancy's other related activities in the employee relations field. The company sees DBM as a valuable tool in the process of organization planning and control. DBM now appears to be a more accessible and practical approach than earlier commentators suggested and one which may have considerable value for first-time users of job evaluation looking for a simple relatively inexpensive scheme to implement.

Acceptability to trade unions is as yet unknown, but there are no obvious reasons why problems in this area should arise given Ernst and Young's emphasis on participative implementation.

Appendix G

Weighting Factors

If a points evaluation scheme has four factors, such as those mentioned in Chapter 5, and if it is decided that the maximum number of points is 100, the decision on how these points should be distributed between the factors – how they should be weighted – is a critical one. It could be decided that factors are equally important and that the maximum number of points for each factor should be the same. But it might be thought that one factor is much more important than the another. If, in these circumstances, it were decided that resources controlled should be allocated, say, 80 points and the remaining 20 points distributed between the other three factors, then the scheme is obviously going to favour staff with large budgets or numbers of people under them rather than the high powered specialist advisers. Either of these alternatives could be right, but it would be unwise to make such an assumption without testing it. This is why standard schemes with predetermined weightings should be used with care.

Weightings can be tested by trial and error. An initial assumption is made about the weighting based upon the preliminary analysis of the jobs and the jobs are evaluated accordingly by the points method. A separate paired comparison exercise is carried out to produce an overall ranking of the jobs. This overall ranking is compared with the ranking produced by the points scheme to determine the degree of correlation between them. The degree of correlation is a measure of the validity of the values or weightings assigned to the factors. Thus, if the paired comparison ranking list is replicated by the points score ranking list it could be assumed that the factor values are probably right. If there is little correlation between the two lists, the values are probably wrong. The degree to which the two lists match can be established by calculating the coefficient of correlation – a statistical formula which if it produces a result of +1 indicates a completely positive correlation while a result of −1 indicates a completely negative correlation. Values between these extremes indicate the degree of positive or negative correlation. Experience of using this technique has shown that a correlation of +0.75 is acceptable, given the inevitable limitations of the original data, although a result of +0.8 or more would be better. If the initial trial produces an unsatisfactory correlation, the weightings are readjusted until an acceptable figure is obtained.

This approach is clumsy and time consuming, especially if the initial assumptions are seriously out of line. A more sophisticated approach is to use the multiple regression analysis technique. Multiple regression analysis is defined as the statistical method for investigating the relationships between independent and dependent variables and obtaining a 'regression equation' for predicting the latter in terms of the former. In a factor weighting exercise the different factors are the independent variables for which points are assessed and added up for each of the jobs to produce the dependent variable of the overall rank order. A multiple regression analysis exercise consists of the following steps:

1. The whole jobs are ranked by paired comparisons. A computer can be used to calculate the rankings, especially if it is decided to increase the accuracy or acceptability of the results by using a number of different judges and reconciling their views for the final ranking.
2. Each factor is ranked separately for all the jobs by paired comparisons, again with the help of a computer.
3. The multiple regression analysis computer program then:
   (a) establishes the degree of correlation between each of the independent variables (the factors) and the dependent variable (the overall rank order)
   (b) ranks each factor in turn (starting with the factor with the highest correlation and finishing with the factor with the least correlation) and reconstructs the whole job ranking order by applying weightings to the ranking orders within the factors
   (c) tests the independent variables by measuring the correlations between them to establish the degree to which they separately contribute to producing the overall rank order (a very high correlation between two factors would suggest a high degree of overlap and might result in one of the factors being eliminated).

Thus multiple regression analysis can indicate which are the most significant factors and weight the degree to which they are significant. As a result, unnecessary factors can be dispensed with.

This is a sophisticated technique which will produce better results than relying on trial and error, as long as the initial assumptions about the overall rank order are correct. In this respect, the approach is somewhat specious. If the subjectively established overall rank order is wrong, what degree of confidence can be attached to the factor weightings? The method has a circular look about it, but it all depends on the degree to which care has been exercised in choosing and analyzing the benchmark jobs. This has to be done thoroughly to ensure that a soundly based scheme is developed for future use.

Appendix H

Computerized Job Evaluation

The need

Whatever basic measuring instrument is used, conventional job evaluation is usually carried out by a process involving:

- collection of data about jobs, typically in the form of job descriptions
- evaluation of jobs, using the selected method, by a group or committee of evaluators. The first stage is frequently the evaluation of a benchmark of jobs to enable the committee to set standards and reference points, against which to test further evaluations
- review of the overall relativities emerging from the evaluations.

Depending on the particular methodology chosen, this can give great sensitivity to individual job design, and thus enable the process to deal with a wide variety of job types. In addition it can yield additional benefits from the evaluation debate, such as input to organizational understanding and clarification.

The conventional process does, however, have a number of disadvantages which are being perceived with increasing acuteness as organizations become more restricted in the resources that they are able, and willing to devote to the process. These include:

- the time and resource needed for conventional job description preparation and committee evaluation
- the need for significant training of evaluators to enable them to operate effectively
- the difficulty in achieving consistency of standards when evaluation is devolved to multiple committees, and the extensive training and control processes which are needed to maintain consistency between committees.

These difficulties have led to the increasing perception that job evaluation is a bureaucratic and time-consuming activity – though it is important to recognize that the degree to which this is justified is a function of the process adopted for evaluation, not of the basic method of measurement itself.

Over the years, many attempts have been made to address these criticisms by more structured approaches to job evaluation. Thus, particularly for large job populations, a variety of techniques such as job matching to generic descriptions, and classification approaches have been used. While these methods gain significantly in speed over 'conventional' committee evaluation where each job is considered individually, they lose sensitivity to job differences because of the degree of 'force-fitting' which is inherent in them, as well as raising questions about equal value from which standpoint a fully analytical method is to be preferred.

In recent years, much effort has been devoted to developing computer-based systems aimed at combining high speed with high sensitivity, and thus addressing directly the criticisms of conventional job evaluation processes. Figure H.1 illustrates the balance between speed and sensitivity for alternative evaluation processes.

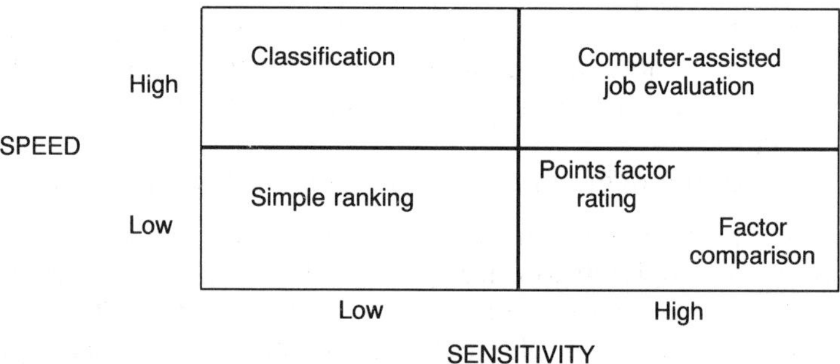

Figure H.1 *Alternative evaluation processes – the balance between speed and sensitivity*

Type of computer assistance

Ways in which computers can assist the process of job evaluation fall into two broad categories:

1. Software systems which support and improve the efficiency and consistency of conventional evaluation processes.
2. Approaches in which evaluations are computer-generated from questionnaire responses.

Within each of these categories, a number of possible approaches exist.

As with conventional job evaluation, a single 'packaged' process solution cannot satisfy the wide range of requirements of different organizations – nor in many cases the diverse needs of different job groups within an organization.

Factors influencing the choice of process include:

- The purpose of the exercise, and the use to which the results are to be put, for example, whether the requirement is purely for a simple grading result, or whether additional outputs or linkages are demanded.
- The scale and diversity of the job population to be covered.
- The resources and time constraints applying both to initial implementation and to maintenance.
- The requirements for communication of, or participation in the process, and the degree of devolution/decentralization needed.

Even within a single organization, consideration of these factors may well indicate the need for different processes to be applied to various job groups.

Thus for example there may be a large clerical and manual job population where the requirement is mainly for an efficient grading process; a group of professional specialists where pay and grading considerations are intimately linked to issues of competency and career development; and a small group of senior managers where a process is required which assists in the clarification of objectives and performance criteria.

For these reasons, computer assisted processes should:

- be capable of being designed to fit the specific organization and job group requirements;
- yield results which are compatible, whatever process options are selected;
- use flexible software capable of supporting, in an integrated way, a variety of processes.

These are the basic design principles which have guided the development and introduction of HayXpert by Hay Management Consultants.

HayXpert

HayXpert provides a powerful and flexible computer environment, in which a range of related and compatible approaches can be operated.

It is built around a high capacity, high speed database, which enables the storage, sorting and retrieval of job and related information, and is equipped with a full range of reporting and output facilities.

Within this environment, specific facilities enable both the provision of computer support to conventional job evaluation, and the use of questionnaire-based CAJE approaches.

Computer support to conventional job evaluation

Within this broad category, two facilities are provided:

1. QED Chart

This is an efficient on-line support tool for conventional evaluation processes using the Guide-Chart Profile technique. It provides a number of 'notepad' screens for recording evaluations, job information, evaluation notes and rationales, and if required, full job descriptions, enabling a 'paperless' evaluation process.

Computerized Guide Charts are incorporated with ratings matrix and logic built in.

During an evaluation, information on any comparator job which is in the database can be called up on to overlay screens, contributing greatly to consistency of standards. Similarly, listings of jobs and evaluations can be called up, sorted by evaluation factor, by job size, function, department, etc – depending on whatever code structure has been put in – enabling rapid 'sore-thumbing' and evaluation reviews. Figure H.2 illustrates a typical screen showing comparator job information.

A flexible report generator enables data to be output in whatever form is required, including the facility to produce organization charts. It is used by organizations who wish to retain the conventional evaluation process, but improve its speed, efficiency and consistency.

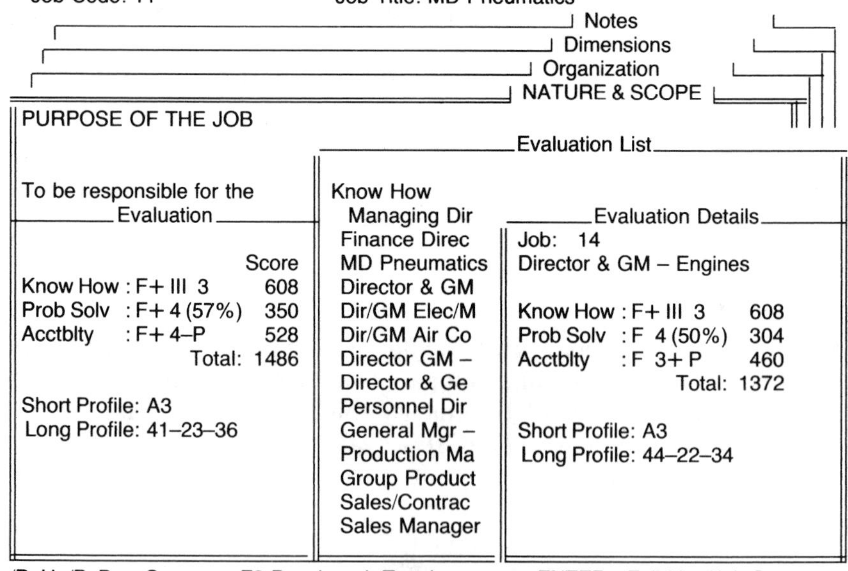

Figure H.2 *Screen from QED Chart showing overlays with comparator job information and listing*

2. QED comparison

This facility is to enable the rapid 'slotting' of large numbers of jobs into a pre-defined framework of benchmark jobs and factor level definitions. The first stage in its use is the evaluation of a benchmark of jobs in the conventional way.

The pattern of results which emerges is carefully analyzed to determine the way that some jobs and evaluations group together, while others are distinguished. From this, a framework of simplified 'slotting' factors and levels can be isolated, enabling rapid evaluation of all remaining jobs by direct comparison with both the slotting factors and the original benchmarks.

The software provides a split-screen facility, in which the factor levels are displayed on one side, with the corresponding benchmark jobs on the other, thus providing the user with the information needed to 'slot' other jobs by direct comparison. That is illustrated in Figure H.3.

Overlay screens can be called up to give more detailed information on the factor level definitions when needed. Similarly, because all the facilities of QED Chart are incorporated, full data on any bench-mark job (or any other job in the database) can be called up to test the slotting, and all the sorethumbing and reporting facilities can be used.

Because the slotting factors can be expressed in plain English rather than evaluation jargon, and can be made highly specific to the organization, it enables extensive devolution of the process to involve line managers with little job evaluation knowledge, but detailed job knowledge.

QED Comparison is typically used for relatively large populations of jobs where the main reason for evaluation is grading, and where a very rapid, simple process is required.

Questionnaire-based techniques

While the above techniques provide computer support and assistance to the evaluation process, questionnaire-based CAJE techniques take this a stage further by:

- gathering job data in structured, quantitative form through a questionnaire
- processing the questionnaire data through a computer-based algorithm to yield, directly, an evaluation result.

Clearly, such approaches offer major advantages over conventional evaluation in terms of process efficiency, because they:

- eliminate the need for the time-consuming process of job description preparation

Job code: 00030 Job title: SR PROJECT ENG

Level description		Code	Reference job
O Manager of a more complex dept. An advanced professional with sufficient technical expertise to be called upon as consultant or for very complex assignments.		00029 00030 00031 00033 00034	BUSINESS SYSTEMS MGR SR PROJECT ENGR MIS MGR FINANCIAL REPORT MGR QUALITY STANDARDS MGR
N Basic level manager of a department. A professional with a thorough knowledge of a technical or specialized area.		00032 00035 00036 00037 00038	SR TECH SLS REP PRODUCTION MGR MATERIALS MANAGER SENIOR CHEMIST SENIOR RES CHEMIST
M Basic level manager of a specialized skill. A journey level professional (i.e. fully qualified) in a non-technical area.		00041 00045 00047 00048 00049	TERRITORY SALES MGR TECH SERV ENGINEER TECH SALES REP MGR DIST COST CONTROL TERRITORY SALES MGR

GRADE: 11 FACTOR: Know-How 304
ESCAbort F2 Slot Change F6 Confirm F8 Zoom F10 Menu
PgUp, DgDnMove F3 Benchmark F7 Exit F9 Evaluation Status

Figure H.3 *Screen from QED Comparison showing part of a slotting factor scale with reference jobs for each level*

- replace the evaluation committee for the bulk of its work by computer processing;
- yield high consistency of results, enabling devolution of the process without the need for heavyweight bureaucratic control mechanisms, or extensive training programmes.

HayXpert provides for two different approaches to questionnaire techniques, designed to satisfy differing requirements.

Universal questionnaire

This is the approach designed for the evaluation of most jobs in an organization quickly and efficiently, using a single instrument in questionnaire format. The questionnaire is tailored to meet the specific needs of the organization and/or job group, and the algorithm is specifically built to reproduce the value standards of the organization. This is accomplished through the following process stages:

1. Having defined the job population to be covered, a representative benchmark sample of jobs is selected.
2. The benchmark jobs are then evaluated, using the Guide Chart Profile Method, in the conventional way. This step enables the organization to set its value standards and relativities, on which to base the computer algorithm.

3. An appropriate questionnaire is then developed, selecting and devising questions to elicit the necessary information about jobs, and building level descriptions for each question. A typical extract from a questionnaire is shown in Figure H.4.
4. The questionnaire is completed for each benchmark job, and a mathematical algorithm built to relate the questionnaire responses to the evaluated job size.
5. Following testing and refinement, the algorithm is then programmed into HayXpert.
6. Evaluations for subsequent jobs can then be generated by completing the questionnaire and processing through the computer – either interactively or by batch processing from paper questionnaires.

IMPACT ON EXTERNAL CONTACTS. To what degree is the job accountable for establishing and/or maintaining (customers, suppliers, consultants, public administrators, etc.).

2. . . .
3. collecting/exchanging information, making or responding to inquiries.
4. . . .
5. ensuring or controlling the delivery of standard or well-defined products or services (for example, follow up of orders, collecting receivables, reordering of supplies or raw material, providing maintenance services, inside sales, etc.).
6. . . .

F1-Help F2-Comments F3-Goto F4-Previous F5-Next F7-Quit F9-Footer F10-Header

Figure H.4 *Part of a typical Questionnaire factor on screen*

While the above sequence describes the main 'technical' steps involved, the application process needs careful design to meet the organization's requirements and yield high quality results. Issues requiring particular attention are listed below:

- What is the process for completing and reviewing the questionnaire – job holder, supervisor, HR specialist, or a combination of these?
- What is the application process? Is the computer to be used as a tool by evaluators, or is it to be the primary process, subject only to quality assurance reviews?
- Quality Assurance (QA) checks. The software itself contains sophisticated checking procedures for flagging up apparent inconsistencies within a questionnaire as illustrated in Figure H.5, but no electronic checks can identify consistent over- or under-stating of a job. QA processes for the review of input data and of output results need to be designed and implemented
- Communication and participation. Universal Questionnaire

offers the potential for much greater devolution and involvement in the process than conventional evaluation, but this opportunity can be lost if it is seen as a 'black box', mechanistic approach. Careful design of the development and implementation processes is needed to ensure that full advantage is taken of this potential.

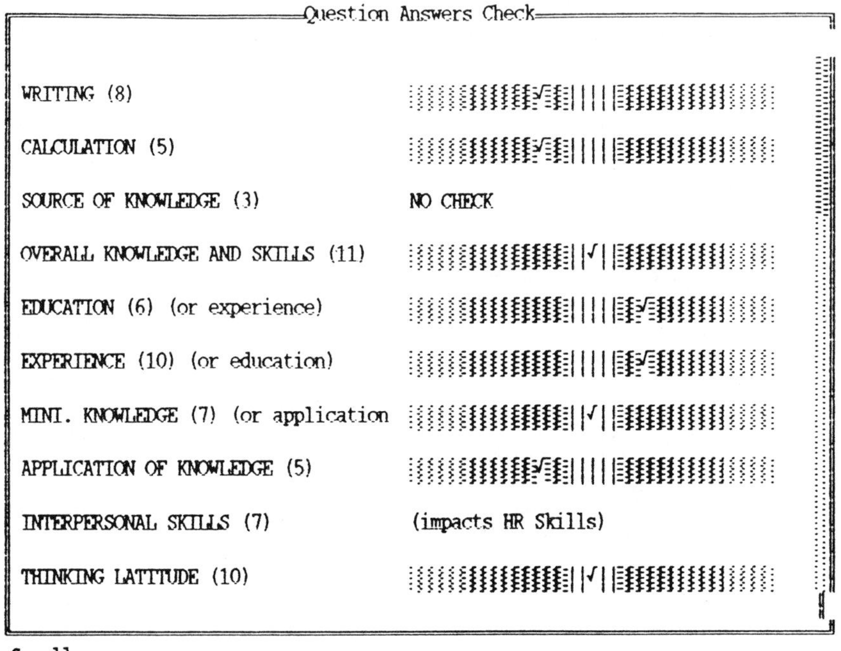

Figure H.5 *QA validation screen showing variance of question responses from expected*

Job family questionnaire

Within many organizations there exist significant groups of jobs which are linked by a commonality of purpose or nature, and where a much more focused approach is required, tailored to the specific needs of that group.

Such groups – Job Families – may be linked by the nature of work undertaken (eg a clerical family), by a professional or technical discipline (eg scientists, engineers), by a common function (eg production management), or may be essentially the same job existing at different levels (eg branch bank managers).

Within such a family, there will be many common factors – these are what make them a family – but jobs will be distinguished by quite specific differentiating factors.

The process of Job Family Modelling concentrates on identifying these differentiating factors and basing questionnaires directly upon them.

In this way, questionnaires can be developed which are short, output oriented and sharply focused on the particular jobs in question. They can be developed in conjunction with members of the family itself, and the questionnaires can be expressed in language familiar to the family.

The technique provides clear links between job evaluation and related HR processes such as career development, performance management and competency analysis, and for these reasons is particularly valuable in environments where the traditional job/person separation is a difficult one – for example, technical/professional hierarchies.

In outline, the process involves the following steps:

1. Definition of the scope of the family and understanding of the range and levels of jobs to be covered.
2. Evaluation of a representative sample of jobs, using conventional Guide Chart process.
3. Identification, in conjunction with members of the family, of the critical differentiating factors.
4. Building of scales and level descriptions for each factor, and presentation of these in questionnaire form.
5. Rating of the benchmark jobs against the factor scales.
6. Development, testing and refinement of an algorithm to enable job size to be predicted from questionnaire responses.
7. Programming into HayXpert.
8. Designing the implementation process, involving similar considerations to those described for Universal Questionnaire.

Particular characteristics of the HayXpert approach

All the facilities described above are contained within the same computer environment, and all are underpinned by the same basic scale of job measurement ratings. Hence evaluation process options can be combined to meet the diverse needs of complex organizations, with consistent results. For example, a Job Family Questionnaire might be applied to a major group of core jobs, with a Universal Questionnaire for the bulk of jobs in other areas. Benchmarks for both of these could be stored in the QED database, while one-off jobs might be dealt with by traditional evaluation.

Underpinning by the Hay Guide Chart Profile Method has two further important implications.

1. It is acknowledged as the world's leading job measurement methodology, and is sufficiently flexible to enable the organization's

values to be fully reflected in the algorithms which are built. All questionnaire-based CAJE approaches require an initial rating or ranking of jobs in order to provide the basic values on which to base the algorithm: this is known as the dependent variable. There are major advantages in using the Guide Chart Profile Method to provide the dependent variable when compared with alternatives which are proxies for job size, for example current grade or pay, or market pay. There are clear weaknesses inherent in these alternatives: using current grade or pay presents difficulties if the object of the exercise is to develop new pay and grading structures because the old ones are deficient; use of market pay requires periodic changes to the algorithm as market relativities change.

2. It provides access to the extensive Hay remuneration databases, which use Hay job size as the basis for analysis and comparison.

Additional features of HayXpert

This description has concentrated on the job evaluation capabilities of HayXpert, but the software also includes facilities for job pricing and salary administration, and for job competency analysis questionnaires, thus enabling much greater integration between these related HR processes than was previously possible.

Computer-assisted job evaluation and HayXpert – summary

For job evaluation to serve its purpose within an organization, it must reflect that organization's values and requirements, and must be seen to do so by both managers and employees. CAJE approaches which are viewed as a 'black box' will not achieve this objective. It is sometimes claimed that CAJE methods eliminate the need for human judgement in the evaluation process. They do not, neither should they seek to. What they do provide is the means of capturing and clarifying the organization's judgements and values about jobs, and reproducing these in a consistent way. Viewed in this light, it is clear that they can provide enormous advances in terms of the efficiency of the job evaluation process and the reduction in the bureaucracy so often associated with traditional processes.

But as with traditional methods, the process must be designed to meet the particular demands and constraints of the user organization. HayXpert has been designed to provide the flexibility and range of approaches needed to satisfy this requirement.

Link Group Consultants Limited – The George computerized job evaluation system

The operation and maintenance of a job evaluation scheme embraces a number of important activities, ie:

- scoring and grading of jobs
- maintenance of an up-to-date rank order
- maintenance of accurate evaluation records
- regular audit of job description within grades
- comparative audits of the grade distribution of jobs within various functions or divisions
- monitoring of the structure for grade drift
- consistency checks on evaluation by different analysts or assessment teams.

Without regular monitoring and audits, inconsistencies creep in and the scheme starts to decay. Such tasks, however, are time consuming and require the allocation of scarce personnel resources to keep on top of them. The George computer program is designed to make job evaluation maintenance simple, quick and highly efficient and gives management the initiative in controlling its job evaluation schemes.

System overview

The system is designed so that users can configure it for their own job evaluation scheme without any outside help. It will accommodate any type of factor based scheme, no matter how complicated the scoring system or grading structure.

As well as job evaluation information, other relevant information about the job can be included, eg department, division, function, location, salary etc.

Entry of job evaluation data is simplified by using predefined entries. For example, all the department titles or site locations can be pre-entered. Once entered, the system scores the job under each factor, applies weights if appropriate, determines the total job score, grades it and displays it at the correct point in the rank order.

If at some later point in time it is felt necessary to change the number of grade lines or the factor weights, this can be performed through the set-up program.

Features of the system

1. Interrogation

Full details of any job, together with its evaluation line, grade and score can be found and displayed instantly, with print-outs available if required.

2. Search and sort

Any group of jobs can be searched for and sorted depending on specified criteria, eg all the accounting jobs within a salary range of £15,000 to £30,000 based in London, Birmingham and Bristol.

Alternatively, the search and sort facilities can be used to monitor consistency of assessment, eg display all jobs which were placed in Factor Level 4 for Responsibility.

3. Audits

Because the job evaluation rank order is up to date and all information is instantly accessible, it is possible to carry out any form of audit the user wishes, eg distribution of jobs and people across the grade structure, comparative spread of jobs by function, location or division.

It is possible to check on whether one analyst assesses more tightly than another.

In a decentralized scheme the consistency with which one division assesses its jobs compared with others can be monitored.

4. Statistics

A range of statistics is available, such as the number of jobs in each grade, spread of jobs above and below the mid-point, average salary in grade, spread of salaries within grade.

5. Salary information

Salary information about each job holder can be entered and either displayed or kept hidden as required. Based on this, the salary structure can be interrogated and analyzed using the search and sort facilities.

A further feature is the facility to transport data to a spreadsheet program and produce a salary curve for all or any part of the job population. This is a useful monitoring tool and can be used when making market comparisons.

6. Job details

George provides five standard fields common to all job populations – job title, date, salary, benchmark and number in job. An additional seven fields can then be defined to capture the information relevant to the scheme.

In addition to the fields described, three lines of text are available to record comments.

7. Job profiles

George can accommodate schemes with up to 15 different factors. For each factor of the scheme the accepted values are defined, whether they be:

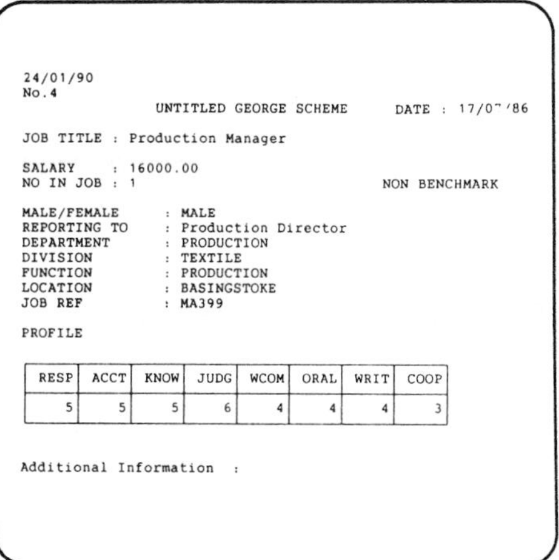

24/01/90
No.4

UNTITLED GEORGE SCHEME   DATE : 17/0[illegible]'86

JOB TITLE : Production Manager

SALARY : 16000.00
NO IN JOB : 1   NON BENCHMARK

MALE/FEMALE : MALE
REPORTING TO : Production Director
DEPARTMENT : PRODUCTION
DIVISION : TEXTILE
FUNCTION : PRODUCTION
LOCATION : BASINGSTOKE
JOB REF : MA399

PROFILE

RESP	ACCT	KNOW	JUDG	WCOM	ORAL	WRIT	COOP
5	5	5	6	4	4	4	3

Additional Information :

24/01/90
No.4

UNTITLED GEORGE SCHEME

Complete rank order

		RESP	ACCT	KNOW	JUDG	WCOM	ORAL	WRIT	COOP	SCORE	GRADE
1	Marketing Manager	5	6	6	6	4	5	4	4	133.0	G11
2	Personnel Manager	6	5	6	5	5	3	4	4	128.5	G10
3	Production Manager	5	5	5	6	4	4	4	3	120.5	G10
4	Advertising Manager	5	5	5	6	4	4	4	3	120.5	G10
5	R&D Manager	5	5	8	4	4	2	3	2	119.5	G9
6	Sales Manager	5	5	6	5	4	3	4	2	117.5	G9
7	Distribution Manager	5	5	4	5	5	4	4	4	116.5	G9
8	Engineering Manager	5	5	5	5	5	4	2	3	115.5	G9
9	Chief Engineer	4	4	5	4	4	3	4	2	101.0	G8
10	Personnel Asst	4	3	4	3	4	5	5	5	100.5	G8
11	EXAMPLE JOB	4	4	4	4	3	3	4	5	99.0	G7
12	Transport Coordinatr	4	5	4	4	4	2	3	3	97.5	G7
13	Project Controller	4	4	4	4	4	3	3	2	94.0	G7
14	Warehousing Supervsr	5	4	4	3	2	3	3	5	94.0	G7
15	Engineer	3	3	4	4	3	4	3	5	91.5	G7
16	Warehouse Controller	4	5	3	3	3	3	3	3	87.5	G6
17	Materials Supervisor	4	4	4	3	3	2	3	2	85.0	G6
18	Advertising Asst	3	3	3	3	4	4	3	4	83.5	G6
19	Asst Engineer	2	3	4	4	3	3	2	4	81.5	G6
20	Salesperson	3	4	3	4	2	5	2	2	81.0	G6

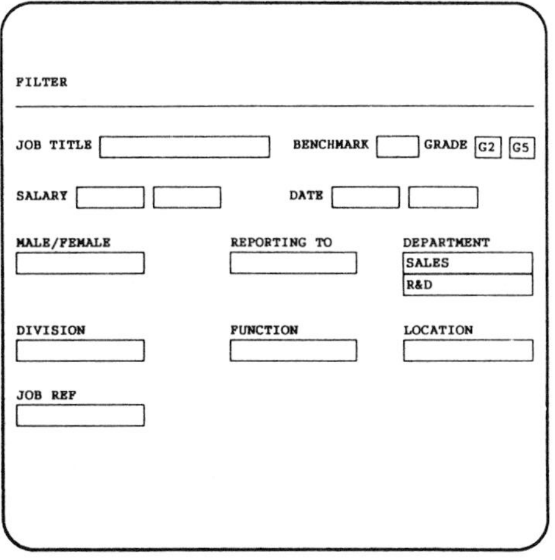

FILTER

JOB TITLE [ ]   BENCHMARK [ ]   GRADE [G2] [G5]

SALARY [ ] [ ]   DATE [ ] [ ]

MALE/FEMALE [ ]   REPORTING TO [ ]   DEPARTMENT [SALES] [R&D]

DIVISION [ ]   FUNCTION [ ]   LOCATION [ ]

JOB REF [ ]

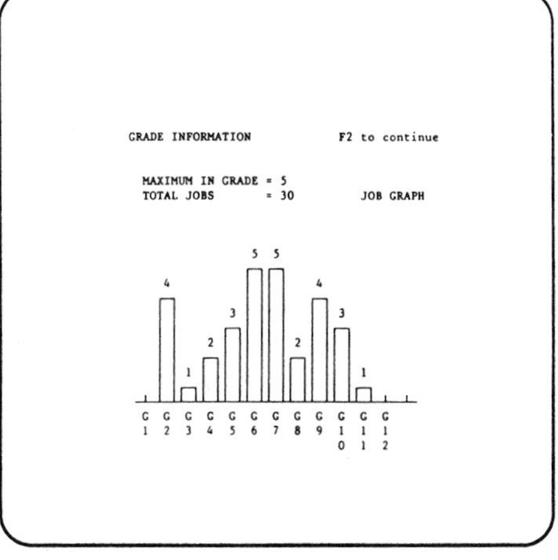

Figure H.6 *Four sample 'George' screens*

- levels (1, 2, 3 etc)
- pre-weighted point scores (15, 25, 55 etc)
- a range (1–200).

In addition, the weights to be applied to factor values can be specified to achieve a weighted points score. Once defined, George allows the user to enter job profiles quickly and accurately.

Sample screens

Figure H.6 shows examples of four screens.

Link Group Consultants Ltd: the 'Jeeves' computerised system

The Jeeves system is tailor-made to assist in the whole process of evaluating jobs rather than simply administering the evaluation scheme, which is what 'GEORGE' does.

Jeeves is an expert system shell which can be tailored to any analytical job evaluation scheme. An expert system shell is a form of computer program into which can be entered a body of expertise in the form of 'rules' which enable decisions to be made on the basis of factual information presented to the computer.

Jeeves assumes that each scheme will have:

- weighted factors
- a demand scale or a matrix for each factor eg points, levels, degrees
- assessment standards for each factor which guide evaluators to the correct rating of jobs; these may take the form of benchmark jobs and/or level definitions.

It also requires that there will be adequate information available on benchmark jobs in the form of job descriptions and factor information.

The rationale behind the Jeeves system is that in every analytical job evaluation scheme there must be clear and discernible reasons why jobs have been placed in the various degree or demand levels of each factor. Indeed if there were no apparent reasons or 'rules', the job evaluation system could not function in a consistent manner. At the same time the system recognises that the 'rules' may be both detailed and complex.

In essence Jeeves has been so constructed that:

1. the evaluation 'rules' can be defined both qualitatively and/or quantitatively;
2. the rules can be enshrined in the system shell;

```
JOB TITLE  : EXAMPLE                          JOB NUMBER : 1
DEPARTMENT : ENGINEERING                      DATE : 10/05/89
JOB HOLDER : John Smith                       ASSESSORS  : AN,NT

                    R E S P O N S I B I L I T Y              page 8/8

Are there major areas of the job where the job holder is expected to sort
things out for himself/herself y/n? y

Please indicate the areas where the job holder is REQUIRED to decide
courses of action without prior reference to supervision:

* PLAN/ORGANISE WORK              RECTIFY ALL FAULTS/JOB PROBS (WITH ASSTNCE)
* DECIDE WORK PRIORITIES          RECTIFY ALL UNRESOLVED FAULTS/PROBS
  MAKE QUALITY DECISIONS          RECOMMEND CHANGES/MODIFICATION
  MAKE MACHN/PLANT ADJUSTMNT      REPAIR MACHINERY/PLANT EQUIPMENT
  RECTIFY SIMPLE FAULTS/PROBS

     Use UP/DOWN arrows to move between selections and <Enter> to choose
                      Press <Esc> to EXIT
```

```
JOB TITLE  : EXAMPLE                          JOB NUMBER : 1
DEPARTMENT : ENGINEERING                      DATE : 10/05/89
JOB HOLDER : John Smith                       ASSESSORS  : AN,NT

                    R E S P O N S I B I L I T Y              page 6/8

Is there an ESSENTIAL need for working carefully and/or accurately
because of the nature of the job y/n? y

If yes, indicate the main reason(s) and whether the responsibiltity is:
                Exercised every shift - <F> (Full Time)
                On a Rota Basis       - <P> (Part time)
By pressing the appropriate key :  <F> or <P>

* ACHIEVE OUTPUT TARGET                     f    SAFEGUARD OTHER PEOPLE
  ACHIEVE MATERIALS YIELD TARGET
  MAINTAIN PRODUCT QUALITY
  MAINTAIN M/C / PLANT EFFICIENCY
  PREVENT ERRORS IN RECORDS/DOCUMENTATION

     Use UP/DOWN arrows to move between selections and <Enter> to choose
                      Press <Esc> to EXIT
```

1. Typical Information Input Screens

```
JOB TITLE  : EXAMPLE                          JOB NUMBER : 001
DEPARTMENT : Factory Department               DATE : 20/04/89
JOB HOLDER : John Smith                       ASSESSORS  :

                          M A I N   M E N U

 PLEASE SPECIFY CHOICE FROM LIST OF OPTIONS

    DISPLAY REPORT                  BENCHMARK COMPARISON
    DISPLAY PROFILE               * VIEW ALL JOBS
    PRINT REPORT                    BEGIN NEW JOB
    PRINT PROFILE                   QUIT
    REPEAT A FACTOR

 Enter PROFILE Password : ******

     Use UP/DOWN arrows to move between selections and <Enter> to choose
                      Press <Esc> to EXIT
```

DEMONSTRATION HOURLY PAID JOB EVALUATION SCHEME : JOB PROFILES

JOB TITLE	RE	KN	WC	JU	PD	CM	WE	WTD	GRADE
1 FITTER	5	5	5	5	4	4	5		H
2 ELECTRICIAN	5	5	5	5	4	4	5		H
3 SECTION MECHANIC, MAKING	4	4	4	4	2	3	3		G
4 TRAINING INSTRUCTOR	4	3	3	3	2	4	2		F
5 DRIVER	4	3	3	3	4	3	3		F
6 COOK	4	4	3	3	2	2	3		F
7 SENIOR ENG. STOREKEEPER	3	3	3	3	2	4	2		E
8 DRIER OPERATOR	3	2	3	3	3	2	3		D
9 FILLER PREPARATION OPERATOR	2	2	2	2	2	2	3		C
10 ASSISTANT COOK	2	2	2	2	2	2	3		C
11 SEWING ROOM ATTENDANT	2	2	2	2	1	2	1		C
12 PACKING MATERIAL SUPPLIER	2	1	2	2	3	2	3		C
13 TRADESMAN'S HELPER	2	1	2	2	4	1	5		C

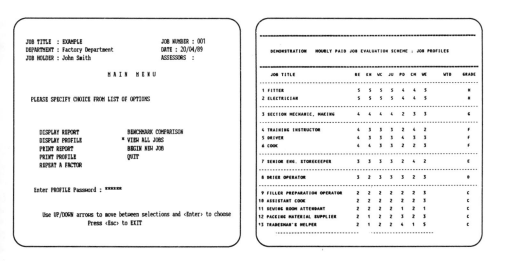

2. Main Menu showing JEEVES facilities **3. Printout of Rank Order by Grade**

Figure H.7 *Three sample 'Jeeves' screens*

3. the computer can be programmed to ask sufficient questions about each factor to enable it to apply the evaluation rules;
4. when the job information has been entered the computer can apply the rules and determine the factor score.

Once the system has been set up Jeeves will therefore consistently apply the rules each time and produce an evaluated score for a factor.

By also entering factor weights and grade line positions to the system, Jeeves can go on to:

- score the job
- grade the job
- sort it into position in the rank order
- store the job information entered in the form of a Factor Analysis.

Sample screens for Jeeves are given in Figure H.7.

Other major market contenders in the area of CAJE are:

- WJQ from Towers Perrin Forster and Crosby,
- Compmaster from Mercer Fraser,
- Equate from KPMG Peat Marwick Human resources consultants.

For contact addresses see Bibliography.

Appendix I

Job Analysis Questionnaire

Job analysis interview

1. Has the purpose of the interview been fully explained?
2. Does the job holder understand what is involved – how the interview will proceed, how the job description will be drafted, checked, signed and countersigned by job holder/immediate superior?
3. Will questions be asked in a sequence which appears sensible to the job holder and from a list which follows the format of the job description?
4. Is it possible to agree the statement of the purpose of the job straight away – or will it be easier to pin this down after going through the main tasks?
5. Has the job holder been encouraged to be rigorous and fair to herself/himself in describing all aspects of the job?
6. Are the statements that emerge specific – so that they neither exaggerate or underplay the importance of the job?
7. Have leading questions (the tendency to put words in to the mouths of job holders) been carefully avoided?

Job description check-list

Job title

1. Does the current job title properly reflect the level and function of job involved? Does it relate sensibly to other jobs at a similar level elsewhere in the organization? Has it been at all inflated as a gesture (especially in their sales/service area) to an external market which prefers to deal with a 'director', 'executive', 'manager' or 'supervisor' when in reality a more junior role is all that is needed?

Direct reporting relationships

2. Is the job holder's immediate superior's job title clear?
3. Is the reporting relationship unambiguous?

4. Are there line/specialist implications (eg in 'matrix' organizations where there are both line managers and those responsible for professional/specialist quality maintenance)?
5. Are the job titles and numbers of staff reporting directly to the job holder fully listed?

Purpose of the job

6. Are the following clear:
   (a) why the job is needed?
   (b) the key role of the job holder?
   (c) the contribution made towards achieving the organization's objectives and those of the function/department/unit in which the individual works?
7. Do these points emerge logically from the list of main tasks which give more detail on the job holder's day-to-day activities?

Description of main tasks

8. Does the list prioritise tasks?
9. Is each main task covered separately?
10. Which of the following methods is used to list tasks:
    (a) frequency with which they occur
    (b) order of importance
    (c) chronological order in relation to the management process of the organization/function.
11. Does the description of each task start with an active verb (eg supervizes, monitors, ensures, controls, liaises, writes, checks) to describe actual responsibilities in each area?
12. Are all unnecessary words avoided so that the nature of each task is clear and unambiguous?
13. Are quantitative illustrations given where these would be helpful to the evaluation panel?
14. Is it clear why each task has to be fulfilled?
15. Can the job be analyzed in relation to the scheme's factors from this description, eg in terms of:
    (a) level of authority and freedom to make decisions
    (b) the range, variety and complexity of tasks
    (c) requirements for creativity and/or complex problem solving skills
    (d) the resources controlled – typically in terms of:
        – staff by job level
        – annual budget
        – value of assets

- sales turnover
- production through put
- floor space.

(e) the experience, knowledge and skills required for:
- professional/technical aspects of the work and the analytical requirements that emerge from these
- people management/supervision
- contacts both within the organization and outside
- written or spoken communications
- computer literacy (in non-IT jobs)
- selling/marketing/commercial activities.

(f) the contacts made – inside and outside the organization

NB: Even where an analytical approach is not being used, attention to these areas is important to ensure full understanding of the job and fair evaluation.

Appendix J

Job Analysis Check list

1. *Knowledge and skills*
   (a) are there any professional or technical qualifications which the job holders *must* possess or it is *desirable* that they possess?
   (b) is there any training that job holders *must* undergo to carry out their job? If so, how long does the training last?
   (c) can job holders acquire the necessary skills and knowledge by experience alone? If so, what sort of experience is required and how much?
   (d) can you give examples of the type and level of knowledge or skills that have to be exercised in each of the job holder's main areas of responsibility?
2. *Responsibility*
   (a) how does this job contribute to achieving the results required from the section, department, unit or organization?
   (b) how easy, or difficult, is it to detect errors?
   (c) what effect could any errors made by the job holder have on the results obtained in the section, department, unit or organization?
   (d) what resources does the job holder control, eg people, finance, equipment, materials, property?
   (e) how much control does the job holder exercise over these resources?
   (f) how difficult is it for the job holder to exercise a proper degree of control?
3. *Decisions*
   (a) to what extent are the job holder's tasks routine?
   (b) how much guidance is available to the job holder on what needs to be done and on how to deal with problems? What form does that guidance take?
   (c) how much supervision is exercised over the job holder?
   (d) on what sort of matters does the job holder have to obtain prior permission from his or her superior before taking action?
   (e) to what extent is the thinking required patterned (ie follows a well-defined course with very little variation)?

(f) to what extent does the job holder have to exercise judgement, initiative and creativity in making decisions?

4. *Complexity*
   (a) what is the range of different tasks that have to be carried out, decisions to be made or problems to be solved?
   (b) to what extent are the differences between these tasks significant in the sense that different skills or knowledge have to be applied or different types of judgement have to be exercised in dealing with any issues that arise?
   (c) what is the variety of skills used by the job holder?
   (d) What is the range and variety of the contacts that the job holder has to make with subordinates, colleagues and individuals or bodies outside the organization?
5. *Contacts*
   (a) what contacts are made by the job holder within and outside the organization?
   (b) what is the level of contacts made?
   (c) how frequently are contacts made?
   (d) to what extent are the contacts dealing with routine matters or significant issues?
   (e) to what extent does the job require out of the ordinary courtesy, tact, persuasive skills or negotiating ability?

Appendix K

Job Analysis Form

<table>
<tr><td>JOB TITLE</td><td>NAME</td></tr>
<tr><td>DEPARTMENT</td><td>SECTION</td></tr>
<tr><td colspan="2">RESPONSIBLE TO</td></tr>
<tr><td colspan="2">RESPONSIBLE TO JOB HOLDER (attach organization chart if appropriate)</td></tr>
<tr><td colspan="2">NATURE AND SCOPE
Describe the nature and scope of the job, indicating in broad terms what the job holder does and amount of responsibility he or she has.

continue overleaf if necessary</td></tr>
</table>

OVERALL PURPOSE Describe as succinctly as possible (one or two sentences) the overall purpose of the job, i.e. what, in general terms the job holder is expected to achieve.
KEY RESULT AREAS Specify the key result areas (not more than 10, each described in one sentence beginning with an active verb) which govern the achievement of the overall purpose of the job.
1.
2.
3.
4.
5.
6.
7.
8.
9.
10.

FACTOR ANALYSIS By reference to the job analysis questionnaire, describe the characteristics of the job with regard to each of the 5 job evaluation factors.
1 KNOWLEDGE AND SKILLS
2 RESPONSIBILITY
3 DECISIONS
4 COMPLEXITY
5 CONTACTS

* Job analysis carried out by (signed) .... Date ....
* Agreed by job holder (signed) .... Date ....
* Agreed by job holder's manager (signed) .... Date ....

Appendix L

Example of a job description

Job description

Job title:

Works manager

Responsible to:

Production director

Responsible to him/her:

- production superintendent
- production controller
- chief inspector
- personnel officer.

Main role

- To achieve agreed budgets, quality standards and delivery requirements by the efficient control of manufacturing operations, by developing and maintaining good labour relations and by ensuring that his/her staff work together as a team.

Main activities

Plans

- Develops manufacturing plans and budgets in line with estimated market demands and ensures that production capacity, equipment and labour are available to achieve agreed output and foreseeable additional demands.

Development

- Continually seeks to improve production methods and techniques and to this end makes full use of company engineering research and development services.

Operations

- Maintains close liaison with company production control to ensure economic loading on the works and to progress availability of supplies
- Ensures that production scheduling fulfils its objectives of meeting programmed delivery dates, minimizing wastage and downtime and optimizing stock levels
- Ensures that all production operations are progressed and the distribution department is informed of expected departures from programmed delivery dates
- Maintains the security of the works and all property, stocks and other assets within it and takes suitable precautions against fire
- Maintains in good order the works and the equipment in it.

Personnel

- Ensures that the works organization is the most appropriate for achieving company objectives
- Recruits, trains and develops effective personnel to meet present and future needs
- Implements company personnel policies and national agreements
- Maintains sound labour relations and morale.

Control

- Develops an effective reporting system on works performance and directs a continuous programme of monitoring productivity, quality and costs.
- Ensures that corrective action is taken where required to meet budgets and standards and reports deviations outside agreed control limits to the production director.

Job analysis

Job title:

Works manager

Resources controlled:

- Assets: £765,000
- Turnover: £3,100,000
- Personnel: 750

Decisions

- The basic production technologies are determined by the company engineering department. The works manager is simply concerned with ensuring that the equipment operates as specified and that it is maintained properly. He/she can introduce changes to meet special requirements but these are minor modifications which do not affect the basic technology and can be installed within one or two days by maintenance craftsman
- The overall production programme and quality and cost standards are laid down at company level. The works manager, however, has complete authority to schedule production within the works
- Buying is conducted centrally but the works manager is responsible for ensuring that stocks are maintained at the minimum level required to maintain an economic production flow and an agreed standard of customer service
- The works manager has authority to spend on revenue items within the agreed annual company budget. Capital expenditure has to be authorized by the production director
- The works manager has complete authority to recruit, discipline and, where necessary, dismiss hourly and weekly paid staff in accordance with company personnel policies and procedures. He/she also has authority to deal with union issues, except those affecting terms and conditions of employment which are dealt with at company level. He/she must report any major issue to the production director.

Complexity

- The product is not a highly technical one and most of the production employees, except in the foundry and in the development shop, are semi-skilled assembly line employees. There are nine product lines and three main processes. Some problems are caused when product lines are changed but they are fairly easy to overcome if scheduling is carried out carefully.
- The main difficulty to overcome is ensuring that quality standards are maintained and that downtime is minimized. Maintenance is a key factor and fairly complex procedures have had to be developed to overcome serious problems in the past
- Labour relations do not present a problem.

Knowledge and skills

- The technical knowledge required is not very high. Anyone with experience in controlling assembly lines or a flow process operation should quickly be able to understand the techniques involved. The main requirement is skill in planning and controlling a high output, fairly high quality plant to meet critical delivery schedules and in motivating a labour force which is engaged on monotonous though well paid work.

Contacts

- Extensive contacts with all levels of management and with trade union officials and shop stewards. Also deals often with supplier and customers on quality and service matters.

Appendix M

The Glaxo Competency-based Job Family Structure

The Glaxo Pharmaceuticals UK pay system for professional, sales and administrative staff is designed to create a more effective link between pay, market rates and performance appraisals.

The previous structure consisted of a number of broad grades which covered all staff, including computer professionals. Salary increases were determined by an across-the-board annual rise and individual merit award, and progression to one common grade maxima was virtually automatic.

Glaxo found this system unsatisfactory on three counts. First, a common grading system provided no flexibility to respond to market pressures for particular groups of specialists. Secondly, there was no facility to award staff delivering consistently good performance once they had reached grade maxima. Thirdly, insufficient incentives existed to reward very good performers, either in terms of accelerated pay progression or progression beyond the normal grade maximum. These problems are, in fact, endemic in typical job grade structures.

New structure

The Company decided to introduce a new structure for all groups which would be flexible enough to cope with these problems.

All staff were allocated to 'job families', which were designed to reflect both market demands for particular groups of staff and the company's internal structure.

All of these families were split into various numbers of competency levels, each of which constitutes a step change in terms of responsibilities, experience and market rates. An example of a competency level description is given at the end of this appendix.

The levels within these job families, as illustrated in figure 1, are linked by a series of 'pay curves' which provide different salary progression tracks according to performance. In this way, annual pay awards are made on the basis of a combination of the performance of individuals and their particular market rates.

Individuals who 'plateau' at a particular level of job family still have the ability to receive salary increases by annual market movements, improved performance, or cash bonuses for consistently good performance standards.

Market settlements

Under this system there is no common level of movements for all grades. Instead, each set of job family pay curves will move on the basis of market demands. Market data is collected from a variety of sources, and is projected forward for the year ahead to ensure that the Company stays in a strong competitive position.

Appraisals

Pay is directly linked to the appraisal process, with the level of increase and the ability to progress to and beyond the standard salary maxima determined by performance ratings.

Performance objectives are set on a cascade basis, beginning with the company objectives and percolating through the system as department and finally individual objectives. An individual's performance is measured by how well they achieve these objectives, with ratings on a bench-mark basis, from 'A' being outstanding, to 'E' unacceptable.

Appraisals are carried out annually, with informal discussions in the interim period to discuss progress. This process is supported by a supplementary overview from a senior manager and a back-up grievance procedure.

Positions in all levels are filled by conventional promotion or appointment, although the new system helps managers to identify candidates who have the skills and potential to progress through a job family.

Competency Level Description

GLAXO PHARMACEUTICALS UK

Job Family: DEVMGR (Development Management)

Level: 1 (of 3)

Typical Job Titles: Analytical Systems Development Manager
Manager, Pharmaceutical Analysis

Main accountabilities/responsibilities

- Will have responsibility for the management of a research unit within the Analytical Development Division
- This will involve the establishing of priorities among analytical

LEVEL	Maximum Salary for Performance Rating				
	E	D	C	B	A
1	14,470	17,570	20,670	21,710	22,740
2	18,040	21,900	25,760	27,050	28,340
3	23,030	27,960	32,890	34,540	36,180

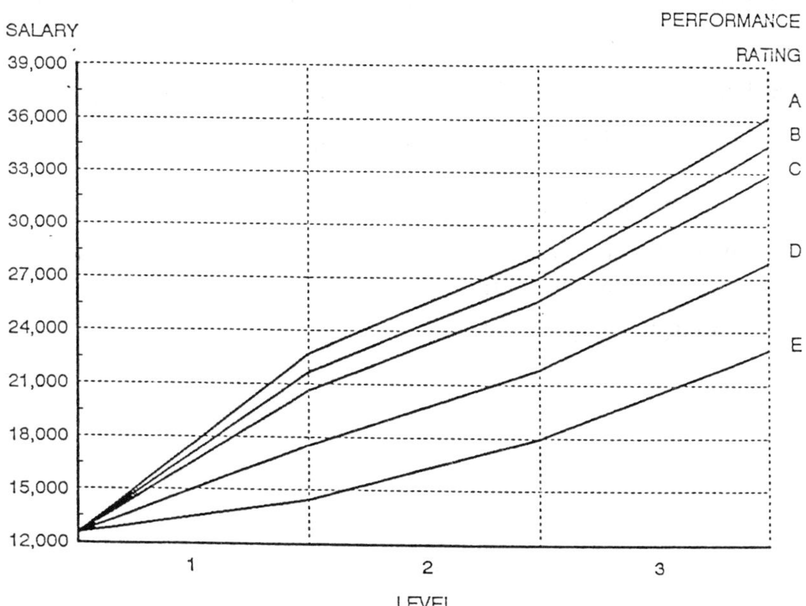

Figure M.1 *Glaxo Pharmaceuticals UK – example of salary ranges and curves for a job*

projects, the co-ordination and control of experiments, and delivery and communication of results within the parameters set by the senior management, at levels 2 and 3.
- Will have budgetary control for the unit, including authority for daily expenditure, and is responsible for ensuring that expenses are kept within agreed limits.
- Has managerial responsibility for a team of professional scientists and technicians, including recruitment, appraisal and development.
- Will maintain close links with managers in customer groups, and relevant external research institutes/universities. Expected to keep abreast of and propose best research practice in industry through these contacts.

Knowledge/experience

- Has expert knowledge of analytical research techniques and general research principles, and a good working knowledge of the organization and activities of customer groups.
- Will have a minimum of five years research experience, includin two years in a supervisory/managerial position.

Education/training

- Chemistry, degree, with relevant professional qualification.

Reporting relationship

- Normally reports to the relevant Level 2 Research Manager, eg

  Technical Development Manager
  Research Manager (Level 2)
  Research Manager (Level 1)

Years in Level: 8
(assuming consistent 'C' rating)

Market matches: PREG 1.18

Appendix N

Performance Management Forms

1. Personal preparation form
2. Performance review form
3. Performance agreement
4. Performance and development plan

1. PERSONAL PREPARATION FORM

Name

Job Title

Department

Period of Plan

From To

YOUR CURRENT JOB

1. In which job objectives have you done well? Why?

2. Which objectives have you found most difficult? Why?

3. Are there any problems which have affected your performance in achieving objectives?

4. What can be done to help you overcome any problems?

5. What are your key skills and areas of strengths?

6. Do you feel that you have any skills or abilities which are under-utilized?

7. What aspects of your job give you most satisfaction?

8. Are there any aspects of your job with which you are less satisfied?

YOUR CAREER INTERESTS

1. What would you like your next career step to be?

2. What are your longer term career interests?

YOUR DEVELOPMENT NEEDS

1. What additional skills, knowledge or experience would help you to further your career?

2. How would you like to acquire these skills, knowledge or experience?

Signature

Date

2. PERFORMANCE REVIEW FORM

Name	Job Title

Department	Review Period			
	From		To	

ACHIEVEMENT OF OBJECTIVES DURING YEAR

Key objectives (*as defined in last year's performance agreement and updated during year)*	Comments on achievement	Level of achievement

Levels of Achievement:
A = far exceeded objective B = exceeded objective C = fully met objective D = partly met objective E = did not meet objective

PROGRESS IN MEETING DEVELOPMENT NEEDS

Development needs (*as defined in last year's performance agreement*)	Comments on progress

REVIEWER'S SUMMARY

Overall level of achievement [ ]

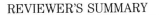

Levels of achievement

Ex = excellent VE = very effective E = effective
D = developing B = basic

Please comment on any notable achievements and areas for action arising from the review

INDIVIDUAL'S COMMENTS

Please comment on any points arising from the review

REVIEWER'S MANAGER'S COMMENTS

SIGNATURES

Individual		Date	
Reviewer		Date	
Reviewer's Manager		Date	

3. PERFORMANCE AGREEMENT

Name

Job Title

Department

Period of Agreement

From To

AGREED OBJECTIVES

Key objectives agreed for next year	Performance indicators

AGREED DEVELOPMENT NEEDS

Development needs agreed for next year	Agreed method of meeting needs

SIGNATURES

Individual Date

Reviewer Date

Reviewer's Manager Date

4. PERFORMANCE AND DEVELOPMENT PLAN

Name

Job Title

Department

Period of Plan

From To

OBJECTIVES

Agreed objectives *(state completion date)*	How they will be achieved	Progress during the year

DEVELOPMENT

Agreed development needs	How they will be met	Progress during year

SIGNATURES

Individual		Date	
Individual's Manager		Date	

Appendix O

Performance-Related Pay (PRP) Check-list

1. Why does the organization want to introduce PRP?
   (a) how does it expect to benefit?
   (b) are those expectations realistic?
2. Is the organization ready for PRP?
   (a) the corporate culture likely to be conducive to its success?
   (b) is the concept of PRP supported at all levels in the organization?
   (c) will the existing systems for objective setting, performance appraisal and reward support the introduction of PRP?
3. To whom is it proposed that PRP should apply and why?
4. What are the key performance issues (critical success factors) which a PRP scheme should address?
5. How much money is the organization prepared to spend on PRP?
6. What are the answers for this organization to the following objections to PRP?
   (a) it is difficult to measure performance objectively and consistently
   (b) it can encourage people to focus too narrowly on short-term tasks
   (c) individual rewards can harm team-work
   (d) it is difficult to prove that PRP schemes do improve performance
   (e) even if performance does improve, the costs of PRP may outweigh the benefits
7. How is it proposed to avoid the following pitfalls when designing the PRP system?
   (a) not matching the culture and value systems of the organization
   (b) performance rewards not linked to the achievement of the overall business strategy
   (c) performance rewards not flexible enough to respond to changes in strategic direction
   (d) failure to identify the key performance issues and critical success factors

(e) failure to establish appropriate performance indicators
(f) failure to link rewards clearly to achievements and levels of competence
(g) setting too mechanistic targets – ignoring the importance of qualitative standards
(h) failure to make provision for monitoring the system to ensure that it can develop and respond to changing needs.

8. How is it proposed to ensure that the PRP system:
   (a) matches the culture
   (b) links incentives to the performance management process
   (c) conforms to the following rules for success:
      - individuals clear about their objectives and standards of performance
      - individuals can track their performance against objectives and standards
      - individuals should be in a position to influence their performance by changing their behaviour or decisions
      - individuals should be clear about the rewards they will receive for achieving the required end results
      - rewards are meaningful enough to make the efforts required worthwhile
   (d) balances quantitative and qualitative measures
   (e) achieves a reasonable degree of flexibility
   (f) promotes team-work as well as individual effort
   (g) encourages long-term thinking. What steps can and should be taken by the organization to provide for longer term motivation and commitment by the use of non-financial rewards?
9. How is it proposed to ensure that managers and staff accept and 'own' the scheme?
10. In the light of an analysis of the organization's mission, strategies, objectives, culture, attitudes to PRP, existing performance management system and the particular requirements for the staff who will receive PRP, which of the following approaches or mix of approaches will be most appropriate for whom:
    (a) individual merit pay
    (b) individual bonus
    (c) group bonus
    (d) company-wide bonus
11. Who will be involved in planning, designing and implementing PRP?
12. Who will manage and control the PRP system?

Appendix P

Examples of Incentive Schemes

To illustrate in more detail the principles set out in Chapter 11, we give here examples of the following forms of incentive scheme:

A a scheme for main board directors of a public company
B a scheme for directors of a subsidiary company of a diversified UK parent multinational
C a senior/middle management incentive plan in a subsidiary of a US multinational in high technology
D a long-term incentive scheme.

They are presented in the form of case-studies to give greater insight into the way in which such schemes are introduced. Although fictionalized, the details are drawn from actual practice in a range of UK employers. They illustrate what can be done, but we cannot emphasize too strongly the need for companies to tailor incentives to meet their own needs and business plans.

Example A – an incentive scheme for main board directors of a public company

The company

A reasonably successful and profitable manufacturer with an annual sales turnover of £50 million. Profit before tax in the year prior to introduction of the incentive scheme was £3.5 million. Although it was operating in a highly competitive market, the directors believed that there was considerable growth potential. The board consisted of five executive and three non-executive directors:

- a non-executive chairman
- managing director
- finance director
- production director
- sales and marketing director
- personnel director
- two non-executive directors.

The chairman and non-executive directors formed the remuneration committee of the board, taking advice on current pay issues from the personnel director. Until 1987 there were no bonus or incentive schemes and directors' pay increased at the chief executive's discretion.

Shortly after a new managing director was appointed in 1986, he proposed introducing an executive incentive plan for full-time directors. His objectives in doing so were:

- to focus the board on the need to improve company profitability
- to provide a 'group reward' to consolidate team-working at board level – the previous managing director had resigned after a boardroom row and the production director had only recently been recruited following the voluntary early retirement of his predecessor
- to match competitive practice in the industry – the managing director felt that despite reasonably competitive basic salaries, the company was slipping behind on the pay front because it did not provide incentives for directors. His previous employer in the same industry had operated an incentive scheme that paid out quite well in response to improved profitability
- to provide further evidence to shareholders and City analysts that this was a forward looking organization, prepared to set itself challenging growth targets and reward success.

The incentive scheme

The board decided to opt for a simple scheme in the first instance. The Remuneration Committee therefore recommended the adoption of a plan linked to the achievement of a target based on growth in profit before tax. The inclusion of targets based on improvements in earnings per share and return on capital employed were also considered, but rejected at least for the first year of the scheme's operation. Instead, the company opted for four non-financial targets – one for each of the executive directors. These were closely related to the business plan which had as the key objective the improvement and updating of existing systems in production, sales and the finance function and the introduction of appraisal and succession planning for the first time by the personnel function.

For the 1987/88 financial year the directors therefore set themselves the following targets:

- an improvement in profit before tax of 10 per cent
- the introduction of a quality management programme based on quality circles in the production area with the objective of

reducing 'rejects' from five per cent of finished articles down to $2\frac{1}{2}$ per cent or less

- the introduction of a performance appraisal scheme for all management and supervisory staff together with the development of a succession plan
- reorganization of the field salesforce to deal with developing markets and completion of a training programme covering the latest thinking in the area of customer care
- the introduction of an improved computer system for producing management accounts to replace one introduced four years ago.

The 1986/7 increase in profit before tax was seven per cent. The 10 per cent target was therefore considered reasonably stretching. The remuneration committee decided to start paying incentive payments once a seven per cent increase was achieved (ie once last year's figure was matched) and to increase payments on the following basis:

% profit increase	% incentive payment
7	10
8	12
9	14
10	16
11	19
12	22
13	25
14	28
15	31
16	35
17	39
18	43
19	47
20	51

This incentive plan was based on a two per cent increase in incentive payment for each one per cent profit improvement between last year's figure and the 10 per cent improvement target, and a three per cent increase between the target and 15 per cent. As an additional reward for exceptional performance, a four per cent increase for each percentage improvement between 16 and 20 per cent would be given. A 'cap' on bonus payments was set at 51 per cent of salary. This was competitive for the industry. The directors also believed that an increase much in excess of 15 per cent over the year was extremely unlikely and would, if it occurred, be almost certainly due to 'windfall' factors beyond the directors' collective control.

The remuneration committee drew up a set of rules covering the scheme. This set out the basic rules affecting payments and included worked examples for each director to show the amounts payable as cash lump sums in relation to the gearing set out above. It decided that incentive payments would not be pensionable but could be 'sacrificed' into the pension scheme as additional voluntary contributions. Progress towards the achievement of non-financial targets would be monitored quarterly. Only if these were met would the full amount of bonus payable in relation to profit improvement be paid.

The scheme was formally introduced following acceptance by shareholders at the annual general meeting. It was launched at a full board meeting at which the chairman gave a presentation explaining how it would work and how it linked in to the achievement of the business plan.

The scheme was to run for one year in the first instance, then to be reviewed with a view to adding in additional financial targets, setting new non-financial targets related to the business plan and providing greater rewards for success.

In the 1987/88 financial year the company achieved a 12 per cent improvement in profit before tax and the directors' non-financial targets were met. They therefore each received lump sum payments of 22 per cent ie:

Title	Basic salary	Incentive
Managing Director	£75,000	£16,500
Finance Director	£61,000	£13,420
Production Director	£54,000	£11,880
Sales and Marketing Director	£60,000	£13,200
Personnel Director	£55,000	£12,100

Profit improvement = £420,000
Additional cost of incentive plan = £67,150

Example B – an incentive plan for directors of a subsidiary

The company

A subsidiary of a diversified major multinational with a £40 million annual sales turnover and well developed and sophisticated reporting systems. The objective in introducing an incentive plan was to pay all directors of subsidiaries on a basis which reflected their contribution to the business and focused their activities on agreed business targets. It was also introduced as a retention factor because several able directors who were being groomed for main board responsibilities had recently been headhunted by rival organizations.

The incentive plan

Each subsidiary is set annual targets by the parent board related to its business plan. These are drawn from the following list of both quantitative and non-quantitive factors. The actual targets are agreed with the subsidiary board at the beginning of the financial year.

- profit before tax
- return on capital employed
- sales turnover
- operating costs
- market share
- new product profitability
- employee turnover
- special project completion
- inventory levels
- company image
- employee relations climate
- succession planning.

The targets set for this organization in 1987/88 were:

- a 15 per cent improvement in profit before tax
- return on capital employed of 20 per cent
- annual sales turnover of £47 million
- a reduction in employee turnover from 12 per cent to 10 per cent
- settlement of the annual shopfloor wage negotiations without industrial action and within six weeks of the annual settlement date
- redesign and successful relaunch of an existing product to boost sales by 20 per cent.

Provided all these targets were met, a maximum pensionable incentive of 25 per cent of basic salary would be paid to all directors. Lower achievement would be less well rewarded at the discretion of the parent company board. If none of the targets were met then no incentive payments would be given. To preserve and foster team working, directors would each be paid the same percentage of their basic salary as an incentive payment.

Because of a downturn in the market for the company's products the outcome for the 1987/88 financial year was somewhat disappointing. Performance in relation to targets was as follows:

- an increase in profit before tax of only 12 per cent
- return on capital employed of 17 per cent
- annual sales turnover of £44 million

- employee turnover reduced to nine per cent (exceeding target)
- wage negotiations completed without problems in time for implementation on the settlement date
- the product/package re-launch happened on schedule but only achieved an increase in sales of 12 per cent.

In view of the partial achievement of the targets, the parent company board decided to pay an incentive payment reflecting reward for reasonable achievement in a difficult market. It was still concerned about executive retention and aware that without the sustained effort of the current directors, the situation would have been much worse. An incentive payment of 12.5 per cent of basic salary was therefore paid, ie half the maximum amount due for full target achievement.

Example C – A senior and middle management incentive plan

The company

This organization is a subsidiary of a US multinational employing about 1,500 people in the UK. Its activities are selling and servicing products manufactured elsewhere in the world. Incentives are paid to senior and some middle managers as part of the company's long-term philosophy of tying rewards to the achievements of the business plan. Management information systems are very sophisticated and the achievement of targets can be closely monitored in all areas. The company pays very competitive basic salaries in relation to its market. All its remuneration practices have a strong US 'flavour' but have been adapted to the UK market.

The incentive plan

There is a separate management plan for sales executives. This plan therefore covers managers across all functions of the business except direct sales. Each year, managers agree between five and eight objectives from the list given below plus others particularly relevant to their activities. The closer they are to the customer, the more emphasis there is on revenue earnings.

Examples of target areas:

- sales revenue
- sales bookings
- consultancy revenue
- contribution
- control of discretionary expenses

- credit control (reducing debtor days)
- cash collection
- discretionary (short term) goals
- staff development
- employee satisfaction

Factors are divided into quarterly and annual targets. Quarterly targets are measured cumulatively throughout the year, so the quarterly incentive payments made are called 'advances' and, to deal with under- or over-payment, these are balanced out in the final payments at the end of the year.

Because the company recognizes the importance of individual control over results, factors are weighted to favour those elements over which each manager has most personal control. Staff development is measured by the number of training days actually undertaken against those required. Employee satisfaction is measured by the use of mandatory employee attitude surveys which provide indicators of subordinates' views of their boss.

To prevent individuals achieving their own goals at the expense of others and to promote team working, the company also has a system of 'shared goals'.

Incentive targets typically range from payment triggered at around 97 per cent of target to a cut off at 105 per cent. On target performance attracts around 75 per cent of the maximum amount payable.

Payments are made on a flat rate basis for each factor irrespective of individual salary. Maximum payments range from 10 to 50 per cent of basic salary. Payments are non-pensionable but can be sacrificed to purchase additional pension.

This system clearly depends on very sensitive performance measurements and excellent management information systems. The use of attitude surveys to measure employee satisfaction is innovative in the UK but reflects a more widespread practice in the US.

Example D – A long-term incentive scheme

(*Source*: Monks Guide to performance related incentives for senior managers.)

The company wishes to emphasize the need for growth in earnings per share (EPS). At a time when inflation is rising at about 7.0 per cent, it decides upon an absolute minimum level of acceptable achievement in EPS growth of 10 per cent compound per year. Bonus may start to be earned at this level.

The company also concludes that growth in excess of 25 per cent compound over three years is a realistic maximum, having regard to the industry in which the company operates. Growth in excess of 25 per cent in any year is likely to be due to a substantial measure of good luck, so 25 per cent compound will be the upper limit for bonus.

The company concludes that, in its circumstances, a payment of 0.75 per cent salary for every 1p increase in EPS between these two thresholds will be paid out at the end of year 3.

In reaching its decision to offer 0.75 per cent for every 1p increase, it assumes a second longer term plan will start at the end of year 3 so that there is some overlap. It would like to see the four participating executives receive a lump sum of about 75 per cent of salary once the accounts are approved by shareholders for year 3, if compound growth of 25 per cent EPS is achieved. The longer term plan complements an annual plan with an upper limit of 40 per cent of salary, plus options over shares worth 4× salary.

The bonus potential is illustrated in the table below. The percentage of salary which can be earned in each year increases, with most weight attached to year 3. The base EPS is 100 pence per share. If the maximum bonus is earned, EPS nearly doubles in 3 years.

Bonus scale – Base Year 100p

End of Year	Min EPS p	Max EPS p	Max EPS Increase for Bonus p	Max Bonus in Year at 0.75% of salary per p
Year 1	110	125	15	11.25%
Year 2	121	156	35	26.25%
Year 3	133	195	62	46.50%
		Maximum Total Bonus		84%

The participants have to stay until the accounts for year 3 are approved before they can receive any bonus, so the plan acts as a tie. At the end of year 2 a new plan will start so the participants should have something more 'under their belt' by the time bonus is paid out in year 3. The new plan may take a different form if objectives have changed.

Appendix Q

A UK Share Option Pricing Model

Increasingly, use is being made of option pricing models to communicate to executives the value of share options at the time they are granted. This is because it is typically hard for them to understand the worth of the options they are being given and assess their value in terms of capital accumulation.

Option pricing is a contentious area and only recently have real studies been made in the pricing of executive options. The IDS Top Pay Unit, in their Personnel Tax Guide 1986/87, published an option valuation matrix, based on forecast share price growth. The Black–Scholes model which is used by short-term options and financial futures traders is widely used in the US but assumes an economist's world of no taxes. Neither of these has proved particularly satisfactory.

On 2 August 1990 Accountancy Age published an article by Alan M Judes, a director of Cockman, Consultants & Partners Limited setting out a model specifically catering for UK tax rates and practices. This appendix explains the Judes model.

The Judes model is based on treating the option to acquire shares as an alternative to a purchase of a similar number of shares at current market value. It treats the option grant as a prelude to share ownership and not as a method of financial speculation. Instead of buying shares now, the option holder who intends to purchase shares in the future would be willing to pay a lesser amount for an option to acquire shares at today's price at a future time, and make an alternative investment with the balance of his funds.

The main information needed to value such an option is the long-term rate of return available to the option holder.

This information can be used to determine the value of an option to subscribe for a share at current market value. Assume a share which pays no dividends and has a market value of £1.00. One way to place a minimum value on the option to buy that share in 5 years' time at £1.00 is to subtract from the current market value the amount needed to accumulate the £1.00 exercise price over the 5 year period. The remaining amount is what the option is worth. In this simple example in Chart 1, it is assumed that the investment can roll up tax free and that rates of interest over the five year period are 10 per cent.

Chart 1

Share value (exercise price)	£1.00
less investment needed to produce £1.00 in 5 years' time	.62p
Value of option	.38p

In the simple world of Chart 1, the option holder would always be in the same position as, or better off than the actual shareholder. Contrast the position as an investor who bought the share at £1.00 (Investor S) and an option holder who bought the option at 38p (Investor O). The details are set out in Chart 2. The conclusion is surprising.

Chart 2

Investor S paid for a share	£1.00
Investor O paid for an option	38p
made an investment of	62p
Outlays of S and O are identical	£1.00

If in 5 years' time the share price has increased say to £3.00.

Investor S has a share worth	£3.00
Investor O has investment worth	£1.00
has an option 'gain' of	£2.00
	£3.00

If the share price has not moved and is still £1.00

Investor S has 1 share worth	£1.00
Investor O has investment worth	£1.00

If the value of the share has fallen to say 50p.

Investor S has 1 share worth	50p
Investor O has investment worth	£1.00

The option holder is better off than the shareholder!

Clearly the real world has dividends paid on shares, tax due on transactions, and volatility of share prices. Consequently a much more sophisticated option pricing model for equities has been developed by two Americans, Black and Scholes, in 1973, and is appropriately known as the Black–Scholes model. The Black–Scholes model is complex mathematically and takes into account the price of the underlying share, the exercise price of the option, the time to maturity, the price volatility of the asset, the risk free rate of interest and the expected level of dividends. It is used by traders of options on the London markets, typically for very short-term transactions. However, it assumes a world without any tax charges.

Judes identified the need for an alternative to the Black–Scholes model which addresses UK taxation issues and UK market practice

Option pricing model for UK equities Chart 3

Variables

8.026%	given after tax yield to redemption for gilt
100p	share price at time of option grant
3.00%	dividend yield
5.00%	assumed future share price growth
7	year life of option (maximum 15)
£25,000	salary of employee at time of option grant
2	multiple of salary placed under option (maximum 4)
40%	marginal rate of income tax
10.00%	risk free rate of interest
140.71p	future value of share at end of option period

Calculation

Value of shares under option	£50,000
Number of shares under option	50,000
After tax yield to redemption	8.026%

Value of option	for holding	for 1 share
		£.p
Initial option value	20,875	0.42
less present value of future dividends	(8,338)	(0.17)
Option value	12,537	0.25

for much longer term option granting. Chart 3 sets out an option pricing model for UK equities. All of the variables can be altered to meet specific circumstances and to calculate a value for an option. The key determinants of the option price are:

(a) the after-tax return that an investor can get on a specific gilt to fund the option exercise;
(b) the dividend yield of the share and the assumed price growth;
(c) the value of shares placed under option, typically as a multiple of salary in the UK context;
(d) the risk-free rate of interest available to investors at the time of the option grant.

Chart 4 proves the model's calculation in the same way that Chart 2 demonstrates the simplistic approach.

Option pricing model for UK equities Chart 4

Demonstration of calculation

	for holding	for 1 share
S buys shares worth	50,000	1.00
Total expense of S	50,000	1.00
O purchases future dividends for	8,338	0.17
O invests in gilt described above	29,125	0.58
O purchases option for option value	12,537	0.25
Total expense of O	50,000	1.00
at end of option period		
S has holding worth	70,355	1.41
O receives proceeds from gilt	50,000	1.00
O has option gain of	20,355	0.41
O's holding is worth	70,355	1.41

S and O have received similar income streams

Appendix R

Profit-Related Pay (PRP) Schemes

In the 1987 budget, the Chancellor of the Exchequer proposed a new income tax relief for employees who receive profit-related pay under registered schemes which link part of their pay to profits.

The main features of PRP as approved by the Government are as follows:

1. In a PRP scheme, a part of pay moves up and down with profits so that employees' pay reflects the profit which has been earned by their work. The Government wants more businesses to set up schemes under which a formula links a part of pay automatically to the profits of the business.
2. Half of PRP will be free of income tax up to the point where PRP is 20 per cent of pay or £4,000 a year, whichever is lower. For a married man on average earnings, the relief could add about £6.00 a week to take-home pay, equivalent to three and a half pence off the basic rate of income tax. If only five per cent is PRP, the relief would be worth one pence off the basic rate of tax.
3. PRP will be subject, like other earnings, to National Insurance Contributions unless it is part of total earnings below the lower earnings limit for employer's National Insurance Contributions. However, PRP which is exempt from employer's NIC (eg, because it is paid through a trust) cannot also qualify for the income tax relief.
4. The relief will be available to all private sector employees paying income tax through PAYE (with the exception of controlling directors).
5. Employers will be free to design their own schemes. They will need to be registered by the employer (in advance of coming into operation) with the Inland Revenue. A scheme must relate to an employment unit which is either a whole incorporated or unincorporated business in the private sector, or a sub-unit of the business. The main qualifying features are:
   (a) schemes must establish a clear relationship between the

PRP of the specified employment unit and the audited profits generated by it

(b) new recruits and part-timers may be excluded, but at least 80 per cent of the other employees in the employment unit must be covered by the PRP scheme

(c) at the outset of the scheme the prospect must be that if profits are unchanged, total PRP produced by the formula at (a) will be at least five per cent of the total pay of participating employees.

(d) a scheme must last for at least one year.

6. The two main choices are the *employment unit* and the *formula* linking profits and PRP (for which a definition of profit is, of course, needed). It must be possible to produce audited profit figures for the employment unit chosen. Subject to that, the employer will be able to choose whatever unit makes sense in the circumstances of the business. Employers will also have a choice between two ways of linking profits and PRP:

   (a) total PRP (or the 'PRP pool') can be a simple proportion of profits

   (b) the PRP pool can be a sum of money which varies in line with year-on-year changes in profits.

   In either case, there will be scope for modifying the effect of large changes in profits, in order to avoid large fluctuations in PRP or to safeguard a minimum level of profit.

7. The basis for calculating the size of a scheme's PRP pool will be the level of profits on the ordinary activities of the employment unit after taxation as defined in the Companies Act 1985. Schemes will, however, be able to provide for a number of adjustments in the production of these profit figures, such as for interest costs. The chosen definition of profit must be used consistently throughout a scheme's life.

8. PRP to be distributed to employees must be determined and paid at least once a year on the basis of audited profits. But it can be calculated on an interim basis as frequently as desired, and paid, for example, in monthly or weekly pay packets.

9. Tax relief will, in effect, be administered by a 'self-assessment' system. The employer will be responsible for:

   (a) ensuring that the scheme complies with the statutory requirements

   (b) calculating PRP profits and the amount of PRP payable to each employee

   (c) giving the tax relief due to each employee as part of the normal operation of PAYE.

10. An independent auditor's report must accompany an employer's application for registration of his or her scheme

(to confirm that it meets the statutory requirements) and his or her return at the end of each PRP period (to confirm that the scheme and the tax relief have been operated properly).

11. New recruits may be excluded from a scheme for up to three years and employers will be able to decide for themselves how to deal with employees who leave before PRP for a particular year can be calculated and paid. The rule will provide flexibility for employers to make special arrangements to deal with reorganizations, etc.
12. PRP can be introduced (or increased in amount) in place of a conventional increase in pay, and this might be coupled with a conversion of some existing pay to PRP.
13. Existing schemes qualify if they meet the criteria and are registered.

The tax relief available from PRP share is shown in Table R.1.

Table R.1 *Illustrative values of tax relief at 1990–91 tax rates and allowances*

	Proportion of pay that is PRP %	Value of[1] tax relief (tax at 25%) £	£	Equivalent pence off basic rate	
		per year	per week	married	single
Average male earnings (estimated at 295.60 a week in 1990–1991)	5	96.07	1.85	0.9	0.8
	10	192.14	3.70	1.7	1.5
	20	384.28	7.39	3.5	3.1

Annual Pay £	Proportion of pay that is PRP %	Value of tax relief[1] £ per year	£ per week
5,000	5	31.25	0.60
	10	62.50	1.20
	20	125.00	2.40
10,000	5	62.50	1.20
	10	125.00	2.40
	20	250.00	4.81
15,000	5	93.75	1.80
	10	187.50	3.61
	20	375.00	7.21
20,000	5	125.00	2.40
	10	250.00	4.81
	20	500.00	9.62
40,000 (40% marginal tax rate)	5	400.00	7.69
	10	800.00	15.38
	20	800.00	15.38

1 No other income, allowances or tax relief

Bibliography and Sources of Information

The section on information sources is divided into four sections:

- Books/reports on salary administration
- Articles
- Salary surveys and sources of information – UK
- International surveys and data on living costs.

It is intended as a guide to the main sources and is therefore selective rather than exhaustive. The fact that a particular source or organization is listed here does not imply the author's recommendation – readers are referred to Chapter 4 and Appendix A for how best to use and interpret remuneration data.

Books/reports on salary administration

This section contains the main recent books and sources of research into pay and benefits practice in the UK. We are indebted to both Incomes Data Services and the Institute of Personnel Management for permission to quote from their bibliographies and directories of sources.

Armstrong M *A Handbook of Human Resource Management*, Kogan Page, London, 1987.

Armstrong M and Murlis H *A Handbook of Salary Administration*, Kogan Page, London, 1980 and *Reward Management – A new Handbook of Salary Administrations*, 1988 (previous edition(s) of this book).

Beer, Michael 'Reward systems' in Michael Beer, Bert Spector, Paul R Laurence, and D Quinn Mills, Managing Human Assets, The Free Press, New York, 1984.

Bell W and Hanson C *Profit Sharing and Profitability – How Profit Sharing Promotes Business Success*, Kogan Page, London, 1987.

Bowey A *Managing salary and wage systems*, Gower Press, Aldershot, 1989.

Equal Opportunities Commission, *Job Evaluation Free From Sex Bias*, EOC, London (New edition) 1985.

Genders J E *Wages and Salaries: Managing Pay Effectively*, Institute of Personnel Management, London 1981.

Greenhill R *Performance Related Pay for the 1990s*, Director Books, London, 1990.

Incomes Data Services/Coopers and Lybrand *Paying for Performance in the Public Sector – A Progress Report*, London, 1989.

Incomes Data Services/Peat Marwick McLintock *Salaries and Benefits in Local Government*, London 1988.

Income Data Services – Top Pay Unit

1. Special Issues:
   - Directory of Salary Surveys 1989
   - Executive Bonus Schemes (published in association with the IPM) 1987
   - Executive Share Options 1985
   - Job Evaluation Review 2nd ed 1986
   - The Merit Factor: Rewarding Individual Performance (published in association with the IPM) 1985
   - Understanding Salary Surveys 1990
   - Putting Pay Philosophies into Practice 1990
2. Research Files:
   - Sales Bonuses and Commissions 1985
   - Pay and Progression for Graduates 1987
   - Communicating the Pay Package 1987
   - Personnel Tax Guide 1990/91
   - Pay and Progression in Research and Development 1987
   - Company Cars 1987
   - Executive Mobility 1988
   - Paying for Performance 1988
   - Pay and Bonuses in Sales 1989

Jaques, Elliot *Equitable payment*, Heinneman, London, 1961.

Kanter, Rosabeth *When giants learn to dance*, Simon & Schuster, London, 1989.

Langley M *Rewarding the Sales Force*, Institute of Personnel Management, London, 1987.

Lupton T and Bowey A *Wages and Salaries*, 2nd edition 1983, Gower, Aldershot, 1983.

Peters, Tom *Thriving on chaos*, Macmillan, London, 1988.

Porter, L W and Lawler, E E *Managerial attitudes and performance*, Irwin-Dorsey, Homewood, Illinois, 1968.

Pinchot Gifford *Intrepreneuring*, Harper and Row, New York.

Vernon-Harcourt A, Shoebridge, and Tulloch C *Employee Share Schemes in Practice*, Marks Publications, Saffron Walden and London, 1991.

Vernon-Harcourt A *Performance Related Bonuses for Senior Management*, Monks Publications, Saffron Walden, 1989.

McBeath G and Rands D *Salary Administration*, Business Books, London, 1976.

Rock L Milton and Berger A Lance (eds) *The Compensation Handbook: A State of the Art Guide to Compensation Strategy and Design*, McGraw Hill Inc, New York, 1991.

Smith I *Incentive Schemes, People and Profits*, 2nd edition, Croner, Kingston-upon-Thames, 1991.

Smith I *The Management of Remuneration: Paying for Effectiveness*, Institute of Personnel Management, London, 1983.

Top Pay Unit *Putting pay philosophies into practice*, Incomes Data Services, London, 1990.

Articles

'Does profit sharing improve employee performance?' V Wright, *Personnel Management*, (IPM), November 1986.

'Merit payment systems: the lessons so far' H Murlis, *Manpower Policy and Practice*, Spring 1988.

'Performance related pay in the public sector' H Murlis, *Public Money*, March 1987.

'The attack on pay' R Moss Kanter, *Harvard Business Review*, March–April 1987.

'Just Rewards' Helen Murlis, *Pensions and Employee Benefits*, February 1990.

Too numerous to mention individually are the many articles appearing as regular commentary on the remuneration scene in the UK from:

Incomes Data Services
- Report
- Focus
- Studies
- Monthly Review of Salaries and benefits (from the Top Pay Unit)
- Pensions Service

Industrial Relations Services
- Pay and Benefits Bulletin
- Industrial Relations Review and Report
- Equal Opportunities Review
- Occupational Pensions

Personnel Management – the monthly journal of the Institute of Personnel Management

PM Plus – The 'News' magazine of the IPM

Salary surveys and sources of information – UK

The listing given below covers all the main producers of published salary and survey data. Space does not permit us to include all the consultants in this area who run small, closed 'participant only' surveys. Further information on these can be obtained from the Management Consultants Association, The Institute of Management Consultants and from the Management Consultancy Information Service who regularly produce a Directory of Management Consultants (enquiries to):

MCIS,
38, Blenheim Avenue
Ilford Essex IG2 6JQ
Tel: 081–554 4695

Regular commentary on and trend data from salary and benefits surveys are given by:

Incomes Data Services – Top Pay Unit
Monthly Review of Salaries and Benefits
193, St John Street
London EC1V 4LS
Tel: 071–250 3434

Industrial Relations Services
Pay and Benefits Bulletin
18–20 Highbury Place
London N5 1QP
Tel: 071–354 5858

Further information on sources can also be obtained from the library and information services of:

The Institute of Personnel Management
IPM House
Camp Road
Wimbledon
London SW19 4UW
Tel: 081–946 9100

The British Institute of Management
Cottingham Road
Corby
Northants NN17 1TT
Tel: 0536–204222

Major published surveys
Note: * = available to participants only

British Institute of Management
National Management Salary Survey – Produced in association with Remuneration Economics (see below)

Charterhouse Group Ltd
Top Management Remuneration – UK
Published by Monks Publications Ltd (see below)

Computer Economics Ltd
Computer Staff Salary Surveys
Survey House
51, Portland Road
Kingston upon Thames
Surrey KT1 2SH
Tel: 081–549 8726

Department of Employment
New Earnings Survey
Her Majesty's Stationery Office
49, Holborn
London WC1V 6HB
(and other Government bookshops)

Hay Management Consultants
Main surveys:

Hay Remuneration Comparison*
Boardroom Pay Survey*
Data Processing Survey*
Survey of Employee Benefits*

Functional Surveys of:

Accountants*
Architects/Surveyors*
Data Processing*
Engineers*
HR/Personnel*
Investment Fund Managers
Retail*
Salesforce*
Solicitors/Legal*
Taxation*
Treasury*
Health Authorities*
Local Authorities

52, Grosvenor Gardens
London SW1W OAU
Tel: 071–730 0833

PE-International
Survey of Executive Salaries and Fringe Benefits
Salary Research Unit
Park House
Wick Road
Egham
Surrey PW20 0HW
Tel: 0784 43411

Korn/Ferry International
Boards of Directors Study
12 Buckingham Street
London WC2N
071–930 0334

Monks Publications
Main Surveys (see also Books section above):
Monks guide to Board and Senior Remuneration in Smaller Companies
Top Management Remuneration UK (with Charterhouse Group Ltd)
Engineering Industry Remuneration*
Property Industry Remuneration
Employment Conditions
Company Car Policy
Management Remuneration in Europe
Debden Green
Saffron Walden
Essex CB11 3LX
Tel: 0371–830939

National Computing Centre
Salaries and Fringe Benefits in Computing
Oxford Road
Manchester M1 7ED
Tel: 061–228 6333

Office of Manpower Economics
Review Body on Top Salaries Report
Her Majesty's Stationery Office
(see address above)

PA Consulting Group
Graduate Salaries and Recruitment Trends
123 Buckingham Palace Road
London SW1W 9SR
Tel: 071–730 9000

Remuneration Economics Ltd

Main surveys:
REL/BIM National Management Salary Survey (see above)
Financial Functions
Engineering Functions
Personnel Functions
Qualified Actuaries and Actuarial Students
Sales and Marketing

Survey House
51, Portland Road
Kingston upon Thames
Surrey KT1 2SH
Tel: 081–549 8726

Reward Group

Main Surveys
Local Salary and Wage Surveys
Research and Development Salary Survey
Salary and Cost of Living Report
Directors Rewards (in association with the Institute of Directors)
Sales and Marketing Rewards (in association with the Institute of Marketing)

Reward House
Diamond Way
Stone Business Park
Staffordshire ST15 OSD
Tel: 0785 813566

Towers Perrin Forster and Crosby

Main Surveys:
Executive Pay in the Electronics Industry*
Executive Pay in UK Subsidiaries of US Companies*
Top Executive Remuneration Survey*

Castlewood House
77–91 New Oxford Street
London WC1A 1PX
Tel: 071–379 4411

The Wyatt Company (UK) Ltd

Main Surveys:
Remuneration Data Service*
Compensation Survey for Electronics Companies*
Survey of Total Compensation for the Insurance Industry*
Survey of Total Compensation for Investment Staff*
Office and Business Automation Data Bank*

Park Gate
21, Tothill Street
London SW1H 9LL
Tel: 071–222 8033

Major professional institutions producing salary surveys:

Bar Association for Commerce Finance and Industry
The Engineering Council
Institute of Directors
Institute of Marketing
Institute of Physics
Institution of Chemical Engineers
Institution of Civil Engineers
Institution of Electrical and Electronics Incorporated Engineers
The Institution of Electrical Engineers
Institution of Geologists
Institution of Mechanical Engineers
Royal Institute of British Architects
Royal Society of Chemistry

International surveys and data on living costs

Employment Conditions Abroad Ltd
Anchor House
15, Britten Street
London SW3
Tel: 071–351 7151

Executive Compensation Service Inc
(A Member of the Wyatt Company)
273 Avenue de Tervuren (Box 4)
1150 Brussels, Belgium
Tel: Brussels 771 99 10

PE-International Salary Research Unit (see previous section)
Hay Management Consultants (see previous sections)

Organisation Resources Counsellors Inc
78, Buckingham Gate
London SW1E
Tel: 071–222 9231

PA Personnel Services (see previous section)
Towers Perrin Forster and Crosby (see previous section)
Articles and commentaries on various aspects of international remuneration and benefits appear in:

Benefits and Compensation International
Pension Publications Ltd
East Wing
4th Floor
45 Grand Peter Street
London SW1P 3LT
Tel: 071–222 0288

Incomes Data Services – European Report (see previous section)
Industrial Relations Services-European Industrial Relations Review
(see previous section)

Mercer Frazer Ltd (Compmaster)
Telford House
14, Tothill Street
London SW1H 9NB
Tel: 071 222 9121

KPMG Peat Marwick Human Resource Consultants (Equate)
PO Box 695
8, Salisbury Square
London EC4Y 8BB
Tel: 071 236 8000

Index